# HISTORIC MANSIONS AND
# HIGHWAYS AROUND BOSTON

*BOOKS BY SAMUEL ADAMS DRAKE*

A BOOK OF NEW ENGLAND LEGENDS AND FOLK LORE

HISTORIC MANSIONS AND HIGHWAYS AROUND BOSTON

OLD LANDMARKS AND HISTORIC PERSONAGES OF BOSTON

OLD WAYSIDE MILL, SOMERVILLE.

# HISTORIC MANSIONS
# AND HIGHWAYS
# AROUND BOSTON

by SAMUEL ADAMS DRAKE

REVISED EDITION

with Numerous Illustrations

CHARLES E. TUTTLE COMPANY
*Rutland, Vermont*

*Representatives*

*Continental Europe:* BOXERBOOKS, INC., *Zurich*
*British Isles:* PRENTICE-HALL INTERNATIONAL, INC., *London*
*Australasia:* PAUL FLESCH & CO., PTY. LTD., *Melbourne*
*Canada:* M. G. HURTIG LTD., *Edmonton*

974.44
D789 h/r
93-0134

*Published by the Charles E. Tuttle Company, Inc.*
*of Rutland, Vermont & Tokyo, Japan*
*with editorial offices at Suido 1-chome, 2–6*
*Bunkyo-ku, Tokyo, Japan*

*Library of Congress Catalog Card No. 73-157256*

*International Standard Book No. 0-8048-0992-5*

*First edition published 1873*
*Revised edition published 1906*
*by Little, Brown, and Company, Boston*
*First Tuttle edition published 1971*

PRINTED IN JAPAN

# TABLE OF CONTENTS

## CHAPTER I.

### THE GATEWAY OF OLD MIDDLESEX.

## CHAPTER II.

### AN HOUR IN THE GOVERNMENT DOCKYARD.

## CHAPTER III.

### BUNKER HILL AND THE MONUMENT.

## CHAPTER IV.

### THE CONTINENTAL TRENCHES.

## CHAPTER V.

### THE OLD WAYSIDE MILL.

## CHAPTER VI.

### THE PLANTATION AT MYSTIC.

## CHAPTER VII.

### LEE'S HEADQUARTERS AND VICINITY.

# CHAPTER VIII.

### OLD CHARLESTOWN ROAD, LECHMERE'S POINT, AND PUTNAM'S HEADQUARTERS.

# CHAPTER IX.

### A DAY AT HARVARD.

# CHAPTER X.

### A DAY AT HARVARD, CONTINUED.

## CHAPTER IV.

### THE CONTINENTAL TRENCHES.

## CHAPTER V.

### THE OLD WAYSIDE MILL.

## CHAPTER VI.

### THE PLANTATION AT MYSTIC.

## CHAPTER VII.

### LEE'S HEADQUARTERS AND VICINITY.

# CHAPTER XIV.

### OLD TORY ROW AND BEYOND.

# CHAPTER XV.

### MOUNT AUBURN TO NONANTUM BRIDGE.

# CHAPTER XVI.

### LECHMERE'S POINT TO LEXINGTON.

# CHAPTER XVII.

### LEXINGTON TO CONCORD.

## CHAPTER XVIII.

### THE RETREAT FROM CONCORD.

## CHAPTER XIX.

### AT THE WAYSIDE INN.

## CHAPTER XX.

### THE HOME OF RUMFORD.

# LIST OF ILLUSTRATIONS

## FULL-PAGE ILLUSTRATIONS

## ILLUSTRATIONS ON WOOD

# PUBLISHER'S FOREWORD TO THE
# NEW EDITION

WHAT were Boston and vicinity like two, three, and even four centuries ago? Because of books like this, that question can be answered readily and well. Because of writers like Samuel Adams Drake, the old has been perpetuated into a veritable gold mine of information for posterity. History thus lives and becomes an imperishable part of our national consciousness.

Drake wrote about Boston and its famous people with an accuracy and authority little short of amazing. His labors of love required decades of diligent and demanding preparation —evident in the end products, which were received with the wide acclaim befitting historic works of this stature.

With his inexhaustible historic lore and his keen appreciation of anecdotes and places, items and relics, the author takes his readers to old Middlesexshire, stopping at almost every port, dwelling, valley, river, and hill, bringing back— through the magic of pen and picture—the sturdy, patriotic men and stirring events of Colonial and Revolutionary times.

He painted his word pictures on an unusually wide canvas, as will be seen in the biographical sketch below, but New England always claimed his greatest attention. It was in this general arena that the colonial stripling suddenly sprang erect, a David planting a blow full on the front of Old England, the insular Goliath—a blow that made the giant reel with the shock. It was here that the people of the "Old Thirteen" first acted together as one nation, and here the separate streams of their existence united into one mighty flood: America.

Samuel Adams Drake was born in Boston on December 20, 1833. His father, Samuel Gardner Drake, established in that city in 1828 one of the first antiquarian bookstores in the United States. A large portion of his stock consisted of books relating to the early history of the country. His brother, Francis Samuel Drake, a writer prominent in literary circles, influenced young Samuel in delving into early New England legend and folk lore.

Upon finishing his education in the public schools of Boston, young Samuel became interested in newspaper work and decided to make journalism his career. In 1858 he went to Kansas (his brother had an antiquarian bookshop in Leavenworth) as telegraphic agent for the New York Associated Press. Later he became a regular correspondent of the *St. Louis Republican* and the *Louisville Journal* and for a while edited the *Leavenworth Times*. His first work published under his own name was a pamphlet entitled *Hints to Emigrants to Pike's Peak*.

Soon after the outbreak of the Civil War, the Kansas State Militia was organized. Drake became adjutant general of the Northern Division and late in 1861 was captain of militia in the Union Army. He rose to the rank of brigadier general of the militia in 1863, and in 1864 he commanded the post at Paola, Kansas, during Price's invasion of Missouri.

Upon retirement from military service in 1871, Drake returned to Massachusetts and resumed work in the literary field. In 1872 he published *Old Landmarks and Historic Personages of Boston* (now available in the Tut Book series) and, in 1873, the present book, *Historic Mansions and Highways Around Boston. Nooks and Corners of the New England Coast* and *Bunker Hill* appeared in 1875.

Drake's later publications include *Around the Hub*, 1881;

*Heart of the White Mountains*, 1881; *A Book of New England Legends and Folk Lore* (now available in the Tut Book series), 1884; *Our Great Benefactors*, 1885; *The Making of New England*, 1886; *The Making of the Great West*, 1887; *Burgoyne's Invasion*, 1889; *The Taking of Louisburg*, 1891; *The Pine Tree Coast*, 1891; *The Battle of Gettysburg*, 1892; *The Making of Virginia*, 1893; *Our Colonial Homes*, 1894; *The Campaign of Trenton*, 1895; *The Watch Fires of '76*, 1895; *On Plymouth Rock*, 1898; *The Myths and Fables of Today*, 1900; and *The Young Vigilantes*, 1904.

Possessed of a remarkable memory, Drake delighted in constructively criticizing the efforts of many contemporary self-styled historians, whom he classified as "textbook hacks." He lived a full life, enjoying the fruits of his labor and glorying in the progress of the American people. He died at Kennebunkport, Maine, in his seventy-second year, beloved by New Englanders, Southerners, and Westerners alike and enshrined in the hearts of the "proper Bostonians," who took great pleasure in reading his literary efforts pertaining to the early history of New England.

# CHAPTER I.

### THE GATEWAY OF OLD MIDDLESEX.

"A sup of New England's Aire is better than a whole draught of Old
England's Ale."

THE charming belt of country around Boston is full of interest to Americans. It is diversified with every feature
that can make a landscape attractive. Town clasps hands with
town until the girdle is complete where Nahant and Nantasket
sit with their feet in the Atlantic. The whole region may be
compared to one vast park, where nature has wrought in savage
grandeur what art has subdued into a series of delightful
pictures. No one portion of the zone may claim precedence.
There is the same shifting panorama visible from every rugged
height that never fails to delight soul and sense. We can
liken these suburban abodes to nothing but a string of precious
gems flung around the neck of Old Boston.

Nor is this all. Whoever cherishes the memory of brave
deeds — and who does not? — will find here the arena in which
the colonial stripling suddenly sprang erect, and planted a blow
full in the front of the old insular gladiator, — a blow that made
him reel with the shock to his very centre. It was here the

people of the "Old Thirteen" first acted together as one nation, and here the separate streams of their existence united in one mighty flood. The girdle is not the less interesting that it rests on the ramparts of the Revolution.

It is in a great measure true that what is nearest to us we know the least about, and that we ignorantly pass over scenes every day, not a whit less interesting than those by which we are attracted to countries beyond the seas. An invitation to a pilgrimage among the familiar objects which may be viewed from the city steeples, while it may not be comparable to a tour in the environs of London or of Paris, will not, our word for it, fail to supply us with materials for reflection and entertainment. Let us beguile the way with glances at the interior home-life of our English ancestors, while inspecting the memorials they have left behind. Their habitations yet stand by the wayside, and if dumb to others, will not altogether refuse their secrets to such as seek them in the light of historic truth. We shall not fill these old halls with lamentations for a greatness that is departed never to return, but remember always that there is a living present into which our lives are framed, and by which the civilization of what we may call the *old régime* may be tested. Where we have advanced, we need not fear the ordeal ; where we have not advanced, we need not fear to avow it.

We suppose ourselves at the water-side, a wayfarer by the old bridge leading to Charlestown, with the tide rippling against the wooden piers beneath our feet, and the blue sky above calling us afield. The shores are bristling with masts which gleam like so many polished conductors and cast their long wavy shadows aslant the watery mirror. Behind these, houses rise, tier over tier, mass against mass, from which, as if disdainful of such company, the granite obelisk springs out, and higher yet, a landmark on the sea, a Pharos of liberty on the shore.

The Charles, to which Longfellow has dedicated some charming lines, though not actually seen by Smith, retained the name with which he christened it. It was a shrewd guess in the bold navigator, that the numerous islands he saw in the bay indicated the estuary of a great river penetrating the interior. It is a curious feature of the map which Smith made of the coast of New England in 1614, that the names of Plymouth, Boston, Cambridge, and many other towns not settled until long afterwards, should be there laid down. Smith's map was the first on which the name of New England appeared.

In the pavement of St. Sepulchre, London, is Smith's tomb-stone. The inscription, except the three Turk's heads, is totally effaced, but the church authorities have promised to have it renewed as given by Stow.

The subject of bridging the river from the old ferry-way at Hudson's Point to the opposite shore — which is here of about the same breadth as the Thames at London Bridge — was agitated as early as 1712, or more than seventy years before its final accomplishment. In 1720 the attempt was renewed, but while the utility of a bridge was conceded, it was not considered a practicable undertaking. After the Revolution the

CAPTAIN JOHN SMITH.

project was again revived, and a man was found equal to the occasion. An ingenious shipwright, named Lemuel Cox, was then living at Medford, who insisted that the enterprise was feasible. Some alleged that the channel of the river was too deep, that the ice would destroy the structure, and that it would obstruct navigation; while by far the greater number rejected the idea altogether as chimerical. But Cox persevered. He brought the influential and enterprising to his views; a charter was obtained, and this energetic and skilful mechanic saw the bridge he had so dexterously planned in his brain become a reality. Captain John Stone, of Concord, Mass., was the architect of this bridge. His epitaph in the old burying-ground there says he was a man of good natural abilities, which seemed to be adorned with modern virtues and Christian graces. He died in 1791.

The opening of the structure upon the anniversary of the battle of Bunker Hill, and only eleven years after that event, attracted upwards of twenty thousand spectators. The day was ushered in by a discharge of thirteen cannon from the opposite heights of Breed's Hill, Charlestown, and Copp's Hill, Boston, accompanied by repeated peals from the bells of Christ Church. At one o'clock, P. M., the proprietors assembled in the State House for the purpose of conducting the several branches of the Legislature over the bridge. The procession, which included not only the public officials, but almost every individual of prominence in the community, moved from State Street, amid a salute from the Castle, and upon its arrival at the bridge the attendant companies of artillery formed two lines to the right and left, through which the cortege passed on to the middle of the bridge, where it halted. The President of the Corporation, Thomas Russell, then advanced alone, and directed Mr. Cox to fix the draw for the passage of the company, which was immediately done. The procession continued its march to Breed's Hill, where two tables, each three hundred and twenty feet long, had been laid, at which eight hundred guests sat down and prolonged the festivities until evening.

When built, this was the longest bridge in the world, and, except the abutments, was entirely of wood. Until West Boston Bridge was constructed, in 1793, it yielded a splendid return to the proprietors; but the latter surpassed it not only in length, but in beauty of architecture, and, with the causeway on the Cambridge side, formed a beautiful drive or prom-

enade of about two miles in extent. It also lessened the distance from Cambridge to Boston more than a mile. In 1828
Warren Bridge was opened, but not without serious opposition
from the proprietors of the old avenue ; and the two bridges
might not inaptly have served some native poet for a colloquy
as famous as that of the rival " Brigs of Ayr."

> " Nae langer thrifty citizens an' douce
> Meet owre a pint, or in the Council-house ;
> But staumrel, corky-headed, graceless Gentry,
> The herryment and ruin of the country;
> Men three-parts made by Tailors and by Barbers,
> Wha' waste your well hain'd gear on d—d *new Brigs* and Harbours ! "

The ferry, which was the original mode of transit between
the two peninsulas, was established in 1635, and five years
later was granted to Harvard College. To compensate for the
loss of the income from this source when Charles River Bridge
was built, the proprietors were required to pay £ 200 per
annum to the University, and in 1792 the same sum was
imposed on the West Boston Bridge Corporation.

Two handbills, each embellished with a rude woodcut of
the bridge, were printed on the occasion of the opening, in
1786. One was from the " Charlestown Press " ; the other was
printed by " E. Russell, Boston, next door to Dr. Haskins',
near Liberty Pole." From the broadside (as it was then
called), published at the request and for the benefit of the
directors and friends of this " grand and almost unparalleled
undertaking," we present the following extract : —

" This elegant work was begun on the First of June 1785, (a day
remarkable in the Annals of America as the Ports of Boston and
Charlestown were unjustly shut up by an arbitrary *British* Administration) and was finished on the seventeenth of the same month
1786, the ever memorable day on which was fought the famous and
bloody Battle of Bunker-Hill, where was shewn the Valour of the
undisciplined NEW ENGLAND MILITIA under the magnanimous
Warren who gloriously fell in his COUNTRY'S CAUSE ! *Blessed Be
His Memory !! And All the People — Say Amen ! ! !* " [1]

[1] A new steel structure is now replacing the old,

The building committee were Hon. Nathaniel Gorham, Richard Devens, David Wood, Jr., Captain Joseph Cordis, Andrew Symmes, Jr., and John Larkin.

Lemuel Cox, the artisan, was born in Boston in 1736, and died in Charlestown in 1806. In 1787 he built the bridge to Malden, which was finished in six months; and in the following year (1788), the Essex Bridge, at Salem, was constructed by him. In 1789 he was living in Prince Street, in Boston, and styled himself a millwright. In 1790, accompanied by a Mr. Thompson, Cox went to Ireland, where he was invited to estimate for the building of a bridge over the Foyle at Londonderry. His proposals being accepted, the two Americans purchased a ship, which they loaded at Sheepscot, Maine, with lumber, and having secured about twenty of their countrymen, skilled in shaping timber, set sail for Ireland. The bridge, which connected the city and county, consisted of fifty-eight arches, all of American oak, and was completed in five months. The Foyle was here about nine hundred feet wide and forty feet deep at high water. What made Cox's achievement the more important was the fact that Milne, an English engineer, had surveyed the river and pronounced the scheme impracticable.

Our pioneer in bridge-building on a great scale in America has received but scanty recompense at the hands of biographers. Dr. Ure has neither noticed his great works in Ireland nor in this country. Before he left Europe, Mr. Cox was applied to by the Corporation of London to take down Wren's monument, which was supposed to threaten a fall; but, as they would not give him his price, he declined. Massachusetts granted him, in 1796, a thousand acres of land in Maine, for being the first inventor of a machine to cut card-wire, the first projector of a powder-mill in the State, and the first to suggest the employment of prisoners on Castle Island to make nails. The rude woodcut which adorned the head of the broadside circulated at the opening of Charles River Bridge was executed, as the printer says, by "that masterpiece of ingenuity, Mr. Lemuel Cox." It shows a detachment of artillery with cannon ready for firing, and a coach with four horses, and a footman behind, driving at full speed over the bridge.

In 1786 no ceremony would have been considered complete without the aid of the Muses, and the Nine were energetically invoked in forty stanzas, of which we submit a fair specimen : —

> " The smiling morn now peeps in view,
>     Bright with peculiar charms,
>   See, *Boston* Nymphs and Charlestown too
>     Each linked arm in arm.

> 2.  " I sing the day in which the BRIDGE
>       Is finished and done,
>     Boston and Charlestown lads rejoice,
>       And fire your cannon guns.

> 3.  " The BRIDGE is finished now I say,
>       Each other bridge outvies,
>     For *London Bridge,* compar'd with ours
>       Appears in dim disguise.

> 23.  " Now Boston, Charlestown nobly join
>       And roast a fatted Ox
>     On noted Bunker Hill combine,
>       To toast our patriot COX.

> 38.  " May North and South and Charlestown all
>       Agree with one consent,
>     To love each one like Indian's rum,
>       On publick good be sent. "

Chelsea Bridge was built in 1803, and the direct avenue to Salem opened by means of a turnpike, by which the distance from Boston was greatly diminished. The bridge was to revert to the Commonwealth in seventy years.

In 1643 the colony of Massachusetts Bay was divided into four shires, of which Middlesex, named after that county in Old England which includes London, was one. It is the most populous of all the counties of the Old Bay State, and embraces within its limits the earliest battle-fields of the Revolution, the first seat of learning in the English colonies, and the manufactures which have made American industry known in every quarter of the globe.

Charlestown, the mother of Boston, resembled in its super-
ficial features its more powerful offspring.   It was a peninsula,
connected with the mainland by a narrow neck ; it had three
principal hills also, but the mutations which have swept over
the one have not left the other untouched.   To remove a
mountain is now only a question of time ; and were Mahomet
to live again, he would see that his celebrated reply has become void of significance.

Like  Shawmut,[1]  Mishawum[2]  had  its  solitary  settler  in
Thomas Walford, the sturdy smith, who was found living
here in 1628, when some of Endicott's company made their way
through the wilderness from Salem.   The next year the settlement received some accessions, and was named Charles Towne
by Governor Endicott, in honor of the reigning prince.   Winthrop's company arrived at Charlestown in June and July,
1630 ; but, owing to the mortality that prevailed and the want
of water, the settlers soon began to disperse, the larger part removing with the governor to Shawmut.   A second dispersion
took place on account of the destruction of the town during
the battle of 1775, leaving nothing but the hills, the ancient
burial-place, and a few old houses that escaped the conflagration in the victors' hands.

After nearly two centuries and a half of separate existence,
Charlestown has at length become part of Boston.   The people simply ratified what History had already decreed.   Now
Bunker Hill and Dorchester Heights lie, as they ought to lie,
within a common municipal government.

The old ferry, besides serving the primitive settlers, is deserving of recognition as the place where the first exchange of
prisoners took place after hostilities began between America
and Great Britain.   This event occurred on the 6th of June
following the battle of Lexington, and was conducted by Dr.
Warren and General Putnam for the colony, and by Major
Moncrieff on behalf of General Gage.   The contending parties
concerned themselves little at that time about what has since

[1] Indian name of Boston; [2] and Charlestown.

been known as "belligerent rights," each being ready to get rid of some troublesome visitors by the easiest and most natural method. Warren and Putnam rode to the ferry in a phaeton, followed by a cavalcade of prisoners, some mounted and others riding in chaises. Arrived at the shore, the Doctor and 'Old Put' signalled the Lively, man-of-war, and Major Moncrieff come off as related. After the performance of their public business, the parties to the exchange adjourned to Mr. Foster's, and had what was then and since known as "a good time." A much worse fate happened to the Bunker Hill prisoners, and it is quite evident that both parties looked upon the collision at Lexington as premature, — the King's commander with misgiving as to whether his conduct would be sustained in England ; the colonists as to whether their resistance had not closed the door against that reconciliation with the throne they professed so ardently to desire.

The great square around which clustered the humble habitations of the settlers ; the "great house," inhabited for a time by the governor, and in which the settlement of Boston was probably planned ; the thatched meeting-house, and even the first tavern of old Samuel Long, — afterwards the sign of the Two Cranes and situated on the City Hall site,* — were what met the eye of Josselyn as he ascended the beach into the market-place in 1638. He describes the rattlesnake he saw while walking out there, and his visit to Long's ordinary. Eventually, the town stretched itself along the street leading to the mainland.

In these times of degeneracy, when man requires the most repressive measures to compel him to abstain from the vice of intemperance, we can but look back with longing eyes upon those halcyon days when a traveller entering a public inn was immediately followed by an officer, who, with the utmost *sang froid*, placed himself near the guest, and when, in his opinion, his charge had partaken of enough strong waters, by a wave of his hand forbade the host to fetch another stoup of liquor. What a companion for a midnight wassail of good fellows ! With his

* Also the site of the "Great House."

gaze riveted upon the countenances of the revellers, he marks each stage of transition from sobriety to that point which we may call the perfect equipoise, where the law steps in. With a rap of his staff upon the floor, or a thwack of his fist on the table, he checks the song or silences the jest. We hardly know how to sufficiently admire such parental care in our forefathers; we hesitate to compare it with the present system.

The night-watch, too, was an institution. With their great-coats, dark-lanterns, and iron-shod staffs, they went their rounds to warn all wayfarers to their beds, admonish the loiterers who might chance to be abroad, or arrest evil-doers. Whether they were marshalled nightly by their officer we know not, but we doubt not they would have diligently executed their commission.

*Dogb.* Well, you are to call at all the alehouses, and bid those that are drunk get them to bed.

2 *Watch.* How if they will not?

*Dogb.* Why, let them alone till they are sober.

The watchman had an ancient custom of crying "All's well!" and the hour of the night, as he went his rounds, at the same time striking his bill upon the pavement. This was to banish sleep altogether from the bed of sickness, or divide it into periods of semi-consciousness for the more robust. Well can we imagine the drowsy guardian, lurking in some dark passage or narrow lane, shouting with stentorian lungs his sleep-destroying watch-cry under the stars, and startling a whole neighborhood from its slumbers. Like the Scot, he murdered sleep; like him, he should have been condemned to sleep no more.

Dr. Bentley, of Salem, who perhaps had a watchman nightly posted under his window, pertinently inquired through a news-paper if it would not be better to cry out when all was not well, and let well enough alone.

Charlestown has given to the world some eminent public characters. Earliest among these is John Harvard, the patron of the college that bears his name. He was admitted a free-man "with promise of such accommodations as we best can," in 1637, but died the following year, leaving half his estate for the use of the infant school of learning. He also left his library of more than three hundred volumes to the College, and has a simple granite shaft, erected to his memory on Burial Hill, in Charlestown, by the graduates of the University he aided to found. Edward Everett delivered the address on the occasion of the dedication. The eastern face of the monument, besides the name of John Harvard, bears the following inscription.

HARVARD'S MONUMENT.

"On the 26th of September, A. D. 1828, this stone was erected by the graduates of the University at Cambridge, in honor of its founder, who died at Charlestown on the 26th of September, 1638."

The western front bears a Latin inscription, recognizing that one who had laid the corner-stone of letters in America should no longer be without a monument, however humble. This memorial, which was raised nearly two hundred years after the decease of Harvard, rests on a suppositive site, his burial-place having been forgotten or obliterated. Unfortunately, less is known of Harvard than of most of his contemporaries, but that little is treasured as a precious legacy to the Alumni of the University. The old graveyard, one of the most interesting in New England, as having received the ashes of many of Winthrop's band, suffered mutilation while the town was held by the British in 1775 – 6. It is stated that the gravestones were in some cases used by the soldiers for thresholds to their barracks.

### THE NIGHT SURPRISE AT DONCASTER.

Charlestown may also lay claim to having given two brave soldiers to Old Noll's army when that hard-hitting Puritan was cracking the crowns of loyal Scot, Briton, or Celt, and sending the ringleted cavaliers over-seas to escape his long arm.

Principal of these was William Rainsborrow who lived here in 1639, and was, with Robert Sedgwick and Israel Stoughton, a member of the Honorable Artillery Company of Boston. Rainsborrow had risen to be colonel of a regiment in the Parliamentary army, in which Stoughton (of Dorchester) was lieutenant-colonel, Nehemiah Bourne, a Boston shipwright, major, and John Leverett, afterwards governor, a captain; William Hudson, supposed to be of Boston, also, was ensign.

In the year 1648, the Yorkshire royalists, who had been living in quiet since the first war, were again excited by intelligence of Duke Hamilton's intended invasion. A plan was laid and successfully carried out to surprise Pomfret Castle, (sometimes called Pontefract) the greatest and strongest castle in all England, and then held by Colonel Cotterel as governor for the Parliament. The castle was soon beseiged by Sir Edward Rhodes and Sir Henry Cholmondly with five thousand regular troops, but the royal garrison made good their conquest.

It being likely to prove a tedious affair, General Rainsborrow was sent from London by the Parliament to put a speedy end to it. He was esteemed a general of great skill and courage, exceedingly zealous in the Protector's service, with a reputation gained both by land and sea, — he having been, for a time, Admiral of Cromwell's fleet. Rainsborrow pitched his headquarters, for the present, at Doncaster, twelve miles from Pomfret, with twelve hundred foot and two regiments of horse.

The castle garrison having learned of Hamilton's defeat at Preston, and that Sir Marmaduke Langdale, who commanded the English in that battle, was a prisoner, formed the bold design of seizing General Rainsborrow in his camp, and holding him a hostage for Sir Marmaduke. The design seemed the more feasible, because the general and his men were in no apprehension of any surprise; the castle being twelve miles distant, closely besieged, and the only garrison for the King in England.

The plan was shrewdly laid, favored by circumstances, and was completely successful except that instead of bringing the general off they were obliged to kill him. With only twenty-two picked men, well mounted, Captain William Paulden penetrated into Doncaster undiscovered. The guards were forced and dispersed, while a party of four made for the general's lodgings. At the door they were met by his lieutenant, who, on their announcing that they had come with despatches from General Cromwell, conducted them to the general's chamber, where he was in bed. While the general was opening the despatch, in which was nothing but blank paper, the king's men told him he was their prisoner, but that not a hair of his head should be touched, if he went quietly along with them. They then disarmed his lieutenant, who had so innocently facilitated their design, and brought them both out of the house. A horse was prepared for the general, and he was directed to mount, which he at first seemed willing to do, and put his foot in the stirrup, but looking about him and seeing only four enemies, while his lieutenant and sentinel (whom they had not disarmed) were standing by him, he pulled his foot out of the stirrup, and cried *Arms! Arms!*

Upon this, one of his enemies, letting fall his sword and pistol,— for he did not wish to kill the general, — caught hold of Rainsborrow, who grappled with him, and both fell to the ground. The general's lieutenant then picked up the trooper's pistol, but was instantly run through the body by Paulden's lieutenant, while in the act of cocking it. A third stabbed Rainsborrow in the neck; yet the general gained his feet with the trooper's sword, with whom he had been struggling, in his hand. The lieutenant of the party then passed his sword through his body, when the brave but ill-fated Rainsborrow fell dead upon the pavement.

Another of Charlestown's worthies whom we cite was

Robert Sedgwick, who became a major-general under the Protector, and is mentioned by Carlyle. Sedgwick was a favorite with the "Usurper" as he was called by the King's party, who sent him with a well-appointed fleet to Jamaica, to replace D'Oyley, a cavalier, who, notwithstanding his success in the West Indies, was disliked by Cromwell. Cromwell had, with his usual astuteness, encouraged the cavaliers to embark in the conquest of Jamaica, where rich booty was expected and whence few of them returned. Sedgwick, unaccustomed to the climate and mode of life, died before he had an opportunity of accomplishing anything.

An original portrait of Leverett in his military garb shows him to be every inch a soldier. He is painted in a buff surcoat fastened with steel frogs, and has a stout blade with steel hilt and guard suspended by an embroidered shoulder-belt, at his thigh.

> "His waistcoat was of stubborn Buff,
>     Some say Fuizee and Ponyard proof";

his head is uncovered, and his curling black locks and beard set off a bronzed and martial countenance. Plumed hat, high jack-boots, and gauntlets complete a military attire of the time by no means unbecoming.

Nathaniel Gorham, a resident of Town Hill, whose name appears among the projectors of Charles River Bridge, was a man eminent in the councils of the State and the nation. He was a member of both the First and Second Provincial Congress; of the General Court, the Board of War, and of the State Constitutional Convention. A delegate to the Continental Congress in 1782 – 83, and president of that body in 1786; he was also a member of Governor Hancock's council in 1789, at the time of Washington's visit. His account of the difference which arose between the President and the Governor, as to which should pay the first visit, and which it is believed is now for the first time in print, sheds some new light on that affair which at the time convulsed all circles of the Massachusetts capital. In regard to the assertion that the Governor expected the first call, Mr. Gorham says : —

" There is nothing further from the truth than this idea; and I do not speak from uncertainties, for the Council was sitting every day for a week before the President's arrival, and met almost every day at the Governor's house to concert proper measures for his reception. I was apprehensive something like what has happened might take place, and proposed that the address which the Governor and Council had agreed to make should be delivered at Cambridge, where the Lieutenant-Governor and Council first saw the President, with a letter from the Governor, or an authorized message, that his indisposition prevented his attending with the Council : but this idea was not supported. The Governor did not oppose it, but on the contrary declared in the most explicit terms that he had no doubt in his mind of the propriety of his making the first visit. This was on Friday. On Saturday the President arrived, and not choosing to come up to the Governor's to dine, the Lieutenant Governor and two of his Council went down to his lodgings in the evening, authorized by the Governor to make the most explicit declaration as to the point in question. This brought some explanation from the President by which it appeared that he had been misinformed as to the state of the Governor's health ; for he had been led to believe that the Governor had dined out some days before, and had rode out every day the preceding week, when to my knowledge he had not been out of his chamber. But the explanation made by the Council on Saturday evening and the Governor's visit on Sunday soon removed every difficulty."

It was during this visit that an incident occurred illustrating Washington's rigid punctuality. He had appointed eight o'clock in the morning as the hour in which he should set out for Salem; and while the Old South clock was striking eight, he was mounting his horse. The company of cavalry which was to escort him, not anticipating this strict punctuality, were parading in Tremont Street after his departure ; and it was not until the President had reached Charles River Bridge, where he stopped a few minutes, that the troop overtook him. On passing the corps, the President with perfect good-nature said, " Major Gibbs, I thought you had been too long in my family, not to know when it was eight o'clock." Charlestown was the first town in Massachusetts to institute public funeral honors on the death of this great man.

What was particularly remarkable in Mr. Gorham was his perspicacity with regard to the destiny of the great West. This led him, at a time when there was neither public nor private credit, to purchase, in connection with Oliver Phelps, an immense tract of land then belonging to Massachusetts, lying on the Genesee, in New York. The area of the purchase comprises ten or twelve counties and includes hundreds of flourishing towns.

Jedediah Morse, the father of American geography, and minister of the first church in Charlestown from 1789 to 1820, describes Charlestown in his Gazetteer of 1797 as containing two hundred and fifty houses and twenty-five hundred inhabitants, with no other public buildings of note than the Congregational meeting-house and almshouse. A traveller who visited the place in 1750 says it then had two hundred houses, and was a pleasant little town " where the Bostoneers build many vessels." The destruction of the town and dispersion of the inhabitants caused the exemption of that part lying within the Neck, that is to say the peninsula, from furnishing troops for the Continental army in 1776. In 1784 Nathaniel Gorham was sent to England on a singular mission by the sufferers from the burning of the town in 1775, — it being for no other purpose than to solicit aid for the consequences of an act of war. The mission resulted in failure, as it deserved, and was condemned by the thinking portion of the community, who did not believe we could afford to ask alms of those whom we had just forced to acknowledge our independence.

Dr. Morse's first work on geography for the use of schools was prepared at New Haven in 1784. This was soon followed by larger works on the same subject and by gazetteers, compiled from the historical and descriptive works of the time, and aided by travel and correspondence. We cannot withhold our astonishment when we look into one of these early volumes ; for it is only by this means we realize the immense strides our country has been taking since the Revolution, or that a vast extent of territory, then a wilderness, has now become the seat of political power for these states and the granary from whence half Europe is fed. What was then laid down as a desert is now seamed by railways and covered with cities and villages. The early volumes of the Massachusetts Historical Society contained many valuable topographical and descriptive papers contributed by Drs. Belknap, Holmes, Bentley, and others, and of which Dr. Morse, an influential member of the society, in all probability availed himself in his later works.

Geography was an original passion with Dr. Morse, which it is said rendered him so absent-minded that once, being asked by his teacher at a Greek recitation where a certain verb was found, he replied, "On the coast of Africa." While he was a tutor at Yale, the want of geographies there induced him to prepare notes for his pupils, to serve as text books, which he eventually printed. Such was the origin of his labors in this field of learning.

The clergy have always been our historians, and New England annals would be indeed meagre, but for the efforts of Hubbard, Prince, the Mathers, Belknap, Gordon, Morse, Holmes, and others. As Hutchinson drew on Hubbard, so all the writers on the Revolution derive much of their material from Gordon, whose work, if it did not satisfy the intense American feeling of his day, seems at this time remarkable for fairness and truth. The meridian of London, where Dr. Gordon's work first appeared, was freely said to have impaired his narrative and to have caused the revision of his manuscript to the suppression of whatever might wound the susceptibilities of his English patrons.

Dr. Morse engaged much in controversy, Unitarianism having begun publicly to assert itself in his time, and in some instances to obtain control of the old Orthodox houses of worship. The struggle of Dr. Holmes to maintain himself against the wave of new ideas forms a curious chapter in religious controversial history. The energy with which Jedediah Morse engaged in the conflict seriously affected his health, but he kept his church true to its original, time-honored doctrines. Dr. Morse, who was the townsman and classmate of Dr. Holmes, is understood to have introduced the latter at Cambridge.

On some occasion, Dr. Gardiner of Trinity Church, Boston, who, by the way, was a pupil of the celebrated Dr. Parr, went to preach in the church at Cambridge, and, as a matter of course, many of the professors went to hear him. Unitarianism had appeared in the Episcopal, as well as the Congregational Church.

Dr. Gardiner began his discourse somewhat in this wise : " My brethren, there is a new science discovered ; it is called Biblical criticism. Do you want to know what Biblical criticism is ? I will tell you.

> ' *Off* with his head ! So much for Buckingham.'   *Cooke.*
> ' *Off with his head !* So much for Buckingham.'   *Kemble.*

Mr. Cooper says neither are right, but that it should be rendered, ' Off with his head ! *so much* for Buckingham !' My friends that is Biblical criticism." We leave the reader to imagine the effect upon the grave and reverend professors of the College.

Dr. Morse was sole editor of the Panoplist from 1806 to 1811, and was prominent in establishing the Andover Theological Seminary. He engaged at times in missionary work, the records of marriages performed by him at the Isles of Shoals being still in existence there. One of his last labors was a visit to the Indian tribes of the Northwest, under the direction of the government, a report of which he published in 1832.

At the time of the excitement in New England against secret societies, when the most direful apprehensions existed that religion itself was to be overthrown by Free-Masonry, the Illuminati, or bugbears of a similar character, Dr. Morse was one of the overseers of Harvard College and a distinguished alarmist. As such, he opposed with all his might the proposal of the Phi Beta Kappa Society to publish " The Literary Miscellany," which afterwards appeared under their auspices. It was conjectured that this literary association, with its then unrevealed Greek initials, was an off-shoot of some order of Masonry, and hence the Doctor's vigilance to prevent the entrance of any corrupting influences within the walls of the seminary.

The old parsonage which was the residence of Dr. Morse was situated in what is now Harvard Street, between the City Hall and Church, the house standing quite near the latter, while the garden extended down the hill on the ground now occupied by Harvard Row, quite to the City Hall. It was a two-story wooden house, removed many years since from its historic site on the ancient Town Hill.

Dr. Morse's more distinguished son, Samuel Finley Breese, known to all the world for making electricity the instantaneous messenger of his will, first saw the light under the shadow of Bunker Hill. His eulogy, thanks to his own invention, was pronounced simultaneously from St. Petersburg to California; his memory received the homage of crowned heads, as well as of our own republican court, such as has rarely, if ever, been accorded to any explorer in the pathways of science. As the *savans* of the Old World have in times past bowed before a Franklin, a Rumford, and a Bowditch, they have once more been called upon to inscribe in their high places of honor the name of an American.

Samuel F. B. Morse was not born at the parsonage, but in the house of Thomas Edes, on Main Street, to which Dr. Morse had removed while his own roof was undergoing some repairs. The house, which is also noted as the first erected in Charlestown after its destruction in 1775, stands at the corner of Main Street Court at a little distance from the Unitarian Church, is of wood, and has three stories.

Young Morse seconded his father's passion for geography by one as strongly marked for drawing, and the blank margin of his Virgil occupied far more of his thoughts than the text. His *penchant* for art, exhibited in much the same manner as Allston's, his future master, did not meet with the same encouragement. A caricature, founded upon some fracas among the students at Yale, and in which the faculty were burlesqued, was seized, handed to President Dwight, and the author, who was no other than our friend Morse, called up. The delinquent received a severe lecture upon his waste of time, violation of college laws, and filial disobedience, without exhibiting any signs of contrition ; but when at length Dr. Dwight said to him, "Morse you are no painter ; this is a rude attempt, a complete failure," he was touched to the quick, and could not keep back the tears.    On being questioned by his fellow-students as to what Dr. Dwight had said or done, "He says I am no painter !" roared Morse, cut to the heart through his darling passion.

A canvas, executed by Morse at the age of nineteen, of the Landing of the Pilgrim's may be seen at the Charlestown City Hall.    He accompanied Allston to Europe, where he became a pupil of West, and, it is said, also, of Copley, though the latter died two years after Morse reached England.    He exhibited his "Dying Hercules" at the Royal Academy in 1813, receiving subsequently from the London Adelphi a prize gold medal for a model of the same in plaster.    In 1815 he returned to America and pursued portrait painting, his price being fifteen dollars for a picture.    Morse became a resident of New York about 1822, and painted Lafayette when the latter visited this country shortly after.

Various accounts have been given of the manner in which Morse first imbibed the idea of making electricity the means of conveying intelligence, the one usually accepted being that, while returning from Europe in 1832, on board the packet ship Sully, a fellow-passenger related some experiments he had witnessed in Paris with the electro-magnet, which made such an impression upon one of his auditors that he walked the deck the whole night.    Professor Morse's own account was that he gained his knowledge of the working of the electro-magnet while attending the lectures of Dr. J. Freeman Dana, then professor of chemistry in the University of New York, delivered before the New York Athenæum.    "I witnessed," says Morse, "the effects of the conjunctive wires in the different forms described by him in his lectures, and exhibited to his audience. The electro-magnet was put in action by an intensity battery ; it was made to sustain the weight of its armature, when the conjunctive wire was connected with the poles of the battery, or the circuit was closed ; and it was made 'to drop its load' upon opening the circuit."

Morse's application to the Twenty-Seventh Congress for aid to put his invention to the test of practical illustration was only carried by a vote of eighty-nine to eighty-seven. The inventor went to Washington with exhausted means and heartsick with despondency. Two votes saved, perhaps, this wonderful discovery to American invention. With the thirty thousand dollars he obtained, Morse stretched his first wires from Washington to Baltimore, — we say wires, because the principle of the ground circuit was not then known, and only discovered, we believe, by accident, so that a wire to go and another to return between the cities was deemed necessary by Morse to complete his first circuit. The first wire was of copper.

The first message, now in the custody of the Connecticut Historical Society, was dictated by Miss Annie G. Ellsworth. With trembling hand Morse must have spelled out the words,—

" WHAT HATH GOD WROUGHT ! "

With an intensity of feeling he must have waited for the "aye, aye " of his distant correspondent. It was done ; and the iron thread, freighted with joy or woe to men or nations, now throbs responsive to the delicate touch of a child. It now springs up from the desert in advance of civilization ; its spark o'erleaps the ocean and well-nigh spans the globe itself. No man can say that its destiny is accomplished ; but we have lived to grasp the lightning and play with the thunderbolt.

The telegraph was at first regarded with a superstitious dread in some sections of the country. Will it be credited that in a Southern State a drouth was attributed to its occult influences, and the people, infatuated with the idea, levelled the wires with the ground? The savages of the plains have been known to lie in ambush watching the mysterious agent of the white man, and listening to the humming of the wires, which they vaguely associated with evil augury to themselves. So common was it for the Indians to knock off the insulators with their rifles, in order to gratify their curiosity in regard to the " singing cord," that it was, at first, extremely difficult to keep the lines in repair along the Pacific railway.

As you go towards Charlestown Neck, when about half-way

from the point where Main and Warren Streets unite, you see
at your right hand the old-fashioned two-story wooden house
in which Charlotte Cushman passed some of her early life.

She was born in Boston, in that part of the town ycleped
the North End, and in an old house that stood within the
present enclosure of the Hancock School yard. It should not
be forgotten that that sterling actor, John Gilbert, was born in
the next house. Here young John spoke his first piece and
here the great curtain was rung up for little Charlotte. When
the lights shall be at last turned off, and darkness envelop the
stage, there will be two wreaths of *immortelles* to be added to
the tributes which that famed old quarter already claims for its
long roll of celebrated names.

It is related that, when a child, Charlotte was one day in-
cautiously playing on Long Wharf, where her father kept a
store, and there fell into the water. She was rescued and
taken home dripping wet, but instead of an ecstatic burst of joy
at the safety of her darling, her mother gave her a sound whipping. Perhaps this was only one of those sudden revulsions
which Tom Hood exemplifies in his " Lost Heir."

After her removal to Charlestown Charlotte went to Miss
Austin's school. This lady was a relative of William Austin,
the author of " Peter Rugg." Charlotte was a good scholar,
and almost always had the badge of excellence suspended from
her neck. She was very strong physically, as some of her
schoolmates bear witness to this day. Although she displayed
considerable aptitude as a reader, her predilection was, at this
time, altogether in favor of a musical career, and she cultivated
her voice assiduously to that end.

Her first appearance in public was at a social concert given
at the hall No. 1 Franklin Avenue, in Boston, March 25th,
1830, where she was assisted by Mr. Farmer, Mr. John F.
Pray, Messrs. Stedman, Morris, and others. She also sang at
one of Mrs. Wood's Concerts, and that lady, pleased with her
fine contralto voice, advised her to turn her attention to the
lyric drama. Mr. Maeder, the husband of Clara Fisher, brought
her out as the Countess, in *Les Noces de Figaro*, in April, 1835,
at the Tremont Theatre.

Her voice failing, she determined to adopt the acting branch of the profession, and studied under the direction of W. E. Burton, the celebrated comedian. Having mastered the part of Lady Macbeth, she appeared with complete success at the New York theatres in this and other leading characters. At this time she brought out her youngest sister, Susan, herself assuming male parts. She was manageress of one of the Philadelphia theatres until Mr. Macready, in 1844, invited her to accompany him in a professional tour of the Northern States, which gave her an opportunity of displaying her tragic powers to advantage.

During her tour with Macready, she played in Boston at the Old Melodeon, with scarcely a single voice of the press raised in her favor. Her benefit, at which the tragedian, with characteristic littleness, refused to appear, was a pecuniary loss to her. But it was during this trip that Macready said to her one day, in his brusque, pompous way, "Girl, you would do well in London." This remark was not lost on the quick-witted Yankee maiden.

The next year found her in London, but she had kept her own counsel, and even Mr. Macready did not know her intention. In vain, however, she solicited an engagement, for she had neither fame nor beauty to recommend her. But at last, when she had spent almost her last farthing, — except the little sum at her banker's, laid aside to take her back home in case all else should fail, — a ray of hope appeared. Maddocks, the manager of the Princess's Theatre, proposed to her to appear in company with Mr. Forrest, who was then, like herself, seeking an opening at the London theatres. The shrewd manager thought that perhaps two American Stars might fill his house.

Charlotte's reply was characteristic of her acuteness. "Give me," she said to the manager, "a chance first. If I succeed, I can well afford to play with Mr. Forrest; if I fail, I shall be only too glad to do so." She made her *début* as Bianca in *Fazio*. The first act, in which the dialogue is tame, passed off ominously. The audience were attentive, but undemonstrative. The actress retired to her dressing-room much depressed with

the fear of failure. "This will never do, Sally," she remarked
to her negro waiting-maid, then and after her affectionate attendant.

"No, indeed, it won't, miss ; but you 'll fetch um bimeby,"
said the faithful creature. The play quietly proceeded until
Bianca spoke the lines, —

*"Fazio, thou hast seen Aldabella!"*

Those words, in which love, anger, and jealousy were all
struggling for the mastery, uttered with indescribable accent
and energy, startled the audience out of its well-bred, cold-
blooded propriety ; cheers filled the house, and Miss Cushman
remained mistress of the situation.

She afterwards appeared in conjunction with Mr. Forrest; but
that gentleman, who had then for the nonce put a curb upon
his fashion of tearing a passion to tatters, was overshadowed by
her. Forrest resented the preference of the public by extreme
rudeness to Charlotte on the stage, and by various unfriendly
acts, which caused a rupture that was never healed. Forrest
played Othello on the occasion above mentioned, Miss Cushman sustaining the part of Emilia. Her performance was
throughout intelligent, impressive, natural, without any strain-
ing after effect ; while her energy, at times, completely carried
the audience along with her.

By the friendship of Charles Kemble and of Mr. Phelps of
Sadler's Wells she attracted the favorable notice of royalty.
It is a fact as singular as it is true, that, on her return from
England, Boston, the city of her birth, was the only place in
which she did not at once meet a cordial reception ; but her
talents compelled their own recognition and buried the few
paltry detractors out of sight. She appeared at the Federal
Street Theatre and won an enthusiastic verdict of popular favor
within that old temple of histrionic art.

The part in which Miss Cushman has achieved her greatest
reputation in this country is that of Meg Merrilies in "Guy
Mannering," a creation peculiarly her own. The character, notwithstanding its repulsive features, becomes in her hands weird,

terrible, and fascinating. Her somewhat masculine *physique* and angular physiognomy have given more character to the assumption of such male parts as Ion and Romeo than is usually the case with her sex. But Miss Cushman was a real artiste, limited to no narrow sphere of her calling. She could play Queen Catharine and Mrs. Simpson in the same evening with equal success, and retained in no small degree, when verging on threescore, the energy and dramatic force of her palmy days.

At the opening of the Cushman School in Boston, Charlotte made an extempore address to the scholars, in which she explained to them her grand principle of action and the secret of her success. "Whatever you have to do," she said, "do it with all your might."

## CHAPTER II.

### AN HOUR IN THE GOVERNMENT DOCKYARD.

"There, where your argosies with portly sail,—
  Like signiors and rich burghers on the flood,
  Or, as it were, the pageants of the sea,—
  Do over-peer the petty traffickers."
                              *Merchant of Venice.*

THERE is a singular fascination in viewing objects created expressly for our destruction. The wounded soldier will make the most convulsive efforts to see the place where he has been struck, and if the leaden bullet which has so nearly threatened his life be placed in his hand, he regards it thereafter with a strange, unaccountable affection. So, when we find ourselves within the government dockyard we cannot pass by the rows of cannon gleaming in the sunshine, or the pyramids of shot and shell, without wondering how many they are destined to destroy. We have not yet learned to dispense with war, and the problem "How to kill" yet taxes the busiest brain, the most inventive genius.

Somehow, too, there is a certain consciousness the moment you set foot within any little strip of territory over which Uncle Sam exercises exclusive authority. The trig, pipe-clayed marine paces stiffly up and down before the entrance, hugging his shining musket as if it were a piece of himself, and looking straight before him, though you would feel yourself more at ease if he would look at you. The officer you see coming, in the laced cap, and to whom you would fain address yourself, never allows your eye to meet his own, but marches straight on, as he would do if he were going to storm a battery. The workmen, even, pursue their labor without the cheerful cries and chaffing which enliven the toil of their brethren outside. The

VIEW OF BUNKER HILL FROM THE NAVY YARD, BEFORE THE ERECTION OF THE MONUMENT, FROM A PAINTING

MADE IN 1825.

calkers' mallets seem to click in unison, the carpenters chip thoughtfully away on the live-oak frame. Everything is systematic, orderly, and precise, but rather oppressive withal.

In the first years of the nation's existence the government was obliged to make use of private yards, and that of Edmund Hartt, in Boston, may be considered the progenitor of this. Several vessels of the old navy, among them the famed Constitution, were built there, under supervision of officers appointed by the government. Henry Jackson, formerly colonel of the Sixteenth Continental Regiment, was appointed naval agent by his bosom friend, General Knox, when the latter was Secretary of War, and Caleb Gibbs, first commander of Washington's famous body-guard, was made naval storekeeper, with an office in Batterymarch Street, Boston. The yard at the bottom of Milk Street was also used for naval purposes by the government.

When Admiral Montague of the royal navy was stationed in our waters, he caused a survey of the harbor to be made, and is reported on good authority to have then said, "The devil got into the government for placing the naval depot at Halifax. God Almighty made Noddle's Island on purpose for a dockyard."

In 1799 the government despatched Mr. Joshua Humphries, the eminent naval architect, to Boston, to examine the proposed sites. The report was favorable to Charlestown, much to the chagrin of the proprietors of Noddle's Island, now East Boston, who had reckoned on a different decision. As Mr. John Harris, the principal owner of the tract selected, and Dr. Putnam, the government agent, were unable to agree upon terms, the affair was decided by a decree of the Middlesex Court of Sessions.

The purchase made by the United States was originally called Moulton's Point, from Robert Moulton, the ship-carpenter; it has also been indifferently styled Moreton's and Morton's Point, in connection with accounts of the battle of Bunker Hill, it being the place where Howe's main body landed on that day. The site also embraced what was known in old times as Dirty Marsh. The point was quite early selected for a fortification, and a small battery, or, as it was then called, a sconce, was thrown up, and armed with light pieces. The guns were secretly removed by the patriots in the autumn of 1774, without exciting the least suspicion of what was taking place on board the British vessels of war in the stream. Upon the evacuation of Boston this was one of the points which Washington directed his chief of artillery to fortify.

That part of the town in the neighborhood of the yard was long ago called Wapping, a circumstance which it has been thought proper to distinguish by a street of that name. In the days of the Great Rebellion this now unsavory locality could not have been much inferior to its prototype by the Thames, and poor Jack, in making his exit from the yard after a long cruise, had to run the gauntlet of all the merciless land-sharks that infested the place. At one time, however, the neighborhood was of quite a different cast, and some of the artisans of the yard found a convenient residence here ; among others, Josiah Barker, for thirty-four years the distinguished naval constructor at this station, lived in Wapping Street, in a house still standing on the north side of the street as you approach the yard from Chelsea Street.

The first records of this station begin in 1815, when an aggregate of forty-four officers and men was borne on the rolls, while it is said as many as six thousand were employed here during the Rebellion. In the beginning of the year mentioned, which was just at the conclusion of war with Great Britain, there was but a single wharf in the yard. The frigates Congress, Macedonian, Constitution, the seventy-fours Washington and Independence, and the brig Chippewa were then lying here.

A lady who visited the yard in 1824, and recorded her impressions, gives a somewhat humorous account of the difficulties she encountered. She says : —

"The United States Navy-Yard is likewise located in Charlestown. A few marines are also stationed here ; the most trifling, abandoned-looking men, from their appearance, to be found. I applied to the Commandant, Major W——, for liberty to inspect the interior of the yard, but this haughty bashaw sent word '*he was engaged*,' and that I must report my business to the lieutenant,' — rather a reproach to Uncle Sam.    As in duty bound, I obeyed his highness, and called on the lieutenant, whom I found unqualified to give the information I wished to obtain ; and, after undergoing sundry indignities from these mighty men of war, I had to give up the design."

Commodore Samuel Nicholson was the first commandant of the yard, and the somewhat peculiar architecture of the house used as a residence by the commodores is a specimen of his taste, —

> "The brave old commodore,
> The rum old commodore."

When the Constitution was building, Nicholson, who was to have her, exercised a general supervision over her construction ; though, notwithstanding anything that has been said, Colonel George Claghorn was the principal and authorized constructor.

In consequence of the narrow limits of Hartt's Yard, it had been agreed that no spectators should be admitted on the day previous to that fixed for the launch, without the permission of Captain Nicholson, Colonel Claghorn, or General Jackson. While the workmen were at breakfast Colonel Claghorn had admitted some ladies and gentlemen to view the ship, but when they attempted to go on board Nicholson forbade their entering.    This was communicated to Colonel Claghorn.    In the afternoon of the same day some visitors who had been denied an entrance to the ship by Nicholson were admitted by Claghorn, who, however, was not aware that they had been previously refused permission.    The captain, who was furious when he saw the men he had just turned away approaching, exclaimed to Claghorn, "D—n it ! do you know whom you have admitted, and that I have just refused them?"    The latter replied that he did not know that circumstance, but, having passed his word, they might go on board.    The whole party being assembled on the Constitution's deck, Colonel Claghorn went up to the captain and desired, with some heat, that he might not treat these visitors as he had done the ladies in the morning; to which Nicholson replied that he should say no more to them, but that he had a right to command on board his own ship. To this Claghorn rejoined that *he* commanded on board the ship, and that if Captain Nicholson did not like the regulations, he might go out of her. Upon this the parties immediately collared each other, and Nicholson, who carried a cane, attempted to strike his adversary, but the bystanders interfered and separated the belligerents. The affair was settled by mutual apologies. Nicholson died in Charlestown in 1811, and was buried under Christ Church, in Boston. It was said that Preble, who was appointed to the Constitution under Nicholson, declined serving with him, and expressed doubts of his courage. General Knox's son, Henry Jackson Knox, was a midshipman on board Old Ironsides on her first cruise.

Hull was one of the early commanders of the yard. The receiving-ship Ohio, now at this station, carried his flag in the Mediterranean in 1839. Bainbridge was commandant at the time of Lafayette's visit in 1824. These two men, famous in the annals of the American Navy, could conquer their invincible adversaries yard-arm to yard-arm, and afterwards gain their hearts by the most kindly offices to them while prisoners. Dacres, whom Hull captured in the Guerrière, became his friend in after time. We may here relate an episode of Bainbridge and the Java.

Early in 1845 the Constitution, then commanded by Mad Jack Percival, cast anchor in the roadstead of Singapore. She had on her way taken out Henry A. Wise, our minister to Brazil, and was on special service in the East Indies and Pacific. The vertical rays of a tropic sun and the deadly breezes of the African coast had made a hospital of the ship; her gun-deck on the starboard side was hung with cots and hammocks. The captain had given up the forward cabin to the sick. The exterior of the old invincible responded mournfully to the interior. Her hull had been painted a dull lead-color at Rio, faintly enlivened by a red streak; but a long passage across the Indian Ocean had brought her old sable color here and there into view, while the streaks of iron-rust down her sides told her condition but too plainly.

Before the anchor was let go a boat with an officer from H. B. M. frigate Cambrian came alongside with the compliments and friendly offers of Commodore Chads. The officer's return brought the gallant commodore on board the Constitution. He was a fine-looking man of about fifty, more than six feet, perfectly erect, and as he stepped over the gangway he simultaneously saluted the officers who received him, at the same time surveying the ship fore and aft, and alow and aloft. The spardeck of the old ship looked passing well, and the commodore's scrutiny was not at all mortifying. He then descended to the cabin, where Captain Percival received him on crutches.

"I have hastened on board your ship," said Commodore Chads, "to offer my services, having heard you were sick, as well as many of your people; and I have brought my surgeon, who has been long out here, and is familiar with the diseases of India."

He then inquired if this was the same ship called the Constitution in 1813. Having been told that she was the same in model, battery, and internal arrangements, although rebuilt, he said he was very glad to meet her *again;* that she was an old acquaintance; and that in the action of the Java he had the honor to fight her after Captain Lambert was disabled; and that, although he had hauled down his colors to the Constitution, there were no reminiscences more pleasing to him than those resulting from the skill, gallantry, and bravery of the noble Bainbridge during and after the action. "The Constitution, sir, was manœuvred in a masterly manner, and it made me regret that she was not British. It was Greek meet Greek, for we were the same blood, after all." These particulars are from a letter supposed to have been from the pen of Mr. Ballestier, our Consul at Singapore. Mrs. Ballestier, who accompanied her husband to the East Indies, was a daughter of the famous Paul Revere.

Commodore Hull was rather short and thick-set, with a countenance deeply bronzed by long exposure to sun and weather, he having gone to sea when a boy. He was a man of plain, unassuming manners, and rather silent than loquacious.

Cooper, who knew him well, describes him as one of the most skilful seamen of history, remarkable for coolness in moments of danger.   He seldom mentioned his exploits, but sometimes, when the famous action with the Guerrière was alluded to, he would speak with enthusiasm of the beautiful day in August on which that battle was fought.

The two Commodores Hull, uncle and nephew,* married sisters belonging to the family of Hart, of Saybrook, Connecticut, and remarkable for their beauty.   Another sister married Hon. Heman Allen, of Vermont, at one time minister to Chili; while still another was the wife of Rev. Dr. Jarvis of St. Paul's, Boston.   The most beautiful of the sisters, Jeanette, never married, but went to Rome and became a nun.   She is said to have been, in her day, the handsomest woman in America. Another nephew of Isaac Hull was the late Admiral Andrew Hull Foote, who was so greatly distinguished in the early part of the Rebellion, receiving, at Fort Donelson, a wound that eventually contributed to cause his death.

It appears, from excellent authority, that the original draft of the Constitution was changed at the suggestion of Colonel George Claghorn, who ought therefore to be regarded as the person most entitled to the credit of having created the pride of the navy, as it was to him her construction was confided.   The subject of an alteration in her dimensions had been verbally broached to the Secretary of War — who also presided over our infant marine at that time — when he was in Boston in 1794.   General Knox consented, in presence of the agent, General Jackson ; but Claghorn, having been a soldier, was not satisfied until he obtained the authority in writing.

At the festival in Faneuil Hall given to Captain Hull on his return from the fight with the Guerrière, Ex-President Adams, who, on account of his infirmities was unable to be present, sent the following toasts, which were read by Hon. Samuel Dexter : —

" May every commodore in our navy soon be made an admiral, and every captain a commodore, with ships and squadrons worthy

* Commodore Joseph B. Hull.

of their commanders and worthy of the wealth, power, and dignity of their country. *Proh dolor ! Proh pudor !*"

"Talbot, Truxtun, Decatur, Little, Preble, — had their country given them the means, they would have been Blakes, Drakes, and Nelsons."

On her return to port from this cruise the Constitution spoke the Dolphin and Decatur, privateers, the latter of which, thinking she was pursued by an enemy, threw her guns overboard. It is at least a coincidence that the news of the surrender of Detroit by General Hull should have reached Boston only a few hours after the arrival of his nephew, Captain Hull, from his successful combat. Shubrick commanded the yard in 1825, Crane in 1826, and Morris from 1827 to 1833, when he was succeeded by Jesse D. Elliott.

The park of naval artillery bears as little resemblance to the cannon of a century ago as do the war-ships of to-day to those commanded by Manley, Jones, or Hopkins. No event will better illustrate the advance in gunnery than the battle between Sampson and Cervera off Santiago. The naval tactics of the first period were to lay a ship alongside her adversary, and then let courage and hard fighting win the day. But nowadays close actions are avoided, or considered unnecessary, and instances of individual gallantry become more rare. Ships toss their heavy shot at each other miles away, without the least knowledge of the damage they inflict, and Old Shylock is now only half right when he says,

> " Ships are but boards, sailors but men,"

for iron succeeds oak, though no substitute is yet found for bone and muscle.

In the beginning of the Revolution cannon was the most essential thing wanted. Ships were built and manned with alacrity, but all kinds of shifts were made to supply them with guns. A fleet of privateers was soon afloat in the waters of Massachusetts Bay, and public vessels were on the stocks, but how they were armed may be inferred from the following extract from a letter dated at Boston, September 1, 1776 : —

"There is so great a demand for guns here for fitting out priva-teers that those old things that used to stick in the ground, particu-larly at Bowes's Corner,* Admiral Vernon, etc., have been taken up, and sold at an immoderate price ; that at Mr. Bowes's was sold by Mr. Jones for fifty dollars. I imagine it will sp.it in the first attempt to fire it."

The Hancock, which was the second Continental frigate launched, and was commanded by Captain Manley, as well as the Old Boston frigate, Captain McNeill, were both armed with guns, chiefly nine-pounders, taken from the works in Boston harbor, and furnished by Massachusetts. The Hancock was built and launched at Newburyport, and not at Boston, as has been stated. Manley, the first sea officer to attack the enemy on that element, received in 1792 a compensation of £150, and a pension of £9 per month for life.

Unlike the celebrated English dockyard and arsenal at Wool-wich, our dockyards are only utilized for naval purposes, while the former is the depot for the royal horse and foot artillery and the royal sappers and miners, with vast magazines of great guns, mortars, bombs, powder, and other warlike stores. The Royal Military Academy was erected in the arsenal, but was not completely formed until 1745, in the reign of George II. It would seem that the same system might be advan-tageously carried out in this country, so far as the corps of engineers and artillery are concerned, with the benefit of com-bining practical with theoretical instruction upon those points where there exists an identity of interest in the military and naval branches of the service.

The area of the great British dockyard is about the same as that of the Charlestown yard, but in depth of water in front the latter has greatly the advantage, the Thames being so shal-low at Woolwich that large ships are now chiefly constructed at the other naval ports. We may here mention that Woolwich is the most ancient arsenal in Great Britain, men-of-war having been built there as early as the reign of Henry VIII., when the Harry Grace de Dieu was constructed in 1512. The Royal

* South Corner of State and Washington Streets.

George, in which Kempenfelt went down at Spithead, and the Nelson, Trafalgar, and other first-rates, were also built at Woolwich.

When we look around upon the wonderful progress of the steam marine during the past quarter of a century, and reflect upon its possibilities, the prediction of the celebrated Dr. Dionysius Lardner, that steam could never be profitably employed in ocean navigation, seems incredible.

THE GREAT HARRY.

Sixty years ago this was demonstrated by the Doctor with facts and figures, models and diagrams.

In the summer of 1781 the port of Boston was almost sealed by the constant presence of British cruisers in the bay, who took many valuable prizes and brought several mercantile houses to the verge of ruin. The merchants accordingly besought Admiral Le Compte de Barras to send some of his frigates from Newport round to Boston; but the Count replied that the efforts already made to induce his men to desert and engage on board privateers compelled him to refuse the request. The merchants then sent a committee composed of Messrs. Sears, Broome, Breck, and others, to assure the Count that his men should not be taken under any circumstances.

The Count's compliance resulted in the loss of one of his ships, the Magicienne, of thirty-two guns, which was taken by the Assurance, a British two-decker, in Boston harbor. The action was so plainly visib'e from the wharves of the town, that the French colors were seen to be struck and the English hoisted in their stead. The French ships Sagittaire, fifty guns, Astrie, thirty-two, and Hermione, thirty-two, were in the

THE NAVY-YARD IN 1873, FROM EAST BOSTON.

harbor when the battle commenced, and immediately got under weigh to go to the assistance of their consort; but the wind being light and the Sagittaire a dull sailer, the enemy escaped with his prize. Many Bostonians went on board the French ships as volunteers in the expected action. Colonel David Sears was among the number who joined the Astrie in the expectation of enjoying some diversion of this sort. The merchants of Boston afterwards gave a splendid dinner to the Marquis de Gergeroux, the commander of the French fleet, and his officers, for the services rendered in keeping the bay clear of the enemy's cruisers.

Nelson, who in 1782 was ordered to cruise in the Albemarle on the

American station, fell in with a fishing schooner on our coast, which he captured, but the master, having piloted the cruiser into Boston Bay, was released with his vessel and the following certificate : —

" This is to certify that I took the schooner Harmony, Nathaniel Carver, master, belonging to Plymouth, but on account of his good services have given him up his vessel again.

"Dated on board His Majesty's ship Albemarle,
            17th August, 1782.

                                    " HORATIO NELSON."

The grateful man afterwards came off to the Albemarle, at the hazard of his life, bringing a present of sheep, poultry, and other fresh provisions, — a most welcome supply, for the scurvy was raging on board.    Nelson exhibited a similar trait of nobility in releasing two officers of Rochambeau's army, who were captured in a boat in the West Indies while on some excursion.    Count Deux-Ponts was one and Isidore Lynch the other captive.    Nelson gave them a capital dinner, and the wine having got into their heads, the secret imprudently came out that Lynch was of English birth.    The poor prisoners were thunderstruck at the discovery, but Nelson, without appearing to have overheard the indiscretion, set both at liberty.

It sounds somewhat strangely at this time to recall the fact that the United States once paid tribute to the ruler of a horde of pirates, to induce him to hold off his hands from our commerce ; and that our captured crews were sold into slavery or held for ransom at the behest of a turbaned barbarian.    Six thousand stand of arms, four field-pieces, and a quantity of gunpowder was the price of the peace granted by the Dey of Algiers to America in 1795.    In May, 1794, an exhibition was given at the Boston Theatre for the relief of our countrymen, prisoners in Algiers, which realized about nine hundred dollars. Dominie Terry & Co. advanced $ 3,000 for the maintenance of these prisoners, without security.

Of the early commanders of our navy Hopkins was described in 1776 as an antiquated-looking person, with a strong ideal resemblance to Van Tromp. He appeared at first angelic, says our authority, until he swore, and then the illusion vanished. Hopkins commanded the first American squadron that set sail from our shores, and carried the colony flag at his gaff.

NAVY-YARD IN 1858.

Paul Jones had the honor not only of hoisting with his own hands the American flag on board the Alfred, in 1775, which he says was then displayed for the first time, but of receiving in the Ranger the first salute to that flag by a foreign power from M. de la Motte Piquet, who, with a French squadron, on board of which was Lafayette, was lying in the bay of Quiberon, ready to sail for America. This occurred February 13, 1778.

Next comes a half-acre of round-shot and shell arranged in pyramids, and waiting till the now torpid Dahlgrens or Parrotts shake off their lethargy and demand their indigestible food. Some of the globes are painted black, befitting their funereal purpose, while we observed that others had received a coat of white, and now looked like great sugar-coated pills, — a sharp medicine to carry off the national bile.

To the field of deadly projectiles succeeds a field of anchors, the last resource of the seaman, the symbol of Hope in all the civilized world.

The invention of the anchor is ascribed by Pliny to the Tyrrhenians, and by other writers to Midas, the son of Gordias, whose anchor Pausanias declares was preserved until his time in a temple dedicated to Jupiter. The most ancient anchors were made of stone, and afterwards of wood which contained a great quantity of lead ; sometimes baskets filled with stones, or shingle, and even sacks of sand were used.

STANCH AND STRONG.

The Greeks used much the same anchor as is now in vogue, except the transverse piece called the stock. Many of the anchors used by our first war-vessels came from the Old Forge at Hanover, Mass.

If we might linger here, it would be to reflect on which of these ponderous masses of metal the fate of some good ship with her precious burden of lives had depended ; with what agony of suspense the tension of the stout cable had been watched from hour to hour as the greedy waves rushed by to throw themselves with a roar of baffled rage upon the flinty shore. Remember, O craftsman, in your mighty workshop yonder, wherein you wield forces old Vulcan might have envied, that life and death are in every stroke of your huge trip-hammer ; and that a batch of rotten iron may cost a thousand lives, therefore,

"Let's forge a goodly anchor, — a bower thick and broad;
For a heart of oak is hanging on every blow, I bode;
And I see the good ship riding all in a perilous road, —
The low reef roaring on her lee ; the roll of ocean poured
From stem to stern, sea after sea ; the mainmast by the board ;
The bulwarks down ; the rudder gone ; the boat stove at the chains ;
But courage still, brave mariners, — the bower yet remains !
And not an inch to flinch he deigns, save when ye pitch sky high;
Then moves his head, as though he said, 'Fear nothing, here am I !'"

We can compare the granite basin, fashioned to receive the great war-ships, to nothing else than a huge bath wherein some antique giant might disport himself. It seems a miracle of intelligence, skill, and perseverance. When Loammi Baldwin was applied to to undertake the building of this Dry Dock, he hesitated, and asked Mr. Southard, then Secretary of the Navy, " What if I should fail ? " " If you do," replied the Secretary, " we will hang you." It proved a great success, worthy to be classed among the other works of this distinguished engineer.

The foundation rests upon piles on which is laid a massive oaken floor. We cannot choose but admire the great blocks of hewn granite, and the exact and elegant masonry. Owing to some defect, when nearly completed, a rupture took place in the wall, and a thundering rush of water came in and filled the excavation, but it was soon pumped out and effectually repaired.

After an examination of the records of the tides in Boston harbor for the previous sixty years, Mr. Baldwin fixed the height of the capping of the dock several inches above the highest that had occurred within that period. In the gale of April, 1851, however, the tide rose to such a height as to overflow the dock, falling in beautiful cascades along its whole length. The basin occupied six years in building ; Job Turner, of Boston, being the master mason, under Colonel Baldwin. It was decided that Old Ironsides should be the first vessel admitted ; and upon the opening of the structure, June 24, 1833, Commodore Hull appeared once more on the deck of his old ship and superintended her entrance within the dock. The gallant old sailor moved about the deck with his head bare, and exhibited as much animation as he would have done in battle. The Vice-President, Mr. Van Buren, the Secretary of War, Mr. Cass, Mr. Southard, and other distinguished guests graced the occasion by their presence, while the officers at the station were required to be present in full uniform.

The Constitution was here rebuilt by Mr. Barker. He had

served in the Revolution both in the army and navy. In the latter service he sailed with Captain Manley in the Hague, formerly the Deane, frigate, on a cruise among the West India Islands. His first ship-yard was within the limits of the present government yard, and here he began to set up vessels as early as 1795. Later, he removed his yard to a site near the state-prison. While naval constructor Mr. Barker built the Independence, Virginia, and Vermont, seventy-fours, and the sloops-of-war Frolic, Marion, Cyane, and Bainbridge. Thatcher Magoun, the well-known shipbuilder of Medford, received his instruction in modelling from Josiah Barker.

Before the Constitution was taken out of dock, a brand-new ship, a figure-head of President Jackson had been fixed to her prow by Commodore Elliott, who then commanded the yard. If it had been desired to test the President's popularity in the New England States no act could have been more happily devised. A universal shout of indignation went up from press and people ; for the old ship was little less than adored by all classes, and to affix the bust of any living personage to her was deemed an indignity not to be borne in silence.

In that immense crowd, which had witnessed the re-baptism of Old Ironsides, stood a young Cape Cod seaman. His father, a brave old captain in the 3d Artillery, had doubtless instilled some strong republican ideas into the youngster's head, for he had accompanied him to Fort Warren * during the War of 1812, and while there the lad had seen from the rampart the doomed Chesapeake lift her anchor, and go forth to meet the Shannon. He had heard the cannonade off in the bay, had noted the hush of the combat, and had shared in the anguish with which all hearts were penetrated at the fatal result.

Old Ironsides was moored with her head to the west, between the seventy-fours Columbus and Independence. The former vessel had a large number of men on board, and a sentinel was placed where he could keep the figure-head in view ; another was posted on the wharf near at hand, and a third patrolled the forecastle of the Constitution ; from an open port

* Now Fort Winthrop.

of the Columbus the light fell full upon the graven features
all these precautions were designed to protect.

On the night of the 2d of July occurred a thunder-storm
of unusual violence. The lightning played around the masts
of the shipping, and only by its lurid flash could any object
be distinguished in the blackness. Young Dewey — he was
only twenty-eight — unmoored his boat from Billy Gray's
Wharf in Boston, and, with his oar muffled in an old woollen
comforter, sculled out into the darkness. He had reconnoitred
the position of the ships by day, and was prepared at all points.
At length he found himself alongside the Independence, the
outside ship, and worked his way along her big black side,
which served to screen him from observation.

Dewey climbed up the Constitution's side by the man-ropes
and ensconced himself in the bow, protected by the headboards,
only placed on the ship the same day. He extended himself
on his back, and in this position sawed off the head. While
here he saw the sentry on the wharf from time to time looking
earnestly towards the spot where he was at work, but the
lightning and the storm each time drove the guard back to the
shelter of his box.

Having completed his midnight decapitation Dewey re-
gained his boat, to find her full of water. She had swung
under the scupper of the ship and had received the torrent that
poured from her deck. In this plight, but never forgetting the
head he had risked his life to obtain, Dewey reached the shore.
We can never think of this scene, with its attendant circumstances, without remembering Cooper's episode of the weird
lady of the Red Rover.

If this act proves Dewey to have been a cool hand, the one
we are to relate must cap the climax. After the excitement
caused by the affair — and it was of no ordinary kind — had
subsided, Dewey packed up the grim and corrugated features
he had decapitated and posted off to Washington. At Philadelphia his secret leaked out, and he was obliged to exhibit his
prize to John Tyler and Willie P. Mangum, afterwards President and acting Vice-President, who were then investigating

the affairs of the United States Bank. These grave and reverend seigniors shook their sides as they regarded the colossal head, now brought so low, and parted with Captain Dewey with warm and pressing offers of service.

The Captain's intention to present the head to General Jackson himself was frustrated by the dangerous illness of the President, to whom all access was denied. He however obtained an audience of Mr. Van Buren, the Vice-President, who at once overwhelmed him with civilities after the manner in which that crafty old fox was wont to lay siege to the susceptibilities of all who approached him. Upon Dewey's announcing himself as the person who had taken off the Constitution's figure-head Mr. Van Buren gave a great start and was thrown off his usual balance. Recovering himself, he demanded the particulars of the exploit, which seemed to afford him no small satisfaction. Captain Dewey wished him to receive the head. "Go to Mr. Dickerson," said the Vice-President, "it belongs to his department; say you have come from me." To Mahlon Dickerson, Secretary of the Navy, our hero accordingly went.

The venerable Secretary was busily engaged with a heap of papers, and requested his visitor to be brief. This hint was not lost on the Captain.

"Mr. Dickerson, I am the person who removed the figure-head from the Constitution, and I have brought it with me for the purpose of returning it to the Government."

The Secretary threw himself back in his chair, pushed his gold-bowed spectacles with a sudden movement up on his forehead, and regarded with genuine astonishment the man who, after evading the most diligent search for his discovery, now came forward and made this voluntary avowal. Between amazement and choler the old gentleman could scarce sputter out,—

"You, sir! you! What, sir, did you have the audacity to disfigure a ship of the United States Navy?"

"Sir, *I took the responsibility.*"

"Well, sir, I'll have you arrested immediately"; and the Secretary took up the bell to summon a messenger.

"Stop, sir," said the Captain, "you cannot inflict any punishment; I can only be sued for a trespass, and in the county where the offence was committed. Say the word, and I will go back to Charlestown and await my trial; but if a Middlesex jury don't give *me* damages, my name's not Dewey." The Captain had explored his ground: there was no statute at that time against defacing ships of war, and he knew it. Mr. Dickerson, an able lawyer, reflected a moment, and then put down his bell. "You are right, sir," said he; "and now tell me all about the affair."

The Captain remained some time closeted with the Secretary, of whose treatment he had no reason to complain.

All these incidents, modestly related by Captain Dewey to the writer, stamp him as a man of no common decision of character. He resolved, deliberated upon, planned, and executed his enterprise without the assistance of a single individual, — one person only receiving a hint from him at the moment he set out, as a precaution in case any accident might befall him. His looks when narrating this adventure are thus recalled. "Captain Dewey shows little sign of decay. A man of middle stature, his sandy hair is lightly touched with gray, his figure but little bent; his complexion is florid, perhaps from the effects of an early seafaring life; his mouth is expressive of determined resolution, and an eye of bluish gray lights up in moments of animation a physiognomy far from unpleasant. He is not the man to commit an act of mere bravado, but is devoted to his convictions of right with the zeal of a Mussulman. We may safely add that he was never a Jackson Democrat."

The names of several of the vessels constructed by Mr. Barker have become historical. The Frolic was captured in 1814 by H. B. M. frigate Orpheus and an armed schooner, after a chase of sixty miles, during which the Frolic threw her lee guns overboard. She was rated as a vessel of 18 guns, but was built to carry twenty 32-pounder carronades and two long 18- or 24-pounders. At the time of her capture she was commanded by Master-Commandant Bainbridge.

The Independence was launched July 20, 1814, during hostilities with Great Britain, and was the first seventy-four afloat in our navy, — if the America, launched in 1782, and given to the French, be excepted. Her first cruise was to the Mediterranean, where she carried the broad pennant of Commodore Bainbridge, and was the first of her class to display our Stars and Stripes abroad. Owing to a defect in her build she was afterwards converted into a serviceable double-banked 60-gun frigate. As such she has been much admired by naval critics, and was honored while lying at Cronstadt by a visit from the Czar Nicholas,* *incognito*.

The Vermont has never made a foreign cruise, though intended in 1853 for the flagship of Commodore Perry's expedition to Japan. The Virginia, sleeping like another Rip Van Winkle, in her big cradle for half a century, until she had become as unsuited to service as the galley of Medina Sidonia would be, remains in one of the ship-houses, a specimen of ancient naval architecture, with her bluff bows and sides tumbling inboard. It would, perhaps, require a nautical eye such as we do not possess to determine which was the stem and which the stern of this ship. The Cumberland went down at Hampton Roads in the unequal conflict with the Merrimac in March, 1862. The Cyane, named after the British ship captured by the Constitution, was broken up at Philadelphia in 1836.

The launch of the Merrimac, in the summer of 1855, is a well-remembered scene. Such was the admiration of her beautiful proportions that it was generally said, if the other five frigates ordered to be built were like her, we should at length have a steam navy worthy of the name. Her model was furnished by Mr. Lenthall, chief of the Bureau of Construction, and she was built by Mr. Delano, then Naval Constructor at this station, under the supervision of Commodore Gregory. Melvin Simmons was the master-carpenter. A year after her keel was laid she glided without accident into the element in which she was destined to play so important a part.

* Captain Preble's Notes on Ship-building in Massachusetts.

She displayed at every available point the flag her batteries were turned against in her first and only battle. Many thousand spectators witnessed from the neighboring wharves, bridges, and shipping her splendid rush into the waters. The Ohio and Vermont, then lying at their moorings in the stream, were thronged with people who welcomed the good ship, at her parting from the shore, with loud huzzas. As she rode on the surface of the river, majestic and beautiful, no conjecture, we will venture to say, was made by any among that vast multitude of the powers of destruction she was destined to exhibit. At that time her size appeared remarkable, and so indeed it was when compared with the smaller craft among which she floated. Her armament was from the celebrated foundry of Cyrus Alger, South Boston.

Returning from a peaceful cruise in the Pacific, she arrived at Norfolk early in February, 1860, and was lying at that station in ordinary when the flag of rebellion was raised at Charleston. But for the prevalence of treason in high places, the Merrimac would have been saved to our navy before the destruction of the dockyard at Norfolk, April 21, 1861. She became a rebel vessel, and, encased in iron, descended the river, appearing among our fleet in Hampton Roads March 8, 1862, where she pursued a course of havoc — her iron prow crashing into our wooden ships — unparalleled in naval annals. Her conflict on the following day with the little Monitor, commanded by the brave Worden, and of which the world may be said, in a manner, to have been spectators, is still fresh in the memories of the present generation.

Napoleon, no mean judge, while candidly admitting the superiority of the English over the French sailors, asserted as his belief, that the Americans were better seamen than the English. It was the general belief in the British Navy, during the War of 1812, that our discipline was more severe than their own. If true, this would have gone far to confute the assertion that our crews were largely composed of British sailors. The truth is, that we always had plenty of the best sailors in the world.

General Hyslop, who was on the quarter-deck of the Java during her contest with the Constitution, stated it as his conviction that the American sailors were far more elastic and active in their habits than the British.   He was astonished, also, at the superior gunnery of the crew of Old Ironsides, who were able to discharge three broadsides to two from the Java, thus adding one third to the weight of their fire.   To this circumstance he attributed the victory of Bainbridge.

It is well known that the royal navy was long indebted to American forests for its masts, the Crown reserving for this purpose the trees of a certain girth, to which an officer affixed the broad-arrow.   The owner of the soil might, if he chose, cut down and haul the king's trees to the nearest seaport, receiving a certain compensation for his labor ; and one of the most notable old-time sights the Maine woods witnessed was the removal of the giant pines by a long train of oxen to the sea.   As was truly said of England,

> " E'en the tall mast that bears your flag on high
> Grew in our soil, and ripened in our sky."

The mast-ship had its regular time for sailing from Piscataqua (Portsmouth) or Falmouth (Portland), convoyed, in time of war with France, by a frigate.   In process of time the increasing scarcity of timber led to the construction of ship's masts in sections.   The first vessel in our navy to carry one of these sticks was the Constitution, whose mainmast, in 1803, when she sailed for Tripoli, was a made mast of twenty-eight pieces.

Copper sheathing for vessels of war was first applied to the Alarm, British frigate, in 1758, but conductors, which we owe to the genius of Franklin, were first used on American ships, and previous to 1790.

The cipher which is used in the United States to designate government property owes its origin, according to Frost's Naval History, to a joke.   When the so-called last war with England broke out there were two inspectors of provisions at Troy, New York, named Ebenezer and Samuel Wilson.   The latter gentleman (universally known as " Uncle Sam ") gen-

erally superintended in person a large number of workmen,
who, on one occasion, were employed in overhauling the provisions purchased by the contractor, Elbert Anderson of New
York. The casks were marked " E. A. — U. S." This work
fell to the lot of a facetious fellow, who, on being asked the
meaning of the mark, said he did not know unless it meant
*Elbert Anderson and Uncle Sam,* alluding to Uncle Sam Wilson. The joke took and became very current.

The Charlestown yard is further distinguished as having the
only ropewalk under the control of the government, in which
an endless twisting of the flexible material — from the slender
thread which flies the youth's kite to the serpent-like folds of
the great ship's cable — is forever going on.

> " At the end an open door;
>   Squares of sunshine on the floor
>     Light the long and dusky lane;
>   And the whirring of a wheel,
>   Dull and drowsy, makes me feel
>     All its spokes are in my brain."

Under cover of houses or temporary roofs are some of those
sea-monsters whose creation dates from the Rebellion ; sub-
marine volcanoes that hurl destruction by the ton, and vomit
fire and smoke from their jaws. As they lie here upon the
river's brink, with their iron scales and their long, low hulks,
we can liken them to nothing else than so many huge alligators
basking themselves in the sunshine to-day, but only waiting
the signal to plunge their half submerged bodies into the stream
and depart on their errand of havoc. Long may ye lie here
powerless by the shore, ye harbingers of ruin ; and long may
your iron entrails lack the food that, breathing life into those
lungs of brass and steel, gives motion to your unwieldy bulk !
May ye lie here tied to the shore, until your iron crust drops
off like the shell of any venerable crustacean, ere the tocsin
again shall sound that lets slip such " dogs of war " !

The lower ship-house marks the beach where the choice
troops of Old England left their boats and began their fatal
march to Breed's Hill ; where the glittering and moving mass,

extending itself like a painted wall, broke off into columns of attack. The light infantry and grenadiers keep the shore of the Mystic, and at length deploy in front of the stern old ranger, John Stark, and of the brave Knowlton, crouched behind their flimsy, simulated rampart of sweet-scented, new-mown hay. A flash, a rattling volley, and the line is enveloped in smoke, which, drifting slowly away before the breeze, reveals what was a wall of living steel rent into fragments, little scattered groups, while the space between is covered with the dead and dying. Reader, do you know the battle-field and its horrors, — an arm tossing here and there; a limb stiffened after some grotesque fashion in the last act of the expiring will, the finger pressed against the trigger, the bayonet at the charge, while the green turf is dotted far and near with little fires fallen from the deadly muzzles?

Many of the slain in this battle were probably buried within the dockyard enclosure; and they once showed you at the Naval Institute a heap of bones brought to light while digging down the hill, — relics of the fight which the earth has given up before their time. We have little sympathy with the exhibition of dead men's bones. These poor memorials of the brave deserve Christian burial at our hands. Fallen far from the Welsh hills or Irish lakes, there is something uncanny and reproachful in their detention above ground; a grave and a stone is due to the remains of those whose fate may one day be our own.

Having thus circumnavigated the hundred acres of Uncle Sam's exclusive domain, we may congratulate that much-abused old gentleman upon the successful speculation he has made. The original estimates included only twenty-three acres, to be obtained from the following proprietors, namely :

| | | | | | |
|---|---|---|---|---|---|
| Seven acres of Harris, estimated worth | $ 12,000 | |
| Three | " | Stearns, | " | " | 500 |
| Two | " | Breed | " | " | 150 |
| Nine | " | " | " | " | 3,600 | $ 16,250 |

Two acres additional were procured in order to alter the road so as to get more room where the ships were to be built, and for which was paid, . . . . . . . . 3,000.

Subsequent purchases, together with the attendant expenses, swelled the first cost of the site to $ 40,000, for about eighty acres of land and marsh ; but the work of filling, which has constantly proceeded, has considerably extended the area.    The government has expended about three and a half millions upon the yard, the value of the land alone being now estimated at nearly six millions.    Efforts have been made to induce the removal to some other locality, in order to secure the site for commerce, but thus far without success.

The Naval Institute, which comprises a museum, a library, and a reading-room, is very creditable to its founders and promoters.    The walls of the museum are decorated with implements of war, or of the chase, belonging to every nation between the poles, while the cabinets are well stocked with curiosities and relics to which every vessel arriving at the station brings accessions.    It will readily be seen, with such unlimited opportunities for bringing, free of cost, articles of value from the most remote climes, what collections might be made at the public dockyards were the government to give a little official stimulus to the object.

The sword which Preble wore before Tripoli, and that of Captain Whynyates of H. M. ship Frolic, are here preserved, together with relics of the Boxer, the figure-head of the General Armstrong, privateer, and some memorials of the ill-fated Cumberland.    The library is valuable and well selected, but the books appear but little used.    A huge aquatic fowl, which stands sentinel near the entrance to these rooms, seems to have been placed there for the convenience of cleaning pens, his downy breast being seamed with inky stains.

There are few trophies within the yard, some field-pieces used in the Mexican War, and one of the umbrellas with which Hull walked his ship away from Broke's squadron, being the most noticeable.    The latter is now stored in the Institute, a fitting memorial to the prowess of

"A Yankee ship and a Yankee crew !"

The great wall of Tartary is not more formidable than is the granite fence which shoulders out the neighborhood, and speaks of the possibilities of invasion of these precincts by the rabble. The appearance without is that of a prison, or a fortress; within, a vista of greensward stocked with cannon, with rows of poplars shading cold granite walls, confounds the vision. Joyous children are warned away from the enclosures by some battered old guardian who will never more be fit for sea. "Keep off!"    "Touch nothing!"    "Your pass!" — So, we are free again.

# CHAPTER III.

### BUNKER HILL AND THE MONUMENT.

"I'd better gone an' sair'd the King,
At *Bunker's Hill.*"
BURNS.

IN June, 1875, was celebrated the centennial of the Battle of Bunker Hill. Never before did the tall gray shaft look down upon such a pageant. Fifty years had elapsed since the corner-stone of the monument was laid, in the presence of General Lafayette, Daniel Webster,

BUNKER HILL MONUMENT.

and of many survivors of the battle. It is not idle sentimentality that has hallowed the spot. A hundred thousand brave men have fought the better because its traditions yet linger among us, and are still recounted around our firesides.

Why is it that we can o'erleap the tremendous conflicts that have taken place since Bunker Hill, and still feel an undiminished interest in that day? It is not the battle, for it was fought without order on the American side, and without skill on the British; it is not the carnage, for many fields have been more bloody in our own times. It is perhaps because the men of New England here cast their first defiance in the teeth of the trained bands of Old England; it is because it was an act of aggression, and showed that our sires were determined to fight and ready to die in their good cause. The battle was as astounding to British arrogance as it was destructive to British prestige; it cannot be doubted that the memory of that day followed Sir William Howe with blighting effect to the end of his military career.

The story of the battle is so familiar that every schoolboy will tell you where the Provincials intrenched, and where the enemy landed; how many times the foe was borne back with slaughter, and how many fell. Here, across the river, is Copp's Hill, where Clinton and Burgoyne watched the varying fortunes of the battle, and from which a battery played upon these heights. The dead sleep as quietly there now as they did on the day when the foundations of the hill were shaken by the discharges of the guns. There, you see the tower and steeple of Christ Church, from which Gage, it is said, witnessed the fray, and whose bells first rang a Merry Christmas peal in 1745, the year of Louisburg. Below us the river ebbs and flows as it did in centuries gone by. Behind us is Bunker Hill proper, its name so tenaciously allied with the battle as to compel the adoption of an historical error. The Neck, over which the Americans advanced and retreated, has disappeared within the body; the Mill Pond, which figured in the military operations, has been filled up to meet the demands of the neighboring railroads for more room.

The British force engaged at Bunker Hill was made up from parts of fourteen regiments, then in Boston, besides the Royal Artillery and two battalions of Marines. Some of these corps were the very *élite* of the army. These were the 4th, or Hodgson's; 5th, Percy's; 10th, Sandford's; 18th, or Royal Irish; 22d, Gage's; 23d, Howe's (Welsh Fusileers); 35th, F. H. Campbell's; 38th, Pigot's; 43d, Cary's; 47th, Carleton's; 52d, Clavering's; 63d, Grant's; 65th, Urmston's. The marching regiments for the American service consisted of twelve com-

panies, and each company mustered fifty-six effective rank and
file.    Two companies of each regiment were usually left at
home on recruiting service.

> " And now they 're forming at the Point, and now the lines advance;
>    We see beneath the sultry sun their polished bayonets glance;
>    We hear anear the throbbing drum, the bugle challenge ring;
>    Quick bursts and loud the flashing cloud, and rolls from wing to wing;
>    But on the height our bulwark stands tremendous in its gloom, —
>    As sullen as a tropic sky, and silent as a tomb."

As these troops disembarked and paraded at the Point below, the spectacle must have extorted the admiration even of
the rude bands who, with compressed lips and bated breath,
awaited their coming.    Let us review the king's regulars as
they stand in battle array.

The scarlet uniforms, burnished arms, and perfect discipline

are common to all the
battalions.    The 4th, or
" King's Own," stands on
the right in the place of
honor.    They have the
king's cipher on a red
ground, within the garter,
with the crown above, in
the centre of their colors.
In the corners of the second color, which every
regiment carried, is the
Lion of England, their
ancient badge.    The grenadiers have the king's

BRITISH FLAG CAPTURED AT YORKTOWN.

crest and cipher on the front of their caps.    Percy's Northum-
berland Fusileers have St. George and the Dragon on their
colors, and on the grenadiers' caps and arms.    The Royal Irish
display a harp in a blue field in the centre of their colors, with
a crown above it ; and in the three corners of the second color
is blazoned the Lion of Nassau, the arms of King William III.
The caps of the grenadiers show the king's crest and the harp

and crown.    An officer of this regiment was the first Briton
to mount the redoubt.

The Royal Welsh have the Prince of Wales arms, — three
feathers issuing out of a coronet.    In the corners of the second
color are the badges of Edward the Black Prince, a rising sun,
red dragon, and plumed cap, with the motto *Ich dien.*    The
marines are clothed and armed in the same manner as his
Majesty's other corps of infantry, their uniform scarlet, turned
up with white, white waistcoats and breeches.    They also wear
caps like those of the fusileer regiments, which caused them to
be called by the French *Les Petits Grenadiers.*

Our readers are probably aware that the Fusileers were so
called, upon their first organization, from the circumstance that
they carried their fusees with slings.    There are three regiments
bearing this designation in the British Army ; namely, 23d or
Royal Welsh, raised in 1688 ; 21st or North British, raised in
1679 ; and 7th or Royal English, raised in 1685.    The grenadiers were a company armed with a pouch of hand grenades, and
originated in France in 1667, but were not adopted in England
until twenty years later.

> " Come, let us fill a bumper, and drink a health to those
>     Who wear the caps and pouches and eke the looped clothes."

In 1774, when the Royal Welsh left New York, Rivington
the bookseller, to whose shop the officers resorted, wrote to a
brother bookseller in Boston as follows : —

" My friends, the gallant Royals of Wales, are as respectable a
corps of gentlemen as are to be found in the uniform of any crowned
head upon earth.    You may depend upon their honor and integrity.
They have not left the least unfavorable impression behind them,
and their departure is more regretted than that of any officers who
ever garrisoned our city.    Pray present my respects to Colonel Bar-
nard, Major Blunt," etc., etc.

This celebrated corps, which had bled freely on the Old
World battle fields, embarked, on the 27th of July, on board
the transports for Boston.    The officers bore the reputation of
" gentlemen of the most approved integrity and of the nicest
punctuality."    Rivington, with the cunning for which he was

distinguished, made use of the gallant and unsuspecting Captain Horsfall to smuggle four chests of tea into Boston as a part of the officers' private luggage. The package was consigned, under strict injunctions of secrecy, to *Henry Knox;* but Rivington, more than suspecting that his consignee would have nothing to do with the obnoxious herb, directed him to turn it over to some one else, in case he should decline the commission. Patriotism and tea were then incompatible, and Knox declined the bait to tempt his cupidity.

The Welsh Fusileers had an ancient and privileged custom of passing in review preceded by a goat with gilded horns, and adorned with garlands of flowers. Every 1st of March, the anniversary of their tutelar saint, David, the officers gave a splendid entertainment to all their Welsh brethren ; and, after the removal of the cloth, a bumper was filled round to his Royal Highness, the Prince of Wales, whose health was always the first drank on that day. The goat, richly caparisoned for the occasion, was then brought in, and, a handsome drummer-boy being mounted on his back, the animal was led thrice around the table by the drum-major. It happened in 1775, at Boston, that the animal gave such a spring from the floor that he dropped his rider upon the table ; then, leaping over the heads of some officers, he ran to the barracks, with all his trappings, to the no small joy of the garrison and populace.

This regiment, which was opposed to Stark's men at the rail-fence, on the left of the redoubt, lost upwards of sixty killed and wounded, but was by no means so cut up as has often been stated. The greatest havoc was made in the ranks of Percy's Northumbrians, who had eight commissioned officers, including two ensigns, and one hundred and forty-four non-commissioned officers and soldiers *hors du combat.* This carnage reminds us of that sustained by the Highlanders in the battle of New Orleans. The British color-bearers at Bunker Hill were specially marked, the 5th, 38th, and 52d having both their ensigns shot down.

Lord George Harris, captain of the grenadier company of the 5th, says of this terrible day : —

"We had made a breach in their fortifications, which I had twice mounted, encouraging the men to follow me, and was ascending a third time, when a ball grazed the top of my head, and I fell, deprived of sense and motion. My lieutenant, Lord Rawdon, caught me in his arms, and, believing me dead, endeavored to remove me from the spot, to save my body from being trampled on. The motion, while it hurt me, restored my senses, and I articulated, ' For God's sake, let me die in peace.'"

Lord Rawdon ordered four soldiers to carry Captain Harris to a place of safety. Of these three were wounded, one mortally, while endeavoring to comply with the order. Such was the terrible fusilade from the redoubt. Captain Harris's life was saved by trepanning, and he recovered to take part in the battle of Long Island and the subsequent operations in New York and the Jerseys. He received another rebel bullet through the leg in 1777 ; was in the expedition to St. Lucie in 1778 as major of the 5th ; served in India with distinction, and was made lieutenant-general in 1801. Lexington was his first battle ; his lieutenant, Francis Rawdon, and himself are among the few British officers who fought at Bunker Hill whose reputations survived the American war.

Captain Addison, a relative of the author of the Spectator, only arrived in Boston the day previous to the battle, and had then accepted an invitation to dine on the next day with General Burgoyne ; but a far different experience awaited him, for he was numbered among the slain.

The agency of the young Bostonian, John Coffin (afterwards a general in the British army), in this battle is said to have been purely accidental ; for, going down to Long Wharf to see the 5th and 38th embark, he became excited with the ardor displayed by his acquaintances among the officers, of whom Captain Harris was one, jumped into a boat and went over to the hill. This was the relation of Dr. Waterhouse. Captain Harris says he had fallen over head and ears in love with a Miss Coffin, — who was a relative of John and Sir Isaac, — or, as he jocosely phrased it, had found a coffin for his heart. The lady had a " remarkably soft hand and red pouting lips." This celebrated family of Coffins also furnished another able officer, Sir Thomas Aston Coffin, to the British cause.

General Coffin is accredited with saying to his American friends after the war, in allusion to Bunker Hill, " You could not have succeeded without it; for *something* was indispensable, in the then state of parties, to fix men *somewhere,* and to show the planters at the South that Northern people were really in earnest, and could and would fight. That, *that* did the business for you." *

Thomas Graves, afterwards an admiral, commanded an armed sloop which assisted in covering the landing of the British troops at Bunker Hill, as did Bouillon and Collingwood (Nelson's famous lieutenant), who were in the boats. Thomas was the nephew of Admiral Samuel Graves, then commanding the fleet in the waters of Boston harbor.

Lord Rawdon, who is represented in Trumbull's picture in the act of waving a flag from the top of the intrenchment, developed, while afterwards commanding in the South, a sanguinary disposition. In view of the numerous desertions taking place in his command, he is reported to have offered, on one occasion, ten guineas for the *head* of any deserter of the Irish Volunteers, but only five for the man if brought in alive.

An American gentleman gives the following account of an interview with the Earl of Moira in 1803, while sojourning on the Isle of Wight : —

" I waited on his Lordship, and was introduced ; my reception was all that could be desired. The Earl then informed me, that, learning from our host that I was from the United States, he had sought my acquaintance in the hope that I would give him some information of some of his old acquaintances of our Revolutionary War. I was pleased to have it in my power to gratify his Lordship far beyond his expectations ; and, after an excellent supper of beefsteak and oysters, with a bottle of old port, we found the night had crept into the morning before we parted. The Earl was a gentleman of most noble appearance."

* Sabine.

Colonel, afterwards General Small, who appears in Trumbull's picture as arresting the thrust of a bayonet aimed at Warren's prostrate form, was greatly respected on both sides, as the following anecdote will illustrate.  "Towards the conclusion of the war, Colonel Small expressing a wish to meet with General St. Clair of the American army, the friend and companion of his early years, a flag of truce was immediately sent by General Greene, with an invitation to come within our lines, and remain at his option therein, free from every restriction.  The invitation was accepted in the same spirit in which it was tendered."  It is perhaps needless to say that the position in which Trumbull has placed Colonel Small is more for artistic effect than for historic accuracy.

General Burgoyne, a spectator only of this battle, lived at one time in Samuel Quincy's house, in South Street, Boston. It was a handsome wooden dwelling of three stories, with a yard and garden, and was for many years the abode of Judge John Davis.  The estate was the third from the corner of Summer Street, according to former lines of division, and on the east side of South Street.  This was the house of which Mrs. Adams remarks, "A lady who lived opposite says she saw raw meat cut and hacked upon her mahogany table, and her superb damask curtains exposed to the rain."

General Pigot, who fought a duel with Major Bruce, without serious result to either combatant, resided in the Hancock House, on Beacon Hill, during the winter of 1775.  To his credit be it said, he left the old family mansion of the proscribed patriot in a cleanly state, and the wines and stores remained as he found them.  Affairs of honor were not uncommon in Boston while the king's troops were stationed there. In September, 1775, a meeting took place between a captain and lieutenant of marines, in which the former was killed and the latter badly wounded.

Duelling was one of the pernicious customs which the British officers left behind them.  The Continental officers sometimes settled their disputes in this wise, and, indeed, carried the fashion into private life; as witness the affair of Burr and

Hamilton. But that the practice obtained a foothold among the gentry in staid Old Boston 'would seem incredible, if we had not the evidence.

Trumbull's great painting of the " Battle of Bunker Hill," except for the portraits it contains, some of which were painted from life, must ever be an unsatisfactory work to Americans. The artist has depicted the moment of defeat for the provincials, with the head of the British column pouring into the redoubt. Warren is extended on the earth in the foreground. Prescott is located in the background, and in a garb that defies recognition. A figure purporting to be that of Lord Rawdon — it might as well be called that of any other officer, — presents its back to the spectator. But for the undoubted likenesses of Putnam, Clinton, Small, and others, the picture would be chiefly valued as commemorating a British victory.

Would that the artist, whose skill as a historical painter we do not mean to depreciate, had seized the instant when Warren, entering the redoubt, his face aglow with the enthusiasm of the occasion, is met by Prescott with the offer of the command ; or that other moment, when that brave old soldier calmly paces the rampart, encouraging his weary and drooping men by his own invincible contempt for danger.

Trumbull's picture was painted in West's studio, and when it was nearly completed the latter gave a dinner to some friends, Sir Joshua Reynolds among others being invited. When Sir Joshua entered the room, he immediately ran up to the " Bunker Hill," and exclaimed, " Why, West, what have you got here? this is better colored than your works are generally." " Sir Joshua, you mistake, that is not mine, it is the work of this young gentleman, Mr. Trumbull." Trumbull relates that he was not sorry to turn the tables upon Sir Joshua, who, only a short time before, had snubbed him unmercifully.

The question of command on the American side, at Bunker Hill, has been in former times one of bitter controversy. It has even mingled to some extent with party politics. The friends of Warren, Putnam, Prescott, Pomeroy, and Stark, each contended manfully to lodge the glory with their particular hero. The opinion has too long prevailed that nobody commanded in chief, and that the battle, taken as a whole, *fought itself*, — or, in other words, was maintained by the individual leaders acting without a responsible head, or any particular concert. Any want of unity is to be ascribed to the chaotic state of the Provincial army, and in no small degree, also, to the jealousy between the officers and soldiers of the different Colonies. The reflection comes naturally, that if there was no general officer present authorized to command, there ought to have been one, and that if Putnam did not hold that authority, the conduct of General Ward cannot be understood. Prescott could not command the whole field when shut up within the redoubt. Warren and Pomeroy fought as volunteers. Putnam endeavored to the last to carry out the original plan, which was to fortify Bunker Hill. Had he succeeded in forming a second line there, the sober judgment is that the enemy would have deferred an attack or lost the battle.

Prescott receives the order and the command of the party to intrench on the hill. When the intention of the enemy is developed, Stark is ordered on and takes his position at the rail-fence, on the left of the redoubt. Putnam is in all parts of the field, and assumes and exercises command at all points, as if by virtue of his rank. Prescott commands within the redoubt he erected; Stark at the rampart of new-mown hay; while Putnam, taking his post on Bunker Hill, where he could observe everything, directs the reinforcements that arrive where to place themselves. As for Warren and Pomeroy, the two other general officers present during the battle, they choose their stations within Prescott's redoubt, and fight like heroes in the ranks. Neither were willing to deprive the veteran of the honor of defending his fort.

At this distance of time Putnam's judgment appears to have been sound and well directed. The evidence goes to show that the lines were well manned. The redoubt could not fight more than five hundred men to advantage, supposing all the sides attacked at once, — that is, admitting the dimensions of the work have been correctly given. Putnam holds a re-

serve, and attempts to intrench himself on Bunker Hill.   He
sends to Cambridge for reinforcements, rallies the fugitives,
and at last plants himself on Prospect Hill like a lion at bay.
It cannot be gainsaid that he alone sustained the duty of commanding the field, in its larger meaning, and was, therefore, in
chief command.   He was in the contest, at the rail-fence, and
was himself there, that is to say, all fire and intrepidity.   The
poet thus depicts him at the retreat : —

> "There strides bold Putnam, and from all the plains
>     Calls the third host, the tardy rear sustains,
>     And, 'mid the whizzing deaths that fill the air,
>     Waves back his sword, and dares the following war."

The statement that Putnam did not give Prescott an order
is irreconcilable with the fact that he rode to the redoubt and
directed the intrenching-tools there to be taken to Bunker
Hill.   Prescott remonstrated, but obeyed the order, as General Heath tells us.

Gordon and Eliot, both contemporary historians, give Prescott the command within the redoubt ; the former attributes to
Putnam the credit of aiding and encouraging on the field at
large.   General Lee, who had every means of knowing the
truth, observes in his defence : —

"To begin with the affair of Bunker Hill, I may venture to pronounce that there never was a more dangerous, a more execrable
situation, than those brave and unfortunate men (if those who die in
the glorious cause of liberty can be termed unfortunate) were placed
in.   They had to encounter with a body of troops, both in point
of spirit and discipline not to be surpassed in the whole world,
headed by an officer of experience, intrepidity, coolness, and decision.   The Am
men, half arme
order, and God

The British
admixture of
lation between Scotch, Irish, Welsh, and Saxon has been the
means of conquering many a field ; for, when placed side by
side in action, neither nationality would give way before the

other.  Of these elements the Irish and Scotch are, of course,
the more distinctive.  It is said to be a fact, that in one of the
Duke of Marlborough's battles, the Irish brigade, on advancing
to the charge, threw away their knapsacks and everything that
would encumber them, all of which were carefully picked up
by a Scotch regiment that followed to support them.  The old
Lord Tyrawley used to say, that, to constitute the *beau ideal* of
an army, a general should take ten thousand fasting Scotch-
men, ten thousand Englishmen after a hearty dinner, and the
same number of Irishmen who have just swallowed their second
bottle.  Sir William Howe so well understood these traits, that
he gave his soldiers their dinner and plentifully supplied them
with grog before advancing to attack the Americans.

The first British regiments (14th and 29th) despatched to Boston in 1768 had negro drummers who were used to whip such
of the soldiers as were ordered for punishment.  The bands on
board derisively played "Yankee Doodle" as the fleet came to
its anchorage before the town.  A little display of force and
a great deal of contempt were deemed sufficient by the ministry and their instruments to overawe the disaffected colonists.

Gage went home to England shorn of his military character,
to explain Lexington and Bunker Hill to the king.  A few
days before he sailed he offered a reward of ten guineas for
the thief or thieves who in September stole from the Council
Chamber, in Boston, the Public Seal of the Province, his
private seal, and the seal of the Supreme Court of Probate.
Upon this announcement the wags suggested whether, as his
Excellency carried his secretary, T. Flucker, with him, "'t is
not as likely that he might have carried them off as any one
else."

On the whole, we feel inclined to call the Battle of Bunker
Hill, like that of Inkerman, the soldiers' battle.  There were
some who cowardly hung back from coming to the assistance
of their brethren, but the Americans as a body displayed great
heroism.  The day was one of the sultriest, and the loose
earth, trampled by many feet, rose in clouds of suffocating dust
within the redoubt.  The men there had marched and worked

all night without relief, and could readily see the enemy's ships
and floating batteries taking positions to prevent reinforcement
or retreat.   The thunder of the cannon to which they could
not reply served to augment the terror of such as were inex-
perienced in war, but still they faltered not.

Most of the provincials fought in their shirt-sleeves.   They
found their outer garments insupportable, and threw them off
as they would have done in a hay-field at home.   More than a
year after the action the General Court was still allowing
claims for guns, coats, and other property lost on the field.
The men were stripped for fighting, while the British at first
came up to the attack in heavy marching order, and arrived in
front of the Americans, breathless and overheated.   But then
those " peasants " in their shirt-sleeves, our ancestors,

> " Fought like brave men, long and well."

The British soldiers, too, deserve the same meed of praise.
They never displayed greater valor, or a more stubborn determination to conquer or die.   Without vanity we might apply
to them the remark of Frederick the Great to Prince Ferdi-
nand : " You are going to fight the French cousin ; it will be
easy for you, perhaps, to beat the generals, but never the
soldiers."   General Howe said of the action on the historic
hill, " You may talk of your Mindens and your Fontenoys,
but for my part, I never saw such carnage in so short a
time."

An instance of *sang-froid* which recalls the celebrated reply
of Junot occurred in the redoubt.   Enoch Jewett of Dunsta-
ble, a young soldier of Captain Ebenezer Bancroft's company,
Bridges's regiment, was standing at one of the angles of the
embankment beside his captain.   Being quite short, he rested
his gun against the breastwork, and arranged some cobble-
stones so that he might be able to get a sight as well as
the rest.   While thus occupied, a cannon-ball from one of the
enemy's frigates passed close above his head, brushing the
dust of the rampart into his musket so that it was quite full.
At this narrow escape Captain Bancroft turned, and said,

" See there, Enoch, they have filled your gun full of dust !"
To this Jewett replied, " I don't care, I'll give them dust
and all !" and, suiting the action to the word, discharged his
piece into the British ranks.

The ever-famous redoubt was only eight rods square, with a
salient in the southern face, which looked towards Charlestown. The entrance was by the north side, in which an opening had been left. Inside the work the men had raised a platform of earth on which to stand while they rested their guns
upon the embankment. The monument stands in the middle
of the space formerly enclosed by the redoubt, the whole area
of which should have been included within an iron fence,
composed of suitable emblems.

The eastern face of the redoubt was prolonged by a wall of
earth breast-high, for a hundred yards towards the Mystic.
Chastellux, who visited the spot a few years after the battle,
said this breastwork had no ditch, but was only a slight intrenchment. It was doubtless intended, had there been time,
to have continued the defences across the intervening space to
the river.

Near the base of Bunker Hill, two hundred yards in rear
of the redoubt, and ranging nearly parallel with its eastern face,
was a stone-wall behind which Knowlton, with the Connecticut
troops and two pieces of artillery, posted himself. In front
of his stone-wall was another fence, the two enclosing a lane.
Knowlton's men filled the space between with the loose hay
recently cut and lying in cocks on the field. This fence
extended to the river-bank, which was nine or ten feet above
the beach below. Stark's men heaped up the loose stones of
the beach until they had made a formidable rampart to the
water's edge.

This made a good defence everywhere except in the space
between the point where the breastwork ended and Knowlton's fence began. Wilkinson says this space was occupied
by a post and rail fence beginning at the northeast angle of the
redoubt, and running back two hundred yards in an oblique line
until it intersected the fence previously described. Frothing-

ham says this line was slightly protected, a part of it, about one hundred yards in extent, being open to the enemy. Howe's engineer-officer calls it a hedge. On another British map (De Berniere's) it appears undefended by any kind of works. By all accounts it was the weak point of the defences, and the fire of the British artillery was concentrated upon it.

After they obtained possession of the hill, the British destroyed the temporary works of the Americans only so far as they obstructed the free movements of their men and material. Dr. John Warren, who visited the spot a few days after the evacuation, probably refers to the removal of the fences when he says the works that had been cast up by our forces were completely levelled. Wilkinson at the same time plainly saw vestiges of the post and rail fences, examined the redoubt, and rested on the rampart. Governor Brooks examined the ground in 1818, and entered the redoubt. A visitor in 1824 says the redoubt was nearly effaced; scarcely a trace of it remaining, while the intrenchment running towards the marsh was still distinct. A portion of this breastwork remained visible as late as 1841. Stones suitably inscribed have been placed to mark the position of the breastwork, of which a little grassy mound, now remaining, is supposed to have formed a part.

The most singular phase which the battle of Bunker Hill presents is that in which we see the provincial officers fighting under the authority of commissions issued to them in the name of the reigning monarch of Great Britain. Yet such was the fact. Probably the greater number of those officers exercised command in the name of that king whose soldiers they were endeavoring to destroy. The situation seems wholly anomalous, and we doubt if there were ever before rebels who carried on rebellion with such means. The officers who were made prisoners — and some of them were captured in this battle — could only prove their rank by the exhibition of the royal warrant, the same under which their captors acted.

This state of things would, perhaps, only go to show that the colonists had not yet squarely come up to the point of throwing off their allegiance, were it not that the measure of continuing, or even issuing commissions to military and civil officers in the king's name, was prolonged by the legislative and executive authority of Massachusetts, long after the Declaration of Independence by the Thirteen United Colonies.

The absurdity of their position seems to have been perfectly comprehended, as the General Court, May 1, 1776, passed an Act, to take effect on the first day of June in that year, by which the style of commissions, civil and military, was thereafter to be in the name of the government and people of Massachusetts Bay, in New England. These commissions were to be dated in the year of the Christian era, and not in that of the reigning sovereign of Great Britain. This renunciation of allegiance to the crown — for such in fact it was — was a bold act, and placed Massachusetts in the van of the movement towards independent sovereignty. It has, in reality, been called a Declaration of Independence by Massachusetts, two months earlier than that by the Congress at Philadelphia.; but as Massachusetts, as a matter of expediency, virtually annulled her own action by subsequent legislation, she cannot maintain her claim in this regard. By the Act referred to, the 19th September, 1776, was fixed as the date when such commissions as had not been made to conform with the new law should be vacated.

But, in consequence of the failure of many of the officers of the militia who were in actual service to have their commissions altered to the new style, and especially in view of the desperate circumstances in which our army found itself after the battle of Long Island, a resolve passed the Massachusetts House on the 16th September, 1776, as follows : —

"It is therefore *Resolved*, That all Military Commissions now in force, shall be and continue in full force and effect on the same nineteenth day of *September*, and from thence to the 19th day of *January* next after, such commissions not being made to conform as aforesaid notwithstanding."

So that the men of Massachusetts continued to fight against George III., with his commissions in their pockets, for more

than six months after the Declaration of Independence by the
Thirteen United Colonies. One of these commissions, dated
in the reign of King George, and as late as the 10th of December, 1776, is in the writer's possession.

Commissions were issued by the Provincial Congress of
Massachusetts before Bunker Hill, and these did not bear the
king's name, but expressed the holders' appointment in the
army raised for the defence of the colony. Some of the officers engaged at Bunker Hill only received their commissions
the day before the battle. The two Brewers were of these.
Samuel Gerrish's regiment, which remained inactive on Bunker Hill during the engagement, Mr. Frothingham supposes
was not commissioned; but Gerrish had received his appointment as colonel, and James Wesson was commissioned major
on the 19th of May, 1775.

After the battle of the 17th of June the Provincial Congress
recommended a day of fasting, humiliation, and prayer to be
observed, in which the Divine blessing is invoked "on our
rightful sovereign, King George III." * The army chaplains
continued to pray for the king until long after the arrival of
General Washington, as we learn from Dr. Jeremy Belknap's
account of his visit to the camps before Boston, in October,
1775, when he observed that the plan of independence was becoming a favorite point in the army, and that it was offensive
to pray for the king. Under the date of October 22d the good
Doctor enters in his journal : —

"Preached all day in the meeting-house. After meeting I was
again told by the chaplain that it was disagreeable to the generals
to pray for the king. I answered that the same authority which
appointed the generals had ordered the king to be prayed for
at the late Continental Fast ; and, till that was revoked, I should
think it my duty to do it. Dr. Appleton prayed in the afternoon,
and mentioned the king with much affection. It is too assuming in
the generals to find fault with it."

John Adams, in a letter to William Tudor, of April 24,
1776, says : —

* Boston Gazette, July 3, 1775.

"How is it possible for people to hear the crier of a court pronounce "God save the King!" and for jurors to swear well and truly to try an issue between our Sovereign Lord the King and a prisoner, or to keep his Majesty's secrets, in these days, I can't conceive. Don't the clergy pray that he may overcome and vanquish all his enemies yet? What do they mean by his enemies? Your army?

"Have people no consciences, or do they look upon all oaths to be custom-house oaths?"*

We have presented the foregoing examples in order to show by what slow degrees the idea of separation germinated in the minds of the colonists. Hostilities were begun to regain their constitutional liberties, just as the war of the Great Rebellion of 1861 was first waged solely in the view of establishing the authority of the Constitution and the laws. If "all history is a romance, unless it is studied as an example," we do not seem to have developed in a hundred years a greater grasp of national questions than those hard-thinking and hard-hitting colonists possessed.

The constitution of the Provincial army was modelled after that of the British. The general officers had regiments, as in the king's service. The regiments and companies were in number and strength similar to those of the regular troops. Thus we frequently meet with mention of the Honorable General Ward's, Thomas's, or Heath's regiments. This custom lapsed upon the creation of a new army. In the British service the generals were addressed or spoken of as Mr. Howe or Mr. Clinton, except the general-in-chief, who was styled "His Excellency." Our own army adopted this custom in so far as the commanding general was concerned; but the subordinate generals, many of whom had come from private life, were little inclined to waive their military designation and continue plain Mister. It is still a rule of the English and American service to address a subaltern as Mr.

To return to the battle, — which was first called by our troops the "Battle of Charlestown," — it is worthy of remem-

---

* Mass. Hist. Collections, II. viii.

brance that the orders to take possession of the hill were issued on the same day that Washington was officially notified of his appointment to command the army. He had scarcely proceeded twenty miles on the way to Cambridge, when he met the courier spurring in hot haste with the despatches to Congress of the battle. The rider was stopped, and the General opened and read the despatch, while Lee, Schuyler, and the other gentlemen who attended him eagerly questioned the messenger. It was on this occasion that Washington, upon hearing that the militia had withstood the fire of the regulars, exclaimed, " Then the liberties of the country are safe ! "

A variety of conflicting accounts have been given of the battle by eyewitnesses ; the narrators, as is usual, seeing only what passed in their own immediate vicinity. On the day of the evacuation of Boston by the British Major Wilkinson accompanied Colonels Reed and Stark over the battle-ground, and the latter pointed out to him the various positions and described the parts played by the different actors. The vestiges of the post and rail fence on the left, and of the stone-wall Stark ordered " his boys " to throw up on the beach of the Mystic, were still plainly visible. It was before this deadly stone-wall where the British light-infantry attacked that John Winslow counted ninety-six dead bodies the next day after the battle. Stark told Wilkinson that " the dead lay as thick as sheep in a fold," and that he had forbidden his men to fire until the enemy reached a point he had marked in the bank, eight or ten rods distant from his line. With such marksmen as Stark's men were, every man covering his adversary, it is no wonder the head of the British column was shot in pieces, or that it drifted in mutilated fragments away from the horrible *feu d'enfer*.

Before the action, when some one asked him if the rebels would stand fire, General Gage replied, " Yes, if one John Stark is there ; for he is a brave fellow." Through his glass the General saw Prescott standing on the crest of the embankment. "Who is he ?" inquired the General of Councillor Willard, Prescott's brother-in-law. He was told. " Will he fight?" demanded Gage. "To the last drop of blood in his veins!" replied Willard. Prescott wore, on this day, a single-breasted blue coat with facings turned up at the skirt, a top-wig and three-cornered hat.

The American field-hospital during the battle was fixed at the old Sun Tavern, on the north side of Bunker Hill. Dr. Eustis, Andrew Craigie, and others officiated there. Some of the wounded early in the engagement were, however, removed to the mainland. The same tavern was one of the places named by the Committee of Safety for granting permits to go into Boston in April, 1775.

The American prisoners were treated with extreme inhumanity. They were conveyed over to Long Wharf in Boston, and allowed to lie there all night without any care for their wounds, or other resting-place than the ground. The next day they were removed to Boston Jail, where several died before their final transfer to Halifax. General Washington earnestly endeavored to mitigate the sufferings of these unfortunate men; but the status of rebel prisoners had not yet been established, or a cartel of exchange arranged.

Both parties were exhausted by the battle. The Americans feared an immediate advance on Cambridge; the British, apprehending an assault from the fresh troops of the Americans, intrenched on the northern face of Bunker Hill, while the 52d regiment bivouacked, on the night of the 17th, in the main street of the town, so as to cover the mill-pond causeway and the approach over the Neck. Dr. Church, in his defence, says, "Your Honor well knows what was our situation after the action of Bunker Hill; insomuch that it was generally believed, had the British troops been in a condition to pursue their success, they might have reached Cambridge with very little opposition."

The minority in Parliament were very severe in their remarks on the conduct of their troops at Lexington and Bunker Hill. Howe's forcing the lines thrown up by a handful of raw, undisciplined militia in the course of a summer's night was ludicrously compared to a Marlborough's victory at Blenheim.

The death of Warren was the greatest loss the American cause sustained on that day. The spot where he fell, while lingering in a retreat his soul rebelled against, is marked by a stone in the northerly part of the monument grounds. The last words he was heard to utter were: " I am a dead man. Fight on, my brave fellows, for the salvation of your country." His remains were buried on the field, with such disregard of the claims of rank, as a man and a citizen, that only the supposition that Gage feared to place them in the hands of his (Warren's) friends for political reasons can account for the indignity with which the body was treated. As for the Americans with whom he fought, it is not known that they made the least effort to obtain the remains. He died and received the burial of an American rebel, a name of which his descendants are not ashamed.

> " No useless coffin enclosed his breast,
> 　　Not in sheet or in shroud we bound him,
> 　　But he lay like a warrior taking his rest,
> 　　　　With his martial cloak around him."

When he entered the redoubt to which Putnam had directed him as the post of honor, Prescott addressed him, saying, " Dr. Warren, do you come here to take the command?" " No, Colonel," replied the Doctor; " but to give what assistance I can, and to let these damned rascals see " — pointing to the British troops — " that the Yankees will fight." This was the relation of Dr. Eustis, who was within the redoubt, to General Wilkinson. Eustis, afterwards governor of Massachusetts, was a student with Warren, and had been commissioned surgeon of Gridley's regiment of artillery. After the battle he attended the wounded, and was placed in charge of the military hospital established at Rev. Samuel Cook's house at Menotomy, now Arlington.

The slaughter of British officers at Bunker Hill was terrible indeed. The bloodiest battles in which British soldiers had been engaged suffered by the comparison. Quebec and Minden were no longer recollected with horror. Spendlove, Major of the 43d, who died of his wounds here, had been gazetted

four times for wounds received in America; namely, with
Wolfe, on the Plains of Abraham, at the reduction of Mar-
tinico, the taking of Havana, and at Bunker Hill. There is no
doubt Pitcairn was singled out for his share in the Lexington
battle; his person was well known in the American ranks.
Dearborn says he was on horseback, and the only mounted
officer of the enemy on the field. Abercrombie, borne away
with a mortal hurt, begged his men not to kill his old friend
Putnam. Each of these officers commanded battalions.

The effect on the new levies in England was marked. An
officer who resigned, upon being asked the reason, replied, that
he wanted to see a little more of the world. "Why don't
you go to America with the troops?" said the querist. "You
will then have an opportunity of seeing the world soon."
"Yes," replied the officer, "*the other world* I believe I should
very soon; but as I am not tired of this, I do not choose to set
out on my journey yet."

These celebrated heights were eventually cultivated, and produced astonishing crops of hemp, etc., so that in this respect
they followed in the train of the memorable Plains of Abraham, which Lord Dalhousie, when he was governor-general of
Canada, ordered to be ploughed up and seeded in grain. This
was laid hold of by the wits, who perpetrated the following
epigram : —

> "Some care for honor, others care for groats, —
>   Here Wolfe reaped glory and Dalhousie oats."

The Freemasons have the honor of taking the initiative in a
structure to commemorate the heroic death of their Grand-
Master, Joseph Warren. In 1794 King Solomon's Lodge of
Charlestown erected a Tuscan column of wood, elevated on a
brick pedestal eight feet square, and surmounted by a gilded
urn, bearing the age and initials of the illustrious dead,
encircled with Masonic emblems. The whole height of the
pillar was twenty-eight feet.

The face of the south side of the base bore the following
inscription : —

Erected, A. D. MDCCXCIV.
By King Solomon's Lodge of Freemasons.
Constituted in Charlestown, 1783,
In Memory of
Major-General Joseph Warren,
And his Associates,
Who were slain on this memorable spot, June 17, 1775.

———

None but they who set a just value on the blessings of Liberty are worthy
to enjoy her.

In vain we toiled ; in vain we fought ; we bled in vain ; if you, our offspring, want valor to repel the assaults of her invaders.

———

Charlestown settled, 1628.
Burnt, 1775.   Rebuilt, 1776.

———

The enclosed land given by the Hon. James Russell.

This structure stood for about thirty years, but was in a
state of ruinous dilapidation before the movement to raise on
the spot its giant successor caused its disappearance. A beautiful model in marble of the first monument may still be seen
within the present obelisk.

William Tudor of Boston, the accomplished scholar, was the
first to draw public attention to the building of a memorial on
Bunker Hill commensurate with the event it was intended to
celebrate. He pursued the subject until the sympathies and
co-operation of many distinguished citizens were secured. Daniel Webster was early enlisted in the cause, and he stated that
it was in Thomas H. Perkins's house, in Boston, that William
Tudor, William Sullivan, and George Blake adopted the first
step towards raising a monument on Bunker Hill. Dr. John C.
Warren, nephew of the General, purchased three acres of land
lying on the hill, in November, 1822, thus preserving for the
monument site an area that was about to be sold. A meeting
of those friendly to the enterprise was held in the Merchants'
Exchange, in Boston, in May, 1823, which resolved itself,
under an act of incorporation passed June 7, 1823, into the
Bunker Hill Monument Association. Governor John Brooks
was the first president.

In 1824 Lafayette, then on his triumphal tour through

the United States, paid a visit to the scene of the battle, and accepted an invitation to assist at the laying of the corner-stone on the ensuing anniversary. Meantime the directors were considering the plan for the monument. A committee for this object was formed of Messrs. Daniel Webster, Loammi Baldwin, George Ticknor, Gilbert Stuart, and Washington Allston, and some fifty plans appeared to compete for the offered premium. This committee, able as it was, did not make a decision; but a new one, of which General H. A. S. Dearborn, Edward Everett, Seth Knowles, S. D. Harris, and Colonel T. H. Perkins were members, eventually made choice of the obelisk as the simplest, and at the same time the grandest, form in which their ideal could be expressed.

It is stated that Horatio Greenough, then an undergraduate at Harvard, sent to the committee a design, with an essay, in which he advocated the obelisk with much power and feeling. The design finally adopted was Greenough's, modified by the taste and judgment of Colonel Baldwin. Solomon Willard, the architect, made the working plan.

The occasion of laying the corner-stone was made as imposing as possible. The day was everything that could be desired. The military and civic bodies appeared to great advantage, while the presence of Lafayette gave an added *éclat* to the pageant. The streets of Boston were thronged with an immense multitude, and again Charlestown was invaded by an army with banners, but with more hospitable intent than the display of fifty years before had witnessed. Some forty survivors of the battle appeared in the ranks of the procession. Their course was followed by the loudest acclamations, and the waving of many handkerchiefs wet with the tears of the gentler sex; while many a manly eye could not refuse its tribute to a spectacle so touching as were these visible relics of the battle. One aged veteran stood up in the midst of the multitude, and exhibited the simple equipments he wore when a soldier of Prescott's Spartan band. Not Webster, not even the noble Frenchman, so moved the hearts of the people, as did these old men, with their white hairs, their bowed forms, and their venerable aspect.

The ceremony of laying the corner-stone proceeded under the direction of King Solomon's Lodge; Mr. Webster, then president of the Monument Association, and the Marquis assisting. The plate, containing a long inscription, was deposited in its place, and the exercises were continued in a spacious amphitheatre erected on the northerly slope of the hill. Here Mr. Webster delivered his oration, and the day finished with a banquet on Bunker Hill. The corner-stone proved not to be deep enough to resist the action of frost, and it was therefore subsequently relaid. The box containing the inscription was eventually placed under the northeast angle of the monument.

The erection of the monument proceeded under continued difficulties, the work frequently halting for want of funds, until its completion on the morning of July 23, 1842, when the last stone was raised to its place. To the patriotic efforts of the ladies is due the final realization of the original design. The association had been compelled not only to sell off a portion of its land, but also to diminish the height of the obelisk; but the proceeds of the fair conducted by the ladies in the hall of Quincy Market (Boston) realized $30,000, and the vote which had been adopted to consider the monument completed at one hundred and fifty-nine feet of altitude was rescinded.

The same great orator who had presided at the incipient stage of the structure addressed another vast audience on the day of dedication in 1843. But of the twoscore living representatives of the army of constitutional liberty there remained but eleven individuals to grace the occasion by their presence. They were, J. Johnson, N. Andrews, E. Dresser, J. Cleveland, J. Smith, P. Bagley, R. Plaisted, E. Reynolds, J. Stephens, N. Porter, J. Harvey, and I. Hobbs.

Mr. Webster was himself on that day, and his apostrophe to the gigantic shaft was as grand and noble as the subject was lofty and sublime. Hawthorne, who certainly did not want for creative power, has declared that he never found his imagination much excited in the presence of scenes of historic celebrity; but this was not the experience of the hundred thousand spectators who stood beneath the majestic shaft, awed by the presence of those men who brought the extremes of our national existence together, and moved by the recollections which the theatre itself inspired.

Mr. Webster applied this test to his auditory when, waving his hand towards the towering structure, he said, " The powerful speaker stands motionless before us." He was himself deeply moved. The sight of such an immense sea of upturned faces — he had never before addressed such a multitude — he afterwards spoke of as awful and oppressive. The applause from a hundred thousand throats surged in great waves around the orator, completing in his mind the parallel of Old Ocean.

Within the little building appropriated to the keeper is a marble statue of General Warren, in citizen's dress, by Dexter. The figure stands on a beautiful pedestal of *verd-antique* marble, the gift of the late Dr. J. C. Warren. The artist's conception was excellent in theory, but the peculiar pose of the head effectually prevents the features being seen by the spectator, except in profile, as the work is now placed. The statue, to be viewed to advantage, should be situated in the middle of a suitable apartment, or where it might have space enough to permit an understanding of the subject at a single *coup d'œil*. Copley's portrait, in Faneuil Hall, was the artist's study for the head. Mr. Dexter has been singularly successful in his studies from life, as well as ideal subjects. Colonel Thomas H. Perkins was the prime mover of the statue, and with John Welles, the two noble brothers Amos and Abbott Lawrence, and Samuel Appleton, contributed half the necessary funds.

We were not a little amused at a little outcropping of that species of flunkeyism in this place which we have hitherto supposed peculiar to our English cousins. The Prince of Wales and suite having visited the spot on the occasion of his sojourn in Boston, the autographs of "Albert Edward," " Newcastle," " Lyons," etc. were carefully removed from the visitors' book, and have been artistically framed, in connection with an account of the visit, in which the names of the gentlemen who were introduced to H. R. H. were not forgotten. We looked around in vain for any memento of the visit of a President of the United

States such as is accorded to the heir presumptive of the British throne. The object of the structure being made known, the Prince is said to have remarked pleasantly, "It is time these old matters were forgotten." Nevertheless, we do not believe he will pull down the Nelson monument or the Wellington statue, when he comes to the throne of his ancestors.

A celebrated statesman of Europe, whom Cromwell named "the wise man of the Continent," once sent his son on a visit to foreign courts with only this admonition, "Go, my son, and see by what fools the world is governed." We do not say that such was Victoria's counsel to her eldest son, but we do affirm that it would not be altogether without significance in this nineteenth century. When shall we so conduct ourselves towards foreign dignitaries as to secure their respect and our own?

> "For you, young potentate o' W——,
>     I tell your Highness fairly,
> Down pleasure's stream wi' swelling sails
>     I'm tauld ye're driving rarely;
> But some day ye may gnaw your nails,
>     An' curse your folly sairly,
> That e'er ye brak Diana's pales,
>     Or rattl'd dice wi' Charlie."

The great Whig convention of September 10, 1840, during the Harrison campaign, brought a monstrous gathering to this spot. The speech of the occasion was made by Daniel Webster, but the exercises were brought to an abrupt close by a violent shower of rain. It was at this time Mr. Webster made his famous remark, "Any rain, gentlemen, but the reign of Martin Van Buren."

Since that time we have had, on Bunker Hill, Mason of Virginia, who little dreamed, we think, that his next view of the monument would be from Fort Warren, as a prisoner of war, with a misty political perspective, — and Davis in Faneuil Hall; but no Toombs has ever called the roll of his slaves here, and now, thanks to the teachings of temple and shaft! not a manacle remains in all the land.

The obelisk is two hundred and twenty feet high, exceeding

the London Monument built by Wren to commemorate the Great Fire, and sometimes stated to be the highest in the world, by eighteen feet. The shaft is composed of ninety courses of stone, of which six are in the foundation. The pinnacle consists of a single mass weighing two and a half tons, fitly crowning the greatest specimen of commemorative architecture America affords. The interior of the shaft is a hollow cone, ascended by a spiral staircase to the summit, where the visitor finds himself within a circular chamber, breathless, perhaps, with his fatiguing climb, but with an unsurpassed prospect of land and sea outspread before him.

> "There architecture's noble pride
>   Bids elegance and splendor rise ;
> Here Justice, from her native skies,
>   High wields her balance and her rod ;
> There Learning, with his eagle eyes,
>   Seeks Science in her coy abode."

Within this chamber are the two little brass cannon, Hancock and Adams, taken out of Boston by stealth in September, 1775, and presented by Massachusetts to the Monument Association in 1825. While the London Monument and the Column Vendôme have been much affected by suicides, we do not remember that such an attempt has ever been made from this shaft.

Of those who will be more prominently identified with Bunker Hill Monument, Amos Lawrence will be remembered as a benefactor, aiding it liberally with purse and earnest personal effort at a time when the friends of the project were almost overcome by their discouragements. He succeeded in obtaining the active co-operation of the Charitable Association, and, by his will, set apart a sum to complete the monument and secure the battle-field, — a provision his executors were not called upon to fulfil, as Mr. Lawrence lived to see the completion of the memorial shaft in which he was so deeply interested.

Although the architect of many noble public edifices, the monument will doubtless be considered as Willard's *chef d'œuvre*. A nominal compensation was all he would accept

for his services.  He secured the quarry from which the granite
was obtained, and appears among the list of contributors set
down for a generous sum.

Edward Everett gave heart and voice to the work, as he
afterwards did to the rescue of Mount Vernon from the hazard
of becoming a prey to private speculation.

In taking our leave of an object so familiar to the citizens
of Massachusetts, and which bears itself proudly up without a
single sculptured line upon its face to tell of its purpose, we
yet remember that its stony finger pointing to the heavens has
a moral which lips by which all hearts were swayed — when
shall we hear their like again ? — disclosed to us in these words.
" To-day it speaks to us.  Its future auditories will be the successive generations of men, as they rise up before it, and gather
around it.  Its speech will be of patriotism and courage, of
civil and religious liberty, of free government, of the moral
improvement and elevation of mankind, and of the immortal
memory of those who, with heroic devotion, have sacrificed their
lives for their country."

Bunker Hill, on which the British erected a very strong fortress, was named for George Bunker, an early settler.  It is
now crowned by the steeple of a Catholic church, which, thanks
to its lofty elevation, can be seen for a considerable distance
inland.  The hill is already much encroached upon, and must
soon follow some of its predecessors into the waters of the
river.  This eminence, Mount Benedict, and Winter Hill are
situated in a range from east to west, each of them on or near
Mystic River.  Mount Benedict (Ploughed Hill) is in the middle, and is the lowest of the three ; its summit was only half a
mile from the English citadel where we stand, and which Sir
Henry Clinton commanded in 1775.

As late as 1840 the summit and northern face of the hill
retained the impress of the enemy's extensive works.  The
utmost labor and skill the British generals could command
were expended to make the position impregnable.  It could
have been turned, and actually was turned, by a force crossing
the mill-pond causeway to its rear ; but its fire commanded

every point of approach, and its strong ramparts effectually protected the garrison. There is evidence that General Sullivan intended making a demonstration in force in this direction during the winter of 1775, but some untoward accident prevented the accomplishment of his design.

It becomes our duty to refer to the almost obliterated vestiges of what was once the great artery of traffic between Boston and the falls of the Merrimack. It seems incredible that the Middlesex Canal, the great enterprise of its day, should have so quickly faded out of recollection. We have traced its scanty remains through the towns of Medford and Woburn, and have found its grass-grown basin and long-neglected tow-path quite distinct at the foot of Winter Hill in the former town, and along the railway to Lowell in the latter. In many places houses occupy its former channel. The steam caravan rushes by with a scream of derision at the ruin of its decayed predecessor, and easily accomplishes in an hour the distance the canal-boats achieved in twelve.

In 1793 James Sullivan of Boston, Oliver Prescott of Groton, James Winthrop of Cambridge, Loammi Baldwin of Woburn, Benjamin Hall, Jonathan Porter, and others of Medford, were incorporated, and begun the construction of the canal. It was at first contemplated to unite the Merrimack at Chelmsford with the Mystic at Medford, but subsequent legislation carried the canal to Charles River by a lock at Charlestown Neck, admitting the boats into the mill-pond, and another by which they gained an entrance to the river. The boats were received into the canal across the town of Boston, and unloaded at the wharves of the harbor. The surveys for the canal were made by Weston, an English engineer, and Colonel Baldwin superintended the excavation, etc. In 1803 the sweet waters flowed through and mingled with the ocean. Superseded by the railway, the canal languished and at length became disused. While it existed it furnished the theme of many a pleasant fiction of perils encountered on its raging stream ; but now it has gone to rest with its fellow, the old stage-coach, and we are dragged with resistless speed on our journey in the train of the iron monster. Peace to the relics of the canal, it was slow but sure. There was not a reasonable doubt but that you would awake in the morning in the same world in which you went to sleep ; but now you repose on a luxurious couch, to awake perhaps in eternity.

## CHAPTER IV.

### THE CONTINENTAL TRENCHES.

" From camp to camp thro' the foul womb of night,
    The hum of either army stilly sounds,
    That the fix'd sentinels almost receive
    The secret whispers of each other's watch."

SHAKESPEARE.

THE military position between the Mystic and Charles will be better understood by a reference to the roads that in 1775 gave communication to the town of Boston.

From Roxbury the main road passed through Brookline and Little Cambridge, now Brighton, crossing the causeway and bridge which leads directly to the Colleges. This was the route by which Lord Percy marched to Lexington.

From Charlestown, after passing the Neck by an artificial causeway, constructed in 1717, two roads diverged, as they now do, at what was then a common, now known as Sullivan Square. Near the point where these roads separated was Anna Whittemore's tavern, at which the Committee of Safety held some of its earliest sessions in 1774, and which had been an inn kept by her father as early as the famous year '45, and perhaps earlier. Malden Bridge is located upon the site of the old Penny Ferry, over which travel to the eastward once passed.

The first of these roads, now known as Washington Street, in Somerville, skirts the base of Prospect Hill, leaving the McLean Asylum on the south, and conducting straight on to

the Colleges. By this road the Americans marched to and
retreated from Bunker Hill. Lord Percy entered it at what is
now Union Square, in Somerville, and led his worn battalions
over it to Charlestown.

The second road proceeded by Mount Benedict to the summit of Winter Hill, where it divided, as at present; one branch
turning northward by General Royall's to Medford, while the
other pursued its way by the powder-magazine to what is now
Arlington, then known as Menotomy. The road over Winter
Hill, by the magazine, which it has been stated was not laid
out in 1775, is denominated a country road as early as 1703,
and appears on the map included in this volume.

Besides these there were no other roads leading to the
colonial capital. The shore between was yet a marsh, unim-
proved, except for the hay it afforded, and reached only at a
few points by unfrequented cartways. A causeway from the
side of Prospect Hill, and a bridge across what is now Miller's
River, gave access to the farm at Lechmere's Point. From the
road first described a way is seen parting at what is now Union
Square, crossing the river just named by a bridge, and leading
by a circuitous route to Inman's house in Cambridgeport, and
from thence to the Colleges. This road, from the nature of the
ground, could have been but little used.

Mount Benedict is the first point where we encounter the
American line of investment during the siege of Boston, after
passing Charlestown Neck. In Revolutionary times it was
called Ploughed Hill, probably from the circumstance of its
being cultivated when the Americans took possession, while
Winter and Prospect Hills were still untilled. The hill was
within short cannon-range of the British post on Bunker Hill,
and its occupation by the Americans on the 26th of August,
1775, was expected to bring on an engagement; in fact,
Washington offered the enemy battle here, but the challenge
was not accepted.

Ploughed Hill was fortified by General Sullivan under a
severe cannonade, the working party being covered by a detachment of riflemen, or riflers, as they were commonly called,

posted in an orchard and under the shelter of stone-walls. Finding they were not attacked, the Provincials contented themselves with stationing a strong picket-guard on the hill, usually consisting of about half a regiment. Poor's regiment performed a tour of duty there in November, 1775. A guard-house was built within the work for the accommodation of the picket, which was relieved every day. General Lee was much incensed because an officer commanding the guard allowed some boards to be pulled off the guard-house for fuel, and administered a sharp reprimand.

The Continental advanced outpost was in an orchard in front of Ploughed Hill. In summer the poor fellows were not so badly off, but in the inclement winter they needed the great watch-coats every night issued to them before they went on duty, and which the poverty of the army required them to turn over to the relieving guard. Here, as at Boston Neck, the pickets were near enough to each other to converse freely, — a practice it was found necessary to prohibit in orders. The reliefs on both sides could be easily counted as they marched down from their respective camps. The rules of civilized warfare which respect sentinels seem, at first, to have been little observed at the Continental outposts. We had some Indians posted on the lines who could not understand why an enemy should not be killed under any and all circumstances. The Southern riflemen, also, were very much of this opinion, each being, Corsican-like, intent on "making his skin." The British officers were soon inspired with such fear of these marksmen that they took excellent care to keep out of range of their dreaded rifles.

It is time to relate an incident which occurred at this out-post, where the parleys and flags that were necessary on this side of the lines were exchanged. Very soon after General Lee's arrival in camp he took occasion to despatch a character-istic letter to General Burgoyne, in which he argued the ques-tion of taxation, lamented while he censured the employment of his quondam friends, Gage, Burgoyne, and Howe, in the army of subjugation, and ridiculed the idea which prevailed in

the British army of the cowardice of the Americans. This letter was written in Philadelphia before the battle of Bunker
Hill, and the general was the bearer of his own missive as far
as Cambridge.

It was probably not later than the morning after his arrival
in camp that Lee went down to the British lines on Charlestown Neck, — then pushed about one hundred and fifty yards
beyond the isthmus, — hailed the sentinel, and desired him to
tell his officers that General Lee was there, and to inform
General Burgoyne that he had a letter for him. The letter
was to have been sent into Boston by Dr. Church, but was
taken by Samuel Webb (afterwards a general), aid to General
Putnam, to the lines near Bunker Hill, where Major Bruce of
the 38th — the same who fought a duel with General Pigot —
came out to receive it.

Webb advanced and said : " Sir, here is a letter from
General Lee to General Burgoyne. Will you be pleased to
give it to him ? As some part of it requires an immediate
answer, I shall be glad you would do it directly; and, also, here
is another letter to a sister of mine, Mrs. Simpson, to whom I
should be glad you would deliver it." The Major gave him
every assurance that he would deliver the letter to Mrs. Simpson himself and also to General Burgoyne, but could not do it
immediately, as the General was on the other lines, meaning
Boston Neck. " General Lee !" exclaimed Major Bruce. " Good
God, sir ! is General Lee there ? I served two years with him
in Portugal. Tell him, sir, I am extremely sorry that my profession obliges me to be his opposite in this unhappy affair. Can't
it be made up ? Let me beg of you to use your influence, and
endeavor to heal this unnatural breach."

Upon hearing that General Lee had a letter for him, Burgoyne had sent out a trumpeter, of his own Light Horse, over
Boston Neck to receive it, but then learned by a second letter
from Lee how his first had been forwarded. In his second communication Lee endeavored to obtain an exact list of the British
losses at Bunker Hill, which great pains had been taken to
conceal. Major Bruce told Mr. Webb that Colonel Aber-

crombie of the 22d was dead of a fever, — suppressing the fact that the fever was caused by a fatal wound, — and it was not until this parley took place that the Americans knew of Pitcairn's death. Lee, on his part, enclosed an account of the American losses in that battle.

As mention has been made of the rifle regiment, the nucleus of Morgan's celebrated corps, and as we are now upon the scene of their earliest exploits, a brief account of the leader and his merry men may not be uninteresting.

FLAG OF MORGAN'S REGIMENT.

The riflemen were raised by a resolve of Congress, passed June 14, 1775, which authorized the employment of eight hundred men of this arm, and on the 22d of the same month two companies additional from Pennsylvania were voted. The expresses despatched by Congress to the persons deputed to raise the companies had in many cases to ride from three to four hundred miles, yet such was the enthusiasm with which officers and men entered into the affair, that one company joined Washington at Cambridge on the 25th of July, and the whole body, numbering 1,430 men, arrived in camp on the 5th and 7th of August. The whole business had been completed in less than two months, and without the advance of a farthing from the Continental treasury. All had marched from four to seven hundred miles, encountering the extreme heat of midsummer, yet they bore the fatigue of their long tramp remarkably well. They were chiefly the backwoodsmen of the Shenandoah Valley, and brought their own long rifles with which they kept the savages from their clearings or knocked over a fat buck in full career.

Michael Cresap, the same whom Logan, the Indian chief, charged with the cold-blooded murder of his women and children, commanded one of these companies, and Otho H. Williams, who afterwards became Greene's able assistant in the South, was lieutenant of another.

It is not to be wondered at that men who in boyhood had been punished by their fathers for shooting their game anywhere except in the head should soon become the terror of their foes, or that they should be spoken of in the British camp as "shirt-tail men, with their cursed twisted guns, the most fatal widow-and-orphan makers in the world."

Their dress was a white or brown linen hunting-shirt, ornamented with a fringe, and secured by a belt of wampum, in which a knife and tomahawk were stuck. Their leggings and moccasins were ornamented in the Indian fashion with beads and brilliantly dyed porcupine-quills. A round hat completed a costume which, it will be conceded, was simple, appropriate, and picturesque. Tall, athletic fellows, they seemed to despise fatigue as they welcomed danger. They marched in Indian file, silent, stealthy, and flitting like shadows though the forests, to fall on the enemy at some unguarded point.

These riflemen were the only purely distinctive body of men our Revolution produced. In costume, as in their mode of fighting, they were wholly American. In physique and martial bearing they were worthy to be compared with the Highlanders of Auld Scotland. The devotion of the men to their leader was that of clansmen to their chief. Indian fare in their pouches and a blanket on their backs found them ready for the march.

We have only to picture to ourselves a "Deer-slayer" or a "Hawk-eye" to see one of these hard-visaged, keen-eyed, weather-beaten woodsmen stand before us. For a skirmish or an ambush such men were unrivalled, but they could not withstand the bayonet, as was shown in the battle of Long Island, where the rifle regiment, then commanded by Colonel Hand, was broken by a charge. Their weapon required too much deliberation to load; for, after emptying their rifles, the enemy were upon them before they could force the patched ball to the bottom of the barrel.

Colonel Archibald Campbell, of the 71st Highlanders, who, with a battalion of his regiment, was taken prisoner in Boston harbor and detained at Reading, admired the rifle-dress so much that it was reported he had one made for his own use, with which it was supposed he meant to disguise himself and effect his escape. The officer who made this discovery described the Highland colonel as "a damned knowing fellow," and adds, "If he should get away, I think he would make a formidable enemy; for he is the most soldier-like, best-looking man I ever saw."

Morgan was a plain, home-bred man. He was very familiar with his men, whom he always called his boys; but this familiarity did not prevent his exacting and receiving implicit obedience to his orders. Sometimes, in case of a secret expedition, the men ordered on duty were to be in readiness by three o'clock in the morning. They were then mounted behind horsemen provided for the purpose, and before daybreak would thus accomplish a day's march for foot-soldiers. Morgan told his men to shoot at those who wore epaulettes rather than the poor fellows who fought for sixpence a day. He carried a conch-shell, which he was accustomed to sound, to let his men know he still kept the field. His corps was sent to Gates to counteract the fear inspired by Burgoyne's Indian allies, who were continually ambushing our outposts and stragglers. It did not take them long to accomplish this task. Burgoyne afterwards said, not an Indian could be brought within sound of a rifle-shot. The British general himself owed his life on one occasion to another officer being mistaken for him, who received the bullet destined for his general. Washington estimated the corps at its true value, and, although he lent it temporarily to Gates, he very soon applied for its return; but Gates begged hard to be permitted to retain it, and his victory at Saratoga was due in no small degree to its presence.

The first colonel of the rifle regiment was William Thompson, by birth an Irishman. He had been captain of a troop of horse in the service of Pennsylvania in the French war of 1759 – 60, and before the Revolution resided at Fort Pitt, since Pittsburg. He was made a brigadier early in 1776, and, having joined General Sullivan in Canada, was made prisoner at *Trois Rivières.* Thompson was succeeded, in March, 1776, by Edward Hand, his lieutenant-colonel, who had accompanied the Royal Irish to America in 1774 as surgeon's mate, but who resigned on his arrival. He was afterwards a brigadier, and fought to the close of the war.

Daniel Morgan, who, in less than a week after the intelligence of the battle of Lexington, enrolled one hundred and seven men, with whom he marched to Cambridge, had been a wagoner in Braddock's army in 1755. For knocking down a British lieutenant he had received five hundred lashes without flinching. He seems at one period to have fallen into the worst vices of the camp, but before the Revolution had become a correct member of society. Washington despatched him with Arnold to Quebec in September, 1775, where, after having forced his way through the first defences, he was made prisoner while paroling some captives that he himself had taken; so that a common fate befell both Morgan and Thompson, and on the same line of operations. Morgan, after his exchange, was appointed colonel of the 11th Virginia, a rifle-corps, November 12, 1776. Of his subsequent career we need not speak.

Chastellux relates that when some of Rochambeau's troops were passing a river between Williamsburg and Baltimore, where they were crowded in a narrow passage, they were met by General Morgan, who, seeing the wagoners did not understand their business, stopped and showed them how to drive. Having put everything in order, he proceeded quietly on his way.

The best account we have of Colonel Morgan's appearance describes him as " stout and active, six feet in height, not too much encumbered with flesh, and exactly fitted for the pomp and toils of war. The features of his face were strong and manly, and his brow thoughtful. His manners plain and decorous, neither insinuating nor repulsive. His conversation grave, sententious, and considerate, unadorned and uncaptivating."

Mount Benedict is associated with an event which has no parallel, we believe, in the history of our country, namely, the destruction of a religious institution by a mob. The ruins of the Convent of St. Ursula long remained an evidence of what popular rage, directed by superstition and lawlessness, has been able to accomplish in a community of high average civilization. For half a century, these ruins served to emphasize a condition which has as completely disappeared as have the ruins themselves, by the grading down of the hill-top, where they stood, to its present level.

THE URSULINE CONVENT IN RUINS.

It must be admitted that the Jesuit fathers who planted the missions of their order in every available spot in the New World possessed an unerring instinct for choosing fine situations. Wherever their establishments have been reared civilization has followed, until towns and cities have grown up and environed their primitive chapels. Whatever may be said of the order, it has left the finest specimens of ancient architecture existing on the American continent. We need only cite Quebec, Mexico, and Panama to support this assertion.

The choice of Mount Benedict, therefore, for the site of a convent is only another instance of the good judgment of the Catholics. The situation, though bleak in winter, commands a superb view of the meadows through which the Mystic winds, and of the towns which extend themselves along the opposite shores. Beyond these are seen the gray, rocky ridges, resembling in their undulations some huge monster of antiquity, which, coming from the Merrimack, form the most remarkable valley in Eastern Massachusetts, and through which, in the dim distance of bygone ages, the river may have found its outlet to the sea. Perched on their rugged sides appear the cottages and villas of a population half city, half rural, but altogether distinctive in the well-kept, thrifty appearance of their homes.

On the night of the 11th of August, 1834, the convent and outbuildings were destroyed by incendiary hands. The flames raged without any attempt to subdue them, until everything combustible was consumed, the bare walls only being left standing. The firemen from the neighboring towns were present with their engines, but remained either passive spectators or actors in the scenes that ensued. A feeble effort was made by the local authorities to disperse the mob, — an effort calculated only to excite contempt, unsupported as it was by any show of force to sustain it. The affair had been planned, and the concerted signal expected.

For some time previous to the final catastrophe rumors had prevailed that Mary St. John Harrison, an inmate of the convent and a candidate for the veil, had either been abducted or secreted where she could not be found by her friends. As this belief obtained currency, an excitement, impossible now to imagine, pervaded the community. Threats were openly made to burn the convent, but passed unheeded. Printed placards were posted in Charlestown, announcing that on such a night the convent would be burned, but even this did not arouse the authorities to action. At about ten o'clock on the night in question a mob, variously estimated at from four to ten thousand persons, assembled within and around the convent grounds. A bonfire was lighted as a signal to those who were apprised of what was about to take place. The Superior of the convent, Mrs. Moffatt, with the other inmates, were notified to depart from the doomed building. There were a dozen nuns, and more than fifty scholars, some of whom were Protestants, and many of a tender age. The announcement filled all with alarm, and several swooned with terror. The unfortunate females were at length removed to a place of security, and the work of destruction began and concluded without hindrance. The mob did not even respect the tomb belonging to the convent, but entered and violated this sanctuary of the dead.

A general burst of indignation followed this dastardly outrage. Reprisals from the Catholics were looked for, and it was many years before the bad blood created by the event subsided. The better feeling of the community was aroused; and few meetings in Old Faneuil Hall have given more emphatic utterance to its voice than that called at this time by Mayor Lyman, and addressed by Harrison Gray Otis, Josiah Quincy, Jr., and others. Measures of security were adopted, and once more, in the language of the wise old saw, "the stable door was shut after the steed had escaped."

The Catholics showed remarkable forbearance. On the day following the conflagration their bishop, Fenwick, contributed by his judicious conduct to allay the exasperation of his flock ; and even Father Taylor, the old, earnest pastor of the seamen, was listened to with respectful attention by a large assemblage of Irish Catholics, who had gathered in the immediate neighborhood of their church, in Franklin Street, Boston, on the same occasion.

In reverting to the conduct of the firemen, it should be remembered that Colonel Thomas C. Amory, then chief engineer of the Boston Fire Department, repaired to the convent at the first alarm, and did all in his power to bring the firemen to their duty. Finding this a hopeless task, he then visited the

bishop, and advised him to take such precautions as the dangerous temper of the mob seemed to demand.

Many arrests were made, and some of the rioters were convicted and punished. Chief Justice Shaw was then on the
bench, and John Davis governor of the State. Both exerted
themselves to bring the offenders to justice, and to vindicate
the name of the old Commonwealth from reproach.

The form of the main building of the convent, which faced
southeast, was a parallelogram of about thirty-three paces long
by ten in breadth ; what appear to have been two wings joined
it on the west side. The buildings were partly of brick and
partly of the blue stone found abundantly in the neighboring
quarries ; the principal edifice being of three stories, with a
pitched roof, and having entrances both in the east and west
fronts. The grounds, which were very extensive, and embraced most of the hill, were terraced down to the highway and
adorned with shrubbery. A fine orchard of several acres, in
the midst of which the buildings stood, extended on the west
quite to the limits of the enclosure, where, until recently, were
visible the remains of the convent tomb. The hill is now being
levelled with a rapidity that is fast obliterating every vestige
of its original appearance, as nature left it. Mount Benedict
already belongs to the past, whatever regret we may feel at
the disappearance of so beautiful an eminence.

The convent was opened on the 17th of July, 1826. It is
but little known that there was a similar establishment in
Boston, contiguous to the Cathedral in Franklin Street,
though no incident drew the popular attention to it. The
information upon which the mob acted in the sack of the
Mount Benedict institution proved wholly groundless.

When we last visited the ruins the scene was one of utter
loneliness. Year by year the walls had been crumbling away,
until the elements were fast completing what the fire had spared.
The snow enshrouded the heaps of *débris* and the jagged outlines of the walls with a robe as spotless as that of St. Ursula
herself. For nearly forty years these blackened memorials of the
little community of St. Angela had been visible to thousands

journeying to and from the neighboring city. The lesson has been sharp, but effectual. Whoever should now raise the torch against such an establishment would be deemed a madman.

Our interest is awakened at the mention of Ten Hills Farm in connection with the plantation of Governor Winthrop, who gave it the name by which it is still known, from the ten little elevations which crowned its uneven surface, but of which few traces remain visible to this day.

The grant to Winthrop was made September 6, 1631, of six hundred acres of land "near his house at Mistick," from which it would appear that the governor already had a house built there which was probably occupied by his servants. We are now speaking of a time nearly coincident with the settlement of Boston, when no other craft than the Indian canoe had ever cleft the waters of the Mystic, and when wild beasts roamed the neighboring forests.

Governor Winthrop tells his own story of what he, the original white inhabitant of Ten Hills, experienced there in 1631 : —

"The governour, being at his farm house at Mistick, walked out after supper, and took a piece in his hand, supposing he might see a wolf, (for they came daily about the house, and killed swine and calves, etc.;) and being about half a mile off, it grew suddenly dark, so as, in coming home, he mistook his path, and went til he came to a little house of Sagamore John, which stood empty. There he stayed, and having a piece of match in his pocket, (for he always carried about him match and a compass, and in summer time snake-weed,) he made a good fire near the house, and lay down upon some old mats which he found there, and so spent the night, sometimes walking by the fire, sometimes singing psalms, and sometimes getting wood, but could not sleep. It was (through God's mercy) a warm night; but a little before day it began to rain, and having no cloak, he made shift by a long pole to climb up into the house. In the morning there came thither an Indian squaw, but, perceiving her before she had opened the door, he barred her out; yet she stayed there a great while essaying to get in, and at last she went away, and he returned safe home, his servants having been much perplexed for him, and having walked about, and shot off pieces, and hallooed in the night, but he heard them not."

Savage supposes that Ten Hills was the governor's summer residence for the first two or three years; Boston being, after the removal of his house there, his constant home. It has also been usually considered as the place where Winthrop built his little bark, the Blessing of the Bay, the first English keel launched in the jurisdiction of Massachusetts Colony. This event occurred on the 4th of July, 1631, and in October the Blessing spread her canvas and bore away on a voyage to the eastward.

The farm of Ten Hills was owned at the time of the Revolution by Robert Temple, a royalist; and the house he occupied stood on the supposed site of Governor Winthrop's until demolished a few years ago. The following description applies to its appearance when the writer last visited it.

The mansion-house has a spacious hall, and a generous provision of large square rooms. As you ascend the stairs, in front of you, at the first landing, is a glass door, opening into a snug little apartment which overlooks the river. This must have been a favorite resort of the family. The wainscoting and other wood-work is in good condition, if a general filthiness be excepted, inseparable from the occupancy of the house by numerous families of the laborers in the neighboring brick-yards. All is now changed by the levelling of the adjacent hills beyond the possibility of recognition.

Robert Temple of Ten Hills was an elder brother of Sir John Temple, Bart., the first Consul-General from England to the United States. His eldest daughter became Lady Dufferin. Mr. Temple sailed for England as early as May, 1775 ; but, the vessel being obliged to put into Plymouth, Massachusetts, he was detained and sent to Cambridge camp. Mr. Temple's family continued to reside in the mansion at Ten Hills after his attempted departure, under the protection of General Ward. The Baronet married a daughter of Governor Bowdoin, while his brother's wife was a daughter of Governor Shirley.

Previous to his coming to Ten Hills, Robert Temple had resided on Noddle's Island, in the elegant mansion there afterwards occupied by Henry Howell Williams. Although himself a tenant, the Temples had in times past owned the island. Sir Thomas, who was proprietor in 1667, had been formerly Governor of Nova Scotia. It is related of him, that once, when on a visit to England, he was presented to Charles II., who complained to him that the colonists had usurped his prerogative of coining money. Sir Thomas replied, that they thought it no crime to coin money for their own use, and presented his Majesty some of Master Hull's pieces, on which was a tree. The king inquiring what tree that was, the courtier answered, " The royal oak which protected your Majesty's life," — a reply which charmed the king and caused him to look with more favor on the offending colony. If one of Master Hull's shillings be examined, we are not greatly surprised that his Majesty so readily believed the pine to be an oak.

Ten Hills was the landing-place of Gage's night expedition to seize the powder in the province magazine, in September, 1774. The next day the uprising in Middlesex took place. And on Saturday, the 3d, the soldiers were harnessed to four field-pieces, which they dragged to Boston Neck, and placed in battery there. The Lively frigate, of twenty guns, came to her moorings in the ferry-way between Boston and Charlestown, and the avenues to the doomed town were shut up as effectually by land as they had been by water.

The vicinity of Ten Hills was that chosen by Mike Martin for the robbery of Major Bray. It was near where the old lane leading to the Temple farm-house, and now known as Temple Street, enters the turnpike, that the robber overtook the chaise of his victim. After his condemnation, Martin related, with apparent gusto, that the pistol which he presented at the Major's head was neither loaded nor cocked, but that the latter was terribly frightened and trembled like a leaf. Mrs. Bray tried to conceal her watch, but was assured by the highwayman that he did not rob ladies. Even now the place seems lonesome, and is not the one we should select for an evening promenade.

On a little promontory which overlooked the Mystic the Americans erected a battery during the siege. At this point the river makes a westerly bend, so that a hostile flotilla must approach for some distance in the teeth of a raking fire from this redoubt. This was fully proved when the enemy brought their floating batteries within range to attack the working party on Ploughed Hill and enfilade the road. A nine-pounder mounted in this redoubt sunk one of the enemy's batteries and disabled the other, while an armed vessel which accompanied them had her foresail shot away, and was obliged to sheer off. The next day (Monday, September 28) the enemy sent a man-of-war into Mystic River, drew some of their forces over from Boston to Charlestown, where they formed a heavy column of attack, and seemed prepared to make a bold push, — as was fully expected in the American camp, — but Bunker Hill was too recent in their memories, and Ploughed Hill had been made much stronger than the position they had carried with so much loss of life on the 17th of June; the combat was declined.

Leaving the redoubt, a hundred yards higher up the hill we found traces of another work, with two of the angles quite clearly defined. Owing to the wholesale demolition which has been going on here, all these years, it has become quite impossible to relocate these very interesting relics of the siege of Boston.

General Sullivan, on first coming to camp, took up his quarters at Medford, where Stark and his New Hampshire men were already assembled. In a letter to the Committee of Safety, the general lamented extremely that the New Hampshire forces were without a chaplain, and were obliged to attend prayers with the Rhode-Islanders on Prospect Hill. We are ignorant whether the men of New Hampshire required more praying for than the men of Rhode Island, but we fully recognize the fact that in those days an army chaplain was not a mere ornamental appendage, dangling at the *queue* of the staff. General Sullivan was absent from camp in November, 1775, having been sent to Portsmouth on account of the alarm occasioned by the burning of Falmouth. He took with him some artillery officers and a company of the rifle regiment. About the same time General Lee went to Rhode Island on a similar mission.

Samuel Jaques, a later resident of Ten Hills Farm, is worthy of remembrance as a distinguished agriculturist. Born in 1776, a few weeks after the declaration of formal separation from England, he died in 1859, just at the dawn of a scarcely less momentous convulsion, thus spanning with his own life the greatest epochs of our history.

Colonel Jaques was in habits and manners the type of the English country gentleman. When a resident of Charlestown, he had, like Cradock's men at Mystic Side in 1632, impaled a deer-park. He also kept his hounds, and often wakened the echoes of the neighboring hills with the note of his bugle or the cry of his pack, bringing the drowsy slumberer from his bed by sounds so unwonted. We trust no incredulous reader will be startled at the assertion that the hills of Somerville have re-sounded with the fox-hunter's "tally-ho!"

Colonel Jaques, who acquired his title by long service in the militia, was engaged for a time during the hostilities of 1812 in the defence of the shores of the bay, being stationed at Chelsea in command of a small detachment. He was twenty-eight years a resident of the old Temple Manor, and discharged the duties of hospitality in a manner that did no discredit to the ancient proprietor. The farm was also occupied at one time by Elias Hasket Derby, who stocked it with improved breeds of sheep.

The place has now been much disfigured with excavations, to procure the clay, which is excellent for brickmaking, and that branch of industry has been extensively carried on for many years by the sons of Colonel Jaques. In time a large portion of the soil has been removed, and is, or was, standing in many a noble edifice in the neighboring city, — a gradual but sure process of annexation. The vein of clay, which is traced from Watertown to Lynn, underlies Ten Hills Farm.

Brickmaking was very early pursued by the settlers, one, at least, of the houses they built in the first decade of the settlement being still in existence. The size of bricks was regulated by Charles I., hence the name statute-bricks. The very first vessels which arrived at Salem had bricks stowed under their hatches, which were doubtless used in the erection of some of the big chimney-stacks that still exist there, their indestructible materials rendering them as useful to-day as when they were originally burnt. In 1745 all the bricks used in reconstructing the works at Louisburg and Annapolis Royal were shipped from Boston to General Amherst. The costly and disastrous examples of Portland, Chicago, and Boston have only confirmed the experience that bricks are more durable than stone. The sun-dried bricks of Nineveh and Babylon are still in existence, while the Roman baths of Caracalla and Titus have withstood the action of the elements far better than the stone of the Coliseum or the marble of the Forum.

Winter Hill was fortified immediately after the battle of Bunker Hill, and garrisoned by the commands of Poor, Stark, Reed, Mansfield, and Doolittle. The policy of placing the soldiers of the same colony together was at first observed, and while Greene on Prospect Hill had his Rhode-Islanders, Sullivan on Winter Hill quartered in the midst of the men of New Hampshire. Webb's and Hutchinson's regiments were under Sullivan's orders in November, 1775.

This, being the extreme left of the American interior line of defence, was fortified with great assiduity, especially as it covered the land approach to the town of Medford, and, to some extent, the navigation of the Mystic. The principal work was thrown up directly across the road leading over the hill, now Broadway, at the point where the Medford road diverges ; and, except at the northwest angle, where it was entered by the last-named highway, was enclosed on all sides. It was in form an irregular pentagon, with bastions and deep fosse. A breastwork conforming with the present direction of Central Street joined the southwest angle. This plan of redoubt and breastwork was the almost stereotyped form of the American works. A hundred yards in advance of the fort were outworks, in which guards were nightly posted. When Central Street was being made, the remains of the intrenchment were exposed, and are also remembered by some of the older people in the vacant land of Mr. Byam on the north side of the road.

Let us take a view of Sullivan's camp and fortress as it was in November, 1775. At eight in the morning the drummers and fifers of all the regiments on the hill assemble in the citadel and beat the troop. The martial sounds are taken up on Prospect Hill, and passed on to Heath at Cambridge. The refrain echoes along the line until it reaches the veteran Thomas at Roxbury, where it is wafted across the waters of the bay to the ears of the king's sentinel on the ramparts of the castle.

The details for pickets and guards are now paraded and inspected by the brave Alexander Scammell, who has followed his general and friend from the law-office at Exeter to be his major of brigade in the Continental service. The camp is now fully astir, and the detachments for fatigue are in motion. Some march to the neighboring forests, where they are employed in cutting wood for fuel and material for fascines. Soon the frosty air is vocal with the blows of their axes. Others are employed in mending the roads, strengthening the works, or deepening the ditches ; still others are busy erecting barracks for the approaching winter. Bustle and preparation have invaded the former solitude of the green slopes, and the beautiful verdure is furrowed with yawning trenches.

There never were such men for building earthworks as the Americans. Fort after fort rose before the astonished vision of the Britons, like the fabled palace of Aladdin. Now Breed's Hill, then Lechmere's Point, and finally Dorchester Heights, showed what workers those Yankees were. Gage was astonished, Howe petrified ; both were outgeneralled before Boston.

In fine weather the men off duty engage in a thousand occupations or amusements. Some read, others write, while not a few are cleaning their trusty firelocks or elaborately carving their powder-horns, to be handed down as heirlooms to their children's children.

Until barracks were built, officers and men made for themselves huts, after the manner described by Mr. Emerson, the general being accommodated in an old house on the hill. The officers exchanged visits, attended garrison courts-martial, — which might be held in Nixon's hut or Doolittle's barracks, — or rambled through the adjacent lines.    Card-playing, the soldiers' favorite pastime, was strongly discountenanced by the commander-in-chief; but we believe we should only have to lift the corner of the old sail that served as a door to the huts to see group after group, rebels that they were, paying court to king and queen.    At night a bit of tallow candle, stuck in the socket of a bayonet, serves to illuminate the soldier's cabin and prolong his pleasures till the drums at tattoo admonish him that the day is done.

Within the lines a regiment went on duty every night.    The tour came round often; the service was hard.    A company was stationed at Medford to prevent the men straggling from camp; and not a few officers, seduced by the comforts of a clean bed or the witchery of a pair of bright eyes, were in the habit of absenting themselves from camp to sleep at Mystic, as Medford was then called.

There was in each brigade a field-officer of the day.    When a colonel mounted guard he was attended by his own surgeon and adjutant.    He was in the saddle from troop to retreat, catching, perhaps, a mouthful at the picket, or sharing pot-luck with some comrade while on his rounds.    The advanced lines must be visited twice a day, and if there should be an alarm, the officer of the day must be at the threatened point.    The post at Ten Hills, the valley redoubts, the detachments at Mystic and the Powder House, were comprised within his charge.    He must not sleep or remove his arms during his tour.

Mrs. John Adams, in her letters, has left some admirable portraits of the distinguished characters of the Revolutionary army.    Speaking of General Sullivan, she says: —

"I drank coffee one day with General Sullivan upon Winter Hill. He appears to be a man of sense and spirit.    His countenance denotes him of a warm constitution, not to be very suddenly moved, but, when once roused, not very easily lulled; easy and social; well calculated for a military station, as he seems to be possessed of those popular qualities necessary to attach men to him."

A London paper said, in 1777 : " General Sullivan, taken prisoner by the king's troops, was an attorney, and only laid down the pen for the sword about eight months ago, though now a general." He was found by the Hessians after the disastrous battle of Long Island, secreted in a cornfield ; was searched, and General Washington's orders taken from him. Among the ridiculous stories with which the foreign officers regaled their home correspondents, the Hessian, Heeringen, in describing this affair, says : " John Sullivan is a lawyer, but before *has been a footman;* he is, however, a man of genius, whom the rebels will very much miss." In the same letter Lord Stirling, who was also made prisoner, is spoken of as an " *échappé de famille,* who is as much like Lord Granby as one egg is like another." General Putnam, says the same authority, is a butcher by trade. This battle of Long Island was where the Hessians became so terrible to their adversaries. They repeatedly halted under a heavy fire to dress their lines and advance with Old-World precision. Their officers took care to tell them the rebels would give no quarter, consequently they put to death all who fell into their hands. Some of the Americans were found after the action pinned to trees with bayonets. At Trenton these bugbears were stripped of their lions' skins.

General Sullivan was rather short in stature, but well-made and active. His complexion was dark, his nose prominent, his eye black and piercing. His countenance, as a whole, was harmonious and agreeable.

Scammell had been a schoolmaster and a surveyor before he became Sullivan's confidential clerk. In 1770 he was a member of the Old Colony Club, the first society in New England to commemorate publicly the landing of the Pilgrim Fathers. He stood six feet two inches, — just the height of the commander-in-chief, — and fought on the hardest fields of the Revolution. Just as final victory was about to crown the efforts of the Americans, Scammell fell at Yorktown, a victim to the ignorance or brutality of a Hessian vidette. When this unlucky event occurred he was in command of a picked corps of light infantry.

There are two actors in the same great drama of which we are
endeavoring to rearrange the scenes, whose acquaintance probably begun here, and whose fates long after became interwoven.
These two were James Wilkinson and Aaron Burr. Both joined
the army at Cambridge as volunteers in 1775. Washington
gave the former, who first united himself with Thompson's rifle-
corps, a captaincy in Reed's regiment. At the time of this
appointment he was a member of General Greene's military
family on Prospect Hill, and did not, therefore, join his regiment until he reached New York. Wilkinson took part in the
possession of Cobble Hill, Lechmere's Point, and Dorchester
Heights, and has recorded his opinion that Howe might have
forced Washington's lines at almost any time prior to January,
1776.

As is well known, Wilkinson became Gates's adjutant-general in the campaign against Burgoyne, and was the bearer of
the official despatches of the surrender to Congress. He was
implicated in the Conway cabal, but became estranged from
Gates, and a challenge passed between them. Wilkinson says
that Gates came to him at the last moment with an apology,
and that the duel did not take place, though it was currently
reported in the army to the contrary. A general officer, writing from White Plains, September, 1778, says: "General
Gates fought a duel with Mr. Wilkinson. General Gates's
pistols would not give fire, but flashed twice. Wilkinson's
gave fire, but the balls did not take effect." "Wilky," as he
was called in the army, was elegant in person and manners.

Burr and Matthias Ogden were recommended to Sullivan by
Gates in November, 1775, for positions, in reward for past services. Both accompanied Arnold to Quebec. Colonel Burr's
eventful career is familiar. His eye was remarkably piercing
and brilliant. With talents equal to any position, he seems to
have been formed by nature for a conspirator. The courtliness
of his manner and address gave him a fatal ascendency over
both sexes, of which he did not scruple to avail himself. The
death of Hamilton and the ruin of Blennerhassett painfully
illustrate the career of Aaron Burr.

It is not a little curious that Arnold, Burr, and Silas Deane, who, it is believed, was more sinned against than sinning, were from the same State. It is also a coincidence that the two former in their young, chivalric days should have fallen in love with two young ladies of the New England capital, both celebrated for their beauty. Arnold lost his heart to the " heavenly Miss Deblois," and laid at her feet the spoils of rich stuffs which he had ignobly plundered from the shops of Montreal. His suit was, however, unsuccessful ; for when did a Boston girl become the mother of traitors ? Burr, on his part, improved a visit which Madam Hancock, the governor's aunt, was paying his uncle at Fairfield, to lay siege to the heart of Dorothy Quincy, who was then under the protection of Madam Hancock. Aaron was then a handsome young fellow of very pretty fortune ; but the dowager, who was apprehensive that he might defeat her purpose of uniting Miss Quincy to her nephew, would not leave them a moment together. If we are to believe report, the lady was not insensible to the insinuating manners of young Burr.

John Vanderlyn, the painter, owed his rescue from the obscurity of a village blacksmith's shop to the acuteness and patronage of Colonel Burr. The latter, while journeying in the interior of New York, was much struck by a little pen-and-ink drawing that hung over the fireplace in the bar-room of a tavern. The lad was sent for, and, on parting, Colonel Burr said to him : " Put a shirt in your pocket, come to New York, and inquire for Aaron Burr ; he will take care of you." The boy followed his patron, who sent him to Paris, where he achieved a reputation that justified the sagacity of the then Vice-President of the United States.

Among the officers who served on Winter Hill, and who subsequently acquired fame, were Henry Dearborn, John Brooks, and Joseph Cilley. Dearborn was a captain in Stark's regiment, Brooks major of Bridges', and Cilley of Poor's regiment. Dearborn and Brooks became very distinguished in military and civil life : both testified their affection for Alexander Scammell by naming a son for that lamented officer ; both fought with conspicuous valor at Saratoga.

During the battle of Monmouth a corps commanded by Colonel Dearborn acquitted themselves with such undaunted bravery that they attracted particular notice. A Southern officer of rank rode up to Dearborn and inquired "who they were, and to what portion of America that regiment belonged." The Colonel replied in this laconic and soldierly manner: "Full-blooded Yankees, by G–d, sir, from the State of New Hampshire." * The same anecdote has been related of Colonel Cilley.

The Germans of Burgoyne's army, to the number of about

HESSIAN FLAG.

nineteen hundred, took up their quarters in the barracks and huts on Winter Hill which had been used by the Americans. General Riedesel, with his family, were accommodated in a farmhouse, where he was obliged to content himself with a room and a garret, with nothing better than straw for a couch. The General's biographer continues the description: "The landlord was very

kind, but his other half was a veritable dragon, doing everything to offend and annoy her obnoxious guests. But, as it was impossible to find another place, they were obliged to put up with everything rather than be driven from the house." After a sojourn here of three weeks, the General and Madame Riedesel were furnished with excellent quarters at Cambridge. Several of the officers were allowed to reside at that place and at Medford, but none were allowed to pass into Boston without special permission. The officers and soldiers had the privilege of going, first a mile, and eventually three miles, from their

* Mrs. Warren.

barracks. Colonel William Raymond Lee commanded on Winter Hill at the time of the arrival of the Hessians.

These mercenaries were employed, it is said, at the instigation of Lord George Germaine. The British government stipulated with the Landgrave of Hesse to pay £ 30 sterling for every man that did not return, and £ 15 sterling for each one disabled, so that it was commonly said, after a battle in which the Hessians were engaged, that their loss was the Landgrave's gain. Similar treaties were made with the Duke of Brunswick and the Count of Hanau.

We make the following extracts, which serve to convey an accurate idea of the condition of things on Winter Hill as they appeared to the German prisoners, from General Riedesel's memoirs : —

" The camp of the prisoners was encircled by a chain of outposts. The officers, who were permitted to go somewhat beyond the camp, were obliged to promise in writing, on their word of honor, to go no farther beyond it than a mile and a half. Within this space are the villages Cambridge, Mystic, or Medford, and a part of Charlestown. In these places the generals and brigadiers could select lodgings, for which, of course, they had to pay dearly. After a while this permission was extended to other staff and subaltern officers. Only a few of the Brunswickers availed themselves of this permission, preferring to remain in their miserable barracks, and thus share all inconveniences with their men.

" The camp was located on a height, which, to a distance of eight miles, was surrounded with woods, thus presenting a splendid view of Boston, the harbor, and the vast ocean. The barracks had been built in 1775, at the time that the Americans first took up arms, and upon these very heights took their first position against General Gage. These heights were fortified.

" When the fatigued and worn-out troops arrived here on the 7th of November they found not the least thing for their support. A little straw and some wood was everything that was furnished to the soldiers. The officers and privates were obliged to repair the barracks as well as they could, although they had neither tools nor materials with which to do it. Necessity, however, which is the mother of invention, accomplished incredible things."

The question, " Will Yankees fight ? " had to be settled in

the Revolution. It might be supposed that Lexington and
Bunker Hill would have given a final answer to such queries,
but they did not. The New England troops, when they came
to join those from the Southern Colonies, were mercilessly ridiculed by the chivalrous Southrons. It was Puritan and Cavalier over again. Hear the avowal of a Pennsylvania officer,
who evidently spoke the feeling of his section : —

" In so contemptible a light were the New England men regarded,
that it was scarcely held possible to conceive a case which could be
construed into a reprehensible disrespect of them."

The officers came in for a degree of ridicule second only to
the rank and file.

" So far from aiming at a deportment which might raise them
above their privates, and thence prompt them to due respect and
obedience to their commands, the object was, by humility, to preserve the existing blessing of equality ; an illustrious instance of
which was given by Colonel Putnam, the chief engineer of the army,
and no less a personage than the nephew of the major-general of
that name. ' What ! ' says a person, meeting him one day with a
piece of meat in his hand, ' carrying home your rations yourself,
Colonel ?' ' Yes,' says he, ' and I do it to set the officers a good
example.' "

This feeling, which the Southerners were at no pains to conceal, was not lost on the objects of it, who, nevertheless, for the
most part quietly endured the opprobrium, trusting to their
deeds to set them right in good time. Sullivan, who was a little
quick-tempered, was rather restive under such treatment. An
officer of Smallwood's Maryland regiment, which " was distinguished by the most fashionably cut coat, the most macaroni
cocked-hat, and hottest blood in the Union," had been guilty
of some disrespect or disobedience to the General. He was
arrested and tried, but, as the narrator ingeniously records, a
majority of the officers being Southern men, the offender was
acquitted with honor. Putnam and Greene were not exempt
from the derision of these blue-blooded heroes.

This was about the time of the disastrous campaign of Long

Island. The battle of Trenton displayed the qualities of the men of New England in such a light that a more creditable feeling began to be discovered by the men of the South. The despised Yankees showed themselves true descendants of the men of Marston Moor, Dunbar, and Worcester ; they became to Washington what Cromwell's Ironsides were to the Protector. The Southern cock crowed less loudly, and Northern courage, proved again and again, asserted, as it ever will assert, to its gainsayers : —

> " If you dare fight to-day, come to the field ;
> If not, when you have stomachs."

We may well pardon one of our generals a little exultation when he writes home, after the battles of Trenton and Princeton : —

" I have been much pleased to see a day approaching to try the difference between Yankee cowardice and Southern valor. The day, or rather the days, have arrived, and all the general officers allowed, and do allow, that Yankee cowardice assumes the shape of true valor in the field, and that Southern valor appears to be a composition of boasting and conceit. General Washington made no scruple to say publicly that the remains of the Eastern regiments were the strength of his army, though their numbers were, comparatively speaking, but small. He calls them in front when the enemy are there. He sends them to the rear when the enemy threaten that way. All the general officers allow them to be the best of troops. The Southern officers and soldiers allow it in time of danger, but not at all other times. Believe me, sir, the Yankees took Trenton before the other troops knew anything of the matter. More than that, there was an engagement, and, what will still surprise you more, the line that attacked the town consisted of but eight hundred Yankees, and there were sixteen hundred Hessians to oppose them. At Princeton, where the 17th regiment had thrown thirty-five hundred Southern militia into the utmost confusion, a regiment of Yankees restored the day. This General Mifflin confessed to me, though the Philadelphia papers tell us a different story. It seems to have been quite forgot that, while the 17th regiment was engaging these troops, six hundred Yankees had the town to take against the 40th and 55th regiments, which they did without loss, owing to the manner of attack."

# CHAPTER V.

## THE OLD WAYSIDE MILL.

*"There watching high the least alarms,*
*Thy rough, rude fortress gleams afar,*
*Like some bold vet'ran gray in arms,*
*And marked with many a seamy scar."*

BY far the most remarkable object to be seen in the vicinity of Boston is the Old Powder House, which stands on a little eminence hard by the road leading from Winter Hill to Arlington, — formerly the old stage-road to Keene, New Hampshire. In the day of its erection it stood at the meeting of the roads from Cambridge, Mystic, and Menotomy, — a situation excellently adapted to the wants of the settlements.

It is the only really antique ruin we can boast of in Massachusetts; and for solitary picturesqueness, in all New England, only its fellow, the Old Mill at Newport, can rival it. Long before you reach the spot its venerable aspect rivets the attention. Its novel structure, its solid masonry, no less than the extraordinary contrast with everything around, stamp it as the handiwork of a generation long since forgotten. We are not long in deciding it to be a windmill of the early settlers.

The Old Mill, as we shall call it, belongs to the early part of the reign of good Queen Anne, and was doubtless erected by John Mallet, who came into possession of the site in 1703 – 04. It remained for a considerable period in the Mallet family, descending at last, in 1747, to Michael, son of Andrew Mallet, by whom it was conveyed in the same year to the Province of the Massachusetts Bay in New England, for the use of " yᵉ Governor, Council and Assembly of said province," with the right of way to and from the high-road. It had, however, ceased to be used as a windmill long before this transfer. So that before Shirley's armada had set sail for Louisburg, its lusty arms had ceased to beat the air. Strange that an edifice erected to sustain life should become the receptacle of such a death-dealing substance as powder!

The walls of the mill are about two feet in thickness, with an inner structure of brick, the outside of which is encased in a shell of blue stone, quarried, probably, on the hillside. Within, it has, or had, three lofts supported by oaken beams of great thickness, and having, each, about six feet of clear space between. A respectable number of visitors have carved their names on these timbers. There were entrances on the northwest and southwest sides, but only the latter belonged to the original edifice, the small brick structure on the northwest having been constructed at a recent date. From this southwest door expands a most charming view. The structure is capped with a conical roof, and stands about thirty feet high, with a diameter of fifteen at the base. To find what was an isolated landmark, not so many years ago, now overlooking a populous neighborhood, is strange indeed. Better yet, it is no longer a neglected ruin.

Mallet's Mill ground for many an old farmstead of Middlesex or Essex. The old farm-house in which the miller dwelt stood by the roadside, where a newer habitation now is. Ten, thirty, sixty miles, and back, the farmers sent their sons to mill. The roads were few and bad. Oxen performed the labor of the fields. Those that came from a distance mounted their horses astride a sack of corn in lieu of saddle, and so performed their journey.

As a historical monument, the mill is commemorative of one of the earliest hostile acts of General Gage, one which led to the most important events. At the instance of William Brattle, at that time major-general of the Massachusetts militia, General Gage sent an expedition to seize the powder in this magazine belonging to the province. About four o'clock on the morning of September 1, 1774, two hundred and sixty soldiers embarked from Long Wharf, in Boston, in thirteen boats, and proceeded up the Mystic River, landing at Ten Hills Farm, less than a mile from the Powder House. The magazine, which then contained two hundred and fifty half-barrels of powder, was speedily emptied, and the explosive mixture transported to the Castle, while a detachment of the expedition proceeded to Cambridge and brought off two field-pieces there. At the time of this occurrence William Gamage was keeper of the magazine.

The news of the seizure circulated with amazing rapidity, and on the following morning several thousand of the inhabitants of the neighboring towns had assembled on Cambridge Common. This appears to have been the very first occasion on which the provincials assembled *in arms* with the intention of opposing the forces of their king. Those men who repaired to the Common at Cambridge were the men of Middlesex ; when, therefore, we place Massachusetts in the front of the Revolution, we must put Middlesex in the van. It was at this time that the lieutenant-governor (Oliver) and several of the councillors were compelled to resign. The Revolution had fairly begun, and accident alone prevented the first blood being shed on Cambridge, instead of Lexington, Common.

We will not leave the old mill until we consider for a moment what a centre of anxious solicitude it had become in 1775, when the word "powder" set the whole camp in a shiver. Putnam prayed for it ; Greene, Sullivan, and the rest begged it of their provincial committees. A terrible mistake had occurred through the inadvertence of the Massachusetts Committee, which had returned four hundred and eighty-five quarter-casks as on hand, when there were actually but thirty-eight barrels in the magazine. When Washington was apprised of this startling error, he sat for half an hour without uttering a word. The generals present — the discovery was made at a general council — felt with him as if the army and the cause had received its death-blow. "The word 'Powder' in a letter," says Reed, "sets us all a-tiptoe." The heavy artillery was useless ; they were obliged to bear with the cannonade of the rascals on Bunker Hill in silence ; and, what was worse than all the rest, there were only nine rounds for the small-arms in the hands of the men. In the whole contest there was not a more dangerous hour for America.

We have had occasion elsewhere to mention this scarcity of ammunition. At no time was the army in possession of abundance. Before Boston the cartridges were taken from the men that left camp, and fourpence was charged for every one expended without proper account. The inhabitants were called upon to give up their window-weights to be moulded into bullets, and even the churchyards were laid under contribution for the leaden coats-of-arms of the deceased. The metal pipes of the English Church of Cambridge were appropriated for a like purpose. On the lines the men plucked the fuses from the enemy's shells, or chased the spent shot with boyish eagerness. In this way missiles were sometimes actually returned to the enemy before they had cooled.

The old name of the eminence on which the Powder House stands was Quarry Hill, from the quarries opened at its base more than a century and a half ago. The region round about was, from the earliest times, known as the Stinted Pasture, and the little rivulet near at hand was called Two Penny Brook. When the province bought the Old Mill there was but a quarter of an acre of land belonging to it. After the Old War the Powder House continued to be used by the State until the erection, more than forty years ago, of the magazine at Cambridgeport. It was then sold, and passed into the possession of Nathan Tufts, from whom the place is usually known as the "Tufts Farm," but it has never lost its designation as the "Old Powder-House Farm," up to the present time.

Except that the sides of the edifice are somewhat bulged out, which gives it a portly, aldermanic appearance, and that it shows a few fissures traversing its outward crust, the Powder House is good for another century if for a day. Fortunately the iconoclasts have not yet begun to sap its foundations. Nothing is wanting but its long arms, for the Old Mill to have stepped bodily out of a canvas of Rembrandt or a cartoon of Albert Dürer. It carries us in imagination beyond seas to the banks of the Scheldt, — to the land of burgomasters, dikes, and guilders.

There is not the smallest doubt that Washington has often dismounted at the Old Mill, or that Knox came here seeking daily food for his Crown Point murtherers. Sullivan, in whose command it was, watched over it with anxious care.

It is pleasant to record the rescue of such a conspicuous and telling landmark as this from the rage of threatened demolition. This fury of progress, which has assailed Somerville in its high places, was here arrested by the joint action of the heirs of Nathan Tufts and of the city fathers, with the result that the permanence of the old building is now fully assured. These heirs, in 1890, proposed to execute a deed of gift to the city, under certain expressed conditions, of the Old Powder House and the surrounding grounds. This being accepted, the city acquired a much larger tract, contiguous to the first, by purchase, and the whole, under skilful and sympathetic treatment, is now converted into a beautiful park, — Nathan Tufts Park — alike a credit to those who gave and those whose taste has turned an unsightly stone quarry into a garden spot. Some necessary repairs were made in the old structure itself at this time without impairment of its general appearance to the most critical eye.

Following close upon these acts, permission was granted to the Massachusetts Society, Sons of the Revolution, to place a bronze tablet upon the old building, reciting the leading events connected with it, as we know them. A smaller tablet, affixed to the grille closing the entrance, gives the names of the city officials under whose direction the good work proceeded. Thus renovated, this ancient landmark tells its story with a new dignity.

Sir Walter Scott has said, "Nothing is easier than to make a legend." We need not invent, but only repeat one of which the Old Mill is the subject.

## A Legend of the Powder House.

In the day of Mallet, the miller, it was no unusual occurrence for a customer to dismount before the farm-house door after dark ; so that when, one sombre November evening, the good-man sat at his evening meal, he was not surprised to hear a horse neigh, and a faint halloo from the rider.

Going to the door, the miller saw, by the light of the lantern he held aloft, a youth mounted on a strong beast, whose steaming flanks gave evidence that he had been pushed at the top of his speed, and whose neck was already stretched wistfully in the direction of the miller's crib.

Mallet, — when was your miller aught else in song or story but a downright jolly fellow, — in cheery tones, bade the lad dismount and enter, at the same time calling his son André to lead the stranger's horse to the stable, and have a care for the brace of well-filled bags that were slung across the crupper.

Once within the house the new-comer seemed to shrink from the scrutiny of the miller's wife and daughters, and, notwithstanding his evident fatigue, could scarcely be prevailed upon to touch the relics of the evening repast, which the goodwife placed before him. He swallowed a few mouthfuls, and then withdrew into the darkest corner of the cavernous fireplace, where a rousing fire blazed on the hearth, crackling, and diffusing a generous warmth through the apartment.

The stranger was a mere stripling, with a face the natural pallor of which was heightened by a pair of large, restless black eyes, that seemed never to rest on any object at which they were directed, but glanced furtively from the glistening fire-irons to the spinning-wheel at which Goodwife Mallet was employed, and from the rude pictures on the wall back to the queen's arm which hung by its hooks above the chimney-piece. " Certes," muttered Mallet, under his breath, " this fellow is no brigand, I 'll be sworn."

The habit of those days among the poorer classes was early to bed, and soon the miller set the example by taking a greasy dip-candle and saying : " Come, wife, Marie, Ivan, to bed ; and you, André, see that all is secured.   Come, lad," — beckoning to his guest, — " follow me."

Leading the way up the rickety stairs, the miller reached the garret, and, pointing to the only bed it contained, bade the wayfarer share a good night's rest with his son André.   The startled expression of the stranger's face, and the painful flush that lingered there, were not observed by the bluff old miller. They were plain folk, and used to entertain guests as they might.

The youth entreated that if he might not have a couch to himself, he might at least sit by the kitchen fire till morning ; but his request was sternly refused by the miller, with marks of evident displeasure.   " Harkye, lad," he blurted out, " your speech is fair, and you do not look as if you would cut our throats in the dark, but if ye can't sleep with the miller's son for a bedfellow, your highness must e'en couch with the rats at the mill, for other place there is none."   To his surprise the boy caught eagerly at the proposal, and, after no little persuasion, he yielded, and conducted his fastidious visitor out into the open air, muttering his disapproval in no stinted phrase as he took the well-trod path that led to the mill.

The old mill loomed large in the obscurity, its scarce distinguishable outline seeming a piece fitted into the surrounding darkness.   The sails, idly flapping in the night wind, gave to the whole structure the appearance of some antique, winged monster, just stooping for a flight.   The boy shivered, and drew his roquelaure closer around him.

Entering the mill, the youth ascended by a ladder to the loft ; the miller fastened the oaken door and withdrew.   Left alone, the strange lad turned to the narrow loophole, through which a single star was visible in the heavens, and, taking some object from his breast, pressed it to his lips.   He then threw himself, sobbing, on a heap of empty bags.   Silence fell upon the old mill.

The slumbers of the lonely occupant were erelong rudely disturbed by the sound of voices, among which he distinguished that of the miller, who appeared to be engaged in unfastening his locks in a manner far too leisurely to satisfy the haste of his companions. Another voice, one which seemed to terrify the boy by its harsh yet familiar accents, bade the miller despatch for a bungling fool. The boy, moved with a sudden impulse, drew the ladder by which, he had gained the loft up to his retreat, and, placing it against the scuttle, ascended yet higher.

The flash of lights below showed that the men were within, as a volley of oaths betrayed the disappointment of the principal speaker at finding access cut off to the object of his pursuit. "Ho there, Claudine!" exclaimed this person, "descend, and you shall be forgiven this escapade; come down, I say. Curse the girl! — Miller! another ladder, and I'll bring her down, or my name's not Dick Wynne."

Another ladder was brought, which the speaker, uttering wild threats, mounted, but, not finding his victim as he expected at the first stage, he was compelled to climb to that above. The fugitive, crouched panting in a corner, betrayed her presence only by her quickened breathing, while the man, whose eyes were yet unaccustomed to the darkness, could only grope cautiously around the cramped area.

Finding it impossible longer to elude her pursuer, the girl, with a piercing cry for help, attempted to reach the ladder, when the man, making a sudden effort to grasp her, missed his footing, and fell headlong through the opening. In his descent, his hand coming in contact with something, he grasped it instinctively, and felt his flight arrested at the moment a yell of horror smote upon his ears. "Damnation!" screamed the miller, "let go the cord, or you're a dead man."

It was too late. In an instant the old mill, shaking off its lethargy, was all astir with life. The ponderous arms were already in quick revolution, and the man was caught and crushed within the mechanism he had set in motion. The mill was stopped; the helpless sufferer extricated and conveyed to the farm-house. He uttered but one word, "Claudine," and became insensible.

The poor Acadian peasant girl was one of those who had been separated from their homes by the rigorous policy of their conquerors. These victims were parcelled out among the different towns like so many brutes, and Claudine had fallen into the power of a wretch. This man, who wished to degrade the pretty French girl to the position of his mistress, had pushed his importunities so far that at last the girl had obtained a disguise, and, watching her opportunity, saddled her master's horse and fled. The man, with a warrant and an officer, was, as we have seen, close upon her track.

At break of day the officer returned from the town with a chirurgeon and a clergyman. The examination of the man of medicine left no room for hope, and he gave place to the man of God. Consciousness returns for a moment to the bruised and bleeding Wynne. Powerless to move, his eyes turn to the bedside, where stands, in her proper attire, the object of his fatal passion, bitterly weeping, and holding a crucifix in her hands. The morning sun gilds the old mill with touches a Turner could not reproduce. His rays fall aslant the farmhouse, and penetrate through the little diamond panes within the chamber, where a stricken group stand hushed and awestruck in the presence of death.

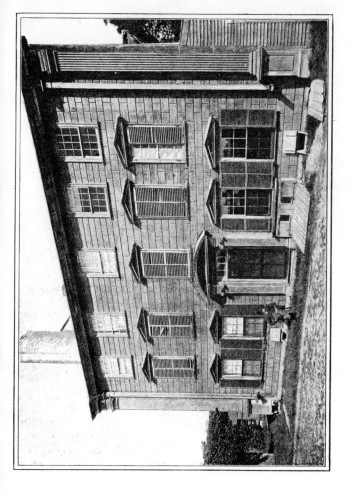

ROYALL HOUSE, MEDFORD.

## CHAPTER VI.

### THE PLANTATION AT MYSTIC.

"Come pass about the bowl to me;
A health to our distressed king."

AS you approach Medford by the Old Boston Road, you
see at your left hand, standing on a rise of ground not
half a mile out of the village, a mansion so strongly marked
with the evidences of a decayed magnificence that your attention is at once arrested, and you will not proceed without a
nearer view of an object which has so justly excited your
interest, or awakened, perhaps, a mere transient curiosity.

Whatever the motive which leads you to thread the broad
avenue that leads up to the entrance door, our word for it you
will not depart with regret that your footsteps have strayed to
its portal. Built by a West-Indian nabob, inhabited by one
whose character and history have been for a hundred years a
puzzle to historians, — a man "full of strange oaths," the very
prince of egotists, and yet not without claim to our kindly consideration, — the old house fairly challenges our inquiry.

Externally the building presents three stories, the upper tier
of windows being, as is usual in houses of even a much later
date, smaller than those underneath. Every pane has rattled
at the boom of the British morning-gun on Bunker Hill ; every
timber shook with the fierce cannonade which warned the invaders to their ships.

The house is of brick, but is on three sides entirely sheathed
in wood, while the south end stands exposed. The reason
which prompted the builder to make the west front by far the
most ornamental does not readily appear ; but certain it is,
that the mansion, in defiance of our homely maxim, " Put
your best foot foremost," seems to have turned its back to the

highway, as if it would ignore what was passing in the outer world.

Sufficient unto himself, no doubt, with his gardens, his slaves, and his rich wines, was the old Antigua merchant, Isaac Royall, who came, in 1737, from his tropical home to establish his seat here in ancient Charlestown. He is said to have brought with him twenty-seven slaves. In December, 1737, he laid before the General Court his petition, as follows, in regard to these "chattels":—

"Petition of Isaac Royall, late of Antigua, now of Charlestown, in the county of Middlesex, that he removed from Antigua with his family, and brought with him, among other things and chattels, a parcel of negroes, designed for his own use and not any of them for merchandise. He prays that he may not be taxed with impost."

The brick quarters which the slaves occupied are situated on the south side of the mansion and front upon the court-yard, one side of which they enclose. These have remained unchanged, and are, we believe, the last visible relics of slavery in New England. The deep fireplace where the blacks prepared their food is still there, and the roll of slaves has certainly been called in sight of Bunker Hill, though never on its summit.

At either end of the building the brick wall, furnished with a pair of stout chimneys, rises above the pitched roof. The cornice and corners are relieved by ornamental wood-work, while the west face is panelled, and further decorated with fluted pilasters. On this side, too, the original windows are seen.

The Royall House stood in the midst of grounds laid out in elegant taste, and embellished with fruit-trees and shrubbery. These grounds were separated from the highway by a low brick wall, now demolished. The gateway opening upon the grand avenue was flanked by wooden posts. Farther to the right was the carriage-drive, on either side of which stood massive stone gate-posts, as antique in appearance as anything about the old mansion. Seventy paces back from the road, along the broad gravelled walk, bordered with box, brings you to the door.

A visitor arriving in a carriage either alighted at the front entrance or passed by the broad drive, under the shade of magnificent old elms, around into the court-yard previously mentioned, and paved with round beach pebbles, through the interstices of which the grass grows thickly. Emerging from the west entrance-door, the old proprietor mounted the steps of the family coach, and rolled away in state to Boston Town-House, where, as a member of the Great and General Court, he long served his fellow-citizens of Charlestown. The driveway has now become a street, to the ruin of its former glory, the stately trees.

Behind the house, as we view it, was an enclosed garden of half an acre or more, with walks, fruit, and a summer-house at the farther extremity. No doubt this was the favorite resort of the family and their guests.

This summer-house, a veritable curiosity in its way, stood upon an artificial mound, with two terraces, ascended by broad flights of red sandstone steps. It was octagonal in form, with a bell-shaped roof, surmounted by a cupola, on which stood a figure of Mercury. At present the statue, with the loss of both wings and arms, cannot be said to resemble the ideal. All of this delightfully suggestive and picturesque affair has now disappeared except the mound itself. We discover that utility led to the elevation of the mound, within which was an ice-house, the existence of which is disclosed by a trap-door in the floor of the summer-house. An artist drew the plan of this little structure, a worthy companion of that formerly existing in Peter Faneuil's grounds in Boston. Doubtless George Erving and Sir William Pepperell came hither to pay their court to the royalist's daughters, and greatly we mistake if its dilapidated walls might not whisper of many a love-tryst.

After having rambled through the grounds and examined the surroundings of the mansion, we returned to the house, prepared to inspect the interior.

Without lingering in the hall of entrance farther than to mark the elaborately carved balusters and the panelled wainscot,

we passed into the suite of apartments at the right hand, the
reception-rooms proper of the house. These were divided in
two by an arch, in which folding-doors were concealed ; and
from floor to ceiling the walls were panelled in wood, the panels
being of single pieces, some of them a yard in breadth. In the
rear apartment, and opening to the north, were two alcoves,
each flanked by fluted pilasters, on which rested an arch enriched with mouldings and carved ornaments. Each recess had
a window furnished with seats, so inviting for a *tête-à-tête*, where
the ladies of the household sat with their needlework ; these
windows were sealed up in winter. The heavy cornice formed
an elaborate finish to this truly elegant saloon.

On the right, as the visitor entered, was a sideboard, which
old-time hospitality required should be always garnished with
wines, or a huge bowl of punch. The host first filled himself
a glass, and drank to his guest, who was then expected to pay
the same courtesy to the master of the mansion. No little of
Colonel Royall's wealth was founded on the traffic in Antigua
rum, and we doubt not his sideboard was well furnished. In
those days men drank their pint of Antigua, and carried it off,
too, with no dread of any enemy but the gout, nor feared to
present themselves before ladies with the aroma of good old
Xeres upon them. But we have fallen upon sadly degenerate,
weak-headed times, when the young men of to-day cannot make
a brace of New-Year's calls without an unsteady gait and tell-
tale tongue.

The second floor was furnished with four chambers, all opening on a spacious and airy hall. Of these the northwest room
only demands special description. It had alcoves similar to
those already mentioned in the apartment underneath, but
instead of panels the walls were finished above the wainscot
with a covering of leather on which were embossed, in gorgeous
colors, flowers, birds, pagodas, and the concomitants of a Chinese
paradise. On this side the original windows, with the small
glass and heavy frames, still remain.

The family of Royall in this country originated with William
Royall, or Ryal, of North Yarmouth, Maine, who was un-

doubtedly the person mentioned by Hazard as being sent over as a cooper or cleaver in 1629. His son, Samuel, followed the same trade of cooper in Boston as early as 1665 – 66, living with old Samuel Cole, the comfit-maker and keeper of the first inn mentioned in the annals of Boston. His father, William Royall, had married Hebe Green, daughter of Margaret, former wife to Samuel Cole. William, another son of William, appears to have settled in Dorchester, where he died, in 1724. His son, Isaac Royall, was a soldier in Philip's War, and built the second meeting-house in Dorchester.

Isaac Royall, the builder of our mansion, did not live long enough to enjoy his princely estate, dying in 1739, not long after its completion. His widow, who survived him eight years, died in this house, but was interred from Colonel Oliver's, in Dorchester, April 25, 1747. The pair share a common tomb in the old burying-place of that ancient town.

Isaac Royall the Second took good care of his patrimony. He was the owner of considerable property in Boston and Medford. Among other estates in the latter town, he was the proprietor of the old Admiral Vernon Tavern, which was standing in 1743, near the bridge.

A visitor preceding us by a century and a quarter thus speaks of the same house we are describing : —

"On our journey past through Mistick which is a small Town of abt a hundred Houses, Pleasantly Situated, near to which is a Fine Country Seat belonging to Mr. Isaac Royall being one of the Grandest in N. America."

When the Revolution begun Colonel Royall fell upon evil times. He was appointed a councillor by mandamus, but declined serving, as Gage says to Lord Dartmouth, from timidity. His own account of his movements after the beginning of "these troubles" is such as to confirm the governor's opinion, while it exhibits him as a loyalist of a very moderate cast.

He had prepared to take passage for the West Indies, intending to embark from Salem for Antigua, but, having gone into Boston the Sunday previous to the battle of Lexington, and remained there until that affair occurred, he was, by the course of events, shut up in the town. He sailed for Halifax very soon, still intending, as he says, for Antigua, but on the arrival of his son-in-law, George Erving, and his daughter, with the troops from Boston, he was by them persuaded to sail for England, whither his other son-in-law, Sir William Pepperell, had preceded him.

Upon his arrival in England he waited upon Lord Dartmouth and Lord Germaine, but was not received by them. Governor Pownall, in the course of a long conversation with Colonel Royall, expressed a strong regard for the Province in general, as being a very fine country and a good sort of people, and, while lamenting the difficulties, said that if his advice had prevailed they would not have happened. Royall also exchanged visits with Governors Bernard and Hutchinson, but, neglecting an invitation to dine with the latter, the acquaintance dropped.

Colonel Royall, after the loss of some of his nearest relatives and of his own health, begged earnestly to be allowed to return "home" to Medford, and to be relieved from the acts which had been passed affecting the absentees. The estate had, however, been taken out of the hands of his agent, Dr. Tufts, in 1788, under the Act of Confiscation.

In Colonel Royall's plea to be permitted to return home, in 1789, half ludicrous, half pathetic, he declares he was ever a true friend of the Province, and expresses the wish to marry again in his own country, where, having already had one good wife, he was in hopes to get another, and in some degree repair his loss. Penelope Royall, sister of Isaac, was married to Colonel Henry Vassall of Cambridge.

Peace be with the absconding royalist for an inoffensive, well-meaning, but shockingly timid old tory! He would fain have lived in amity with all men and with his king too, but the crisis engulfed him even as his valor forsook him. His fears counselled him to run, and he obeyed. But he is not forgotten. His large-hearted benevolence showed itself in many bequests to that country to which he was alien only in name. The Royall Professorship of Law at Harvard was founded by his bounty. He has a town (Royalston) in Massachusetts named for him, and is remembered with affection in the place of his former abode.

After inspecting the kitchen, with its monstrous brick oven still in perfect repair, its iron chimney-back, with the Royall arms impressed upon it, we inquired of the lady who had kindly attended us if she had ever been disturbed by strange visions or frightful dreams. She looked somewhat perplexed at the question, but replied in the negative. "They were all good people, you know, who dwelt here in bygone times," she said.

When the yeomen began pouring into the environs of Boston, encircling it with a belt of steel, the New Hampshire levies pitched their tents in Medford. They found the Royall mansion in the occupancy of Madam Royall and her accomplished daughters, who willingly received Colonel John Stark into the house as a safeguard against insult or any invasion of the estate the soldiery might attempt. A few rooms were set apart for the use of the bluff old ranger, and he, on his part, treated the family with considerate respect. Stark's wife afterwards followed him to camp, and when Dorchester Heights were occupied was by him directed to mount on horseback and watch the passage of his detachment over to West Boston. If his landing was opposed, she was to ride into the country and spread the alarm. These were the men and women of 1776.

John Stark was formed by nature for a leader. Though the reins of discipline chafed his impetuous spirit, few men possessed in a greater degree the confidence of his soldiers. The very hairs of his head seem bristling for the fray. A countenance strongly marked, high cheek-bones, eyes keen and thoughtful, nose prominent, — in short, the aspect of an eagle of his own mountains, with a soul as void of fear. He was at times somewhat "splenetive and rash." While stationed here he one day sent a file of his men to arrest and bring to camp a civilian accused of some extortion towards his men. Such acts, without the knowledge of his general, were sure to bring reproof upon Stark, which he received with tolerable grace. But he was always ready to render ample satisfaction for a wrong. The election for colonel of the New Hampshire regiment was held in the public hall of Billings's tavern in Medford, afterwards called the New Hampshire Hall. It was a hand vote, and some, they say, held up both hands for John Stark.

In the fall of 1776 a small party of the British came up the lake before Ticonderoga to take soundings of the depth of water. From the prospect of attack Gates summoned a council of war. There were no officers who had been in actual service except Gates and Stark. Gates took Stark aside, and the following dialogue ensued : —

*Gates.* What do you think of it, John ?

*Stark.* I think if they come we must fight them.

*Gates.* Psho, John ! Tell me what your opinion is, seriously.

*Stark.* My opinion is, that they will not fire a shot against this place this season, but whoever is here next must look out.

Stark and Gates were very intimate ; they addressed each other familiarly by their given names. The events justified Stark's sagacity.

It is also related that at the memorable council of war where the movement to Trenton was decided upon, Stark, who came in late, said to Washington, " Your men have long been accustomed to place dependence upon spades, pickaxes, and hoes for safety, but if you ever mean to establish the independence of the United States, you must teach them to put confidence in their fire-arms." Washington answered, " That is what we have agreed upon ; we are to march to-morrow to the attack of Trenton ; you are to take command of the right wing of the advanced guard, and General Greene the left." Stark observed he could not have been better suited. It is noticeable that several officers attached to the brigade on Winter Hill served in this action, namely, Sullivan, Stark, Scammell, and Wilkinson.

One of Washington's most trusted officers thus wrote to a friend in Boston of the battle of Bennington : —

" The news of the victory at the northward, under General Stark, must give you singular satisfaction; indeed, it was a most noble stroke for the oldest troops, but the achievement by militia doubly enhances the value of the action. America will ever be free if all her sons exert themselves equally."

This battle, like that of Trenton, was an act of inspiration. We cannot, at this distance of time, appreciate its electric effect upon the public mind, then sunk in despondency by the fall of Ticonderoga, and the rapid and unchecked advance of Burgoyne. It was generally believed that Boston was the British general's destination. Great alarm prevailed in consequence, and many families removed from the town. The news of Bennington, therefore, was received with great joy. At sundown about one hundred of the first gentlemen of the town, with all the strangers then in Boston, met at the Bunch of Grapes in State Street, where good liquors and a side table were provided. In the street were two brass field-pieces with a detachment of Colonel Craft's regiment. In the balcony of the Old State House all the musicians of Henry Jackson's regiment were assembled, with their fifes and drums. The ball was opened by the discharge of thirteen cannon, and at every toast three guns were fired, followed by a flight of rockets. About nine o'clock two barrels of grog were brought into the street for the people that had collected there. The whole affair was conducted with the greatest propriety, and by ten o'clock every man was at his home.

The effect on enlistments was equally happy. In the back parts of the State the militia turned out to a man. The best farmers went into the ranks, and Massachusetts soon enrolled the finest body of militia that had taken the field. The seaports were more backward. The towns that had not secured their quotas for the continental army were giving £100, lawful money, bounty for men. Some towns gave as much as five hundred dollars for each man enlisted.

Captain Barns, who brought the news of the battle of Bennington to Boston, related that, " after the first action, General Stark ordered a hogshead of rum for the refreshment of the militia ; but so eager were they to attack the enemy, upon being reinforced, that they tarried not to taste of it, but rushed on the enemy with an ardor perhaps unparalleled."

Stark sent to Boston not long after the battle the trophies, presented to the State, now placed in the Senate Chamber.

The drum is one of several captured on the field, while the sword, carried by one of Riedesel's dragoons, required no pygmy to wield it; in fact, the hat and sword of a German dragoon were as heavy as the whole equipment of a British soldier.

There are other memorials of the battles of Bennington and of Saratoga preserved in Boston. The original orders of Burgoyne to Baum were deposited with the Massachusetts Historical Society by General Lincoln, while the capitulation of Saratoga is in the Public Library. It is not a little remarkable, too, that the original draft of the surrender of Cornwallis was found among the papers of General Knox, now in the archives of the Historic Genealogical Society. All these are memorials of great events, and are of inestimable value. What is really noticeable about the battle of Bennington is, that Baum, finding himself surrounded, had strongly intrenched himself. His works were attacked and carried by raw militia, of whom Baum took little note because they were *in their shirt-sleeves.* He held his adversaries cheaply and paid dearly for his confidence. Of Stark he doubtless thought as one

> " That never set a squadron in the field,
> Nor the division of a battle knows
> More than a spinster."

The Bennington prisoners arrived at Boston on Friday, September 5, 1777, and were confined on board guard-ships in the harbor. Some of the officers were permitted to quarter in farm-houses along the route, where they soon had the melancholy pleasure of welcoming their brethren of the main army.

Of the Hessians confined on board the guard-ships, ten made their escape on the night of the 26th of October, in a most daring manner. Having, through the connivance of their friends outside, obtained a boat, in which arms were provided, they boarded the sloop Julia off the Hardings, took possession of her, and bore away for the southward, expecting, no doubt, to fall in with some of the enemy's vessels of war in Long Island Sound.

Some of the guns captured at Bennington by Stark fell

again into British possession at the surrender of Detroit. The inscriptions were read with much curiosity by the captors, who observed that they would now add a line to the history. The British officer of the day directed the evening salutes to be fired from them. When Stark heard of the loss of his guns he was much incensed. These pieces again became American at the capture of Fort George. Two of the lightest metal were presented by Congress to the State of Vermont.

In 1819 Stark was still living, the last survivor of the American generals of the Revolution. His recollections were then more distinct in relation to the events of the Old French War than of that for independence. Bunker Hill, Trenton, and Bennington should be inscribed upon his tomb.

Not long after his arrival at the camp General Lee took up his quarters in the Royall mansion, whose echoing corridors suggested to his fancy the name of Hobgoblin Hall. But Washington, as elsewhere related, caused him to remove to a point nearer his command. After Lee, Sullivan, attracted no doubt by the superior comforts of the old country-seat, unwarily fell into the same error. He, too, was remanded to his brigade by the chief, who knew the impulsive Sullivan would not readily forgive himself if anything befell the left wing of the army in his absence. In these two cases Washington exhibited his adhesion to the maxim that a general should sleep among his troops.

The Royall mansion came, in 1810, into the possession of Jacob Tidd, in whose family it remained half a century, until its identity with the old royalist had become merged in the new proprietor. It has been subsequently owned by George L. Barr and by George C. Nichols, but is now unoccupied. The Tidd House is the name by which it is best known, and all old citizens have a presentiment that it will not much longer retain a foothold among its modern neighbors. The surveyor has appeared on the scene with compass and level. Not one of the granite gate-posts remains in the driveway, while the stumps of the once splendid elms, planted by Royall, lie scattered about.

Nothing goes to our heart more than to see one of these gigantic old trees, which it has cost a century to grow, struck down in an hour; but when whole ranks of them are swept away, how quickly the scene changes from picturesque beauty to insignificance ! At the forks of every road leading into their villages the old settlers were wont to plant an elm, where weary travellers and footsore beasts might, in time, gather under its spreading branches, sheltered from the burning rays of the noonday sun. In the market-place, too, they dug their wells, but planted the tree beside. Many of these yet remain; and if in any one thing our New England towns may claim pre-eminence, it is in the beauty of these trees, — the admiration of every beholder, the gigantic fans that cool and purify the air around our habitations. Dickens, no mean observer, said our country-houses, in their spruce tidiness, their white paint, and green blinds, looked like houses built of cards, which a breath might blow away, so fragile and unsubstantial did they appear. Reader, if you could stand upon one of those bluffs that rise out of our Western prairies, like headlands out of the ocean, and, after looking down upon the town at your feet, wellnigh treeless and blistering in the sun, could then descend into the brown and dusty streets, and note the care bestowed upon the growth of a few puny poplars or maples, you would come back to your New England home, all glorious in its luxuriance and wealth of every form of forest beauty, prepared to make the destruction of one of these ancestral elms a penal offence.

" God the first garden made, and the first city Cain !"

Medford possesses other elements of attraction to the antiquary besides its old houses. Until Malden Bridge was built the great tide of travel north and east passed through the town. The visitor now finds it a very staid, quiet sort of place. Travel has so changed both its mode and its channels that we can form little idea of a country highway even fifty years ago. Travellers of every condition then pursued their route by the public roads : the wealthy or well-to-do generally in chaises or phaetons ; the professional gentleman on horseback, — a custom so graceful and health-giving that we should not be sorry to see its revival in New England. Whole families — men, women, and even little children — passed and repassed on foot, carrying with them their scanty effects. Then there was the mail-coach, — a puffy, groaning vehicle, bulging out at the top and sides, and hung on thoroughbraces. On a rough road it lurched like a Chinese junk in a heavy sea-way, and the passengers not unfrequently provided themselves with brandy, lemons, and other palliatives against sea-sickness. Besides these well-marked constituents of the stream, a nondescript element of stragglers drifted along the edges of the current until caught in some eddy which cast them up at the tavern door.

The public inn then had a relative importance to the world of wayfarers that is not now represented by any brown-stone or marble front hotel. The distances from Boston in every direction were reckoned to the taverns. The landlord was a man of note. He was the village newsmonger, oracle, and referee in all disputes. When he had a full house his guests were distributed about the floors, and the dining-table commanded a premium. The charge for meals or for baiting a horse was a quarter of a dollar. If the world moved then more slowly than it now does, it was not the less content.

The tavern was also the political centre where caucuses were held and the state of the country discussed. It was ofttimes there town-meetings were convened, and in war times it was the recruiting rendezvous. Proclamations, notices of that multifarious character pertaining to the interior economy of the village, from the reward for the apprehension of a thief to the loss of a favorite brooch, were affixed to the bar-room walls. The smell of old Santa Cruz or other strong waters saluted the nostrils of all who entered the public room, and yet there was call for neither fumigation nor exorcism. The mail-coach, which only stopped to change horses, occupied forty-eight hours in going over this route from Boston to Portland. Concord coaches succeeded the old English pattern, and still traverse here and there a few byways into which the railway disdains to turn aside.

The mail-coach, too, bore its fixed relation to the population along the line. It marked the time of day for the laborers in the fields, who leaned on hoe or scythe until it was lost to view. The plough stopped in the furrow, the smith rested his sledge on his anvil, while the faces of young and old were glued to the window-panes as this moving piece of the far-away metropolis rolled along. Entering the town, the driver cracked his whip, his leaders sprang out into a brisker gait, and the lumbering vehicle drew up with a flourish beside the tavern door.

The first of the Medford ordinaries, so far as known, goes back to about 1690, Nathaniel Pierce being mine host. The General Court licensed him to sell not less than a gallon of liquor at a time to one person, and prohibited the sale of smaller quantities by retail. The house was at one time owned by Colonel Royall, being known at different times by the name of the "Royal Oak" and "Admiral Vernon." In 1775 it became the Revolutionary headquarters, kept by Roger Billings, and was long afterward the principal tavern in the town. The house stood on the corner of Main and Union Streets, and was destroyed by fire in 1850.

The old Fountain Tavern, so called from its sign representing a fountain pouring forth punch, is no more standing on the old Salem road, at the corner of Fountain Street. Brooks, in his History of Medford, says it was first called the "Two Palaverers." The two large trees in front had each a platform in its branches, connected with each other and with the house by wooden bridges. In summer these retreats were resorted to by the guests for tea-parties or punch-drinking. The house was built in 1725, and is extremely unique in appearance.

The name of Medford is known in every seaport under the sun for its stanch and well-built ships. Of the thousands that float the ocean bearing any flag aloft, none sail more proudly than those of Curtis or Magoun. This industry, which has dated from the time when Englishmen first set foot on the shores of the Mystic, has of late years fallen into decay, but once more the familiar sound of the shipwright's beetle is

OLD CRADOCK HOUSE.

beginning to be heard on its banks. Cradock sent over skilled artisans, who at once laid down the keels that have increased so prodigiously. Although we are told his men had a vessel of a hundred tons on the stocks in 1632, the earlier craft were chiefly pinnaces, galleys, and snows, — the latter being rigged somewhat after the fashion of our barks. No branch of mechanical skill appears to have developed with such rapidity in New England as shipbuilding. The timber, which is now brought hundreds of miles to the yards, then grew along the shores. We now bring the keel from Virginia, the frame from the Gulf States, and the masts from Canada. New England, which does not furnish a single product entering into the construction of the ship, forges the anchor which holds her to the bottom; twists the hemp into shrouds, rigging, and those spiders'-webs aloft whose intricacies confound the eye; spins the cotton which hangs from the yards, and weaves the colors that float at the mast-head.

In the public square of Medford is an excellent specimen of the architecture of the last century, now occupied by offices, but originally a dwelling. A few rods distant in a westerly direction, where the Savings Bank now is, was the house which Governor Brooks inhabited, and at the corner was the stone where he was accustomed to mount his horse. A plain granite shaft is erected over the remains of this distinguished soldier and civilian in the old burial-ground. Behind the Savings Bank, on a rising ground, is one of the early garrison-houses, built of brick, and looking none the worse for its long conflict with time, thanks to the owner, Gen. Samuel C. Lawrence, beside whose elegant mansion it stands conspicuous, a foil to the symmetry and gracefulness of modern art.

As a soldier Governor Brooks appeared to his greatest advantage in the battle of Bemis's Heights, where he was in command of the old Eighth, Michael Jackson's regiment. His own relation of the incidents of that day to General Sumner is not, even now, devoid of interest.

" On the 7th of October, the day of the last battle with General Burgoyne, General Arnold and several officers dined with General

Gates. I was among the company, and well remember that one of the dishes was an ox's heart. While at table we heard a firing from the advanced picket. The armies were about two miles from each other. The firing increasing, we all rose from table ; and General Arnold, addressing General Gates, said, 'Shall I go out and see what is the matter ?' General Gates made no reply, but upon being pressed, said, 'I am afraid to trust you, Arnold.' To which Arnold answered, 'Pray let me go ; I will be careful ; and if our advance does not need support, I will promise not to commit you.' Gates then told him he might go and see what the firing meant."

Colonel Brooks repaired to his post, and under the impetuous Arnold, who seemed fully imbued on this day with the *rage militaire*, stormed Breyman's Fort, and thus mastered the key to the enemy's position. Arnold, once in action, forgot his promise to Gates, who vainly endeavored to recall him from the field. Had his life been laid down there, his name would have been as much revered as it is now contemned by his countrymen.

The object of paramount interest which Medford contains is the plantation house of Governor Cradock, or " Mathias Charterparty," as the malcontent Morton styled him. This house is the monarch of all those now existing in North America. As we trace a family back generation after generation until we bring all collateral branches to one common source in the first colonist, so we go from one old house to another until we finally come to a pause before this patriarch by the sea. It is the handiwork of the first planters in the vicinity of Boston, and is one of the first, if not the very first, of the brick houses erected within the government of John Winthrop.

Every man, woman, and child in Medford knows the " Old Fort," as the older inhabitants love to call it, and will point you to the site with visible pride that their pleasant town contains so interesting a relic. Turning your back upon the village, and your face to the east, a brisk walk of ten minutes along the banks of the Mystic, and you are in presence of the object of your search.

A very brief survey establishes the fact that this was one of those houses of refuge scattered through the New England settlements, into which the inhabitants might fly for safety upon any sudden alarm of danger from the savages.

The situation was well chosen for security. It has the river in front, marshes to the eastward, and a considerable extent of level meadow behind it. As it was from this latter quarter that an attack was most to be apprehended, greater precautions were taken to secure that side. The house itself is placed a little above the general level. Standing for a century and a half in the midst of an extensive and open field, enclosed by palisades, and guarded with gates, a foe could not approach unseen by day, nor find a vantage-ground from which to assail the inmates. Here, then, the agents of Matthew Cradock, first Governor of the Massachusetts Company in England, built the house we are describing.

In the office of the Secretary of the Commonwealth, at Boston, hangs the charter of "The Governor and Company of the Massachusetts Bay in New England," brought over by Winthrop in 1630. The great seal of England, a most ponderous and convincing symbol of authority, is appended to it.

It is well known that the settlement at Salem, two years earlier, under the leadership of Endicott, was begun by a commercial company in England, of which Matthew Cradock was Governor. In order to secure the emigration of such men as Winthrop, Dudley, Sir R. Saltonstall, Johnson, and others, Cradock proposed, in July, 1629, to transfer the government from the company in England to the inhabitants here. As he was the wealthiest and most influential person in the association, his proposal was acceded to.

We cannot enter, here, into the political aspects of this *coup d'état*. It must ever arrest the attention and challenge the admiration of the student of American history. In defiance of the crown, which had merely organized them into a mercantile corporation, like the East India Company, with officers resident in England, they proceeded to nullify the clear intent of their charter by removing the government to America. The project was first mooted by Cradock, and secrecy enjoined upon

the members of the company.    That he was the avowed author
of it must be our apology for introducing the incident.    This
circumstance renders Matthew Cradock's name conspicuous in
the annals of New England.

Cradock never came to America, but there is little doubt that
he entertained the purpose of doing so.    He sent over, however, agents, or " servants," as they were styled, who established the plantation at Mystic Side.    He also had houses at
Ipswich and at Marblehead, for fishery and traffic.

For a shrewd man of business Cradock seems to have been
singularly unfortunate in some of his servants.    One of these,
Philip Ratcliff, being convicted " *ore tenus* of most foul and
slanderous invectives " against the churches and government,
was sentenced to be whipped, lose his ears, and be banished the
plantation.    Winthrop was complained of by Dudley because
he stayed the execution of the sentence of banishment, but
answered that it was on the score of humanity, as it was winter
and the man must have perished.    Ratcliff afterwards, in conjunction with Thomas Morton and Sir Christopher Gardiner,
procured a petition to the Lords of the Privy Council, before
whom Cradock was summoned.

Morton, who was sent away to England for his mad pranks
and contempt of Puritan authority, wrote as follows of this
examination : —

" My Lord Canterbury having with my Lord Privy Seal caused all
Mr. Cradock's letters to be viewed, and his apology in particular for
the brethren here, protested against him and Mr. Humfry [another
of the undertakers] that they were a couple of imposterous knaves,
so that for all their great friends they departed the council chamber
in our view with a pair of cold shoulders.

" As for Ratcliff, he was comforted by their lordships with the
croppings of Mr. Winthrop's ears, which shows what opinion is held
among them of King Winthrop with all his inventions and his
Amsterdam fantastical ordinances, his preachings, marriages, and
other abusive ceremonies, which do exemplify his detestation of the
Church of England and the contempt of his majesty's authority and
wholesome laws which are and will be established here *invita
Minerva.*"

In the letter to Winthrop which follows, printed in the Massachusetts Historical Society's Collections, the old merchant complains bitterly of the conduct of another of his agents : —

"LONDON 21 Febr. 1636.

" Jno. Joliff writes mee the manner of Mr Mayheues accounts is, that what is not sett down is spent ; most extremely I am abused. My seruants write they drinke nothing but water & I haue in an account lately sent me Red Wyne, Sack & Aqua Vitae in one yeere aboue 300 gallons, besides many other intollerable abuses, 10 *l* for tobacco etc.   My papers are misselayd but if you call for the coppyes of the accounts sent me and examine vppon what ground it is made you shall find I doubt all but forged stuffe.

"MATHEWE CRADOCK."

Wood, one of the early chroniclers, tells us that Master Cradock had a park impaled at Mystic, where his cattle were kept until it could be stocked with deer ; and that he also was engaged in shipbuilding, a vessel of a " hundred tunne " having been built the previous year (1632).   It may be, too, that Cradock's artisans built here for Winthrop the little " Blessing of the Bay," launched upon the Mystic tide July 4, 1631, — an event usually located at the governor's farm, at Ten Hills.

This house, a unique specimen of the architecture of the early settlers, must be considered a gem of its kind.   It is not disguised by modern alterations in any essential feature, but bears its credentials on its face.   Two hundred and thirty odd New England winters have searched every cranny of the old fortress, whistled down the big chimney-stacks, rattled the window-panes in impotent rage, and, departing, certified to us the stanch and trusty handiwork of Cradock's English craftsmen.

Time has dealt gently with this venerable relic.   Like a veteran of many campaigns, it shows a few honorable scars. The roof has swerved a little from its true outline.   It has been denuded of a chimney, and has parted reluctantly with a dormer-window.   The loopholes, seen in the front, were long since closed ; the race they were to defend against has hardly an existence to-day.   The windows have been enlarged, with an effect on the *ensemble*, as Hawthorne says in a similar case, of rouging the cheeks of one's grandmother. Hoary with age, it is yet no ruin, but a comfortable habitation.

How many generations of men — and our old house has seldom if ever been untenanted — have lived and died within those walls! When it was built Charles I. reigned in Old England, and Cromwell had not begun his great career. Peter the Great was not then born, and the house was waxing in years when Frederick the Great appeared on the stage. We seem to be speaking of recent events when Louis XVI. suffered by the axe of the guillotine, and Napoleon's sun rose in splendor, to set in obscurity.

The Indian, who witnessed its slowly ascending walls with wonder and misgiving; the Englishman, whose axe wakened new echoes in the primeval forest; the colonist native to the soil, who battled and died within view, to found a new nation, — all have passed away. But here, in this old mansion, is the silent evidence of those great epochs of history.

It is not clear at what time the house was erected, but it has usually been fixed in the year 1634, when a large grant of land was made to Cradock by the General Court. The bricks are said to have been burned near by. There was some attempt at ornament, the lower course of the belt being laid with moulded bricks so as to form a cornice. The loopholes were for defence. The walls were half a yard in thickness. Heavy iron bars secured the arched windows at the back, and the entrance-door was encased in iron. The fire-proof closets, huge chimney-stacks, and massive hewn timbers told of strength and durability. A single pane of glass, set in iron, and placed in the back wall of the western chimney, overlooked the approach from the town.

The builders were Englishmen, and, of course, followed their English types. They named their towns and villages after the sounding nomenclature of Old England; what more natural than that they should wish their homes to resemble those they had left behind? Such a house might have served an inhabitant of the Scottish border, with its loopholes, narrow windows, and doors sheathed in iron. Against an Indian foray it was impregnable.

Cradock was about the only man connected with the settlement in Massachusetts Bay whose means admitted of such a house. Both Winthrop and Dudley built of wood, and the former rebuked the deputy for what he thought an unreasonable expense in finishing his own house. Many brick buildings were erected in Boston during the first decade of the settlement, but we have found none that can claim such an ancient pedigree as this of which we are writing. It is far from improbable that, having in view a future residence in New England, Cradock may have given directions for or prescribed the plan of this house, and that it may have been the counterpart of his own in St. Swithen's Lane, near London Stone.

> "Then went I forth by London Stone
> Throughout all Canwick Street."

The plantation, with its green meadows and its stately forest-trees, was a manor of which Cradock was lord and master. His grant extended a mile into the country from the river-side in all places. Though absent, he was considered nominally present, and is constantly alluded to by name in the early records. Cradock was a member of the Long Parliament, dying in 1641. The euphonious name of Mystic has been supplanted by Medford, the Meadford of Dudley and the rest.

It is not to be expected that a structure belonging to so remote a period, for New England, should be without its legendary lore. It is related that the old fort was at one time beleaguered for several days by an Indian war-party, who at length retired baffled from the strong walls and death-shots of the garrison. As a veracious historian, we are compelled to add that we know of no authentic data of such an occurrence. Indians were plenty enough in the vicinity, and, though generally peaceful, they were regarded with more or less distrust. The settlers seldom stirred abroad without their trusty matchlocks and well-filled bandoleer. We cannot give a better picture of the times than by invoking the aid of MacFingal : —

> " For once, for fear of Indian beating,
>     Our grandsires bore their guns to meeting;
>     Each man equipped on Sunday morn
>     With psalm-book, shot, and powder-horn;
>     And looked in form, as all must grant,
>     Like the ancient, true church militant;
>     Or fierce, like modern deep divines,
>     Who fight with quills, like porcupines."

In all probability this most interesting landmark of the beginnings of New England, so suggestive too of the many changes wrought by the passing centuries under its own shadow, as one might say, so knit with the fortunes of an infant commonwealth, would have gone to irremediable ruin and decay but for the patriotic action of General Samuel C. Lawrence, who bought the Cradock House to save it from threatened demolition.

TUFTS HOUSE.

# CHAPTER VII.

## LEE'S HEADQUARTERS AND VICINITY.

> " Night closed around the conqueror's way,
>     And lightnings showed the distant hill,
>   Where those who lost that dreadful day
>     Stood few and faint, but fearless still."

DESCENDING into the valley between Winter and Prospect Hills, any search for traces of the works which existed here in 1775 – 76 would be fruitless ; every vestige had disappeared fifty years ago. The site of the star fort laid down on the map was a little north of Medford Street and east of Walnut Street. The structure of the ground shows that there was once a considerable elevation here, which commanded the approach by the low land between Prospect, Winter, and Ploughed Hills.

On the little byway now dignified with the name of Sycamore Street stands the old farm-house which was the headquarters for a time of General Charles Lee. Long ago, I found there Oliver Tufts, whose father, John Tufts, resided there in Revolutionary times, and planted with his own hands the beautiful elm that now stretches its protecting branches over the old homestead.

When the house was occupied by the mercurial Lee it had one of those long pitched roofs descending to a single story at the back, and which are still occasionally met with in our interior New England towns. The elder Tufts altered the exterior to what we now see it ; and although the date of the erection of the house, which once sheltered so notable an occupant, has not remained extant in the family, it evidently belongs to the earlier years of the eighteenth century.

The name and career of Charles Lee are not the least interesting subjects in our Revolutionary annals. A mystery, not

wholly cleared away, has enshrouded the concluding incidents
of Lee's connection with the American army.   Whether the
name of traitor is to accompany his memory to posterity or not,
there is no question that he was at the beginning of the contest a zealous partisan of the American cause.   It is in this light
we prefer to consider him.

When Lee came to join the forces assembled around Boston
he was certainly regarded, in respect to military skill, as the
foremost man in the army.   His experience had been acquired
on the same fields with the men he was now to oppose, and it
is evident that neither Gage, Howe, Clinton, nor Burgoyne
underrated his ability.

In a "separate and secret despatch" Lord Dartmouth wrote
to General Gage to have a special eye on Lee, whose presence
in Boston in the autumn of 1774 was known to his lordship.
Lord Dartmouth's letter says : —

"I am told that M^r Lee, a major upon half pay with the rank
of Lieut Colonel, has lately appeared at Boston, that he associates
only with the enemies of government, that he encourages the discontent of the people by harangues and publications, and even
advises to arms.   This gentleman's general character cannot be unknown to you, and therefore it will be very proper that you should
have attention to his conduct, and take every legal method to prevent his effecting any of those dangerous purposes he is said to have
in view."

General Lee was five feet eight, and of rather slender make,
but with unlimited powers of endurance, as was fully proved
in his rapid movements from Boston to New York, and from
New York to the defence of the Southern seaports.   His capacity to resist fatigue was thoroughly tested at Monmouth, the
only instance recorded where he admitted that he was tired out.
Lee had visited most of the courts of Europe, and was a good
linguist.   He wrote well, but rather diffusely ; and although
his language is marred by a certain coarseness, it is not con-
spicuously so when compared with that of his contemporaries
in the profession of arms.

"And more than that he can speak French, and therefore he is a traitor."

Lee had lived for some time among the Mohawks, who made him a chief, and who, on account of his impetuous temper, named him, in their figurative and highly expressive way, "Boiling Water." He was more than half Indian in his extreme carelessness of his personal appearance, of what he ate or drank, or where he slept. He had lost two fingers in a duel in Italy, — one of many personal encounters in which he was engaged during his lifetime. Lee was cool, clear-headed in action, and possessed true military insight. The following is probably an accurate pen-portrait of this extraordinary man : —

"A tall man, lank and thin, with a huge nose, a satirical mouth, and restless eyes, who sat his horse as if he had often ridden at fox-hunts in England, and wore his uniform with a cynical disregard of common opinion."

There is a caricature of General Lee by Rushbrooke, which, if allowed to resemble the General, as it is claimed it does, would fairly establish his title to be regarded as the ugliest of men, both in form and feature. It should, however, be considered as a caricature and nothing else.

Mrs. John Adams, who first met General Lee at an evening party at Major Mifflin's house in Cambridge, describes him as looking like a "careless, hardy veteran," who brought to her mind his namesake, Charles XII. "The elegance of his pen far exceeds that of his person" says this accomplished lady.

Lee was very fond of dogs, and was constantly attended by one or more ; his favorite being a great shaggy Pomeranian, which Dr. Belknap says resembled a bear more than a harmless canine. Spada — that was the dog's name — was constantly at his master's heels, and accompanied him in whatever company he might happen to be.

It appears from a letter of John Adams to James Warren, — the then President of the Provincial Congress, — which was intercepted by the British, that Colonel Warren had no great opinion of General Lee, for Mr. Adams tells him he must bear with his whimsical manners and his dogs for the sake of his military talents. "Love me, love my dog," says Mr. Adams.

General Lee used to relate with great gusto an anecdote of one of his aides who showed a little trepidation under fire, and who expostulated with his general for exposing himself. The general told his officer that his Prussian majesty had twenty aides killed in one battle. The aide replied that he did not think Congress could spare so many. Lee's first aide-de-camp was Samuel Griffin, who was succeeded by Colonel William Palfrey, the same who afterwards served Washington in a similar capacity.

Lee's slovenliness was the occasion of a rather amusing *contretemps*. On one of Washington's journeys to reconnoitre the shores of the bay he was accompanied by Lee, who, on arriving at the house where they were to dine, went straight to the kitchen and demanded something to eat. The cook, taking him for a servant, told him she would give him some victuals directly, but he must first help her off with the pot, — a request with which he readily complied. He was then requested to take a bucket and go to the well for water, and was actually engaged in drawing it when found by an aide whom Washington had despatched in quest of him. The poor girl then heard for the first time her assistant addressed by the title of " general." The mug fell from her hands, and, dropping on her knees, she began crying for pardon, when Lee, who was ever ready to see the impropriety of his own conduct, but never willing to change it, gave her a crown, and, turning to the aide-de-camp, observed: " You see, young man, the advantage of a fine coat ; the man of consequence is indebted to it for respect ; neither virtue nor abilities without it will make you look like a gentleman."

It is somewhat remarkable that most of the officers of the Revolutionary army who had seen service in that of Great Britain, and of whom so much was expected, either left the army before the close of the war with damaged reputations or in disgrace. Lee and Gates, who stood first in the general estimation, suffered a complete loss of favor, while the fame of Schuyler and St. Clair endured a partial eclipse. Montgomery bravely fell before Quebec. St. Clair married a Boston lady

(Phœbe Bayard), a relative of Governor Bowdoin, and during the war placed his daughter in that town to be educated.

In the memorable retreat through the Jerseys Lee's conduct began to be distrusted. He was perhaps willing to see Washington, whose life only intervened between himself and the supreme command, defeated; but we need not go back a century to find generals who have been unwilling to support their commanders, even when within sound of their cannon.

Lee had a good private fortune. He was sanguine and lively, and a martyr to gout. He was fearless and outspoken, never concealing his sentiments from any man, and in every respect was the antipodes of a conspirator. Men, indeed, might say of him, —

> "Yond' Cassius has a lean and hungry look;
> He thinks too much; such men are dangerous."

By his brother officers he was evidently considered a rival of the commander-in-chief, but we find no contemporary evidence that he was looked upon as a traitor until the day of Monmouth. The present generation, however, much wiser, has decreed him faithless upon the evidence of a manuscript said to be in Lee's handwriting, and purporting to be a plan for subjugating the States. This precious document is without date or signature, but is indorsed by another hand, "Mr. Lee's plan — 29th March, 1777." At this time the General was a prisoner in New York. The writing, which bears an extraordinary resemblance to that of General Lee, is relied upon mainly to convict him of treason.

The so-called proofs of the treachery of Lee have been skilfully put together by George H. Moore, but they contain other fatal objections besides the want of a signature to the "plan." Proof is adduced to show that Lee was not a general, and at the same time he is accredited with having induced General Howe to adopt his "plan" and abandon one carefully matured by his brother and himself, as early as April 2, or four days after the date indorsed on the "plan." Moreover, a motive for Lee's defection is not supplied. He did not want money, nor sell himself, like Arnold, for a price. His fate, which at one time had trembled in the balance, — the king had ordered him sent home to be tried as a deserter, — was practically decided by Washington's firmness long before the date of the " plan." There is no evidence to show he ever received the least emolument from the British government. Lee rejoined his flag, and his conduct at Monmouth appears more like vacillation than treachery ; for it will hardly be doubted that, had he so intended, he might easily have betrayed his troops into the hands of Sir Henry Clinton. If opportunity was what he sought to give effect to his treason, it must be looked for elsewhere than in this campaign, which he had opposed with all his might, and executed, so far as in him lay, with languor and reluctance. We can conclude Lee erratic, wayward, ambitious beyond his abilities, devoured by egotism, but not a traitor ; or if one, he was the most disinterested that the pages of history have recorded.

A British officer who knew Lee well gives this account of his capture : —

" He was taken by a party of ours, under Colonel Harcourt, who surrounded the house in which this arch-traitor was residing. Lee behaved as cowardly in this transaction as he had dishonorably in every other. After firing one or two shots from the house, he came out and entreated our troops to spare his life. Had he behaved with proper spirit I should have pitied him, and wished that his energies had been exerted in a better cause. I could hardly refrain from tears when I first saw him, and thought of the miserable fate in which his obstinacy had involved him. He says he has been mistaken in three things : 1st, That the New England men would fight ; 2d, That America was unanimous ; and 3d, That she could afford two men for our one."

Opposed to this narration is that of Major (afterwards General) Wilkinson, who was with the General at the moment of his capture, but who made his escape. He was the bearer of a letter from General Gates, to which Lee was penning a reply, and saw from the window the approach of the British dragoons. He says : —

" Startled at this unexpected spectacle, I exclaimed, ' Here, sir, are the British cavalry !' ' *Where ?*' replied the General, who had signed his letter in the instant. ' Around the house'; for they had opened files and encompassed the building. General Lee appeared alarmed, yet collected, and his second observation marked his self-possession: 'Where is the guard? Damn the guard, why don't they fire?' and after a momentary pause, he turned to me and said, 'Do, sir, see what has become of the guard.' The women of the house at this moment entered the room, and proposed to him to conceal himself in a bed, which he rejected with evident disgust."

The exact language used by Washington in the hurried altercation with Lee at Monmouth has been a matter of much curiosity. The officers who overheard this celebrated colloquy exhibited at the trial a remarkable forgetfulness on this point. They agree, however, that His Excellency addressed his lieutenant "*with much warmth*," the conventional expression for strong language. Lafayette, who was both on the field and at the trial, is accredited with having related to Governor Tompkins, in 1824, that Washington called Lee "a damned poltroon." "This," said Lafayette, "was the only time I ever heard Washington swear." *

After the battle Lee certainly wrote two very impudent and characteristic letters to the commander-in-chief. His subsequent trial, equalled only in interest in our military annals by that of André, failed to fix any treasonable design on the general, though it punished his insubordination by a year's suspension from command. His military peers evidently considered him unfit to command in conjunction with Washington.

Lee's encounter with the beautiful Miss Franks of Philadelphia forms a humorous episode. The lady, who had been one of the bright stars of Sir William Howe's entertainment of the Mischianza, and was celebrated for her keen wit, had asserted that General Lee wore green breeches patched with leather. The General met the allegation by sending the unmentionables in question to the lady, accompanied by a letter, which Miss Franks received in very bad part.

The will of General Lee contains this singular request : —

" I desire most earnestly that I may not be buried in any church or churchyard, or within a mile of any Presbyterian or Anabaptist

* Note to Custis's Recollections, p. 218.

meeting-house; for since I have resided in this country I have kept so much bad company when living that I do not choose to continue it when dead."

General Lee died at an obscure inn (the sign of the Conestoga Wagon, in Market Street, Philadelphia), October 2, 1782. The last words he distinctly articulated were : " Stand by me, my brave grenadiers."

Prospect Hill, second in the line of investment, had formerly two eminences, both of which were strongly fortified. The citadel, defended by outworks, was on the most easterly summit, and covered with its fire the road coming from Charlestown, which winds around its base, Cobble Hill (McLean Asylum), and the low ground towards Mount Benedict. Both eminences were connected by a rampart and ditch, which, after being carried the whole length of the summit, were continued along the lower plateau of the hill in a northerly direction, till they terminated in a strong redoubt situated very near the present High School. On the Cambridge side the works joined Fort No. 3 by redoubts placed on each side of the road from Charlestown.

It was here Putnam took his stand after the retreat from Bunker Hill, and the next day found him busy intrenching himself in full view of the late battle-field. Putnam was, perhaps, the only general officer then willing to take and hold so advanced a position. He says he halted here without orders from anybody ; it was expected the British would follow up their success, and he placed himself resolutely in their path.

A foreign officer of distinction, who examined the works on Prospect Hill five years after the events of the siege, says of them : —

" All these intrenchments seemed to me to be executed with intelligence; nor was I surprised that the English respected them during the whole winter of 1776."

Nearly fifty years afterwards a visitor thus records his observations of the same lines : —

" The forts on these hills were destroyed only a few years ago, but their size can be distinctly seen. On the southern eminence the fort is still entire, and the southwest face of the hill is divided into several platforms, of which I cannot exactly understand the use. There are also evident marks of the dwellings of the soldiers. The extensive view from this hill, the walk on the ancient ramparts, and the site of the various stations occupied by the American army, will render this hill at a future period a favorite resort."

After the arrival of General Washington the army was regularly brigaded, and General Greene was assigned, under the orders of Lee, to the command at Prospect Hill. He accordingly took up his quarters there on the 26th of July, with Sullivan on his left at Winter Hill, Patterson at his feet in No. 3, and Heath on his right. Greene had with him his own Rhode-Islanders that had been encamped at Jamaica Plain, and the regiments of Whitcomb, Gardner, Brewer, and Little, — a fluctuating garrison of from three to four thousand men. The leader was the right man in the right place.

Nathaniel Greene is one of the grandest figures of the Revolution. He is known to us as the man whom Washington deemed most worthy to be his lieutenant, and how he vindicated that confidence the pages of history relate. It is said he was the only general officer who testified his gratification at the appointment of Washington by presenting an address from himself and his officers to the General upon his arrival at Cambridge, — a circumstance not likely to escape the memory of the commander-in-chief. At his decease, which occurred in 1786, Congress voted to raise a monument to his memory. It was never erected, and we are left to reflect

> "How nations slowly wise and meanly just,
> To buried merit raise the tardy bust."

General Knox, the bosom friend of Greene, said to a distinguished son of Carolina : —

"His knowledge is intuitive. He came to us the rawest and most untutored being I ever met with, but in less than twelve months he was equal in military knowledge to any general officer in the army, and very superior to most of them."

John Dewey Library
Johnson State College
Johnson, VT. 05656

His ability as commissary-general of the army is well known, as is the fact that he would not retain the office unless permitted to command in the field. On relieving General Gates after the disastrous battle of Camden, Greene sat up the whole night with General Polk of Gates's commissariat, investigating the resources of the country; and, as was stated by that officer, Greene better understood what those resources were on the following morning than Gates had done in the whole period of his command. His treatment of General Gates on this trying occasion was remarkable for delicacy and magnanimity.

Greene was seen, in 1774, in a coat and hat of the Quaker fashion, attentively watching the exercises of the British troops on Boston Common. Perhaps Knox, whose shop in Cornhill he frequented for certain treatises on the art of war, was his companion. Such was the primary school in which these two great soldiers were formed.

When Greene was selected by the commander-in-chief to command the Southern army, he urged in the strongest terms the superior qualifications of Knox for that position. With his usual modesty, the Quaker General said : " Knox is the man for that difficult undertaking; all obstacles vanish before him ; his resources are infinite." Washington, in admitting the truth of all Greene had advanced, replied, in effect, that these were the very reasons that impelled him to retain Knox near his person.

It was General Greene's fortune to preside over the board of officers at Tappan which condemned the chivalric but ill-starred André. That board was composed of the most distinguished men of the army. Among them all, we will venture to say, no heart was wrung more acutely by the inexorable necessity for the vindication of military law than was that of the president. Alexander Hamilton said, near the close of the war, while opposing reprisals for the death of Captain Huddy : " The death of André could not have been dispensed with ; but it must still be viewed as an act of rigid justice."

General Greene retired from the army in very embarrassed circumstances. Like the other general officers, he had received no equivalent for the sums he was compelled to disburse for his support while in the field.   These officers were obliged to apply to Congress for " relief," such being then, as now, the legal phraseology of an application of a creditor when government is the debtor.   Greene met with losses at the South which hurt him.   He turned to the soil; but the season was unkind, and his first crop was a failure.   Congress voted him military trophies, but these did not afford him the means of living.

It is pleasant to turn from the contemplation of the neglect which Greene experienced as a general to examine the inner characteristics of the man.   These cannot better be illustrated than by the following extracts from a letter written by him in the autumn of 1781, from his camp on the High Hills of Santee. Henry Jackson, of whom the General speaks, was the burly, good-natured colonel of the 16th, sometimes called the Boston Regiment.

" We have fought frequently and bled freely, and little glory comes to our share.  Our force has been so small that nothing capital could be effected, and our operations have been conducted under every disadvantage that could embarrass either a general or an army. . . . .

" How is my old friend Colonel Jackson ?  Is he as fat as ever, and can  he still eat down a plate of fish that he can't see over ?  God bless his fat soul with good health and good spirits to the end of the war, that we may all have a happy meeting in the North."

One who had frequent opportunities of observing the General has admirably painted his portrait.   Fortunately for us, beards were not worn at the Revolution, so that we are enabled to trace the lineaments of celebrated public characters of that time with a degree of satisfaction that will hardly reward the future biographers of the men of the present day.

" Major-General Greene in person was rather corpulent, and above the common size.  His complexion was fair and florid, his countenance serene and mild, indicating a goodness which seemed to soften and shade the fire and greatness of its expression.  His health was delicate, but preserved by temperance and regularity."

> " On martial ground the school of heroes taught,
>   He studied battles where campaigns were fought;
>   By valor led, he traced each scene of fame,
>   Where war had left no spot without a name.
>   Great by resolve, yet by example warned,
>   Himself the model of his glory formed."

General Greene's wife (Catharine Littlefield) was every way worthy of her distinguished husband. Her conversation and manner were fascinating and vivacious. It is noteworthy that Eli Whitney conceived the idea of his wonderful machine while under Mrs. Greene's roof at Mulberry Grove, Georgia, in 1792. Whitney, then a poor law-student, was protected by Mrs. Greene, who provided him an apartment, where he labored and produced his cotton-gin.

The high elevation of Prospect Hill exposes it on all sides to the chill wintry winds. Even now a residence there has its drawbacks, in spite of the charming panorama constantly unfolded to the eyes of the residents. What, then, was it during the winter of '75–'76, when the ground was held by men who slept in barracks rudely constructed of boards, through the crevices of which the snow drifted until it sometimes covered their sleeping forms? Greene wrote to his neighbor, Sullivan, the last of September, that his fingers were so benumbed he could scarcely hold his pen. The General occupied a hut in the rear of his encampment, where he was visited by his wife shortly after he assumed the command on Prospect Hill.

As what we desire to give the reader is as accurate a view as possible of the Continental camps during the period we are considering, we cannot do better than to exhibit their resources, and especially how they were provided with artillery to defend such extensive lines. In so far as such testimony is attainable, the evidence of the actors themselves or of eyewitnesses is preferred.

Dr. Thacher, who was a surgeon's mate in Asa Whitcomb's regiment in barracks on Prospect Hill, in 1775, says : —

" Before our privateers had fortunately captured some prizes with cannon and other ordnance, our army before Boston had, I believe, only four * small brass cannon and a few old honey-comb iron pieces with their trunnions broken off ; and these were ingeniously bedded in timbers in the same manner as stocking a musket.   These machines were *exceedingly* unwieldy and inconvenient, requiring much skill to elevate and depress them."

CARRIAGE FOR CANNON WITHOUT TRUNNIONS, USED BEFORE BOSTON.

As early as January, 1775, four brass pieces, two seven-inch mortars, and an unknown number of battering cannon, were in possession of the provincial committees.   Besides these, others are obscurely hinted at without mentioning the number. Worcester and Concord were selected as the places of deposit for all the artillery and munitions of war.   Even as far back as November, 1774, the committees had begun to purchase heavy cannon, which could be found in all the seaports from Boston to Falmouth.   Many of these were ship's guns.   Others had been purchased to defend the ports during the frequent wars with France ; and not a few had come from the fortifications of Louisburg and Annapolis Royal.   It appears that the Revolutionary executive had voted to equip a park of sixteen field-pieces, in which those brought out of Boston were to be included.   This will serve to show that, long before Lexington, the Americans were earnestly preparing for war, and that although the artillery in their hands was generally of light calibre, they were by no means as defenceless as has been supposed.   The sixteen field-pieces were, in February, voted to be distributed among the seven regiments of militia, in the pro-

* This was an underestimate.

portion of two to each, and two to the Boston company, lately Paddock's, it being the intention to have an artillery company in each regiment of minute-men. In March eight field-pieces and two brass mortars, with their ammunition, were ordered to be deposited at Leicester.

At Concord, on the 19th of April, the British disabled three iron 24-pounders by knocking off the trunnions. These were too heavy to remove as readily as had been done in the case of the lighter pieces, but Yankee ingenuity made the guns serviceable. Dr. Preserved Clap invented the carriage which is described by Thacher, and in our drawing made by an officer of artillery present at the siege. There were also field-pieces concealed at Newburyport, and cannon at Malden, Watertown, and Marlborough. Four light brass pieces (3-pounders), two of which had belonged to Paddock's Artillery, were, in the early days of the blockade, brought out of Boston under the very noses of the British officers.

Two days after the battle of Lexington the Provincials began to collect their warlike material, and couriers were despatched to Gridley, at Stoughton, and to David Mason,* then upon furlough at Salem. Mason was ordered to provide the necessary implements for eight 3- and three 6-pounders.

On the 29th of April the Committee of Safety reported to the Provincial Congress that there were in Cambridge six 3-pounders complete, with ammunition, and one 6-pounder. In Watertown there were sixteen pieces of artillery of different sizes. The Committee say : —

" The said 6-pounder and sixteen pieces of artillery will be taken out of the way; and the first-mentioned six pieces will be used in a proper way of defence." †

Measures were taken on the same day to organize two companies of artillery, Captain Joseph Foster being appointed to the command of one and Captain William Lee of Marblehead to the other. This appears to be the first step taken towards organizing the subsequently famous regiment of Massachusetts

* Afterwards major of Knox's Artillery.
† Records of the Provincial Congress.

artillery, which Gridley, Knox, and Crane commmanded.   The pieces first used were 3-pounders, and were those taken to Bunker Hill, where five of the six were captured by the enemy.

Among the Rhode Island troops which arrived at Cambridge early in June was a fine company of artillery, with four excellent field-pieces.   On the 12th of June Edes's Gazette stated that

"Many large pieces of battering cannon are expected soon from different places; twelve pieces, 18 and 24 pounders, with a quantity of ordnance-stores, we are informed, are already arrived from Providence."

A train with four field-pieces had also arrived in camp from Connecticut.   We have been thus circumstantial because much curiosity has existed in relation to the Provincial artillery before the arrival of Knox from Crown Point with fifty-five pieces of various calibres.   In the autumn of 1776 Massachusetts began to cast cannon.

With regard to small-arms the difficulties were even greater. Spears were largely used to supply the want of bayonets, and were kept within all the works to repel assault.   They were frequently examined, cleaned, and kept ready for service.   As for muskets, the General Court, as far back as 1770, had tried to wheedle Hutchinson out of the Province arms, but he refused to distribute them to the militia as recommended.   The arms were seized, however, in February, 1775, and removed from Harvard College, where they were deposited, to Worcester, to be out of Gage's clutches.   Private sources were soon exhausted, and there were no public workshops.   Washington paid £3 for a gun on his arrival at Cambridge; and by September, 1776, the price for a serviceable musket with bayonet made in the State was £4.   During the siege the scarcity became so great that the muskets had to be taken by force from soldiers whose term of enlistment had expired, and who brought their own guns, in order to supply those coming to take their places.

Rev. William Emerson, grandfather of Ralph Waldo Emerson, who was a chaplain in the army at this time, affords us glimpses of the Continental camps after the arrival of Washington : —

" My quarters are at the foot of the famous Prospect Hill, where such great preparations are made for the reception of the enemy. It is very diverting to walk among the camps. They are as different in their form as the owners are in their dress, and every tent is a portraiture of the temper and taste of the persons who encamp in it. Some are made of boards and some of sail-cloth. Some partly of one and some partly of the other. Again, others are made of stone and turf, brick and brush. Some are thrown up in a hurry; others curiously wrought with doors and windows done with wreaths and withes in the manner of a basket. Some are your proper tents and marquees, looking like the regular camp of the enemy. In these are the Rhode-Islanders, who are furnished with tent-equipage and everything in the most exact English style. However, I think this great variety is rather a beauty than a blemish in the army."

Rhode Island has always sent her sons to the field in a manner highly creditable to herself. As in the Revolution so in the late Rebellion her troops presented themselves supplied with every necessary for active service. When the Rhode-Islanders reached Washington, in 1861, their commander was asked, " What are your wants ? " " Nothing," was the reply ; " my State has provided for everything."

It was on Prospect Hill that Putnam raised, on the 18th of July, 1775, his celebrated flag, bearing on one side the motto, " An Appeal to Heaven ! " and on the reverse the three vines, which are the armorial bearings of Connecticut, with the legend, " *Qui Transtulit Sustinet !* " The shouts that rent the air when Old Put gave the signal are said to have caused the British on Bunker Hill to rush to arms, in the fear of an immediate attack.

Among Greene's officers Colonel Whitcomb of Lancaster has been mentioned. The Deacon, as he was usually called, was left out in the new organization of the army, on account of his age. His men, who were much attached to him, highly resented this treatment of the old man, and declared they would not re-enlist. The Colonel told them he did not doubt there were good reasons for the regulation, and said he would enlist as a private soldier. Colonel Brewer, who heard of this determination, offered to resign in favor of Whitcomb. The affair coming to Washington's knowledge, he permitted Brewer to carry his proposal into effect, giving him at the same time an appointment as barrack-master until a vacancy should occur in the line. The General then published the whole transaction in orders.

On New-Year's Day, 1776, the Union Flag, bearing thirteen stripes, was hoisted at Prospect Hill, and saluted with thirteen guns. This was the birthday of the new Continental army of undying fame. Now, for the first time, the thirteen united Colonies had a common flag. From this lofty height the colors were plainly distinguishable in the enemy's camps, and were at first thought to be a token of submission, — the king's speech having been sent to the Americans the same day. But the enemy were speedily undeceived; the proclamation was not received until after the flag had been flung to the breeze. There it continued to fly until raised in triumph on the abandoned works of the British.

Prospect Hill is occasionally mentioned as Mt. Pisgah. It could be reached by the enemy's battery at West Boston, which threw a 13-inch shell into the citadel during the bombardment preceding the possession of Dorchester Heights. The missile exploded without doing any injury. The hill, too, is associated with the last days of the siege by two incidents. An accidental fire which occurred in the barracks was conceived by Howe to be a signal for calling in the militia from the country, and probably accelerated his preparations to depart. The following order was issued to the army from headquarters, March 4, 1776 : —

"The flag on Prospect Hill and that at the Laboratory on Cambridge Common are ordered to be hoisted only upon a general alarm: of this the whole army is to take particular notice, and immediately upon these colors being displayed every officer and soldier must repair to his alarm-post. This to remain a standing order until the commander-in-chief shall please to direct otherwise."

Prospect Hill next demands attention from the circumstance that in November, 1777, it became the quarters of the British portion of Burgoyne's army; the Hessians occupied the barracks on Winter Hill.   The British arrived at Cambridge on Thursday the 6th, and the Germans on the following day.

The English entered Cambridge, *via* Watertown, in the midst of a pelting storm, and, without halting, proceeded quickly onward to Prospect Hill.   The officers had their side-arms, which they were allowed by the treaty to retain; but the men, unarmed, gloomy, and sullen, wore little of the defiant air of British soldiers.

As for the Hessians, the appearance they presented was truly pitiable.   The men were ragged and filthy, from the effects of the long marches and bivouacs without shelter.   Most of them had their tobacco-pipes, with which, with the national phlegm, they were solacing their misfortunes, so that a cloud of smoke enveloped them as they moved along.   They were followed by numbers of their women, staggering under the burdens of camp utensils, with huge hampers on their backs, from which peeped infants, some of them born on the road.   That the Germans were regarded with the utmost curiosity by the population we can well believe, for the most frightful stories were current concerning their prowess and bloodthirstiness. The American ladies, ignorant that at home these women performed their share of the labor of the fields, looked with compassion on what they considered evidence of the brutality of the men.   What with the tobacco-smoke and effluvia arising from this motley horde, the air was tainted as they passed by.

The Hessian officers politely saluted the ladies whom they saw at the windows, but the Britons, ever selfish and intractable in misfortune, kept their eyes upon the ground.   Burgoyne rode at the head of his men, behind the advanced guard.   He and his officers went to Bradish's tavern, afterwards Porter's, where they remained temporarily.   The animals which drew the prisoners' baggage-wagons seemed to partake of the sorry condition of their masters, being lean and half starved.

General Phillips, during the early part of the march from Saratoga, is said to have expressed his astonishment that so great an expenditure of money and life should have been made to conquer so barren and unattractive a region as that through which they were then passing. When they came to the beautiful and fertile valley of the Connecticut, General Whipple observed : " This, General, is the country we are fighting for." " Ah ! " replied Phillips, " this is a country worth a ten years' war."

The British officers soon became familiar objects to the people of Cambridge, some of whom did not care to conceal their discontent at the airs these sons of Mars gave themselves. They lived on the best the country and the times afforded, promenading the College grounds, and appearing in public with their swords belted about them. A slight check to their self-sufficiency was the sight of their whole train of artillery, which was parked on the Common.

There were two rows of barracks situated outside the citadel. These barracks were enclosed by a fence, at the entrance gate of which a sentinel was posted. Within the citadel was the guard-house, always occupied by a strong detachment of our troops. Sentinels were placed on the Charlestown and Cambridge roads, and at the provision barracks at the foot of the hill. A chain of sentinels extended across the valley between Prospect and Winter Hills, the line passing immediately in rear of Oliver Tufts's farm-house. The peculiarity of the terms granted to Burgoyne and his soldiers under the convention with Gates caused the British officers and men to reject the name of prisoners. They were styled " the troops of the Convention."

The American guards were drawn from the militia of Massachusetts expressly for this service. They were, for the most part, ignorant of camp discipline, and were ridiculed and abused by the prisoners whenever an opportunity presented itself. The guards, therefore, did not go beyond the letter of their orders to show respect to the prisoners.

The Britons, on the other hand, were not of a better class than was usual in the rank and file of that service. Many robberies were committed by them on the roads and even within the towns. Moreover, the apprehensions caused by the presence of so large a body of turbulent spirits near a populous place justified the enforcement of stringent regulations. As for the officers, they were supercilious to a degree, and one of them was shot dead for neglecting to answer the challenge of a sentry.

Inside their·barracks the Convention troops were allowed to manage for themselves. They were paraded, punished, and received from their own officers orders pertaining to their comfort or discipline precisely as if under the protection of their own flag. There was a British and a Hessian officer of the day who saw that the police of the barracks was properly performed. The barracks were, of course, at all times subject to the inspection of the Continental officer of the guard.

Many of the Germans were received into families in Boston as servants, or found employment as farm-laborers in the neighboring towns by their own desire. Numbers of them, after having been clothed and well fed, absconded. Five of the British were in Boston jail at one time, charged with highway robbery ; on one of them was found a watch taken from a gentleman on Charlestown Common. Numerous instances occurred where houses in and around Boston were. robbed of weapons only, while more valuable booty was left untouched. This created an impression that a conspiracy existed among the prisoners to obtain their freedom, especially after the refusal of Congress to carry out the provisions of the capitulation became known in the camp of the Convention troops.

Matters soon came to a crisis. Some of the British one day knocked down a sentinel and took away his gun, which they concealed in their quarters and refused to give up. At another time they rescued a prisoner from a guard, and showed every disposition to turn upon their jailers. After this last occurrence, Colonel David Henley, who commanded at Cambridge, ordered a body of the prisoners who had collected in front of his guard on Prospect Hill to retire to their barracks. One of the prisoners refusing to obey, Colonel Henley wounded him with his sword. On a previous occasion he had, in endeavoring to silence an insolent prisoner, seized a firelock from the guard and slightly wounded the man in the breast.

For these acts Colonel Henley was formally accused by General Burgoyne " of behavior heinously criminal as an officer and unbecoming a man ; of the most indecent, violent, vindictive severity against unarmed men, and of intentional murder." Colonel Henley was placed in arrest and tried by a military court at Cambridge, of which Colonel Glover was president, and Colonel William Tudor judge-advocate. General Burgoyne appeared as prosecutor. His address to the court was a model of wheedling, cajolery, and special pleading. He complimented the president for his honorable treatment of the Convention troops on the march to Boston. To Colonel Wesson, who had immediate command in the district when the troops arrived, he also paid his respects, and even the judge-advocate came in for a share of his persuasive eloquence.

It was believed that Burgoyne undertook the *rôle* of prosecutor, not only to recover in some degree his waning influence with his troops, but to retrieve, if possible, his reputation at home, by appearing in the guise of the champion of his soldiers.

Henley owed his acquittal mainly to the exertions of Colonel Tudor in his behalf. The evidence showed that the prisoner had acted under great provocation ; but what most influenced the result was the startling testimony adduced of the mutinous spirit prevalent among the British soldiers.

A day or two after this trial the judge-advocate and Colonel Henley met at Roxbury in making a visit to a family where a lady resided to whom Colonel H. was paying his addresses. He fancied himself coldly received, and was in rather a melancholy humor as they rode into town together. In coming over the Neck he abruptly said to his companion, " Colonel Tudor, I will thank you to shoot me ! " " Why, what is the matter now ? " asked Tudor. " You have ruined me." " I thought I had rendered you some assistance in the trial." " You said I was a man of passionate, impetuous temper ; this has destroyed me in the estimation of the woman I love ; you see she received me coldly. You have destroyed my happiness. You may now

do me a favor to shoot me." Colonel Tudor was vexed for a
moment at this sort of return for the services he had rendered, but these feelings were transient on both sides; they
continued friends, and Colonel Henley married the lady he
loved.*

Henley had served at the siege of Boston as brigade-major to
General Heath. In December, 1776, he was lieutenant-colonel
of Rufus Putnam's regiment. He commanded the rear-guard
in the disastrous retreat through the Jerseys, gaining the
opposite shore of the Delaware at midnight, just as Cornwallis
reached the river.

Colonel William Tudor presided over the courts-martial at
Cambridge after the arrival of Washington. He was the classmate and chum of Chief Justice Parsons at Harvard, graduating
in the class of 1769. In 1777 he was appointed lieutenant-
colonel of Henley's regiment. His courtship of the lady who
afterwards became his wife was prosecuted under very romantic
circumstances. By the hostilities which had broken out he was
separated from the object of his affections, who was residing on
Noddles Island (East Boston), in the family of Henry Howell
Williams. The British fleet, which lay off the island, rendered
it dangerous to approach it in a boat. A boyish acquisition
was now of use to the gallant colonel. He was an excellent
swimmer. Tying his clothes in a bundle on his head, he, like
another Leander, swam the strait between the island and the
main, paid his visit, and returned the way he came. Miss Delia
Jarvis — that was the lady's name — became Mrs. Tudor. The
Colonel's son, William, is well known in literature as one of
the founders of the Anthology Club, and first editor of the
North American Review. The eldest daughter of Colonel
Tudor married Robert Hallowell Gardiner, of Gardiner, Maine;
the youngest married Commodore Charles Stuart of the United
States Navy.

It is related of Colonel Tudor, that when a boy, being on a
visit on board an English line-of-battle ship in Boston harbor,
the conversation turned upon swimming. Tudor proposed to

* Mass. Historical Collections.

jump from the taffrail rail, which in ships of that time was at a considerable height from the water, if any one would do the same.    A sailor accepted the challenge.  The boy took the leap, but the man was afraid to follow.

As mention has been made of Colonel James Wesson in connection with the trial of Henley, we may be permitted to introduce an anecdote of the manner in which that brave officer's active career was brought to a close.  He had been commissioned major of Samuel Gerrish's regiment as early as the 19th May, 1775, by Joseph Warren, and served at the siege of Boston.  In November, 1776, he was made colonel.  He fought with credit at Saratoga and Monmouth.  In the latter battle our artillery under Knox opened an unexampled cannonade, to which the British guns fiercely replied.   Colonel Wesson, who then commanded the 9th Massachusetts, was in the front line.   Leaning over his horse's neck to look under the cannon smoke, which enveloped everything, a ball from the enemy grazed his back, tearing away his clothing, and with it fragments of his flesh.   Had he remained upright an instant longer he would have been killed; as it was, he remained a cripple for life.

In the summer of 1778 the British prisoners were transferred to Rutland, Massachusetts; a certain number went to Barre, in the same State.   Some thirty or forty of the worst characters, known to have been implicated in the riots which preceded the Henley affair, were placed on board the guard-ships at Boston.

On the 28th July the 20th British regiment, numbering then about four hundred men, marched for Rutland, under escort of a detachment of Colonel Thatcher's regiment.   They were followed on the 2d of September by the 21st and 47th, and on the 5th by the 24th regiment.   The last of the English troops marched for the same destination on the 15th of October, and the people of Boston breathed freer than they had done for months.

Mrs. Warren, who was an eyewitness, thus speaks of the effects produced by the presence of the British soldiery: —

"This idle and dissipated army lay too long in the vicinity of Boston for the advantage of either side.  While there, in durance, they disseminated their manners; they corrupted the students of Harvard College and the youth of the capital and its environs, who were allured to enter into their gambling-parties and other scenes of licentiousness. They became acquainted with the designs, resources, and weaknesses of America; and there were many among them whose talents and capacity rendered them capable of making the most mischievous use of their knowledge."

As might have been expected, there were a great many desertions among the foreign troops. Before the end of December four hundred of the English were missing, while the Brunswickers lost no fewer than seventy-three in a single month. Colonels Lee, Henley, and Jackson were all recruiting in Boston in 1777 – 78, and, as men were very scarce, they were not averse to enlisting the English soldiers. Burgoyne gave out publicly that neither he nor his troops were prisoners, but only an unarmed body of men marching through a country to the nearest seaport to embark for their homes. The men themselves, or many of them, were anxious to enlist, and the regiments then in Boston would have had no difficulty in filling up, had it not been that this course was discountenanced at the headquarters of the army as repugnant to the good of the service. The Hessian general was obliged to place non-commissioned officers as sentinels, — privates could not be trusted, — to prevent his men from running away. Some of them entered the American service, and the descendants of some are now living among us.

We obtain the following account of the manner in which the Convention troops were quartered at Rutland from the statement of one of the prisoners: —

" Here we were confined in a sort of pen or fence, which was constructed in the following manner: A great number of trees were ordered to be cut down in the woods. These were sharpened at each end and drove firmly into the earth, very close together, enclosing a space of about two or three acres. American sentinels were planted on the outside of this fence, at convenient distances, in order to prevent our getting out. At one angle a gate was erected, and on the outside thereof stood the guard-house. Two sentinels were constantly posted at this gate, and no one could get out unless he had a pass from the officer of the guard ; but this was a privilege in which very few were indulged.  Boards and nails were given the British, in order to make them temporary huts to secure them from the rain and the heat of the sun.  The provisions were rice and salt pork, delivered with a scanty hand.  The officers were allowed to lodge in the farm-houses which lay contiguous to the pen ; they were permitted likewise to come in amongst their men for the purpose of roll-call and other matters of regularity."

On the 9th November, 1778, the British and Germans, in accordance with a resolve of Congress, began their march for Virginia in six divisions, each of which was accompanied by an American escort.  Each nationality formed a division.  The first English division consisted of the artillery, grenadiers, and light infantry, and the 9th (Taylor's) regiment, under command of Lieutenant-Colonel Hill.  The second English division consisted of the 20th (Parr's) and 21st (Hamilton's) regiments, commanded by Major Forster ; and the third, composed of the 24th (Fraser's), 47th (Nesbitt's), and 62d (Anstruther's) regiments, were under the command of Brigadier Hamilton. The first German division consisted of the dragoons, grenadiers, and the regiment Von Rhetz, under Major Von Mengen.  In the second division were the regiments Von Riedesel and Von Specht, led by General Specht ; the third was made up of the Barner Battalion, the regiment Hesse Hanau, and the artillery, under Brigadier Gall.  The divisions marched respectively on the 9th, 10th, and 11th, keeping one day in advance of each other on the route.  Burgoyne having been permitted to return to England, General Phillips was in command of all the Convention troops.  He had been placed in arrest by General Heath for using insulting expressions in connection with Lieutenant Brown's death, but Gates, who now succeeded to the command, relieved the fiery Briton from his disability.

The story of the sojourn of the British army in the interior of Massachusetts closes with a domestic tragedy.  Bathsheba Spooner was the daughter of that tough old tory, Brigadier Ruggles, of Sandwich, Massachusetts, who fought with Sir

William Johnson in 1755. He had been at the head of the bench of the Court of Common Pleas, and a delegate to the Congress of 1765, where his course subjected him to reprimand from the Massachusetts House. In 1774 he was a Mandamus Councillor, and in the following year, after taking refuge in the then tory asylum of Boston, he attempted to raise a loyal corps there, of which Howe appointed him commandant. In some respects Ruggles was not unlike Putnam, — he was brave and impetuous. Like him, also, he was a tavern-keeper; but he wanted the love of country and rough good-humor which made every one admire Old Put.

Bathsheba proved to be a sort of female Borgia. Her husband, Joshua Spooner, was a respected citizen of Brookfield, Massachusetts. His wife, who had conceived a lawless passion for another, found in William Brooks and James Buchanan — soldiers of Burgoyne — two instruments fit for her bloody purpose. She employed them to murder her husband, which they did without remorse. The murderess, her two assassins, and another participant were tried, convicted, and executed at Worcester in July, 1778, for the crime. There is not in the criminal annals of Massachusetts a more horrible and repulsive record than this trial affords. For such a deed we can but think of the invocation of Lady Macbeth : —

> " Come, come, you spirits
> That tend on mortal thoughts, unsex me here ;
> And fill me, from the crown to the toe, top-full
> Of direst cruelty ! make thick my blood,
> Stop up the access and passage to remorse,
> That no compunctious visitings of nature
> Shake my fell purpose, nor keep peace between
> The effect and it ! "

Buchanan, one of the criminals, is supposed to be the same who was a corporal in the 9th regiment. He had been a leader in the mutiny on Prospect Hill, and was in arrest at the time of the Henley trial. In taking leave for the present of the Convention troops, we recall the pertinent inquiry : " Who would have thought that Mr. Burgoyne's declaration would have been so soon verified when he said in Parliament that at the head of five thousand troops he would march through the continent of America ? "

The march of improvement has left no traces of the old works that once crowned the brow of Prospect Hill so threateningly. A telling reminder of them, however, exists in an artificial battery, terminating the little park, near the new High School, on Central Hill, where the old defences on this side formerly ended. A mere glance shows how important the position was to the Americans, who considered it impregnable.

From here the lines ran in a generally southwesterly direction to the banks of the Charles. Before the work of grading was undertaken the line of the ditch could easily be traced to where it was crossed by Highland Avenue. The position on Central Hill is notable from the fact of its having been chosen by General Putnam as a rallying-point for the Americans, after the battle of Bunker Hill.

Leaving this, the northerly of the two eminences of Prospect Hill, we pass on to the extreme summit, where an enchanting view bursts upon the sight. The homes of half a million of people are before you. The tall chimneys of East Cambridge, the distant steeples of the city and of its lesser satellites, whose hands are grasped across the intervening river, form a wondrous and instructive exhibition of that prosperity which our fathers battled to secure.

Could the shades of those who by day and night kept watch and ward on this embattled height once again revisit the scene of their trials and their triumphs, we could scarcely expect them to recognize in the majestic, dome-crowned city the gray old town which they beheld through the morning mists of a century gone by, or even to identify the winding river on whose bosom lay moored the hostile shipping, and from whose black sides,

> " Sullen and silent, and like couchant lions,
>     Their cannon through the night,   .
>   Holding their breath, had watched in grim defiance
>     The sea-coast opposite."

A narrow strip of the high, northern summit, reached by Monroe Street, is all that is now left of this once proud eminence, around which now cluster the homes of a more peaceful population. " Grim visaged war " has here indeed " smoothed his wrinkled front " to such purpose that the old tale seems more like a dream than like sober reality.

# CHAPTER VIII.

### OLD CHARLESTOWN ROAD, LECHMERE'S POINT, AND PUTNAM'S HEADQUARTERS.

> " Poor *Tommy Gage* within a cage
> Was kept at Boston *ha'*, man,
> Till Willie Howe took o'er the knowe
> For *Philadelphia,* man."

OF the many whose custom it is to pass over the high-road leading from Charlestown to Cambridge Common it is likely that few are aware that they follow the course over which condemned criminals were once transported for execution. Its antecedents may not be as prolific of horrors as the way from Newgate to Tyburn, which counts a life for every rod of the journey, but its consequence as one of the most frequented highways of colonial days caused its selection for an exhibition which chills the blood, and carries us back within view of the atrocious judicial punishments of the Dark Ages.

To kill was not enough. The law was by no means satisfied with the victim's life. The poor human shell must be hacked or mangled with all the savagery which barbarous ingenuity could devise ; and at last Justice erected her revolting sign by the public highway, where the decaying corse of the victim creaked in a gibbet, as it mournfully obeyed the behest of the night-wind. Gibbeting, burning, impaling, have all a precedent in New England, of which let us relate an incident or two.

In the year 1749 a fire broke out in Charlestown, destroying some shops and other buildings belonging to Captain John Codman, a respectable citizen and active military officer. It transpired that Captain Codman had been poisoned by his negro servants, Mark, Phillis, and Phœbe, who were favorite domestics, and that the arson was committed to destroy the evidence of the crime.   The man had procured arsenic and the women administered it.   Mark was hanged, and Phillis was burnt at the usual place of execution in Cambridge.   Phœbe, who was said to have been the most culpable, became evidence against the others.   She was transported to the West Indies. The body of Mark was suspended in irons on the northerly side of Cambridge road, now Washington Street, a little west of and very near the stone quarry now there.   The gibbet remained until a short time before the Revolution, and is mentioned by Paul Revere as the place where he was intercepted by a patrol of British officers on the night he carried the news of the march of the regulars to Lexington.   A specimen of one of these bar-

NIX'S MATE.

barous engines of cruelty was once kept in the Boston Museum.   It was brought from Quebec, and looked as though it might have been put to horrid purpose.

This was, in all probability, the latest occurrence of burning and gibbeting in Massachusetts.   Earlier it was not uncommon to condemn malefactors of the worst sort to be hung in chains.   As long ago as 1726 the bodies of the pirates, William Fly, Samuel Cole, and Henry Greenville, were taken after execution to Nix's Mate, in Boston harbor, where the remains of Fly were suspended in chains; the others were buried on the island, which then contained several acres.   Hence the superstitious awe with which the place is even now regarded by mariners, and which the disappearance of the island has served so firmly to establish.

We must confess that while our humanity revolts at these barbarous usages of our ancestors, we cannot but admit that punishment followed crime in their day with a certainty by no means paralleled in our own.   The severity of the code, the infliction of death for petty crimes, we must abhor and condemn; but we may still contrast that state of things, in which the criminal's life was held so cheaply, with the present time, in which condemned malefactors repose on luxuriant couches, while the law jealously guards them from the penalty of crime, and justice, uncertain of itself, repeals its sentence and sets the guilty free. To something we must attribute the startling increase of crime. Can it be the laxity of the law?

Thomas Morton, the Merry Andrew of Mount Wollaston, relates, in his New English Canaan, an occurrence which, he says, happened to Weston's colony, in what is now Weymouth; and upon this slight foundation Hudibras built his humorous account of the hanging of a weaver for the crime of which a cobbler had been adjudged guilty:—

> "Our brethren of New England use
> Choice mal-factors to excuse,
> And hang the guiltless in their stead,
> Of whom the churches have less need;
> As lately happened."

Morton's story goes that, one of Weston's men having stolen corn from an Indian, a parliament of all the people was called to decide what punishment should be inflicted. It was agreed that the crime was a felony under the laws of England, and that the culprit must suffer death. Upon this a person arose and harangued the assembly. He proposed that as the accused was young and strong, fit for resistance against an enemy, they should take the young man's clothes and put them upon some old, bedridden person, near to the grave, and hang him in the stead of the other. Although Morton says the idea was well liked by the multitude, he admits that the substitution was not made, and that the course of justice was allowed to take effect upon the real offender.

Branding was not an unusual punishment in former times. A marine belonging to one of his Majesty's ships lying in Boston harbor, in 1770, being convicted of manslaughter, was immediately branded in the hand and dismissed. Montgomery and Killroy, convicted of the same crime for participation in the 5th of March massacre, were also branded in the same manner.

Directly in front of Mount Prospect, of which it is a lesser satellite, is the hill on which once stood the Asylum for the Insane, named for noble John McLean. During the siege this elevation was indifferently called Miller's and Cobble Hill, and subsequently Barrell's Hill from Joseph Barrell of Boston, whose superb old mansion has been demolished.

The work on Cobble Hill was laid out by General Putnam and Colonel Knox. It was begun on the night of November

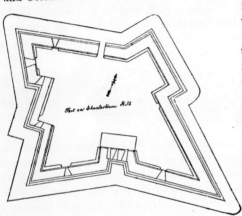

Fort on Charlestown Hill

22, 1775, and was considered, when completed, the best specimen of military engineering the Americans could yet boast of, — receiving the name of Putnam's impregnable fortress. To Washington's great surprise, he was allowed to finish the work without the least interruption from the enemy.

Cobble Hill was within point-blank range of the enemy's lines on Bunker Hill, and the post was designed to command the ferry between Boston and Charlestown, as well as to prevent the enemy's vessels of war from moving up the river at pleasure, — a result fully accomplished by arming the fort with 18 and 24 pounders.

As Colonel Knox had a principal share in laying out the fort on Cobble Hill, the only one of the works around Boston he is certainly known to have designed, the eminence should retain some association with the name of this distinguished soldier of the Revolution.

At the time he quitted Boston to repair to the American camp, Knox rented of Benjamin Harrod a store in old Cornhill (now the site of the "Globe" newspaper), who readily consented that Knox's goods might remain there, in the belief that his tory connections — he had lately married the daughter of Secretary Flucker — would be a safeguard for both. The store, however, was rifled by the British, and the landlord put in a claim against Knox for the time it was shut up, which Knox indignantly refused to allow. After the evacuation, William Knox, brother of the general, continued the business of a bookseller at the same stand.

When the Revolution began, Knox was a lieutenant of the Boston Grenadiers, commanded by Thomas Dawes, with the rank of major. Dawes was an officer of activity and address, and had exerted himself to bring the militia to a high standard of excellence. The presence of some of the best regiments in the British service offered both a model and incentive for these efforts. The company was composed of mechanics and professional men, selected with regard to their height and martial bearing, no member being under five feet ten inches, and many six feet in height. Joseph Peirce was a lieutenant with Knox, and Lemuel Trescott (afterwards a distinguished officer in the Massachusetts line) was orderly-sergeant. The company made a splendid appearance on parade, and Knox was considered a remarkably fine-looking officer. So at least thought one young lady, who, it is said, became captivated with her tall grenadier through those broad avenues to the female heart, admiration and pity, and by the following circumstance : —

Harry Knox had been out gunning some time previous, when the piece he carried, bursting in his hands, occasioned the loss of several of his fingers. "He made his appearance in the company," says Captain Henry Burbeck, "with the wound handsomely bandaged with a scarf, which, of course, excited the sympathy of all the ladies. I recollect the circumstance as well as though it had only happened yesterday. I stood at the head of Bedford Street and saw them coming up."

It is probable that Lucy Flucker was a frequent visitor to Knox's shop, for he reckoned the cream of the old Bostonians, as well as the debonair officers of his Majesty's army and fleet, among his customers. Longman was his London correspondent, and that arch-knave, Rivington, his New York ally in trade; be it known that New York relied on Boston chiefly for its advices from England before the Revolution. There is evidence that the affair of Knox and Miss Flucker was a love-match not sanctioned by her family. Lucy Flucker, with a true woman's faith and self-devotion, espoused the cause and embraced the fortunes of her husband. She followed him to the camp and to the field.

Knox's great reputation as an officer of artillery had its beginning here before Boston. He succeeded Gridley in the command of the Massachusetts regiment of artillery, a regiment of which Paddock's company formed the nucleus, and of which some twenty members became commissioned officers in the army of the Revolution. That company nobly responded when Joseph Warren demanded of them how many could be counted on to serve in the Army of Constitutional Liberty when it should take the field. And David Mason, who had raised the company, subsequently Paddock's, made no effort to obtain promotion for himself, but declared his willingness to serve under Knox, if the latter could be appointed colonel of the artillery.

Knox became very early a favorite with Washington. We know not whether the general-in-chief was of Cæsar's way of thinking, but it is certain Knox would have fulfilled the Roman's desire when he exclaims from his heart : —

> " Let me have men about me that are fat ;
> Sleek-headed men, and such as sleep o' nights."

We have seen that Washington told Greene he meant to keep Knox near him. On the other hand, Knox loved and revered his commander as a son. At that memorable leave-taking at Francis's tavern in New York, which no American can read without emotion, the General, after his few, touching words of farewell, invites his comrades to take him by the hand. " Knox, being nearest, turned to him. Incapable of utterance, Washington, in tears, grasped his hand, embraced, and kissed him. In the same affectionate manner he took leave of each succeeding officer." History does not record such another scene as this.

Wilkinson says Knox facilitated the passage of the Delaware before Trenton by his stentorian lungs and extraordinary exertions. He was in the front at Monmouth, placing his pieces at a critical moment where they stemmed the British onset and restored the battle. But Harry Knox " won his spurs " by his successful exertions in removing the artillery from Crown Point to the camp at Cambridge. At one time failure stared him in the face. The advanced season and contrary winds were near preventing the transportation of his ponderous treasures across the lake. The bateaux were rotten, and some, after being loaded with infinite difficulty, either sunk or let the cannon through their leaky bottoms. With joy at last Knox saw his efforts crowned with success. He writes to Washington, " Three days ago it was very uncertain whether we could have gotten them until next spring, but now, please God, they must go."

The cannon and mortars were loaded on forty-two strong sleds, and were dragged slowly along by eighty yoke of oxen, the route being from Fort George to Kinderhook, and from thence, *via* Great Barrington, to Springfield, where fresh cattle were provided. The roads were bad, and suitable carriages could not be had, so that the train could not proceed without snow. Fortunately the roads became passable, and the singular procession wound its tedious way through the mountains of Western Massachusetts and down to the sea. " We shall cut no small figure in going through the country with our cannon, mortars, &c., drawn by eighty yoke of oxen," says Knox.

General Knox, notwithstanding his later pecuniary difficulties, in which some of his best friends were unfortunately involved, was the soul of honor. When the war broke out he was in debt to Longman and other London creditors to a considerable amount, but at the peace he paid the greater part of these debts in full. Well might Mrs. Knox, after her bereavement, speak of " his enlarged soul, his generous heart, his gentleness of demeanor, and his expansive benevolence." He deserved it all.

When the General became a resident of Boston again, ten years after he had quitted it for the service, he was a tenant of Copley's house on Beacon Hill. He was then very fat, and wore in summer a high-crowned Leghorn hat, a very full shirt-frill, and usually carried a green umbrella under his arm. His injured hand was always wrapped in a silk handkerchief, which he was in the habit of unwinding when he stopped to speak with any one. Knox County and Knoxville in East Tennessee were named for the General while Secretary of War.

Mrs. Knox was a fine horsewoman. She was affable and gracious to her equals, but was unbending and unsocial with her inferiors, so that when her husband went to live in his elegant home at Thomaston, Maine, she found the society but little congenial. Her winters were chiefly passed in Boston, among her former friends, where she was often to be seen at the evening parties. When at home the General and lady received many notable guests, and many are the absurd stories still related of the General's prodigality. Mrs. Knox is said to have had a *penchant* for play, which, it must be remembered, was the rule and not the exception of fashionable society in her day. To show to what extent this practice prevailed in the good old town of Boston in 1782, we give the testimony of the high-bred Marquis Chastellux, to whom such scenes were familiar : —

"They made me play at whist, for the first time since my arrival in America. The cards were English, that is, much handsomer and dearer than ours, and we marked our points with Louis d'ors. When the party was finished the loss was not difficult to settle ; for the company was still faithful to that voluntary law established in society from the commencement of the troubles, which prohibited playing for money during the war. This law, however, was not scrupulously observed in the clubs and parties made by the men themselves. The inhabitants of Boston are fond of high play, and it is fortunate, perhaps, that the war happened when it did to moderate this passion, which began to be attended with dangerous consequences."

When General Knox was with the army under Washington, in the neighborhood of New York, his wife remained at a certain town in Connecticut, awaiting an opportunity of rejoining her husband after the event of the campaign should be decided. Mrs. Knox had for a companion the wife of another Massachusetts officer. The person who let his house for a short time to the ladies asserted that, after their departure, twenty-five gallons of choice old rum which he had in his cellar, and of which Mrs. Knox had the key, were missing.

It is not a little curious that while the splendid seat erected by Knox after the war, at Thomaston, which he named Montpelier, has been demolished, the old wooden house in Boston in which the General was born was, until quite recently, standing on Federal Street, near East Street, — that part of Boston being formerly known as Wheeler's Point. General Heath says in his memoirs that, being well acquainted with Knox before the war, he urged him to join the American army, but that Knox's removal out of Boston and the state of his domestic concerns required some arrangement, which he effected as soon as possible, and then joined his countrymen.

Cobble Hill was, in December, 1777, the quarters of a portion of Burgoyne's troops, who were suspected of setting fire to the guard-house there at the same time a plot was discovered on board one of the guard-ships in the harbor for the release of the Bennington prisoners.

Joseph Barrell was an eminent Boston merchant, who, while a resident of that town, had inhabited one of the most elegant old places to be found there. The evidences of his taste were until lately seen in the house which he built after the Revolutionary War, and in the grounds which he laid out. Barrell's palace, as it was called, was reached by passing through a noble avenue, shaded by elms planted by the old merchant. It was erected in 1792, and was furnished with glass of American manufacture from the first works erected in Boston. The house, which was of brick, does not demand a particular description here, but it was in all respects a noble old mansion, worthy a magnate of the Exchange. The interior arrangement of the ground-floor is thus described. Entering a vestibule opening into a spacious hall, across which springs the staircase, supported by wooden columns, you pass under this bridge into an oval reception-room in the rear of the building, an apartment of elegance even for our day, and commanding a view of the gardens and fish-pond so much affected by the old proprietor, — a souvenir of the estate in Summer Street. In this room is hanging a portrait of McLean, the beneficent founder of the asylum, by Alexander. Mr. Barrell spared no expense in the interior decoration of his house, as the rich woodwork abundantly testifies. He it was who first introduced the tautog into Boston Bay, a fish of such excellence that all true disciples of Izaak Walton should hold his name in grateful remembrance.

Poplar Grove, as Mr. Barrell's place was called, was purchased in 1816, by the corporation of the Massachusetts General Hospital, — of which the asylum is an appendage, — of Benjamin Joy, and the Barrell mansion became, and until recently remained, the residence of the physician and superintendent. Rufus Wyman, M. D., was, from the first opening in 1818 until 1835, the physician here.

But the topography of all this region is now strangely altered, not only by the demolition of the buildings, but also by the levelling of the hill itself, once such a beautiful and interesting feature in the otherwise dreary landscape. The demands of the railroads, entering the city at this point, for more room, have been imperative, and the dome-capped buildings with their shady walks and extensive orchard have silently obeyed the relentless mandate. It is true that the noise caused by the frequent passing of hurrying trains, to and fro, was bad for the hospital patients.

Here the poor patients whose wits are out may ramble in the pleasant paths and " babble o' green fields." Here we may see a Lear, there an Ophelia, — old and young, rich and poor, but with an equality of wretchedness that levels all worldly condition. Though dead in law as to the world, we know not that the lives of the inmates are a blank, or that some mysterious affinity may not exist among them. From the incurable maniac

down to the victim of a single hallucination, who is only mad
when the wind is north-northwest, the principles of an enlarged
philanthropy have been found to be productive of the most
happy results. Their former lives are studied, and, as far as
practicable, grafted upon the new. Your madhouse, perhaps
the most repulsive of all earthly objects, becomes, under wise
and kindly influences, the medium by which the insane are in
very many instances returned into the world. Such have been
for fifty years the fruits of McLean's exalted charity.

None but the antiquary, who is ready to discard every sense
but that of smell need explore the margin of Miller's River.
If he expects to find a placid, inviting stream, with green
banks and clumps of willows, — a stream for poetry or medita-
tion, — let him beware. If he looks for a current in which to
cast a line, or where he may float in his skiff and dream the
day away, building his aerial *châteaux*, let him discard all
such ideas and pass by on the other side. Miller's River in
time became a public nuisance, and for sanitary reasons was
filled up. Such draughts of air as are wafted to your nostrils
from slaughter-houses, where whole hecatombs of squealing
victims are daily sacrificed, are not of the chameleon's dish.

Lechmere's Point, now East Cambridge, was so called from
its ownership by the Lechmere family. Hon. Thomas Lechmere, who died in 1765, was for many years Surveyor-General
for the Northern District of America, and brother of the then
Lord Lechmere. Richard Lechmere, a royalist refugee of 1776,
married a daughter of Lieutenant-Governor Spencer Phips, and
by her inherited that part of the Phips estate of which we are
now writing. This will account to the reader for the name of
" Phips's Farm," which was sometimes applied to the Point in
Revolutionary times. About 1806 Andrew Craigie purchased
the Point. The site of the old farm-house, which was the only
one existing there prior to the Revolution, was near where the
Court House now stands.

This locality is celebrated as the landing-place of the British
grenadiers and light infantry, under Lieutenant-Colonel Smith,
on the night of April 18, 1775. It would not be unworthy

the public spirit of the citizens of East Cambridge to erect some memorial by which this fact may be perpetuated. At high tide the Point was an island, connected only with the mainland by a causeway or dike. Willis's Creek or Miller's River, was on the north, and received the waters of a little rivulet which flowed through the marsh on the west.

The access to the Point before the Revolution was by a bridge across Willis's Creek, and a causeway now corresponding nearly with Gore Street. This causeway was probably little more than a footway slightly raised above the level of the marsh, and submerged at high water. The troops lying on and around Prospect Hill were therefore nearest the Point. Washington, in December, 1775, built the causeway now coinciding with Cambridge Street when he had resolved to fortify Lechmere's Point. By this means he was enabled to reinforce the garrison there from Cambridge as well as Charlestown side, and by a route less circuitous than that leading from the camps above and at Inman's, which, diverging at Inman's, passed through his lane about as far as the present line of Cambridge Street, when it curved to the eastward, crossed the creek, and united with Charlestown road at the foot of Prospect Hill.

The possession of a siege-train at last enabled Washington to plant batteries where they would seriously annoy the enemy in Boston. Among the most important of these were the forts on Cobble Hill and Lechmere's Point.

Lechmere's Point was first fortified by the erection of a bomb-battery on the night of November 29, 1775. The fortunate capture by Captain Manly of a British ordnance brig in Boston Bay gave, among other valuable stores, a 13-inch brass mortar to the besieging army. Colonel Stephen Moylan relates that the arrival of this trophy in camp was the occasion of great rejoicing. The mortar was placed in its bed in front of the laboratory on Cambridge Common for the occasion, and Old Put, mounted astride with a bottle of rum in his hand, stood parson, while Godfather Mifflin gave it the name of "Congress."

The mortar was eventually placed in battery at the Point, where Washington had so far modified his original plan of a bomb-battery only as to cause the construction of two redoubts. The approach to the causeway and bridge leading to the Point from Charlestown side had previously been secured by a small work on the main shore. After constructing a covered way and improving the causeway, — a task which a heavy fall of snow much retarded, — Washington directed Putnam to throw up the redoubts. The enemy did not at first offer the least impediment to the work, and the General could only account for this silence by the supposition that Howe was meditating some grand stroke ; but as soon as the Americans had carried their covered way up to the brow of the hill and broke ground there, the British opened a heavy fire, which continued for several days, without, however, interrupting the work. Owing to the frozen condition of the ground, which made the labor one of infinite difficulty, it was not until the last days of February that the redoubts were completed.

With proper ordnance the Americans were now able to render the west part of Boston, which was only half a mile distant, untenable to the enemy, and to drive his ships and floating-batteries, from which they had experienced the greatest annoyance, out of the river. The arrival of Colonel Knox with the heavy artillery from Ticonderoga and Crown Point supplied the want that had all along been so keenly felt. On the 25th of February, 1776, Knox orders Burbeck, his lieutenant-colonel, to arm the batteries at Lechmere's Point with two 18 and two 24 pounders, to be removed from Prospect Hill ; and on the 26th Washington announces the mounting there of heavy ordnance and the preparation of two platforms for mortars, but laments the want of *the* thing essential to offensive operations. An officer writes in January of this poverty of ammunition : —

" The bay is open, — everything thaws here except Old Put. He is still as hard as ever crying out for powder, powder ! ye gods, give us powder ! "

From this point Boston was successfully bombarded on the 2d March, 1776. A number of houses in what is now the West End were struck, — Peter Chardon's, in Bowdoin Square, where the granite church now stands, being hit several times. The ball which so long remained in Brattle Street Church, a visible memorial of the siege, was undoubtedly thrown from Lechmere's Point. The fort here, which we are justified in considering the most important of all the American works, commanded the town of Boston as fully as the hills in Dorchester did on that side. It was to resist the works here and on Cobble Hill that the British erected batteries on Beacon Hill and at Barton's Point in Boston, — the point where Craigie's Bridge leaves the shore.

The following extracts from the letter of a British officer of rank, begun on the 3d of March, 1776, and continued in the form of a journal until the embarkation, give an account of the bombardment and manner in which the American artillery was served by Colonel Knox : —

" For the last six weeks, or near two months, we have been better amused than could possibly be expected in our situation. We had a theatre, we had balls, and there is actually a subscription on foot for a masquerade. England seems to have forgot us, and we endeavored to forget ourselves. But we were roused to a sense of our situation last night in a manner unpleasant enough. The rebels have been erecting for some time a bomb battery, and last night they began to play upon us. Two shells fell not far from me. One fell upon Colonel Monckton's house and broke all the windows, but luckily did not burst until it had crossed the street. Many houses were damaged, but no lives lost. What makes this matter more provoking is, that their barracks are so scattered and at such a distance that we cannot disturb them, although from a battery near the water-side they can reach us easily.

" 4th. The rebel army is not brave, I believe, but it is conceded on all hands that their artillery officers are at least equal to our own. In the number of shells that they flung last night not above three failed. This morning we flung four, and three of them burst in the air.

" 5th. We underwent last night a severe cannonade, which damaged a number of houses and killed some men."

The Royal Artillery endeavored for fourteen days unsuccessfully to silence the American batteries on the east and west of

Boston.  On the 6th orders were issued to embark the artillery and stores.  Colonel Cleaveland writes as follows of the difficulties he encountered : —

" The transports for the cannon, etc., which were ordered to the wharf were without a sailor on board and half stowed with lumber. At the same time most of my heavy cannon and all the field artillery, with a great quantity of arms, was to be brought in from Charlestown and other distant posts.  I was obliged to send iron ordnance to supply their places, to keep up a fire on the enemy and prevent their breaking ground on Forster Hill (South Boston).  On the fifth day most of the stores were on board, with the exception of four iron mortars and their beds, weighing near six tons each.  With great difficulty I brought three of them from the battery, but on getting them on board the transport the blocks gave way, and a mortar fell into the sea, where I afterwards threw the other two."

Four companies of the 3d Battalion of Artillery had joined before the troops left Boston.  Until their arrival there was not a relief for the men who were kept constantly on duty.  One hundred and fifty vessels were employed in transporting the army and stores to Halifax.

It was related by Colonel Burbeck that the battery containing the " Congress " mortar was placed under the command of Colonel David Mason.  With this mortar Mason was ordered to set fire to Boston.  His first shell was aimed at the Old South, and passed just above the steeple.  The next shell was aimed more accurately at the roof, which it would doubtless have entered had not the mortar burst, grievously wounding the colonel and killing a number of his men.  From this and similar accidents at the batteries, Boston escaped destruction. Through the inexperience of those who served them, four other mortars were burst during the bombardment which preceded the occupation of Dorchester Heights.

Early in March Washington evidently expected an attack, as his dispositions were made with that view.  That Lechmere's Point was the object of his solicitude is clear from the precautions taken to guard that important post.  Upon any alarm Patterson, whose regiment garrisoned No. 3, was ordered to march to the Point, leaving a strong guard in the work leading to the bridge. Bond's was to garrison Cobble Hill, and Sargeant's the North, South, and Middle Redoubts. Heath's, Sullivan's, Greene's, and Frye's brigades were, in rotation, to march a regiment an hour before day into the works at Lechmere's Point and Cobble Hill, — five companies to the former and three to the latter post, where they were to remain until sunrise.

The fort was situated on the summit of the hill, which has lost considerable of its altitude, the southeast angle being about where the old Unitarian Church now stands, and the northern bastion on the spot now occupied by Thomas Hastings's house, on the corner of 4th and Otis Streets; the latter street is laid out through the fort. A breastwork parallel with the creek and flanking it extended some distance down the hill.

Lechmere's Point obtained an unenviable reputation as the place of execution for Middlesex. Many criminals were hung here; among others the notorious Mike Martin, sometimes called "the last of the highwaymen."

Michael Martin, *alias* Captain Lightfoot, after a checkered career as a highway robber in Ireland, his native country, and in Scotland, became a fugitive to America in 1819, landing at Salem, where he obtained employment as a farm laborer of Elias Hasket Derby. A life of honest toil not being congenial, Martin, after passing through numerous vicissitudes, again took to the road, making Canada the theatre of his exploits.

At length, after committing many robberies in Vermont and New Hampshire, Martin arrived at Boston, and at once commenced his bold operations. His first and last victim here was Major John Bray of Boston, who was stopped and robbed by Martin as he was returning to town in his chaise over the Medford turnpike. Martin had learned that there was to be a dinner-party at Governor Brooks's house on that afternoon, and, with native shrewdness, had guessed that some of the guests might be worth plundering.

Martin fled. He was pursued and arrested in bed at Springfield. After being removed to East Cambridge jail, he was tried, convicted of highway robbery, and sentenced to be hanged. This was the first trial that had occurred under the statute for such an offence, and naturally created great interest. The knight of the road was perfectly cool during his trial, and, after sentence was pronounced, observed : "Well, that is the worst you can do for me."

While awaiting his fate, Martin made a desperate effort to escape from prison. He had succeeded in filing off the chains by which he was secured, so that he could remove them at pleasure ; and one morning when Mr. Coolidge, the turnkey, came to his cell, the prisoner struck him a savage blow with his irons, and, leaving him senseless on the floor, rushed into the prison yard. By throwing himself repeatedly and with great force against the strong oaken gate, Martin at last emerged into the street, but was, after a short flight, recaptured and returned to his cell. After this attempt he was guarded with greater vigilance, and suffered the penalty of his crimes.

Of the two half-moon batteries which Washington caused to be thrown up in November, between Lechmere's Point and the mouth of Charles River, the vestiges of one only are remaining. They were not designed for permanent occupation, but only for occasional use, to repel an attempt by the enemy to land. The good taste of the authorities of Cambridge has preserved the little semicircular battery situated on the farthest reach of firm ground on the Cambridge shore. It is protected by a handsome iron fence, composed of military emblems, and is called Fort Washington, — a name rather too pretending for a work of this class. Looking towards Boston, we see in front of us the southerly side of the Common, where the enemy had erected works. The battery has three embrasures, and on a tall flagstaff is the inscription : —

"1775    Fort Washington    1857
This battery thrown up by Washington Nov. 1775."

Struck with the perfect condition of the earthwork, we found upon inquiry that the city of Cambridge had, about forty years ago, thoroughly restored the rampart, which was then in good preservation. The guns now mounted there were, at that time, furnished by the United States government. The situation is very bleak and exposed, and the cold north-winds must have pierced the poor fellows through and through as they delved in the frozen gravel of the beach to construct this work. The other battery was probably on the little hill where the powder-magazine now stands.

Having arrived at the limit of the exterior or offensive lines between the Mystic and Charles, we may briefly sketch the remaining positions on this side, constructed for defence only, in the earlier stages of the investment. These lines connected Prospect Hill with Charles River by a series of detached forts and redoubts. Of the former there were three, numbered from right to left. No. 1 was on the bank of Charles River, at the point where it makes a southerly bend. Next was a redoubt situated a short distance south of the main street leading to the Colleges, and in the angle formed by Putnam Street. The eminence is being levelled as rapidly as possible, and no marks of the work remain. Connected with this redoubt were the Cambridge lines, called No. 2, a series of redans, six in number, joined together by curtains. These were carried across the road, and up the slope of what was then called Butler's, since known as Dana Hill, terminating at their northerly extremity in another redoubt, situated on the crest and in the angle of Broadway and Maple Avenue, on the Greenough estate. The soil being a hard clay, the earth to build this work was carried from the lower ground on the Hovey estate to the top of the hill. To the north of Cambridge Street a breastwork was continued in a northeasterly direction through Mr. C. M. Hovey's nursery. Cannon-shot and other vestiges of military occupation have been unearthed there by Mr. Hovey. A hundred yards behind this line, but of less extent, was another rampart of earth, having a *tenaille*, or inverted redan, in the centre. The right flank rested on the main road, which divided the more advanced work nearly at right angles. Remains of these works have existed within forty odd years.

Continuing to trace the lines eastward, — their general direc-

INMAN HOUSE.

tion being from east to west, — we find that two little half-moons were thrown up on each side of the Charlestown road at the point where it crossed the west branch of Willis's Creek.

No. 3 lay to the southwest of Prospect Hill, a little south of the point where the main road from Charlestown (Washington Street) was intersected by that from Medford and Menotomy, and which pass it was designed to defend. It was a strong, well-constructed work, and should be placed very near Union Square, in Somerville. These defences were, for the most part, planned by Richard Gridley, the veteran engineer, assisted by his son and by Captain Josiah Waters, of Boston, and Captain Jonathan Baldwin, of Brookfield, afterwards colonel of engineers. Colonel Knox occasionally lent his aid before receiving his rank in the army.

In coming from Charlestown or Lechmere's Point by the old county road hitherto described, and before the day of bridges had created what is now Cambridgeport out of the marshes, the first object of interest was the farm of Ralph Inman, a well-to-do, retired merchant of the capital. His mansion-house and outbuildings formed a small hamlet, and stood in the angle of the road as it turned sharp to the right and stretched away to the Colleges.

The world would not have cared to know who Ralph Inman was had not his house become interwoven with the history of the siege as the headquarters of that rough, fiery genius, Israel Putnam. It could not have been better situated, in a military view, for Old Put's residence. The General's own regiment and most of the Connecticut troops lay encamped near at hand in Inman's green fields and fragrant pine woods. It was but a short gallop to the commander-in-chief's, or to the posts on the river. Remove all the houses that now intervene between Inman Street and the Charles, and we see that the gallant old man had crouched as near the enemy as it was possible for him to do, and lay like a watch-dog at the door of the American lines.

Ralph Inman was, of course, a royalist. Nature does not more certainly abhor a vacuum than does your man of substance a revolution. Strong domestic ties bound him to his allegiance. He was of the Church of England too, and his associates were cast in the same tory mould with himself. He had been a merchant in Boston in 1764, and the agent of Sir Charles Frankland when that gentleman went abroad. He kept his coach and his liveried servants for state occasions, and the indispensable four-wheeled chaise universally affected by the gentry of his day for more ordinary use. If he was not a Scotsman by descent, we have not read aright the meaning of the thistle, which Inman loved to see around him.

The house had a plain outside, unostentatious, but speaking eloquently of solid comfort and good cheer within. It was of wood, of three stories, with a pitched roof. From his veranda Inman had an unobstructed outlook over the meadows, the salt marshes, and across the bay, to the town of Boston. What really claim our admiration about this estate were the trees by which it was glorified, and of which a few noble elms have been spared. Approaching such a house, as it lay environed by shrubbery and screened from the noonday sun by its giant guardians, with the tame pigeons perched upon the parapet and the domestic fowls cackling a noisy refrain in the barn-yard, you would have said, " Here is good old-fashioned thrift and hospitality ; let us enter," and you would not have done ill to let instant execution follow the happy thought.

Besides his tory neighbors — and at the time of which we write what we now call Old Cambridge was parcelled out among a dozen of these — Inman was a good deal visited by the loyal faction of the town. The officers of his Majesty's army and navy liked to ride out to Inman's to dine or sup, and one of them lost his heart there.

John Linzee, captain of H. M. ship Beaver, met with Sukey Inman (Ralph's eldest daughter) in some royalist coterie, — as like as not at the house of her bosom friend, Lucy Flucker, — and found his heart pierced through and through by her bright glances. He struck his flag, and, being incapable of resistance, became Sukey's lawful prize. He came with Dalrymple, Montague, and his brother officers ostensibly to sip Ralph's mulled port or Vidania, but really, as we may believe, to see the daughter of the house. For some unknown cause the father did not favor Linzee's suit. There was an aunt whom Sukey visited in town, and to whose house the gallant captain had the *open sesame*, but who manœuvred, as only aunts in 1772 (and they have not forgot their cunning) knew how, to keep the lovers apart.

But John Linzee was no faint-heart, and he married Sukey Inman. George Inman, her brother, entered the British army. Linzee commanded the Falcon at the battle of Bunker Hill, where he did us all the mischief he could, and figured elsewhere on our coasts. In 1789 he happened again to cast anchor in Boston harbor, and opened his batteries this time with a peaceful salute to the famous stars and stripes flying from the Castle. It is well known that Prescott, the historian, married a granddaughter of Captain Linzee.

The interior of Inman's house possessed no striking features. It was roomy, but so low-studded that you could easily reach the ceilings with your hand when standing upright. The deep fireplaces, capacious cupboards, and secret closets were all there. Our last visit to the mansion was to find it divided asunder, and being rolled away to another part of the town, where we have no wish to follow. It was not a pleasant sight to see this old house thus mutilated, with its halls agape and its cosey bedchambers literally turned out of doors, — a veritable wreck ashore.

Inman was arrested in 1776. He had been of the king's council and an addresser of Hutchinson. He became a refugee in Boston, and his mansion passed into the custody of the Provincial Congress, who assigned it to General Putnam.

Putnam, as we remember, commanded the centre of the American position, comprising the works and camps in Cambridge. The commission of major-general was then no sinecure, and we may opine that Old Put had his hands busily employed. Those long summer days of 1775 were full of care and toil, but the summer evenings were not less glorious than now, and the General must have often sat on the refugee's lawn, watching the camp-fires of the investing army, or tracing in the heavens the course of some fiery ambassador from the hostile shore.

One day while Putnam was on Prospect Hill he summoned all his captains to headquarters. It was stated to them that a hazardous service was contemplated, for which one of their number was desired to volunteer. A candidate stepped forward, eager to signalize himself. A draft of six men from each company was then made. At the appointed time the chosen band appeared before the General's quarters, fully armed and equipped. Old Put complimented their appearance and commended their spirit. He then ordered every man to lay aside his arms for an axe, and directed their march to a neighboring swamp to cut fascines.

When Putnam was with Amherst in Canada, that general, to his great annoyance, found that the French had a vessel of twelve guns stationed on a lake he meant to pass over with his army. While pondering upon the unexpected dilemma he was accosted by Putnam with the remark, "General, that ship must be taken." "Ay," says Amherst, "I'd give the world she were taken." "I'll take her," says Old Put. "Give me some wedges, a beetle, and a few men of my own choice." Amherst, though unable to see how the ship was to be taken by such means, willingly complied. At night Putnam took a boat, and, gaining the ship's stern unperceived, with a few quick blows drove his wedges in such a manner as to disable the rudder. In the morning the vessel, being unmanageable, came ashore, and was taken.

With the single exception of Washington there is not a name on the roll of the Revolution more honored in the popular heart than that of Putnam. He was emphatically a man of action and of purpose. At what time he received his famous sobriquet we are unable to say, but he was Old Put at Cambridge, and will be to posterity.

We can imagine the young fledglings of the army calling the then gray-haired veteran by this familiar nickname, but when it comes to the dignified commander-in-chief, it shows us not only that he had a grim sense of the humorous, but that he was capable of relaxing a little from his habitual dignity of thought and expression. " I suppose," says Joseph Reed, in a letter to Washington, — " I suppose ' Old Put ' was to command the detachment intended for Boston on the 5th instant, as I do not know of any officer but himself who could have been depended on for so hazardous a service." And the General replies : " The four thousand men destined for Boston on the 5th, if the ministerialists had attempted our works at Dorchester or the lines at Roxbury, were to have been headed by Old Put."

He had nearly attained threescore when the war broke out, but the fires which a life filled with extraordinary adventures had not dimmed still burned brightly in the old man's breast. Only think of a sexagenarian so stirred at the scent of battle as to mount his horse and gallop a hundred and fifty miles to the scene of conflict. Whether we remember him in the wolf's lair, at the Indian torture, or fighting for his country, we recognize a spirit which knew not fear and never blenched at danger.

If the General sometimes swore big oaths, — and we are not disposed to dispute it, — they were, in a measure, inocuous ; such, for example, as Uncle Toby used at the bedside of the dying lieutenant. Your camp is a sad leveller, and though the Continental officers could not have had a more correct example than their illustrious chief, yet it was much the fashion among gentlemen of quality of that day, and especially such as embraced the military profession, to indulge themselves in a little profanity. Say what we will, our Washingtons and our Havelocks are the *rara aves* of the camp. We have history for it that " our army swore terribly in Flanders." We believe the Revolution furnishes a similar example ; and we fear the Great Rebellion tells the same story.

It was perhaps to remedy this tendency, and that the spiritual wants of the soldiery might not suffer, that a prayer was composed by Rev. Abiel Leonard, chaplain to General Putnam's regiment, and printed by the Messrs. Hall in Harvard

College in 1775. Putnam was no courtier, but brusque, hearty, and honest. The words attributed to the Moor might have been his own : —

> " Rude am I in my speech,
> And little blessed with the set phrase of peace ;
> For since these arms of mine had seven years' pith,
> Till now some nine moons wasted, they have used
> Their dearest action in the tented field."

Putnam's summer costume was a waistcoat without sleeves for his upper garment. Across his brawny shoulders was thrown a broad leathern belt, from which depended a hanger, and thus he appeared as he bestrode his horse among the camps at Cambridge. Those sneering Marylanders scouted this carelessness in the bluff old captain's attire, and said he was much better to head a band of sicklemen or ditchers than musketeers.

The day following the battle of Bunker Hill, a young lady who had been assisting Dr. Eustis in the care of our wounded wished to send a letter to her parents in Boston. Her heart was full of anguish at the death of Warren, and her pen unskilled in cold set phrase. The officer at the lines to whom she handed her missive, in order that it might go in with the first flag, returned it, saying, " It is too d—d saucy." The lady went to General Ward, who advised her to soften the expressions a little. General Putnam, who was sitting by, read the letter attentively, and exclaimed, " It shall go in if I send it at the mouth of a cannon ! " He demanded a pass for it, and the fair writer received an answer from her friends within forty-eight hours.

Putnam's old sign of General Wolfe, which he displayed when a tavern-keeper at Brooklyn, Connecticut, is still preserved at Hartford, Connecticut.

Before we depart from Cambridgeport the reader will permit us a pilgrimage to the homes of Margaret Fuller and Washington Allston. Margaret was born in a house now standing in Cherry Street, on the corner of Eaton Street, with three splendid elms in front, planted by her father on her natal day. The large square building, placed on a brick basement, is removed about twenty feet back from the street. It is of wood, of three stories, has a veranda at the front reached by a flight of steps, and a large L, but the splendid elms have been cut down. Miss Fuller went to Edward Dickinson's school, situated in Main Street, nearly opposite Inman, where Rev. S. K. Lothrop and O. W. Holmes were her classmates. Her father, Timothy Fuller, and herself are still remembered by the elder people wending their way on a Sabbath morn to the old brick church of Mr. Gannett.

Allston lived in a house at the corner of Magazine and Auburn Streets. His studio was nearly opposite his dwelling, in the rear of the Baptist church, in a building erected for him. It was confidently asserted by Americans in England, that had Allston remained there he might have reached a high position in the Royal Academy ; but he was devotedly attached to his country and to a choice circle of highly prized friends at home.

Allston realized whatever prices he chose to ask for his pictures. Stuart only demanded $ 150 for a kit-kat portrait and $ 100 for a bust, but Allston's prices were much higher. Being asked by a lady if he did not require rest after finishing a work, he replied : " No, I only require a change. After I finish a portrait I paint a landscape, and then a portrait again." He delighted in his art.

He was received in Boston on his return from England with every mark of affection and respect, and his society was courted in the most intelligent and cultivated circles. Even the young ladies, the belles of the period, appreciated the polish and charm of his manners and address, and were well pleased when he made choice of one of them as a partner in a cotillon, then the fashionable dance at evening parties.

Besides his immediate and gifted family connections, Allston was much attached to Isaac P Davis and Loammi Baldwin, the eminent engineer. The painting of " Elijah in the Wilderness " remained at the house of the former in Boston until it was purchased by Labouchiere, who saw it there. It has been repurchased by Mrs. S. Hooper, and placed in the Athenæum Gallery. No distinguished stranger went away from Boston without seeing Allston; among others he was visited by Mrs. Jameson, who was taken by the artist to his studio, where he exhibited to her several of his unfinished works and sketches. It was a most interesting interview.

Allston's "Jeremiah," an immense canvas, with figures larger than life, was ordered by Miss Gibbs. "Saul and the Witch of Endor" and "A Bookseller and a Poet" were painted for Hon. T. H. Perkins. "Miriam on the Shore of the Red Sea," a magnificent work, with figures nearly life-size, was executed for Hon. David Sears. The "Angel appearing to Peter in Prison" was painted for Dr. Hooper. A landscape and exquisite ideal portrait, finished for Hon. Jonathan Phillips, were destroyed in the great fire of 1872. "Rosalie," an ideal portrait, was painted for Hon. N. Appleton. "The Valentine," another ideal subject, became the property of Professor Ticknor. "Amy Robsart" was done for John A. Lowell, Esq. Besides these the painter executed works for Hon. Jonathan Mason, N. Amory, F. C. Gray, Richard Sullivan, Loammi Baldwin, — for whom the exquisite "Florimel" of Spenser was painted, — Theodore Lyman, Samuel A. Eliot, Warren Dutton, and others. This catalogue will serve to show who were Allston's patrons. For each subject the price varied from seven to fifteen hundred dollars. About 1830 a number of Boston gentlemen advanced the artist $10,000 for his unfinished "Belshazzar."

## CHAPTER IX.

### A DAY AT HARVARD.

"Ye fields of Cambridge, our dear Cambridge, say
Have you not seen us walking every day?
Was there a tree about which did not know
The love betwixt us two?"

CAMBRIDGE seems to realize the injunction of a sagacious
statesman of antiquity: "If you would have your city
loved by its citizens, you must make it lovely."

The location of this settlement was, according to Governor
Dudley, due to apprehensions of the French, which caused the
colonists to seek an inland situation. They decided to call it
Newtown, but in 1638 the name was changed in honor of the
old English university town. Cambridge was made a port
of entry in 1805, hence Cambridgeport. It became a city
in 1846.

The broad, level plain where Winthrop, Dudley, Bradstreet,
and the rest bivouacked in the midst of the stately forest in
1631, and looked upon it as

"That wild where weeds and flowers promiscuous shoot";

where they posted their trusty servants, with lighted match, at
the verge of the encampment, and the moon's rays glittered on
steel cap and corselet; where they nightly folded their herds
within the chain of sentinels, until they had hedged themselves
round about with palisades; where they repeated their simple
prayers and sung their evening hymn; where learning erected
her first temple in the wilderness; and where a host of armed
men sprung forth, Minerva-like, ready for action, — the abode
of the Muses, the domain of Letters, — this is our present walk
among the habitations of the living and the dead.

Old William Wood, author of the first printed account of Massachusetts, says : —

" Newtown was first intended for a city, but upon more serious consideration, it was thought not so fit, being too far from the sea ; being the greatest inconvenience it hath. This is one of the neatest and best compacted towns in New England, having many fair structures, with many handsome contrived streets. The inhabitants most of them are very rich."

Old Cambridge a hundred years after its settlement was, as we have mentioned, the peculiar abode of a dozen wealthy and aristocratic families. Their possessions were as extensive as their purses were long and their loyalty approved. They were of the English Church, were intermarried, and had every tie — social position, blood, politics, religion, and we know not what else — to bind them together in a distinct community. The old Puritan stock had mostly dispersed. Many had passed into Connecticut, others into Boston ; and still others, finding their ancient limits much too narrow, had, in the language of that day, " sat down" in what are now Arlington and Lexington, and were long known distinctively as the " farmers." These latter, with the fragment still adhering to the skirts of the ancient village, had their meeting-house and the College, which they still kept free from heresy, — not, however, without continual watchfulness, nor without attempts on the part of the Episcopalians to obtain a foothold.

It was believed before the Revolution that the Ministry seriously contemplated the firmer establishment of the Church of England by creating bishoprics in the colonies, — a measure which was warmly opposed by the Congregational clergy in and out of the pulpit. Tithes and ceremonials were the bugbears used to stimulate the opposition and arouse the prejudices of the populace. Controversy ran high, and caricatures appeared, in one of which the expected bishop is seen taking refuge on board a departing vessel, while a mob on the wharf is pushing the bark from shore and pelting the unfortunate ecclesiastic with treatises of national law.

The large wooden mansion standing well back from Harvard

APTHORP HOUSE, CAMBRIDGE.

Street, directly opposite Gore Hall, was built by the Rev. East
Apthorp, D. D., son of Charles Apthorp, an eminent Boston
merchant of Welsh descent. It was probably erected in 1761,
the year in which Dr. Apthorp was settled in Cambridge, and
was regarded, on account of its elegance and proximity to the
University, with peculiar distrust by Mayhew and his orthodox
contemporaries. It was thought that if the ministerial plan
was carried out Dr. Apthorp had an eye to the Episcopate, and
Ifis mansion was alluded to as " the palace of one of the humble
successors of the Apostles." So uncomfortable did his antagonists render his ministry, that Dr. Apthorp gave up his charge
and removed to England in the latter part of 1764.

The pleasant old house seems next to have been occupied by
John Borland, a merchant of the capital, who abandoned it on
the breaking out of hostilities, and took refuge in Boston, where
he died the same year (1775) from the effects of a fall.

Under the new order of things the mansion became the
headquarters of the Connecticut troops, with Old Put at their
head, on their arrival at Cambridge, and Putnam probably remained there until after the battle of Bunker Hill. It continued a barrack, occupied by three companies, until finally
cleared and taken possession of by the Committee of Safety,
the then executive authority of the province.

Its next inhabitant was " John Burgoyne, Esquire, lieutenant-general of his Majesty's armies in America, colonel
of the queen's regiment of light dragoons, governor of Fort
William in North Britain, one of the representatives of the
Commons of Great Britain, and commanding an army and fleet
on an expedition from Canada," etc., etc., etc. Such is a faithful enumeration of the titles of this illustrious Gascon as pre-
fixed to his bombastic proclamation, and which must have left
the herald breathless long ere he arrived at the " Whereas."
For a pithy history of the campaign which led to Burgoyne's
enforced residence here, commend us to the poet : —

> " Burgoyne gaed up, like spur an' whip,
>   Till *Fraser* brave did fa', man ;
> Then lost his way ae misty day,
>   In *Saratoga* shaw, man."

The house fronts towards Mount Auburn Street, and overlooked the river when Cambridge was yet a conservative, old-
fashioned country town. That street was then the high-road,
which wound around the foot of the garden, making a sharp
curve to the north where it is now joined by Harvard Street.
It was, therefore, no lack of respect to the Rev. Edward Holyoke, the inhabitant of the somewhat less pretending dwelling
of the College presidents, that caused Dr. Apthorp to turn his
back in his direction.

The true front bears a strong family resemblance to the
Vassall-Longfellow mansion, the design of which was perhaps
followed by the architect of this. The wooden balustrade
which surmounted, and at the same time relieved, the bare
outline of the roof was swept away in the great September gale
of 1815. A third story, which makes the house look like an
ill-assorted pair joined in matrimonial bands for life, is said to
be the work of Mr. Borland, who required additional space for
his household slaves. The line of the old cornice shows where
the roof was separated from the original structure. The position of the outbuildings, now huddled together in close contact with the house, has been changed by the stress of those
circumstances which have from time to time denuded the estate
of portions of its ancient belongings. The clergyman's grounds
extended to Holyoke Street on the one hand, and for an equal
distance on the other, and were entered by the carriage-drive
from the side of Harvard Street.

As it now stands, about equidistant from the avenues in
front and rear, it seems a patrician of the old *régime*, withdraw-
ing itself instinctively from contact with its upstart neighbors.
The house which John Adams's apprehensions converted into a
Lambeth Palace was, happily for its occupant, never the seat
of an Episcopal see, or it might have shared the fate with which
Wat Tyler's bands visited the ancient castellated residence of
the Archbishops of Canterbury.

We found the interior of the house worthy of inspection.
There is a broad, generous hall, with its staircase railed in with
the curiously wrought balusters, which the taste of the times

required to be different in form and design. A handsome reception-room opens at the left, a library at the right. The former was the state apartment, and a truly elegant one. The ceilings are high, and the wainscots, panels, and mouldings were enriched with carvings. The fireplace has still the blue Dutch tiles with their Scripture allegories, and the ornamental fire-back is in its place.

Directly above is the state chamber, a luxurious apartment within and without. We say without, for we looked down upon the gardens, with their box-bordered walks and their unfolding beauties of leaf and flower, — the fruit-trees dressed in bridal blossoms, the *Pyrus Japonica* in its gorgeous crimson bloom, with white-starred *Spiræa* and *Deutzia gracilis* enshrouded in their fragrant mists.

> " A brave old house ! a garden full of bees,
> Large dropping poppies, and queen hollyhocks,
> With butterflies for crowns, — tree peonies,
> And pinks and goldilocks."

In this bedchamber, which wooed the slumbers of the sybarite Burgoyne, the walls are formed in panels, ornamented with paper representing fruit, landscapes, ruins, etc., — a species of decoration both rare and costly at the period when the house was built. Mr. Jonathan Simpson, Jr., who married a daughter of Mr. Borland, became the proprietor after the old war. Mrs. Manning, a later occupant, had lived to see many changes from her venerable roof, and the prediction that her prospect would never be impaired answered by the overtopping walls of contiguous buildings.

We crave the reader's indulgence while we return for a moment upon our own footsteps to Dana Hill, upon which we have hitherto traced the defensive lines. The family for whom the eminence is named have been distinguished in law, politics, and letters, — from Richard Dana, of pre-Revolutionary fame, to his descendants of to-day.

The Dana mansion, surrounded by beautiful grounds, formerly stood some two hundred feet back from the present Main Street, and between Ellery and Dana Streets. It was a

wooden house, of two stories, not unlike in general appearance
that of Mr. Longfellow, but was many years since destroyed
by fire.

Judge Francis Dana, a law-student with Trowbridge, and
who was succeeded as chief justice of Massachusetts by Theophilus Parsons, filled many positions of high trust and responsibility both at home and abroad.   The name of Ellery Street
happily recalls that of the family of Mrs. Judge Dana.   With
the career of Richard H. Dana, poet and essayist, son of the
judge, and with that of the younger Richard H. and Edmund
his brother, grandsons of the jurist, the public are familiar.

When William Ellery Channing was an undergraduate he
resided in the family mansion of the Danas, the wife of the

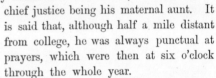
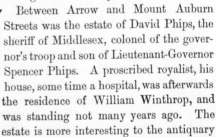

chief justice being his maternal aunt.   It
is said that, although half a mile distant
from college, he was always punctual at
prayers, which were then at six o'clock
through the whole year.

Between Arrow and Mount Auburn
Streets was the estate of David Phips, the
sheriff of Middlesex, colonel of the governor's troop and son of Lieutenant-Governor
Spencer Phips.   A proscribed royalist, his
house, some time a hospital, was afterwards
the residence of William Winthrop, and
was standing not many years ago.   The
estate is more interesting to the antiquary

GOOKIN.

as that of Major-General Daniel Gookin, Indian superintendent
in the time of Eliot, and one of the licensers of the printing-
press in 1662, — an office supposed not to have been too arduous
in his time, and not considered compatible with liberty in our
own.   What this old censor would have said to many of the
so-called respectable publications of to-day is not a matter of
doubtful conjecture.   It was under Gookin's roof, and perhaps
on this very spot, that Generals Goffe and Whalley were sheltered until the news of the Restoration and Act of Indemnity
caused them to seek another asylum.

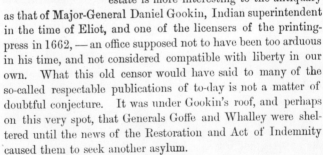

The large, square wooden house at the corner of Harvard and Quincy Streets, and which stands upon the extreme limit of the College grounds in this direction, was the first observatory at Harvard. It long continued the residence of Rev. Dr. Peabody, chaplain of the College. William Cranch Bond, subsequently professor of astronomy, was a skilful optician, who had, from innate love of the science of the heavens, established a small observatory of his own in Dorchester, where he pursued his investigations. He was invited to Harvard, and, with the aid of such instruments as could be obtained, founded in this house what has since grown to be a credit to the University and to America. He had the assistance of some of the professors, and of President Hill and others. Triangular points were established in connection with this position at Milton Hill and at Bunker Hill. It was the intention to have erected an observatory on Milton Hill, but difficulties of a financial character interposed, and President Quincy purchased Craigie Hill, the present excellent location.

We are now trenching upon classic ground. We have passed the sites of the old parsonage of the first parish, built in 1670, and in which all the ministers, from Mr. Mitchell to Dr. Holmes, resided, taken down in 1843 ; the traditional Fellows' Orchard, on a corner of which now stands Gore Hall ; the homes of Stephen Sewall, first Hancock Professor, and of the Professors Wigglesworth, long since demolished or removed, to find all these former landmarks included within the College grounds.

If the reader obeys our instincts he will not fail to turn aside and wend his way to the Library, erected in 1839 – 42, through the munificence of Governor Gore, enlarged by the addition of a wing in 1877. Within are the busts of

> " Those dead but sceptred sovereigns, who still rule
> Our spirits from their urns."

The cabinets of precious manuscripts, some of them going before the art of printing, and almost putting it to blush with their beautifully illuminated pages ; the alcoves, inscribed with

the benefactors' names, and garnered with the thoughts and
deeds of centuries, — each a storehouse of many busy brains,
and each contributing to the aggregate of human knowledge ; —
all these seemed like so many ladened hives of human patience,
industry, and, perchance, of ill-requited toil.

GORE HALL, 1873.

Here is your dainty fellow in rich binding, glittering in gold
title, and swelling with importance, — a parvenu among books.
You see it is but little consulted, — the verdict of condemnation.   Here is a Body of Divinity, once belonging to Samuel
Parris, first minister of Danvers, in whose family witchcraft
had its beginning in 1692.   His name is on the fly-leaf, the
ink scarcely faded, while his bones have long since mouldered.
Truly, we apprehend such bulky bodies must have sadly lacked
soul!   Many of Hollis's books are on the shelves, beautifully
bound, and stamped with the owner's opinions of their merits
by placing the owl, his family emblem, upside down when he
wished to express his disapproval.

Somehow we cannot take the book of an author, known

or unknown, from its accustomed place without becoming as deeply contemplative as was ever Hamlet over the skull of Yorick, or without thinking that each sentence may have been distilled from an overworked, thought-compressed brain. But if one laborer faints and falls out of the ranks, twenty arise to take his place, and still the delvers in the mine follow the alluring vein, and still the warfare against ignorance goes on.

The library was originally deposited in Old Harvard, which was destroyed by fire on the 24th January, 1764, and with it the College library, consisting of about five thousand volumes of printed books and many invaluable manuscripts. The philosophical apparatus was also lost. This was a severe and irreparable blow to the College, for the books given by John Harvard, the founder, Sir Kenelm Digby, Sir John Maynard, Dr. Lightfoot, Dr. Gale, Bishop Berkely, and the first Thomas Hollis, together with the Greek and Hebrew types belonging to the College, perished in the flames. Only a single volume of the donation of Harvard remains from the fire. Its title is "Douname's Christian Warfare."

A picture of the library as it existed before this accident is given by a visitor to the College in 1750 : —

"The library is very large and well stored with books but much abused by frequent use. The repository of curiosities which was not over well stock'd. Saw 2 Human Skellitons a peice Neigro's hide tan'd &c. Hornes and bones of land and sea animals, fishes, skins of different animals stuff'd &c. The skull of a Famous Indian Warrior, where was also the moddell of the Boston Man of Warr of 40 Gunns compleatly rig'd &c."

We can only indulge in vain regrets that so many valuable collections relative to New England history have been swept away. The fire which destroyed Boston Town House in 1747; the mobs which pillaged the house of Governor Hutchinson, and also the Admiralty archives ; the mutilation of the invaluable Prince library stored in the tower of the Old South, of the destruction of which Dr. Belknap related that he was a witness, and which was used from day to day to kindle the fires of the vandal soldiery ; the plunder of the Court of Common Pleas by the same lawless soldiery, — all have added to the havoc among our early chronicles, which the conflagration at Harvard assisted to make a lamentably conspicuous funeral-pyre to learning.

After the fire the library was renewed by contributions, among the most valuable of which was the gift of a considerable part of Governor Bernard's private library. John Hancock was the donor, in 1772, of a large number of books, and also of a carpet for the floor and paper for the walls. The library and apparatus were packed up on the day before the battle of Bunker Hill, under the care of Samuel Phillips, assisted by Thompson, afterwards Count Rumford, and removed, first to Andover, and a part subsequently to Concord, to which place the government and many of the students had retired. Many of the books, however, were probably scattered in private hands, as we find President Langdon advertising for the return of the apparatus and library to Mr. Winthrop, the librarian, early in 1778.

Here are works on which the writers have expended a lifetime of patient research, and which are highly prized by scholars ; but their laborious composition has failed to meet such reward as would keep even the body and soul of an author together. And here are yet others that have struck the fickle chord of transient popular favor, requiting their makers with golden showers, and perhaps advancement to high places of honor. In our own day it is literary buffoonery that pays the best. Once master the secret how " to set the table in a roar," be it never so wisely, and we warrant you success. Perhaps it is because, as a people, we laugh too little that we are willing to pay so well for a little of the scanty wit and a good deal of the chalk and sawdust of the circus.

Among other treasures which the library contains is a copy of Eliot's Indian Bible, the first Bible printed on the continent of America, perhaps in the Indian College, certainly on Samuel Green's Cambridge press, though where this press was set up diligent inquiry has failed to enlighten us. In 1720, as we gather from an English authority, the press was kept either in Harvard or Stoughton, the only two buildings then existing.

Last, but not least, we have chanced on Father Rale's Dictionary of the Abenaquis, captured, with the priest's strong-box, at Norridgewock, in 1721. Sebastian Rale exercised great influence over the eastern Indians, among whom he resided after his coming to Canada in 1689. This influence, which was exerted on behalf of the French, by exciting the Indians to commit depredations upon the frontier settlements of the English, caused an attempt to be made to seize Rale at his house at Norridgewock by a party led by Colonel Westbrook. The priest escaped, but his strong-box was taken, and in it were found the letters of M. de Vaudreuil, Governor of Canada, which exhibited Rale in the light of a political agent.

This attempt was retaliated by the Indians, and Lovewell's War ensued. In 1724 Norridgewock was surprised and Rale killed, refusing, it is alleged, the quarter offered him. Rale was slain near a cross which he had erected near the middle of the village, and with him some Indians who endeavored to defend him. The father went boldly forth to meet his enemies, and died, like a martyr, at the foot of the cross. He was scalped, his chapel destroyed, and the plate and furniture of the altar, with the devotional flag, brought away as trophies. The strong-box passed into the possession of the family of Colonel Westbrook, the commander of the Eastern forces. The story is harrowing, but true.

All the librarians have been noted men. John Langdon Sibley had presided over it since 1856, with previous service as assistant for many years after his graduation in 1825. Himself a scholar, and an author whose energies have been chiefly exerted in behalf of his Alma Mater, his long experience had made of him a living encyclopedia, with brain arranged in pigeon-holes and alcoves, and where the information accumulated for so many studious years was always at command, — not pressed and laid away to moulder in its living receptacle.

The idea of a secure depository for the College library originated in an attempt, in April, 1829, to blow up Harvard Hall.

Leaving the castellated granite Library, the first attempt at architectural display these precincts knew, we pass on to the ancient dwelling-place of the governors of the College, known as the President's House.

It is a venerable gambrel-roofed structure, of no mean consideration in its day, and certainly an object remarkable enough for its antiquated appearance, standing, as it does, solitary and alone, of all its companions that once stretched along the lane. A tall elm at its back, another at its side, droop over it lovingly and tenderly. These are all that remain of a number planted by President Willard, the exigencies of improvement having cut off a portion of the grounds in front, now turned into the street.

The house is of two stories, with a chimney at either end, and a straggling collection of buildings at its back, which the necessities of various occupants have called into being. It was literally the habitation of the presidents of the College for a hundred and twenty years, beginning with Benjamin Wadsworth, minister of the First Church in Boston, and son of the old Indian fighter, for whom it was erected. The entry from the President's MS. book, in the College Library, which follows, fixes the date with precision : —

" The President's House to dwell in was raised May 24, 1726. No life was lost nor person hurt in raising it ; thanks be to God for his preserving goodness. In y* evening those who raised y* House, had a supper in y* Hall ; after wch we sang y* first stave or staff in y* 127 Psalm.

" 27 Oct. 1726. This night some of our family lodged at y* New House built for y* President; Nov. 4 at night was y* first time y* my wife and I lodg'd there. The house was not half finished within."

Miss Eliza Susan Quincy, daughter of President Quincy, who resided in this house for sixteen years, has lately given the annexed description of the old mansion.* She says : —

" My sketch represents the house as Washington saw it, except that there were only two windows on each side the porch in the

* Charles Deane, in Mass. Hist. Society's Proceedings.

PRESIDENT'S HOUSE, CAMBRIDGE.

lowest story. The enlargement of the dining and drawing rooms, which added a third, was subsequently made under the direction of Treasurer Storer, as his daughter informed me. The room in the rear of the drawing-room, on the right hand as you enter, was the President's study, until the presidency of Webber, when the end of the house was added, with a kitchen and chamber and dressing-room, very commodiously arranged, I was told, under the direction of Mrs. Webber. The brick building was built at the same time for the President's study and Freshman's room beneath it, and for the preservation of the college manuscripts. I went over the house with my father and mother and President Kirkland, soon after his accession. As there were no regular records kept during his presidency of eighteen years, he did not add much to the manuscripts. We then little imagined that we should be the next occupants of the mansion, should repair and arrange the house under Mrs. Quincy's direction, and reside in it sixteen very happy years. I regret its present dilapidated state, and rejoice, in view of ' the new departure,' as it is termed, that I sketched the antiquities and old mansions of Old Cambridge."

The brick building alluded to, and which now joins the ex treme rear additions, formerly stood on the left-hand side of the mansion as the spectator faces it, and communicated with it. This part was built under the supervision of President Webber, and was, in 1871, removed to its present situation. It is now the office of the College Steward.

Probably no private mansion in America has seen so many illustrious personages under its roof-tree as the President's House. Besides its occu- pancy by Wadsworth, Holyoke, Locke, Langdon, Willard, Webber, Kirkland, Quincy, and Everett, the royal governors have assembled there on successive anniver- saries, and no distinguished traveller passed its door without paying his respects to the administration for the time being. No doubt the eccentric Dr. Witherspoon broke bread at the table of Holyoke when he visited Boston in the memorable year 1768.

WILLARD.

The office of president, though for a long time, either through policy or parsimony, a dependent one, was always an eminent mark of distinction, and its possessor was regarded — outside the College walls at least, if not always within — with veneration and respect. The earlier incumbents were men who had acquired great influence for their piety and learning as teachers

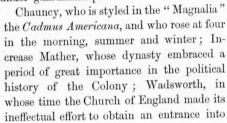

CHAUNCY.

of the people, whose spiritual and temporal wants were in those primitive days equally under guardianship.

Chauncy, who is styled in the "Magnalia" the *Cadmus Americana*, and who rose at four in the morning, summer and winter ; Increase Mather, whose dynasty embraced a period of great importance in the political history of the Colony ; Wadsworth, in whose time the Church of England made its ineffectual effort to obtain an entrance into the government ; Holyoke, whose term is memorable as the longest of the series ; and Langdon, who left his office at the dictation of a cabal of students, — all are honored names, and part of the history of their times.

Upon the coming of General Washington to Cambridge the Provincial Congress assigned the President's House for his use, not because it was the best by many the place could afford, but probably because it was the only one then unoccupied by the provincial forces or their military adjuncts. The house not being in readiness when the General arrived, on the 2d of July, 1775, he availed himself, temporarily, of another situation, and within a week indicated his preference for the Vassall House, which he had not passed down the old Watertown road without observing. There is no conclusive evidence that the General ever occupied the President's House, and the absence of any tradition involves it in doubt.

Washington made a passing visit to Cambridge in 1789, and was welcomed on behalf of the governors of the College by President Willard. He was then accompanied by Tobias Lear, who had owed his confidential position as Washington's secretary to the good offices of Willard.

With President Willard departed the day of big wigs at the President's House. He always appeared abroad in the full-bottomed white periwig sanctioned by the custom of the times; this was exchanged in the study for a velvet cap, such as adorn the heads of some of the portraits in Old Massachusetts Hall.

It is related that when Congress was sitting in New York, during Washington's term, President Willard visited that place. It chanced that he wore his full-bottomed wig, which attracted so great a crowd when he walked about as to occasion on his part apprehensions of ill usage from the mob. With what satisfaction he must have shaken off the dust of that barbarous city, where the sight of his periwig aroused a curiosity akin to that exhibited by the Goths when they beheld the long white beards of the Roman senators.

In Willard's time a club of gentlemen were accustomed to assemble at his house on certain evenings, of which, besides the President and resident professors, Judge Dana, Governor Gerry, Mr. Craigie, Mr. Gannett, and others, were members. Bachelors were excluded, which caused Judge Winthrop, the former librarian and one of the tabooed, to say they met to talk over their grievances.

President Kirkland, an elegant scholar and most fascinating companion, was noted for his pithy sayings as well as for his wit. On one occasion an ambitious young fellow, who had a pretty good opinion of himself, having asked the Doctor at what age a man would be justified in becoming an author, replied, "Wait until you are forty; after that you will never print anything." To a student who observed in his presence that dress of itself was of little consequence, he made this shrewd remark : "There are many things which there is no particular merit in doing, but which there is positive demerit in leaving undone."

The rare abilities of Dr. Kirkland make it a never-failing regret that he was by nature indolent, and indisposed to call into action the full powers of his mind, or to bring forward his reserves of information except in brilliant conversation. He talked apparently without effort, and could unite the merest minutes of a discourse with little or no preparation and with marvellous address.

President Kirkland is described as of middling stature, portly, with fair complexion, a round and comely face, with blue eyes, a small mouth, regular and beautiful teeth, and a countenance noble, frank, and intelligent.

Josiah Quincy, after an active political life, became President in 1849. During his occupancy of the chair Gore Hall was built, and the security of the library, which had given him much solicitude, was assured against ordinary contingencies. The sixteen years of Mr. Quincy's administration were a period of great usefulness and prosperity to the College. In 1840 the President published his History of Harvard University, — a work of much value, in which he was assisted by his daughter, Eliza, a lady whose culture and tastes eminently qualified her for the work.

Mr. Everett's excessive sensitiveness contributed to make his contact with so many young and turbulent spirits at times disquieting. His elegant, classic diction and superb manner have gained for him an enviable name as an orator. He would never, if possible, speak extemporaneously, but carefully prepared and committed his addresses. His mind was quick to grasp any circumstance and turn it to account; the simile of a drop of water, used by him with much force, occurred to him, it is said, through the dropping from a leak over his head while performing his morning ablutions. Similarly, while once on his way to deliver an address at Williams College, he happened to pass the night at Stockbridge, where a gentleman exhibited to him the watch of Baron Dieskau. The next day this little relic furnished the theme for a beautiful passage, into which the defeat of Dieskau and the death of Colonel Williams, on the same field, were effectively interwoven.

Rev. Sydney Smith, with whom Mr. Everett passed some time in Somersetshire, thus spoke of him : —

" He made upon us the same impression he appears to make universally in this country. We thought him (a character which the English always receive with affectionate regard) an amiable American, republican without rudeness, and accomplished without ostentation. 'If I had known that gentleman five years ago (said one of my guests), I should have been deep in the American funds ; and, as it is, I think at times that I see nineteen or twenty shillings in the pound in his face.' "

Increase Mather was the first person to receive the degree of Doctor of Divinity from Harvard. When he became President he refused to accede to the requirement that the President should reside at Cambridge, and finally resigned rather than comply with it. Vice-President Willard is the only person who has administered the affairs of the College under that title, which was assumed to evade the rule of residence, and to enable him to continue his functions as pastor of the Old South, Boston.

It was Increase Mather, then (1700) President, who ordered Robert Calef's " wicked book "— a satire on witchcraft, entitled " More Wonders of the Invisible World," and printed in London — burnt in the College yard, and the members of the reverend Doctor's church (*The Old North*) published a defence of their pastors, Increase and Cotton Mather, called " *Truth will come off Conqueror.*" This publication proved even a greater satire than Calef's, as the authors were erelong but too glad to disavow all sympathy with the wretched superstition.

The President's chair, an ancient relic, used in the College, from an indefinite time, for conferring degrees, is preserved in Gore Hall. Report represents it to have been brought to the College during the presidency of Holyoke as the gift of Rev. Ebenezer Turell. It has a triangular seat, and belongs to the earliest specimens of our ancestors' domestic furniture.

In Dunster Street we salute the name of the first President of the College, whose habitation, it is conjectured, stood near. It was at first called Water Street, and in it were situated the first church erected in Newtown, which stood on the west side, a little south of the intersection of Mount Auburn Street, upon land formerly owned by Thaddeus M. Harris, and also the house of Thomas Dudley, the deputy of Governor Winthrop, whose extravagance in ornamenting his habitation with a wain-

scot made of clapboards the latter reproved. At the foot of
Water Street was the old ferry by which communication was
had with the opposite shore.

The old meeting-house stood till about 1650, when the town
took order for building a new church on the Watch House Hill,
of which presently. A vote of the town in the year mentioned
directs the repair of the old house " with a 4 square roofe and
covered with shingle." The new house was to be forty foot
square, covered in the same manner as was directed for the old,
the repair of which was discontinued, and the land belonging
to it sold in 1651.

Dudley, the tough old soldier of *Henri Quatre*, with whom
he had fought at the siege of Amiens in 1597, with a captain's
commission from Queen Bess, finally settled in Roxbury, and
left a name that has been honored in his descendants. His
house stood on the west side of Water Street, near its southern
termination at Marsh Lane. Governor Belcher says : " It was
wrote of him,

> ' Here lies Thomas Dudley that trusty old stud,
> A bargain 's a bargain and must be made good.' "

A brief glance at the topography of our surroundings will
enable the reader to understand in what way the Englishmen
laid out what they intended for their capital town. They first
reserved a square for a market-place, after the manner of the
old English towns. This is the present Harvard Square, upon
which the College grounds abut, and in its midst was perhaps
placed a central *milliarium*, which marked the home points of
the converging roads. The plain, as level as a calm sea, admitted the laying out of the town in squares, the streets crossing each other at right angles. Between the market-place and
the river were erected the principal houses of the settlement,
and some of the oldest now standing in Cambridge will be
found in this locality.

We have noticed the ferry. About 1660 this was superseded by "the great bridge," rebuilt in 1690, and standing at
the Revolution in its present situation at the foot of Boylston

Street. Over this bridge came Earl Percy with his reinforcement on that eventful morning in April which dissolved the
British empire in America. The people, having notice of his
approach, removed the "leaves" or flooring of the bridge, but,
as they were not conveyed to any distance, they were soon
found and replaced by the Earl's troops. A draw was made in
the bridge at Washington's request in 1775.

The street leading from the market-place to the bridge was
the principal in the town for a long period, it being in the
direct route of travel from Boston *via* Roxbury and Little Cambridge (Brighton) to what is now Lexington, and from the
capital again by Charlestown Ferry to the Colleges, and thence
by the bridge to Brookline and the southward.

It was intended to make Newtown a fortified place, and a
levy was made on the several towns for this purpose. Rev.
Abiel Holmes, writing in 1800, says : —

"This fortification was actually made, and the fosse which was
then dug around the town is, in some places, visible to this day. It
commenced at Brick Wharf (originally called Windmill Hill) and
ran along the northern side of the present Common in Cambridge,
and through what was then a thicket, but now constitutes a part of
the cultivated grounds of Mr. Nathaniel Jarvis, beyond which it
cannot be distinctly traced. It enclosed above one thousand acres."

The road to Watertown, now Brattle Street, and formerly
the great highway to the south and west, left the market-place,
as now, by the rear of the English Church, but communicated
also more directly with Charlestown road by the north side of
the Common. It was by this road that Washington arrived
in Cambridge and the army marched to New York. By it,
also, Burgoyne's troops reached their designated camps. The
reader will go over it with us hereafter. All these particulars
are deemed essential to a comprehension of the military operations of the siege of Boston when Cambridge was an intrenched
camp.

Not far from the Square, and on the west side of Boylston
Street, is the site of Ebenezer Bradish's tavern, of repute in
Revolutionary times. Its situation near the bridge was com-

patible with the convenience of travellers ; nor was it too remote from the College halls for the requirements of the students
when Latin classics became too dry, and Euclid too dull for
human endurance.   Many, we will venture to say, were the
plump, big-bellied Dutch bottles smuggled from mine host's
into Old Harvard, Massachusetts, or Stoughton.   Bradish kept
a livery too, which was no doubt well patronized by the collegians, though here he encountered some disgrace by letting
his horses to David Phips to carry off the province cannon at
Gage's behest.   Bradish seems, however, to have been well
affected to the patriot cause.   His inn was long the only one
in the town, and had the honor of entertaining Generals Burgoyne, Philips, and the principal British officers on their first
arrival in Cambridge.   This tavern, also later known as Porter's,
was for a time the annual resort of the Senior Class of the College on Class Day, for a dinner and final leave-taking of all
academical exercises.   Bradish's was the rendezvous of Rufus
Putnam's regiment in 1777.

The first publican in Old Cambridge was Andrew Belcher,
an ancestor of the governor of that name, who was licensed in
1652 " to sell beare and bread, for entertainment of strangers
and the good of the towne."   It is at least a coincidence that a
Belcher still dispenses rather more dainty viands in the same
locality.

It is a relief to find that in the year 1750 there were some
convivial and even thirsty souls about, as we learn from the
journal of a rollicking sea-captain, who was having his ship
repaired at Boston while he indulged in a run on shore : —

" Being now ready to Sale I determined to pay my way in time,
which I accordingly did at M$^{rs}$ Graces at the Request of M$^r$ Heyleg-
her and the Other Gentlemen Gave them a Good Supper with Wine
and Arack Punch Galore, where Exceeding Merry Drinking Toasts
Singing Roaring &c. untill Morning when Could Scarce see One
another being Blinded by the Wine Arack &c. we where in all ab$^t$ 20
in comp$^y$."

The tavern bills of the General Court in 1768 – 69 would
astonish the ascetics of Beacon Hill.   We remark a great dis-

parity between the quantity of fluids and edibles. In a document now before us eighty dinners are flanked with one hundred and thirty-six bowls of punch, twenty-one bottles of sherry, and brandy at discretion. Truly! we are tempted to exclaim with Prince Hal on reading the bill of Falstaff's supper, —

"O monstrous! but one half-pennyworth of bread to this intolerable deal of sack,"

What, then, would Prince Hal have said to a bill of your modern alderman?

Returning into the Square, we continue our peregrinations around the College enclosure. As you turn towards the Common, in approaching from Harvard Street, you pass over the spot whereon the second edifice of the first church was erected. A little elevation which formerly existed here is supposed to have been the Watch-house Hill, before mentioned, and later called Meeting-house Hill. In 1706 the third church was erected on this ground, and in 1756 the fourth house was raised, somewhat nearer Dane Hall. This church was taken down in 1833, when the site became the property of the College.

In the meeting-house which stood here the First Provincial Congress held their session in 1774, after their adjournment from Salem and Concord. The Congress first met in the old Court House on the 17th of October, but immediately adjourned to the meeting-house, of which Rev. Nathaniel Appleton was then pastor, and who officiated as their chaplain. This was the period of the Port Act, and the crisis of the country. The Congress was earnestly engaged in measures for the relief of the distressed and embargoed town of Boston, the formation of an army, a civil administration, and other revolutionary measures. Here was made the organization of the celebrated minutemen, the appointment of Jedediah Preble, Artemas Ward, and Seth Pomeroy as general officers; and of the famous Revolutionary committee of nine, of which Hancock, Warren, Church, Devens, White, Palmer, Quincy, Watson, and Orne were members. This body, called the Committee of Safety, wielded the executive power, and in the recess of Congress were vested with almost dictatorial authority. The members of the Second Continental Congress were also chosen at this time.

Space does not permit us to linger among those giants who welded the Old Thirteen together with the fire of their eloquence. One incident must have created no little sensation in an assembly of which probably a majority were slaveholders. A letter was brought into the Congress directed to Rev. Dr. Appleton, which was read. It represented the propriety while Congress was engaged in efforts to free themselves and the people from slavery, that it should also take into consideration the state and circumstances of the negro slaves in the province. After some debate the question " was allowed to subside."

> " A ! freedome is a nobill thing!
> Freedome mayse man to haiff liking!
> Freedome all solace to man giffis;
> He levys at ese that frely levys!
> A noble hart may haiff nane ese,
> Na ellys nocht that may him plese,
> Gyff fredome failythe ; for fre liking
> Is yearnyt our all other thing
> Na he, that ay hase levyt fre,
> May nocht knaw well the propryte,
> The angyr, na the wretchyt dome,
> That is cowplyt to foul thryldome."

In the olden time people were summoned to church by beat of drum, — until a bell was procured, a harsh and discordant appeal for the assembly of a peaceful congregation, — but those were the days of the church militant. On the contrary, our grandsires, whose ears were not attuned to the sound, could as little endure the roll of British drums near their sanctuaries on a Sabbath morn, as could the poet the clangor of the bell of Tron-Kirk which he so rudely apostrophized : —

> " Oh! were I provost o' the town,
> I swear by a' the powers aboon,
> I 'd bring ye wi' a reesle down ;
>         Nor should you think
> (So sair I 'd crack and clour your crown)
>         Again to clink."

The old Court House, which has been named in connection with the Henley trial, stood at first bodily within the Square, but was later removed to the site of the present Lyceum building, and perhaps is even now existing in its rear, where it is utilized for workshops. It was built in 1756, and continued to be used by the courts until the proprietors of Lechmere Point obtained their removal to that location by the offer of a large bonus. The old wooden jail stood at the southwest corner of the Square, and was but little used for the detention of criminals after the erection of the stone jail at Concord in 1789. The Court House witnessed the trials of many notable causes, and furnished the law-students of the University with a real theatre, of which they were in the habit of availing themselves.

As late as 1665 declarations and summonses were published by sound of trumpet. The crier opened the court in the king's name, and the judges and barristers in scarlet robes, gown, and wig, inspired the spectator with a wholesome sense of the majesty of the law. The usual form of a document was "To all Xtian people Greeting."

Under the first charter, or patent as it was usually called, the Governor and Assistants were the sole depositaries of all power, whether legislative, executive, or judicial. When the patent was silent the Scriptures were consulted as the proper guide. The ministers and elders were, in all new exigencies, the expounders of the law, which was frequently made for the occasion and applied without hesitation. The cause of complaint was briefly stated, and there were no pleadings. Hutchinson says, that for more than the first ten years the parties spoke for themselves, sometimes assisted, if the cause was weighty, by a *patron*, or man of superior abilities, but without fee or reward. The jury — and this marks the simplicity of the times — were allowed by law, if not satisfied with the opinion of the court, "*to consult any by-stander.*" Such were the humble beginnings of our courts of law.

The following is extracted from the early laws of Massachusetts : —

" Everie marryed woeman shall be free from bodilie correction or stripes by her husband, unlesse it be in his owne defence upon her assalt. If there be any just cause of correction complaint shall be made to Authoritie assembled in some court, from which onely she shall receive it."

The common law of England authorized the infliction of chastisement on a wife with a reasonable instrument. It is related that Judge Buller, charging a jury in such a case, said, " Without undertaking to define exactly what a reasonable instrument is, I hold, gentlemen of the jury, that a stick no bigger than my thumb comes clearly within that description." It is further reported that a committee of ladies waited on him the next day, to beg that they might be favored with the exact dimensions of his lordship's thumb.

Dane Hall, which bears the name of that eminent jurist and statesman through whose bounty it arose, was erected in 1832 and enlarged in 1845. The south foundation-wall of Dane is the same as the north wall of the old meeting-house, so that Law and Divinity rest here upon a common base.

The first law-professorship was established through the bequest of Isaac Royall, the Medford loyalist, who gave by his will more than two thousand acres of land in the towns of Granby and Royalston for this purpose. In 1815 Hon. Isaac Parker, Chief Justice of the Supreme Court, was appointed first professor, and in 1817, at his suggestion, a law school was established. Judge Parker's lectures were delivered in what was then known as the Philosophy Chamber, in Harvard Hall. Both the Law and Divinity Schools were established during Dr. Kirkland's presidency. It is worthy of mention that the first doctorate of laws was conferred on Washington for his expulsion of the British from Boston.

Nathan Dane, LL. D., a native of Ipswich and graduate of Harvard, is justly remembered as the framer, while in Congress, of the celebrated " Ordinance of 1787 " for the government of the territory northwest of the Ohio, by which slavery was excluded from that immense region. In 1829 the Law School was reorganized through the liberality of Mr. Dane, who had offered a competent sum for a professorship, with the right of nominating the first incumbent. The person who had been selected for the occupancy of the chair was Joseph Story, whose fame as a jurist had culminated on the Supreme Bench of the United States.

Judge Story remained in the Dane Professorship until his death in 1845, a period of sixteen years. It is believed that his life was shortened by his prodigious intellectual labors and the demands made upon him for various kinds of literary work. As a writer he belonged to the intense school, if such a characterization be admissible, and this mental tension appeared in the quick changes of his countenance and in his nervous movements as well as in the rapidity of his pen. A great talker, he never lacked interested auditors; for his was a mind of colossal stamp, and he never wanted language to give utterance to his thoughts.

The first settlers in Massachusetts Bay did not recognize the law of England any further than it suited their interests. The common law does not appear, says Sullivan, to have been regarded under the old patent, nor for many years after the Charter of 1692. In 1647 the first importation of law books was made; it comprised, —

2 copies of Sir Edward Coke on Littleton,
2    "    of the Book of Entries,
2    "    of Sir Edward Coke on Magna Charta,
2    "    of the New Terms of the Law,
2    "    of Dalton's Justice of the Peace,
2    "    of Sir Edward Coke's Reports.

This was four years after the division of the Colony of Massachusetts Bay into four shires. Norfolk included that part of the present county of Essex north of the Merrimac, and also the settled part of New Hampshire.

There were attorneys here about ten years after the settlement. Lechford, who came over in 1631, and returned to England in 1641, where he published a pamphlet called "Plain Dealing," says that "every church member was a bishop, and, not inclining to become one himself, he could not be admitted a freeman among them ; that the General Court and Quarter Sessions exercised all the powers of King's Bench, Common Pleas, Chancery, High Commission, Star Chamber, and of all the other courts of England." For some offence Lechford, debarred from pleading and deprived of practice, returned to England, to bear witness against the colonial magistrates. But from other authority than Lechford's, we know that the distinction between freeman and non-freeman, members and nonmembers, appeared as striking to new-comers as that between Cavalier and Roundhead in Old England.

In 1687, almost sixty years from the first settlement of this country, there were but two attorneys in Massachusetts. The noted crown agent, Randolph, wrote to a friend in England, in that year, as follows : —

"I have wrote you the want we have of two or three *honest attorneys*, if there be any such thing in Nature. We have but two ; one is Mr. West's creature, — came with him from New York, and drives all before him. He takes *extravagant fees*, and for want of more, the country cannot avoid coming to him."

The other appears to have been George Farewell, who said in open court in Charlestown that all causes must be brought to Boston, because there were not honest men enough in Middlesex to make a jury to serve their turns.

Our two oldest Universities have never displayed a political bias like Oxford and Cambridge in Old England, where the distinction between Whig and Tory was so marked that when George I. gave his library to Cambridge, the following epigram appeared : —

> " King George observing with judicious eyes
> The state of both his Universities,
> To Oxford sent a troop of horse ; for why ?
> That learned body wanted loyalty.
> To Cambridge books he sent, as well discerning
> How much that loyal body wanted learning."

## CHAPTER X.

### A DAY AT HARVARD, CONTINUED.

" It will be proved to thy face that thou hast men about thee that usually talk of a noun and a verb, and such abominable words." — *Jack Cade.*

THE Marquis of Wellesley is accredited with having said to an American, "Establishing a seminary in New England at so early a period of time hastened your revolution half a century." This was a shrewd observation, and aptly supplements the forecast of the commissioners of Charles II., who said, in their report, made about 1666 : —

" It may be feared this collidg may afford as many scismaticks to the Church, and the Corporation as many rebells to the King, as formerly they have done if not timely prevented."

The earliest contemporary account of the founding of the College is found in a tract entitled " New England's First Fruits," dated at " Boston in New England, September 26, 1642," and published in London in 1643. This is, in point of time, nearly coeval with the University, and is as follows : —

" After God had carried us safe to New England, and wee had builded our houses, provided necessaries for our liveli-hood, rear'd convenient places for God's worship, and settled the civill government ; One of the next things we longed for and looked after was to advance learning and perpetuate it to posterity ; dreading to leave an illiterate ministry to the churches when our present ministers shall lie in the dust. And as wee were thinking and consulting how to effect this great work ; it pleased God to stir up the heart of one Mr. Harvard (a godly gentleman and a lover of learning, then living amongst us) to give the one half of his estate (it being in all about 1700 *l.*) towards the erecting of a Colledge and all his Library; After him another gave 300 *l.* others after them cast in more, and the publique hand of the State added the rest : The Colledge was by common consent, appointed to be at Cambridge, (a place very pleasant and accommodate) and is called (according to the name of its first founder) Harvard Colledge."

The account, with its quaint and pertinent title, gives also the first description of the College itself : —

" The edifice is very faire and comely within and without, having in it a spacious hall ; where they daily meet at commons, lectures and Exercises ; and a large library with some bookes to it, the. gifts of diverse of our friends, their chambers and studies also fitted for, and possessed by the students, and all other roomes of office necessary and convenient with all needful offices thereto belonging : And by the side of the Colledge a faire Grammar Schoole for the training up of young scholars and fitting them for Academical learning, that still as they are judged ripe, they may be received into the Colledge of this schoole : Master Corlet is the Mr. who hath very well approved himself for his abilities, dexterity, and painfulnesse in teaching and education of the youths under him."

Edward Johnson's account of New England, which appeared in 1654, mentions the single College building, which was of wood, as the commissioners before quoted say : —

" At Cambridge, they have a wooden Collidg, and in the yard a brick pile of two Cages for the Indians, where the Commissioners saw but one. They said they had three or more at scool."

The Indian seminary was built by the corporation in England, and in 1665 contained eight pupils, one of whom had been admitted into the College. It was torn down in 1698, and its bricks were probably used in Stoughton, as the old building was bought by Willis, the builder.

There existed formerly, in lieu of the low railing at present dividing the College grounds from the highway, a close fence, with an entrance opening upon the old College yard between Harvard and Massachusetts. This was superseded in time by a more ornamental structure, with as many as four entrances, flanked by tall gateposts. The present streets, then but lanes, were enlarged at the expense of the College territory, thus reducing its area very materially.

The first building, or Old Harvard, was rebuilt of brick in 1672 by the contributions of the Colony. Of the £1890 raised for this purpose, Boston gave £800.

The old structures ranging along the street which separates the College enclosure from the Common are, with the exception of Stoughton, on their original sites, and were, when erected, fronting the principal highway through the town. Harvard, which is upon its old ground, was the nucleus around which the newer halls ranged themselves. Stoughton, second in the order of time, was built in 1698, and Massachusetts in 1720. These are the three edifices shown in an illustration, of which the original was published by William Price at the "King's Head and Looking Glass," in Cornhill (Boston), and is dedicated to Lieutenant-Governor Spencer Phips. It is entitled "A Prospect of the Colledges in Cambridge in New England."

The first Stoughton was placed a little in the rear of, and at right angles with, Harvard and Massachusetts, fronting the open space between, so as to form three sides of a quadrangle. It stood nearly on a line with Hollis, was of brick, and had the name of Governor Stoughton, the founder, inscribed upon it. The foundation-stone was laid May 9, 1698, but, after standing nearly a century, having gone to irremediable decay, it was taken down in 1781. A facsimile of this edifice appears in the background of Governor Stoughton's portrait, in the gallery in Massachusetts Hall.

As has been remarked, there is a probability that the College press was kept in either Harvard or Stoughton as early as 1720, and the fact that the types belonging to the College were destroyed by the fire which consumed Harvard in 1764 gives color to the conjecture that the press was there. In May, 1775, the Provincial Congress, having taken possession of the College, assigned a chamber in Stoughton to Samuel and Ebenezer Hall, who printed the "New England Chronicle and Essex Gazette" there until the removal of the army from Cambridge. From this press, says a contemporary, "issued streams of intelligence, and those patriotic songs and tracts which so pre-eminently animated the defenders of American liberty."

John Fox, who was born at Boston, in England, in 1517, thus speaks of the art of printing : —

"What man soever was the instrument [whereby this invention was made] without all doubt, God himself was the ordainer and disposer thereof, no otherwise than he was of the gift of tongues, and that for a similar purpose."

In 1639 the first printing-press erected in New England was set up at Cambridge by Stephen Daye, at the charge of Rev. Joseph Glover, who not only brought over the printer, but everything necessary to the typographic art. "The first thing printed was 'The Freeman's Oath,' the next an Almanac made for New England by Mr. Pierce, mariner; the next was the Psalms newly turned into metre." * John Day, who lived in Elizabeth's time at Aldersgate, London, was a famous printer, who is understood to have introduced the italic characters and the first font of Saxon types into our typography.

Samuel Green, into whose possession the press very early came, and who is usually considered the first printer in America, was an inhabitant of Cambridge in 1639, and pursued his calling here for more than forty years, when he removed to Boston. Green printed the "Cambridge Platform" in 1649 ; the Laws in 1660 ; and the "Psalter," "Eliot's Catechism," "Baxter's Call," and the Bible in the Indian language in 1685. Daye's press, or some relics of it, are said to have been in existence as late as 1809 at Windsor, Vt. All these early publications are of great rarity.

Massachusetts, which is the first of the old halls reached in coming from the Square, is the oldest building now standing. It is but one remove from, and is the oldest existing specimen in Massachusetts of, our earliest types of architecture as applied to public edifices. Like Harvard, it presents its end to the street, and faces upon what was the College green a century and a half gone by, — perhaps the very place where Robert Calef's wicked book was, by an edict which smacks strongly of the Inquisition, burnt by order of Increase Mather.

* Winthrop's Journal.

VIEW OF THE ANCIENT BUILDINGS BELONGING TO HARVARD COLLEGE, CAMBRIDGE, NEW ENGLAND.

The building, with its high gambrel roof, dormer windows, and wooden balustrade surmounting all, has a quaint and decidedly picturesque appearance. Though nominally of three stories, it shows five tiers of windows as we look at it, above which the parapet terminates in two tall chimneys. Between each range of windows is a belt giving an appearance of strength to the structure. On the summit of the western gable was a clock affixed to an ornamental wooden tablet, which is still in its place, although the clock has long since disappeared. Massachusetts contained thirty-two rooms and sixty-four studies, until its dilapidated condition compelled the removal of all the interior woodwork, when it was converted into a gallery for the reception of the portraits since removed to Memorial Hall.

Many of these portraits are originals of Smibert, Copley, and Stuart, which makes the collection one of rare value and excellence. Of these, two of the most characteristic are of old Thomas Hancock, the merchant prince, and founder of the professorship of that name, and of Nicholas Boylston, another eminent benefactor, — both Copleys. Hancock, who was the governor's uncle, and who became very rich through his contracts for supplying Loudon's and Amherst's armies, kept a bookseller's shop at the "Bible and Three Crowns" in Ann Street, Boston, as early as 1726.

Copley has delineated him in a suit of black velvet, white silk stockings, and shoes with gold buckles. One of the hands is gloved, while the other, uncovered, shows the beautiful member which plays so important a part in all of that painter's works. The old gentleman's clothes fit as if he had been melted down and poured into them, and his ruffles, big-wig, cocked hat, and gold-headed cane supply materials for completing an attire suited to the dignity of a nabob of 1756. The artist gives his subject a double chin, shrewd, smallish eyes, and a general expression of complacency and good-nature. What we remark about Copley is his ability to paint a close-shaven face on which the beard may still be traced, with wonderful faithfulness to nature; every one of his portraits has a character of its own.

Boylston is represented in a *négligé* costume, with a dressing-gown of blue damask, the usual purple-velvet cap on his head, and his feet encased in slippers. This portrait was painted at the request of the corporation in partial acknowledgment of the bequest of £1500 lawful money by Boylston, to found a professorship of oratory and rhetoric, of which John Quincy Adams was the first professor. The portrait ordered by the College was a copy from the original by Copley, and was directed to be hung in the Philosophy Room beside those of Hancock and Hollis.

The portraits of Thomas Hollis, one of a family celebrated for its many benefactions to the College, and of President Holyoke, are also by Copley; that of John Lovell, the tory schoolmaster of Boston, is a Smibert. The full length of John Adams exhibits a figure full of animation, attired in an elegant suit of brown velvet, with dress sword and short curled wig. As a whole, it may fairly claim to take rank with the superb portrait of Colonel Josiah Quincy in the possession of his descendants, and overshadows the full length of J. Q. Adams by Stuart, hanging near it. There is also a portrait of Count Rumford.

All these portraits are admirable studies of the costumes of their time, and as such have an interest rivalling their purely artistic merits. One of the irreparable consequences of the great fire in Boston, of November, 1872, was the loss of a score or more of Copley's portraits which were stored within the burnt district.

In 1806 the College corporation having represented to the General Court that the proceeds of the lottery granted for the use of the University by an act passed June 14, 1794, were insufficient, and that great and expensive repairs were necessary to be made on Massachusetts Hall, they were empowered by an act passed March 14, to raise $30,000 by lottery, to erect the " new building called Stoughton Hall," and for the purpose of repairing Massachusetts, under direction of the President and Fellows, who were to appoint agents and publish the schemes in the papers.

A lottery had been authorized as early as 1765 to raise

funds for the "new building" (Harvard Hall), another in 1794, — in which the College itself drew the principal prize (No. 18,547) of ten thousand dollars, — and still another in 1811.

When the camps were formed at Cambridge, the College buildings were found very convenient for barracks; but as the greater part of the troops encamped during the summer of 1775, they were made available for every variety of military offices as well as for a certain number of soldiers. In June Captain Smith was ordered to quarter in No. 6, and Captain Sephens in No. 2 of Massachusetts, while Mr. Adams, a sutler, was assigned to No. 17. The commissariat was in the College yard, where the details from all the posts came to draw rations. Nearly two thousand men were sheltered in the five College buildings standing in the winter of 1775 – 76, of which Harvard received 640, Stoughton 240, and the chapel 160.

Harvard Hall, as it now appears, was rebuilt in 1765. The fire which destroyed its predecessor was supposed to have originated under the hearth of the library, where a fire had been kept for the use of the General Court, which was then

ILLIARD & METCALF, Print.

Harvard College Lottery.

Sixth Class.

THIS TICKET will entitle the bearer to such PRIZE, as may be drawn against its number; agreeably to an act of the General Court of Massachusetts, passed the 14th day of March, 1806.

BOSTON, JULY, 1811.

No. 4400

Manager.

sitting there on account of the prevalence of small-pox in Boston. Two days after this accident the General Court passed a resolve to rebuild Harvard Hall. The new edifice contained a chapel, dining-hall, library, museum, philosophy chamber, and an apartment for the philosophical apparatus.

Several interesting incidents are associated with the rebuilding of Harvard. When the Rev. George Whitefield was first in New England he was engaged in an acrimonious controversy with the President and some of the instructors of the College. Upon learning of the loss the seminary had sustained, Whitefield, putting all animosities aside, solicited contributions in England and Scotland with generous results. On the occasion of the last visit of this celebrated preacher to America every attention was paid him by the President and Fellows of the University. Dr. Appleton, who had moderately opposed Whitefield's teachings, invited him to preach in his pulpit, and the scene is said to have been one of great interest.

Harvard Hall was planned by Governor Bernard, — a great friend of the College, whatever else his demerits, — and while it was building he would not suffer the least departure from his plan. It is said he could repeat the whole of Shakespeare. That he was somewhat sensitive to the many lampoons levelled at him may be inferred from his complaint to the council of a piece in the Boston Gazette, which ended with these lines : —

> "And if such men are by God appointed,
> The devil may be the Lord's anointed."

Shortly after the arrival of the troops from England in 1768, which was one of Bernard's measures, the portrait of the Governor which hung in Harvard Hall was found with a piece cut out of the breast, exactly describing a heart. The mutilated picture disappeared and could never be traced.

After Bernard's return home it was reported, and currently believed, that he was driven out of the Smyrna Coffee House in London, by General Oglethorpe, who told him he was a dirty, factious scoundrel, who smelled cursed strong of the hangman. The General ordered the Governor to leave the room as one unworthy to mix with gentlemen, but offered to give him the satisfaction of following him to the door had he anything to reply. The Governor, according to the account, left the house like a guilty coward.

Harvard, the building of which Thomas Dawes superintended, stands on a foundation of Braintree stone, above which is a course of dressed red sandstone with a belt of the same material between the stories. It is composed of a central building with a pediment at either front, to which are joined two wings of equal height and length, each having a pediment at the end. There are but two stories, the lower tier of windows being arched, and the whole structure surmounted by a cupola. It was in the Philosophy Room of Harvard that Washington was received in 1789, and after breakfasting inspected the library, museum, &c.

The three buildings which we have described are those seen by Captain Goelet in 1750.* He says : —

" After dinner Mr. Jacob Wendell, Abraham Wendell, and self took horse and went to see Cambridge, which is a neat, pleasant village, and consists of about an hundred houses and three Colleges, which are a plain old fabrick of no manner of architect, and the present much out of repair, is situated on one side of the Towne and forms a large Square ; its apartments are pretty large. Drank a glass wine with the collegians, returned and stopt at Richardson's where bought some fowles and came home in the evening which we spent at Wetherhead's with sundry gentlemen."

Hollis and the second Stoughton Hall, both standing to the north of Harvard, are in the same style of architecture. The first, named for Thomas Hollis, was begun in 1762 and completed in 1763. It was set on fire when Old Harvard was consumed, and was struck by lightning in 1768. Thomas Dawes was the architect. Stoughton was built during the years 1804, 1805. They have each four stories, and are exceedingly plain " old fabrics " of red brick. Standing in front of the interval between these is Holden Chapel, built in 1745 at

* N. E. Hist. and Gen. Register.

the cost of the widow and daughters of Samuel Holden, one of the directors of the Bank of England. It was first used for the College devotions, subsequently for the American courts-martial, and afterwards for anatomical lectures and dissections. It became in 1800 devoted to lecture and recitation rooms for the professors and tutors. Holworthy Hall, which stands at right angles with Stoughton, was erected in 1812. Besides the five brick edifices standing in 1800, was also what was then called the College House, a three-story wooden building, standing without the College yard, containing twelve rooms with studies. It was originally built in 1770 for a private dwelling, and purchased soon after by the College corporation. University Hall, built in 1812 – 13 of Chelmsford granite, is placed upon the site of the old Bog Pond and within the limits of the Wigglesworth Ox Pasture. This building had once a narrow escape from being blown up by the students, the explosion being heard at a great distance. A little southeast of Hollis is the supposed site of the Indian college.

It does not fall within our purpose to recite the history of the more modern buildings grouped around the interior quadrangle, with its magnificent elms and shady walks ; its elegant and lofty dormitories, and its classic lore. Our business is with the old fabrics, the ancient pastimes and antiquated customs of former generations of Senior and Junior, Sophomore and Freshman.

It was a warm spring afternoon when we stood within the quadrangle and slaked our thirst at the wooden pump. A longing to throw one's self upon the grass under one of those inviting trees was rudely repelled by the painted admonition, met at every turn, to " Keep off the Grass." The government does not waste words ; it orders, and its regulations assimilate to those of the Medes and Persians, which altereth not. Nevertheless, a few benches would not seem out of place here, when we recall how the sages of Greece instructed their disciples as they walked or while seated under some shady bough, as Socrates is described by Plato.

Looking up at the open windows of the dormitories, we saw

QUADRANGLE, HARVARD COLLEGE.

that not a few were garnished with booted or slippered feet. This seemed the favorite attitude for study, by which knowledge, absorbed at the pedal extremities, is conducted by the inclined plane of the legs to the body, finally mounting as high as its source, siphon-like, to the brain. Any movement by which the feet might be lowered during this process would, we are persuaded, cause the hardly gained learning to flow back again to the feet. Others of the students were squatted in Indian fashion, their elbows on their knees, their chins resting in their palms, with knitted brows and eyes fixed on vacancy, in which, did we possess the conjurer's art, the coming University boat-race or the last base-ball tournament would, we fancy, appear instead of Latin classics. Perhaps we have not rightly interpreted the expressions of others, which seemed to say, in the language of one whose brain was stretched upon the same rack a century and a quarter ago : —

> " Now algebra, geometry,
> Arithmetick, astronomy,
> Opticks, chronology and staticks,
> All tiresome parts of mathematics,
> With twenty harder names than these,
> Disturb my brains and break my peace."

It was formerly the practice of the Sophomores to notify the Freshmen to assemble in the Chapel, where they were indoctrinated in the ancient customs of the College, the latter being required " to keep their places in their seats, and attend with decency to the reading." Among these customs, descended from remote times, was one which forbade a Freshman "to wear his hat in the College yard, unless it rains, hails, or snows, provided he be on foot, and have not both hands full." The same prohibition extended to all undergraduates when any of the governors of the College were in the yard. These absurd " relics of barbarism " had become entirely obsolete before 1800.

The degrading custom which made a Freshman subservient to all other classes, and obliged him to go of errands like a pot-boy in an alehouse, the Senior having the prior claim to his service, died a natural death, without the interposition of authority. It became the practice under this state of things for a Freshman to choose a Senior as a patron, to whom he acknowledged service, and who, on his part, rendered due protection to his servitor from the demands of others. These petty offices, when not unreasonably required, could be enforced by an appeal to a tutor. The President and immediate government had also their Freshmen. It is noteworthy that the abolition of this menial custom was recommended by the Overseers as early as 1772; but the Corporation, which, doubtless, derived too many advantages from a continuance of the practice, rejected the proposal.

Another custom obliged the Freshman to measure his strength with the Sophomore in a wrestling-match, which usually took place during the second week in the term on the College playground, which formerly bounded on Charlestown road, now Kirkland Street, and included about an acre and a half. This playground was enclosed by a close board fence, which began about fifty feet north of Hollis and extended back about three hundred feet, separating the playground from the College buildings. The playground had a front on the Common of about sixty-five feet, and was entered on the side of Hollis.

"This enclosure, an irregular square, contained two thirds or more of the ground on which Stoughton stands, the greater part of the land on which Holworthy stands, together with about the same quantity of land in front of the same, the land back of Holworthy, including part of a road since laid out, and perhaps a very small portion of the western extremity of the Delta, so called."

This was the College gymnasia, where the students, after evening prayers, ran, leaped, wrestled, played at quoits or cricket, and at good, old-fashioned, obsolete bat and ball, — not the dangerous pastime of to-day, but where you stood up, man-fashion, with nothing worse resulting than an occasional eye in mourning.

In the early days offending students were punished by the imposition of fines or whipping. There is a record of an order to this effect in the Massachusetts archives.

Any account of Harvard which ignored the clubs would be incomplete. Besides the Phi Beta Kappa was the Porcellian, founded by the Seniors about 1793. It was originally called the Pig Club, but, for some unknown reason, this homely but expressive derivation was translated into a more euphonious title. A writer remarks that learned pigs have sometimes been on exhibition, but, to our mind, to have been educated among them would be but an ill passport into good society. There was also the Hasty Pudding Club, — a name significant of that savory, farinaceous substance, the dish of many generations of New-Englanders. Whether this society owed its origin to sumptuary regulations we are unable to say ; but a kettle of the article, steaming hot, suspended to a pole, and borne by a brace of students across the College yard, were worth a visit to Old Harvard to have witnessed.

Commencement, Neal says, was formerly a festival second only to the day of the election of the magistrates, usually termed "Election Day." The account in "New England's First Fruits" gives the manner of conducting the academical exercises in 1642 : —

"The students of the first classis that have beene these foure yeeres* trained up in University learning (for their ripening in the knowledge of tongues and arts) and are approved for their manners, as they have kept their public Acts in former yeares, ourselves being present at them ; so have they lately kept two solemn Acts for their Commencement, when Governour, Magistrates and the Ministers from all parts, with all sorts of schollars, and others in great numbers were present and did heare their exercises ; which were Latine and Greeke Orations, and Declamations, and Hebrew Analasis, Grammaticall, Logicall and Rhetoricall of the Psalms ; And their answers and disputations in Logicall, Ethicall, Physicall, and Metaphysicall questions ; and so were found worthy of the first degree (commonly called Bachelour pro more Academiarum in Anglia) ; Being first presented by the President to the Magistrates and Ministers, and by him upon their approbation, solemnly admitted unto the same degree, and a booke of arts delivered into each of their hands, and the power given them to read Lectures in the hall upon

* Fixing the founding in 1638.

any of the arts, when they shall be thereunto called, and a liberty of studying in the library."

Commencement continued to be celebrated as a red-letter day, second only to the republican anniversary of the Fourth of July. The merry-makings under the tents and awnings erected within the College grounds, for the entertainment of the guests, who had assembled to do honor to the literary triumphs of their friends or relatives, were completely eclipsed by the saturnalia going on without on the neighboring Common. This space was covered with booths, within which the hungry and thirsty might find refreshment, or the unwary be initiated into the mysteries of sweat-cloth, dice, or roulette.  Side-shows, with performing monkeys, dogs, or perhaps a tame bear, less savage than his human tormentors, drew their gaping multitudes, ever in movement, from point to point.  Gaming was freely indulged in, and the Maine Law was not.  As the day waxed, the liquor began to produce its legitimate results, swearing and fighting taking the place of the less exciting exhibitions.  The crowd surged around the scene of each pugilistic encounter, upsetting the booths, and vociferating encouragement to the combatants.  The *best man* emerged with battered nose, eyes swelled and inflamed, his clothes in tatters, to receive the plaudits of the mob and the pledge of victory in another bowl of grog, while the vanquished sneaked away amid the jeers and derision of the men and the hootings of the boys.  These orgies, somewhat less violent at the beginning of the present century, were by degrees brought within the limits of decency, and finally disappeared altogether.  This was one of those " good old time " customs which we have sometimes known recalled with long-drawn sigh and woful shake of the head over our own days of State police, lemonade, and degeneracy.  During the early years of the Revolution, and as late as 1778, there was no public Commencement at Harvard.

Dress was a matter to which students gave little heed at the beginning of the century.  The College laws required them to wear coats of blue-gray, with gowns as a substitute, in warm weather, — except on public occasions, when black gowns were permitted. Little does your spruce young undergraduate of to-day resemble, in this respect, his predecessor, who went about the College grounds, and even the village, attired in summer in a loose, long gown of calico or gingham, varied in winter by a similar garment of woollen stuff, called lambskin. With a cocked hat on his head, and peaked-toed shoes on his feet, your collegian was not a bad counterpart of Dominie Sampson in dishabille, if not in learning. Knee-breeches began to be discarded about 1800 by the young men, but were retained by a few of the elders until about 1825, when pantaloons had so far established themselves that it was unusual to see small-clothes except upon the limbs of some aged relic of the old *régime*. Top-boots, with the yellow lining falling over, and cordovans, or half-boots, made of elastic leather, fitting itself to the shape of the leg, belonged to the time of which we are writing. The tendency, it must be admitted, has been towards improvement, and the present generation fully comprehends how

> " Braid claith lends fouk an unca heeze ;
> Maks mony kail-worms butterflees ;
> Gies mony a doctor his degrees,
> For little skaith ;
> In short you may be what you please,
> W'i guid braid claith."

An example of the merits of dress was somewhat ludicrously presented by a colloquy between two Harvard men who arrived at eminence, and who were as wide apart as the poles in their attention to personal appearance. Theophilus Parsons was a man very negligent of his outward seeming, while Harrison Gray Otis was noted for his fine linen and regard for his apparel. The elegant Otis, having to cross-examine a witness in court whose appearance was slovenly in the extreme, commented upon the man's filthy exterior with severity, and spoke of him as a " dirty fellow," because he had on a dirty shirt. Parsons, whose witness it was, objected to the badgering of Otis.

" Why," said Otis, turning to Parsons, with ill-concealed irony, " how many shirts a week do you wear, Brother Parsons ? "

"I wear one shirt a week," was the reply. "How many do you wear?"

"I change my shirt every day, and sometimes oftener," said Otis.

"Well," retorted Parsons, "you must be a 'dirty fellow' to soil seven shirts a week when I do but one."

There was a sensation in the court-room, and Mr. Otis sat down with his plumage a little ruffled.

> "For though you had as wise a snout on,
>   As Shakespeare or Sir Isaac Newton,
> Your judgment fouk would hae a doubt on,
>   I'll tak my aith,
> Till they would see ye wi' a suit on
>   O' guid braid claith."

The silken "Oxford Caps," formerly worn in public by the collegians, are well remembered. These were abandoned, in public places, through the force of circumstances alone, as they drew attentions of no agreeable nature upon the wearer when he wandered from the protecting ægis of his Alma Mater. In the neighboring city, should his steps unfortunately tend thither, the sight of his headpiece at once aroused the war-cries of the clans of Cambridge Street and the West End. "An Oxford Cap! an Oxford Cap!" reverberated through the dirty lanes, and was answered by the instant muster of an ill-omened rabble of *sans-culottes*. Stones, mud, and unsavory eggs were showered upon the wretched "Soph," whose conduct on these occasions justified the derivation of his College title. Sometimes he stood his ground to be pummelled until within an inch of taking his degree in another world, and finally to see his silken helmet borne off in triumph at the end of a broomstick; generally, however, he obeyed the dictates of discretion and took incontinently to his heels. At sight of these ugly black bonnets, worthy a familiar of the Inquisition, the whole neighborhood seemed stirred to its centre with a frenzy only to be assuaged when the student doffed his obnoxious casque or fled across the hostile border.

The collegians, with a commendable *esprit du corps*, and a

valor worthy a better cause, clung to their caps with a chivalric
devotion born alone of persecution.   They learned to visit the
city in bands instead of singly, but this only brought into
action the reserves of " Nigger Hill," and enlarged the war.
The North made common cause with the West, and South End
with both.   The Harvard boys armed themselves, and some
dangerous night-affrays took place in the streets, for which the
actors were cited before the authorities.   Common-sense at
length put an end to the disturbing cause, in which the students were obliged to confess the game was not worth the
candle.   The Oxford Caps were hung on the dormitory pegs,
and order reigned in Warsaw.

It is not designed to enumerate the many distinguished sons
of Old Harvard whose names illuminate history.   This has
been done in a series of biographies from an able pen.*   One
of the first class of graduates was George Downing, who went
to England and became Chaplain to Colonel Okey's regiment,
in Cromwell's army, — the same whom he afterwards betrayed
in order to ingratiate himself in the favor of Charles II.   He
was a brother-in-law of Governor Bradstreet and a good friend
to New England.   Doctor Johnson characterized him as the
" dog Downing."   He was ambassador to the states of Hol-
land, and notwithstanding his reputation, soiled by the betrayal
of some of his republican friends to the block, was a man of
genius and address.   No other evidence is needed to show that
he was a scoundrel than the record of his treatment of his
mother, in her old age, as related by herself : —

" But I am now att ten pounde ayear for my chamber and 3
pound for my seruants wages, and haue to extend the other tene
pound a year to accomadat for our meat and drinck ; and for my
clothing and all other necessaries I am much to seeke, and more
your brother Georg will not hear of for me ; and that it is onely
couetousness that maks me aske more.   He last sumer bought another town, near Hatly, called Clappum, cost him 13 or 14 thousand pound, and I really beleeue one of us 2 are couetous."

Downing Street, London, was named for Sir George when

* John L. Sibley, Librarian.

the office of Lord Treasurer was put in commission (May, 1667), and Downing College, Cambridge, England, was founded by a grandson of the baronet, in 1717.

The class of 1763 was in many respects a remarkable one, fruitful in loyalists to the mother country. Three refugee judges of the Supreme Court, of which number Sampson Salter Blowers lived to be a hundred, and, with the exception of Dr. Holyoke, the oldest of the Harvard alumni ; Bliss of Springfield and Upham of Brookfield, afterwards judges of the highest court in New Brunswick ; Dr. John Jeffries, the celebrated surgeon of Boston, and others of less note. On the Whig side were Colonel Timothy Pickering, General Jedediah Huntington, who pronounced the first English oration ever delivered at Commencement, and Hon. Nathan Cushing.

Benjamin Pratt, afterwards Chief Justice of New York under the crown, was a graduate of 1737. He had been bred a mechanic, but, having met with a serious injury that disabled him from pursuing his trade, turned his attention to study. Governors Belcher, Hutchinson, Dummer, Spencer Phips, Bowdoin, Strong, Gerry, Eustis, Everett, T. L. Winthrop, the two Presidents Adams and the Governor of that name, are of those who have been distinguished in high political positions. The names of those who have become eminent in law, medicine, and divinity would make too formidable a catalogue for our limits.

The Marquis Chastellux, writing in 1782, says : —

"I must here repeat, what I have observed elsewhere, that in comparing our universities and our studies in general with those of the Americans, it would not be to our interest to call for a decision of the question, which of the two nations should be considered an infant people."

A University education, upon which, perhaps, too great stress is laid by a few narrow minds who would found an aristocracy of learning in the republic of letters, is unquestionably of great advantage, though not absolutely essential to a successful public career. It is a passport which smooths the way, if it does not guarantee superiority. Perhaps it has a

tendency to a clannishness which has but little sympathy with
those whose acquirements have been gained while sternly
fighting the battle of life in the pursuit of a livelihood.
Through its means many have achieved honor and distinction,
while not a few have arrived at the goal without it.   Franklin,
Rumford, Rittenhouse, and William Wirt are examples of so-
called self-made men which it would be needless to multiply.
Even in England the proportion of collegians in public life is
small.   Twenty-five years ago Lord Lyndhurst said in a speech
that, when he began his political career a majority of the House
of Commons had received a University education, while at the
time of which he was speaking not more than one fifth had
been so educated.   The practice which prevails in our country,
especially at the West, of distinguishing every country seminary with the name of college, is deserving of unqualified
reprobation.

It would be curious to trace the antecedents of the posses-
sors of some of the great names in history.   Columbus was
a weaver ; Sixtus V. kept swine ; Ferguson and Burns were
shepherds ; Defoe was a hosier's apprentice ; Hogarth, an en-
graver of pewter pots ; Ben Jonson was a brick-layer ; Cer-
vantes was a common soldier ; Halley was the son of a soap-
boiler ; Arkwright was a barber, and Belzoni the son of a barber ; Canova was the son of a stone-cutter, and Shakespeare
commenced life as a menial.

The historic associations of Harvard are many and interesting.   The buildings have frequently been used by the legislative
branches of the provincial government.   In 1729 the General
Court sat here, having been adjourned from Salem by Governor
Burnet, in August.   Again in the stormy times of 1770 the
Court was prorogued by Hutchinson to meet here instead of at
its ancient seat in Boston.   Wagers were laid at great odds
that the Assembly would not proceed to do business, considering
themselves as under restraint.   They, however, opened their
session under protest, by a vote of 59 yeas to 29 nays.   Urgent
public business gave the Governor a triumph, which was rendered as empty as possible by every annoyance the members in

their ingenuity could invent. The preceding May the election
of councillors had been held in Cambridge, conformably to
Governor Hutchinson's orders, but contrary to the charter and
the sense of the whole province. This was done to prevent
any popular demonstration in Boston, but the patriotic party
celebrated the day there, and their friends flocked into town
from the country as usual. An ox was roasted whole on the
Common and given to the populace.

The tragic events of the 5th of March, 1770, had occasioned
great indignation and uneasiness, which the acquittal of Captain Preston and his soldiers contributed to keep alive. The
following is a copy of the paper posted upon the door of Boston
Town House (Old State House), December 13, 1770, and for
which Governor Hutchinson offered a reward of a hundred
pounds lawful money, to be paid out of the public treasury.
Otway's "Venice Preserved" seems to have furnished the text
to the writer : —

> "To see the sufferings of my fellow-*townsmen*
> And own myself a man ; To see the *Court*
> Cheat the INJURED people with a shew
> Of *justice*, which *we* ne'er *can taste* of ;
> Drive us like wrecks down the rough tide of power,
> While no hold is left to save us from destruction,
> All that bear this are *slaves*, and *we as such*,
> Not to rouse up at the great call of Nature
> And *free the world from such* domestic *tyrants*."

Harvard has not been free from those insurrectionary ebulli-
tions common to universities. In most instances they have
originated in Commons Hall ; the grievances of the stomach,
if not promptly redressed, leading to direful results. Sydney
Smith once remarked, that "old friendships are destroyed by
toasted cheese, and hard salted meat has led to suicide." The
stomachs of the students seem, on sundry occasions, to have
been no less sensitive.

In 1674 all the scholars, except three or four whose friends
lived in Cambridge, left the College. In the State archives
exists a curious document relative to a difficulty about commons at an early period in the history of the College. It is the

confession of Nathaniel Eaton and wife, who were cited before the General Court for misdemeanors in providing diet for the students.   In Mrs. Eaton's confession the following passage occurs : —

" And for bad fish, that they had it brought to table, I am sorry there was that cause of offence given them.   I acknowledge my sin in it.   And for their mackerel, brought to them with their guts in them, and goat's dung in their hasty pudding, its utterly unknown to me ; but I am much ashamed it should be in the family and not prevented by myself or servants and I humbly acknowledge my negligence in it."

The affair of the resignation of Dr. Langdon has been mentioned.   In 1807 there was a general revolt of all the classes against their commons, which brought the affairs of the College nearly to a stand for about a month.   The classes, having *en masse* refused to attend commons, were considered in the light of outlaws by the government, and were obliged to subscribe to a form of apology dictated by it to obtain readmission.   Many refused to sign a confession a little humiliating, and left the College ; but the greater number of the prodigals accepted the alternative, though we do not learn that any fatted calf was killed to celebrate the return of harmony.   This was during Dr. Webber's presidency.

The students have ever been imbued with strong patriotic feelings.   In 1768 the Seniors unanimously agreed to take their degrees at Commencement dressed in black cloth of the manufacture of the country.   In 1812 they proceeded in a body to work on the forts in Boston harbor.   In the great Rebellion the names of Harvard's sons are inscribed among the heroic, living or dead for their country.

The seal of Harvard was " adopted at the first meeting of the governors of the College after the first charter was obtained. On the 27th of December, 1643, a College seal was adopted, having, as at present, three open books on the field of an heraldic shield, with the motto *Veritas* inscribed."   This, says Mr. Quincy, is the only seal which has the sanction of any record.   The first seal actually used had the motto "*In Christi*

*Gloriam*," which conveys the idea of a school of theology, and is indirectly sanctioned by the later motto, *Christo et Ecclesiæ*.

The Americans threw up works on the College green in 1775, which were probably among the earliest erected by the Colony forces. They were begun in May, and extended towards the river. An aged resident of Cambridge informed the writer that a fort had existed in what is now Holyoke Place, leading from Mount Auburn Street, — a point which may be assumed to indicate the right flank of the first position. The lines in the vicinity of the College were carefully effaced, some few traces being remarked in 1824. They were, in all probability, hastily planned, and soon abandoned for the Dana Hill position, by which they were commanded.

The first official action upon fortifications which appears on record is the recommendation of a joint committee of the Committee of Safety and the council of war — a body composed of the general officers — to throw up works on Charlestown road, a redoubt on what is supposed to have been Prospect Hill to be armed with 9-pounders, and a strong redoubt on Bunker Hill to be mounted with cannon. These works were proposed on the 12th of May. The reader knows that the execution of the last-named work brought on the battle on that ground.

Ever since Lexington the Americans looked for another sally of the royal forces. They expected it would be by way of Charlestown, and have the camps at Cambridge for its object. By landing a force on Charlestown Neck, which the command of the water always enabled them to do, the enemy were within a little more than two miles of headquarters, while a force coming from Roxbury side must first beat Thomas's troops stationed there, and then have a long *détour* of several miles before they could reach the river, where the passage might be expected to be blocked by the destruction of the bridge, and would at any rate cost a severe action, under great disadvantage, to have forced. A landing along the Cambridge shore was impracticable. It was a continuous marsh, intersected here and there by a few farm-roads, impassable for artillery, without which the king's troops would not have moved. The Lexing-

ton expedition forced its way through these marshes with
infinite difficulty.    The English commander might land his
troops at Ten Hills, as had already been done ; but to prevent
this was the object of the possession of Bunker Hill.    He was
therefore reduced to the choice of the two great highways leading into Boston, with the advantages greatly in favor of that
which passed on the side of Charlestown.

The advanced post of the Americans on old Charlestown
road, which was meant to secure the camp on this side,
was near the point where it is now intersected by Beacon
Street.    It was distant about five eighths of a mile from Cambridge Common.    The road, which has here been straightened,
formerly curved towards the north, crossing the head of the
west fork of Willis Creek (Miller's River), by what was called
Pillon Bridge.    The road also passed over the east branch of
the same stream near the present crossing of the Fitchburg
Railway, where nothing now appears to indicate its vicinity.
The works at Pillon Bridge were on each side of the road ; that
on the north running up the declivity of the hill now crossed
by Park Street, and occupying a commanding site.    The existence of a watercourse here might long be traced in the venerable willows which once skirted its banks, and even by the dry
bed of the stream itself.    The bridge, according to appearances,
was situated seventy-five or a hundred yards north of the present point of junction of the two roads, now known as Washington and Beacon Streets.    At the Cambridge line the former
takes the name of Kirkland Street.    Quite near this point, at
Dane Street, a memorial tablet marks the spot where John
Woolrich, the first settler in what is now Somerville, lived.

## CHAPTER XI.

### CAMBRIDGE CAMP.

" Father and I went down to camp
    Along with Captain Gooding,
    And there we see the men and boys
    As thick as hasty pudding."

THERE is a certain historical coincidence in the fact that
the armies of the Parliament in England and of the
Congress in America were each mustered in Cambridge. Old
Cambridge, in 1642 – 43, was generally for the king, and the
University tried unsuccessfully to send its plate out of Oliver's
reach. In 1775 the wealth and influence of American Cambridge were also for the king, but the University was stanch
for the Revolution.

We confess we should like to see, on a spot so historic as
Cambridge Common, an equestrian statue to George Washington, " *Pater, Liberator, Defensor Patriæ.*" Besides being the
muster-field where the American army of the Revolution had
its being, it is consecrated by other memories. It was the
place of arms of the settlers of 1631, who selected it for their
strong fortress and intrenched camp. Within this field the
flag of thirteen stripes was first unfolded to the air. We have
already had occasion to refer to the uprising of Middlesex in
1774, when the crown servitors resident in Cambridge had their
judicial commissions revoked in the name of the people. It
was also the place where George the Third's speech, sent out by
the " Boston gentry," was committed to the flames.

Before reviewing the Continental camp, a brief retrospect of
the military organization of the early colonists will not be
deemed inappropriate. In the year 1644 the militia was organized, and the old soldier, Dudley, appointed major-general.
Endicott was the next incumbent of this new office ; Gibbons,

the third, had first commanded the Suffolk regiments; Sedgwick, the fourth, the Middlesex regiment.    After Sedgwick
came Atherton, Denison, Leverett, and Gookin, who was the
last major-general under the old charter.    These officers were
also styled sergeants major-general, a title borrowed from Old
England.    They were chosen annually by the freemen, at the
same time as the governor and assistants, while the other military officers held for life.

Old Edward Johnson, describing the train-bands in Gibbons's
time, says his forts were in good repair, his artillery well
mounted and cleanly kept, half-cannon, culverins, and sakers,
as also fieldpieces of brass, very ready for service.

A soldier in 1630 – 40 wore a steel cap or head-piece, breast
and back piece, buff coat, bandoleer, containing his powder, and
carried a matchlock.    He was also armed with a long sword
suspended by a belt from the shoulder.    In the time of Philip's
War the Colony forces were provided with blunderbusses and also
with hand-grenadoes, which were found effectual in driving the
Indians from an ambush.    A troop at this time numbered sixty
horse, besides the officers', all well mounted and completely
armed with back, breast, head-piece, buff coat, sword, carbine,
and pistols.    Each of the twelve troops in the Colony were
distinguished by their coats.    In time of war the pay of a captain of horse was £ 6 per month; of a captain of foot, £ 4; of a
private soldier, one shilling a day.    Military punishments were
severe; the strapado, or riding the wooden horse so as to bring
the blood, being commonly inflicted for offences one grade below the death-penalty.    The governor had the chief command,
but the major-generals did not take the field, their offices being
more for profit than for fighting.

With improved fire-arms, when battles were no more to be
decided by hand-to-hand encounters, armor gradually went out
of fashion.

> " Farewell, then, ancient men of might !
> Crusader, errant-squire, and knight !
> Our coats and customs soften ;
> To rise would only make you weep ;
> Sleep on, in rusty iron sleep,
> As in a safety coffin."

Bayonets as first used in England (about 1680) had a wooden haft, which was inserted in the mouth of the piece, answering thus the purpose of a partisan. The French, with whom the weapon originated, anticipated the English in fixing it with a socket. A French and British regiment in one of the wars of William III. encountered in Flanders, where this difference in the manner of using the bayonet was near deciding the day in favor of the French battalion. This weapon, once so important that the British infantry made it their peculiar boast, is now seldom used, except perhaps as a defence against cavalry. Some confidence it still gives to the soldier, but its most important function in these days of long-range small-arms is the splendor with which it invests the array of a battalion as it stands on parade. We do not know of a commander who would now order a bayonet-charge, although in the early battles of the Revolution it often turned the scale against us.

After the battle of Lexington the Committee of Safety resolved to enlist eight thousand men for seven months. A company was to consist of one captain, one lieutenant, one ensign, four sergeants, a drummer and fifer, and seventy privates. Nine companies formed a regiment, of which the field-officers were a colonel, lieutenant-colonel, and major. Each of the field-officers had a company which was called his own, as each of the general officers, beginning with Ward himself, had his regiment. The aggregate of the rank and file was, two days afterward, reduced to fifty. This must be considered as the first organization of the army of the Thirteen Colonies, — as they afterwards adopted it as their own, — the army which fought at Bunker Hill, and opened the trenches around Boston.

This Common was the grand parade of the army. Here were formed every morning, under supervision of the Brigadier of the Day, the guards for Lechmere's Point, Cobble Hill, White House, North, South, and Middle Redoubts, Lechmere's Point *tête du pont*, and the main guards for Winter Hill, Prospect Hill, and Cambridge. Hither were marched the detachments which assembled on their regimental parades at eight o'clock. Arms, accoutrements, and clothing underwent the scrutiny of Greene, Sullivan, or Heath. This finished, the grand guard broke off into small bodies, which marched to their designated stations to the music of the fife and drum.

We may here mention that the " ear-piercing fife " was introduced into the British army after the campaign of Flanders in 1748. This instrument was first adopted by the Royal Regiment of Artillery, the musicians receiving their instruction from John Ulrich, a Hanoverian fifer, brought from Flanders by Colonel Belford when the allied army separated. Nothing puts life into the soldier like this noisy little reed. You shall see a band of weary, footsore men, after a long march, fall into step, close up their ranks, and move on, a serried phalanx, at the scream of the fife.

Fortunate indeed was he who witnessed this old-fashioned guard-mount, where the first efforts to range in order the nondescript battalia must have filled the few old soldiers present with despair. There was no uniformity in weapons, dress, or equipment, and until the arrival of Washington not an epaulette in camp. The officers could not have been picked out of the line for any insignia of rank or superiority of attire over the common soldiers. Some, perhaps, had been fortunate enough to secure a gorget, a sword, or espontoon, but all carried their trusty fusees. All that went to make up the outward pomp of the soldier was wanting. Compared with the scarlet uniforms, burnished arms, and compact files of the troops to whom they were opposed, our own poor fellows were the veriest ragamuffins ; but the contrast in this was not more striking than were the different motives with which each combated : the Briton fought the battle of his king, the American soldier his own.

The curse of the American army was in the short enlistments. Men were taken for two, three, and six months, and scarcely arrived in camp before they infected it with that dangerous disease, homesickness. The same experience awaited the nation in the great civil war. In truth, if history is philosophy teaching by example, we make little progress in forming armies out of the crude material.

If the Americans were so contemptible in infantry, they were even more so in artillery, — as for cavalry, it was a thing as yet unknown in an army in which many field-officers could not obtain a mount. The enemy was well supplied with field and siege pieces, abundant supplies of which had been sent out, while the reserves of the Castle and fleet were drawn upon as circumstances demanded. The unenterprising spirit of the British commander rendered all this disparity much less alarming than it would have been with a Carleton or Cornwallis, instead of a Gage or Howe. An eyewitness relates that

"The British appeared so inoffensive that the Americans enjoyed at Cambridge the conviviality of the season. The ladies of the principal American officers repaired to the camp. Civility and mutual forbearance appeared between the officers of the royal and continental armies, and a frequent interchange of flags was indulged for the gratification of the different partisans."

The earliest arrangement of this chrysalis of an army was about as follows. The regiments were encamped in tents as fast as possible, but as this supply soon gave out, old sails, contributed by the seaport towns, were issued as a substitute. Patterson's, Whitcomb's, Doolittle's, and Gridley's pitched their tents, and were soon joined under canvas by Glover. Nixon's lay on Charlestown road ; a part of the regiment in Mr. Foxcroft's barn. The houses were at first used chiefly as hospitals for the sick. Patterson's hospital was in Andrew Boardman's house, near his encampment ; Gridley's, in Mr. Robshaw's. Sheriff Phip's house was hospital No. 2, over which Dr. Dunsmore presided. Drs. John Warren, Isaac Rand, William Eustis, James Thacher, Isaac Foster, and others officiated in the hospitals, under the chief direction of Dr. Church. John Pigeon was commissary-general to the forces.

We are able to give an exact return of all the regiments in Cambridge on the 10th of July, 1775, with the number of men in each : —

| | | | |
|---|---|---|---|
| Jonathan Ward, | 505. | James Scammon, | 529. |
| William Prescott, | 487. | Thomas Gardner, | 334. |
| Asa Whitcomb, | 571. | Jonathan Brewer, | 373. |
| Ephraim Doolittle, | 351. | B. Ruggles Woodbridge, | 343. |
| James Fry, | 473. | Paul Dudley Sargeant, | 192. |
| Richard Gridley, | 445. | Samuel Gerrish, | 258. |
| John Nixon, | 482. | John Mansfield, | 507. |
| John Glover, | 519. | Edmund Phinney, | 163. |
| John Patterson, | 492. | Moses Little, | 543. |
| Ebenezer Bridge, | 509. | | |

Two companies of Bond's and two of Gerrish's were at Medford, Malden, and Chelsea. Phinney had only three companies in camp. This seems to have been before the troops were arranged in grand divisions and newly brigaded by Washington. The aggregate of the troops in Cambridge presented by the above return was 8,076, of which probably not many in excess of six thousand were for duty. Under the new arrangement of forces Scammon's was ordered to No. 1 and the redoubt on the flank of No. 2, Heath's to No. 2, Patterson to No. 3, and Prescott to Sewall's Point. On the 10th of January, 1776, when the returns of the whole army only amounted to 8,212 men, but 5,582 were returned fit for duty.

Gridley calls for fascines, gabions, pickets, etc., for the batteries, and makes requisitions for the service of a siege-train. The artillery, such as it was, but lately dragged from places of concealment, was without carriages, horses, or harness. There were no intrenching tools except such as could be obtained of private persons, no furnaces for casting shot, — no anything but pluck and resolution, and of that there was enough and to spare.

Armorers were set to work repairing the men's firelocks. Knox, Burbeck, Crane, Mason, and Crafts mounted the artillery. Sailmakers were employed making tents, carpenters to build barracks, and shoemakers and tailors as fast as they could be obtained, — the former in making shoes, cartouch-boxes, etc., the latter in clothing the soldiers. Shipwrights were building bateaux on the river. In this condition of activity and chaos Washington found his army, and realized, perhaps for the first time, the magnitude of the work before him. From the Mystic to the Charles and from the Charles to the sea the air echoed to the sound of the hammer or the blows of the axe, the crash of falling trees or the word of command. Another Carthage might have been rebuilding by another Cæsar, and the ground trembled beneath the tread of armed men.

Imagine such an army, without artillery or effective small-arms, without magazines or discipline, and unable to execute the smallest tactical manœuvre should their lines be forced at any point, laying siege to a town containing ten thousand troops, the first in the world. It was, moreover, without a flag or a commander having absolute authority until Washington came.

Picture to yourself a grimy figure behind a rank of gabions, his head wrapped in an old bandanna, a short pipe between his teeth, stripped of his upper garments, his lower limbs encased in leather breeches, yarn stockings, and hob-nailed shoes, industriously plying mattock or spade, and your provincial soldier of '75 stands before you. Multiply him by ten thousand, and you have the provincial army.

It is certain that no common flag had been adopted by any authority up to February, 1776, though the flag of thirteen stripes had been displayed in January. The following extract from a regimental order book will answer the oft-repeated inquiry as to whether the contingents from the different Colonies fought under the same flag in 1775 : —

"HEAD QUARTERS 20th February 1776.
"Parole Manchester : Countersign Boyle.

"As it is necessary that every regiment should be furnished with colours and that those colours bear some kind of similitude to the regiment to which they belong, the colonels with their respective Brigadiers and with the Q. M. G. may fix upon any such as are proper and can be procured. There must be for each regiment the standard for regimental colours and colours for each grand division, the whole to be small and light. The number of the regiment is to be marked on the colours and such a motto as the colonels may choose, in fixing upon which the general advises a consultation among them. The colonels are to delay no time in getting the matter fix'd that the Q. M. General may provide the colours for them as soon as possible.                           G? WASHINGTON."

Washington's first requisition on arriving in camp was for one hundred axes and bunting for colors. At the battle of Long Island, fought August, 1776, a regimental color of red damask, having only the word "Liberty" on the field, was captured by the British. As late as Monmouth there were no distinctive colors.

The whipping-post, where minor offences against military law were expiated, was to be met with in every camp. The prisoners received the sentence of the court-martial on their naked backs; from twenty to forty lashes (the limit of the Jewish law) with a cat-o'-nine-tails being the usual punishment. This barbarous custom, inherited from the English service, was long retained in the American army. Its disuse in the navy is too recent to need special mention. Incorrigible offenders were drummed out of camp ; but though there are instances of the death-penalty having been adjudged by courts-martial, there is not a recorded case of military execution in the American army during the whole siege.

The men in general were healthy, — much more so in Roxbury than in Cambridge, and Thomas had the credit of keeping his camps in excellent order. In July, 1776, a company of ship carpenters was raised and sent to General Schuyler at Albany for service on the lakes. A company of bread-bakers was another feature of our camp.

The troops did not pile or stack their arms. They had few bayonets. The custom was to rest the guns upon wooden horses made for the purpose. In wet weather they were taken into the tents or quarters. We have dwelt upon details that may appear trivial, unless the reconstruction of the Continental camps, with fidelity in all things, and dedicated in all honor to the patriot army, be our sufficient warrant.

Pope Day, the anniversary of Guy Fawkes's abortive plot

(November 5, 1605), had long been observed in the Colonies. It was proposed to celebrate it in the American camp on the return of the day in 1775, but General Washington characterized it as a ridiculous and childish custom, and expressed his surprise that there should be officers and men in the army so void of common-sense as not to see its impropriety at a time when the Colonies were endeavoring to bring Canada into an alliance with themselves against the common enemy. The General argued that the Canadians, who were largely Catholic, would feel their religion insulted. The British, on the contrary, celebrated the day with salvos of artillery. As the crisis of the siege approached, Washington sternly forbade all games of chance.

The glorious evening in June came, when the dark clusters of men gathered on the greensward for Breed's Hill. Silently they stood while Dr. Langdon knelt on the threshold of yonder house and prayed for their good speed. The men tighten their belts and feel if their flints are firmly fixed. Their faces we cannot see, but we warrant their teeth are shut hard, and a strange light, the gleam of battle, is in their eyes. A nocturnal march, with conflict at the end of it, will try the nerves of the stoutest soldier. What will it then do for men who have yet to fire a shot in anger? They whisper together, and we know what they say, —

> "To-morrow, comrade, we
> On the battle plain must be,
> There to conquer or both lie low!"

Some one who has fairly judged of the raw recruit in general doubts if the Americans reserved their fire at Bunker Hill. The answer is conclusive. As the enemy marched to the attack a few scattering shots were fired at them, soon checked by the leaders. This is the testimony of both sides, and is, in this case, perhaps, exceptional. But the best answer is in the enemy's frightful list of casualties, — a thousand and more men are not placed *hors du combat* in less than two hours by indiscriminate popping.

The first attempts at uniforming the Continentals were anything but successful, the absence of cloth, except the homespun of the country, rendering it impracticable. Chester's company, which was clothed in blue turned up with red, is the only one in uniform at the battle of Bunker Hill of which we have any account. In Edmund Phinney's regiment, stationed in Boston after the departure of the English, the men were supplied with coats and double-breasted jackets of undyed cloth, just as it came from the looms, turned up with buff facings. They had also blue breeches, felt hats with narrow brims and white binding. Another regiment, being raised in the same town, wore black faced with red. The motto on the button was, "*Inimica Tyrannis,*" above a hand with a naked sword. During this year (1776) homespun or other coats, brown or any other color, made large and full-lapelled, with facings of the same or of white, cloth jackets without sleeves, cloth or leather breeches, large felt hats, and yarn stockings of all colors, were purchased by the Continental agents. Smallwood's Maryland regiment was clothed in red, but Washington eventually prohibited this color, for obvious reasons. In November, 1776, Paul Jones captured an armed vessel, which had on board ten thousand complete sets of uniform, destined for the troops in Canada under Carleton and Burgoyne. The American levies in the British service were first attired in green, which they finally and with heavy hearts exchanged for red, as a prelude to their being drafted into British regiments.

The term "Continent" was applied to the thirteen Colonies early in 1776, to distinguish their government from that of the Provinces, and hence the name Continental, as applied to the army of their adoption.

The surroundings of Cambridge Common invite our attention, and of these the old gambrel-roof house, formerly standing on what is now Holmes Place, naturally claims precedence. To the present generation it was known as the birthplace of our Autocrat of the Breakfast-table, our songster in many keys, ever welcome in any guise, whether humorous, pathetic, or even a little satirical withal. It was a good house to be born in, and does honor to the poet's choice, as his bouquet of

BIRTHPLACE OF OLIVER WENDELL HOLMES.

fragrant memories, culled for the readers of the " Atlantic,"
does honor to the poet's self.   It is certainly no disadvantage
to have first drawn breath in a house which
was the original headquarters of the American army of the Revolution, and in which
the battle of Bunker Hill was planned and
ordered.   The old house was pleasant to look
at, though built originally for nothing more
pretending than a farm-house.   It had a
thoroughly sturdy and honest look, like its
old neighbor, the President's house, and in
nothing except its yellow and white paint
did it seem to counterfeit the royalist man-

WENDELL.

sions of Tory Row.   The Professor tells us it once had a row
of Lombardy poplars on the west, but now not a single specimen of the tree can be found of the many that once stood
stiffly up at intervals around the Common.   The building
fronted the south, with the College edifices of its own time
drawn up in ugly array before it.   Beyond, in unobstructed
view, are the Square, the church with its lofty steeple, and its
Anglican neighbor of the lowlier tower, where, —

> "Like sentinel and nun they keep
>     Their vigil on the green;
> One seems to guard and one to weep
>     The dead that lie between."

The west windows overlooked the Common, with its beautiful
monument in its midst, and bordered by other houses with
walls as familiar to the scenes of a hundred years ago as are
those of our present subject.   Were we to indulge our fancy,
we might as easily invest these old houses with the gift of
vision through their many glassy eyes, as to give ears to their
walls ; we might imagine their looks of recognition, doubtful of
their own identity, amid the changes which time has wrought
in their vicinage.

It is at least a singular chance that fixed the homes of Longfellow, Holmes, Lowell, Hawthorne, and Everett in houses of
greater or less historic celebrity ; but it is not merely a coinci-

dence that has given these authors a decided preference for historical subjects. All are students of history; all either are or have been valued members of our historical societies. Evangeline, The Scarlet Letter, and Old Ironsides are pledges that the more striking subjects have not escaped them.

In the roll of proprietors of the old gambrel-roof house, which Dr. Holmes supposed to be about one hundred and fifty years old, but which, we believe, was even more ancient, the first to appear is Jabez Fox, described as a tailor, of Boston, to whom the estate was allotted in 1707, and whose heirs sold it to Farmer Jonathan Hastings thirty years later, with the four acres of land pertaining to the messuage.

The first Jonathan Hastings is the same to whom Gordon attributes the origin of the word "yankee." He says : —

"It was a cant, favorite word with Farmer Jonathan Hastings of Cambridge about 1713. Two aged ministers who were at the College in that town have told me they remembered it to have been then in use among the students, but had no recollection of it before that period. The inventor used it to express excellency. A Yankee good horse, or Yankee good cider, and the like, were an excellent good horse and excellent cider. The students used to hire horses of him, and the use of the term upon all occasions led them to adopt it, and they gave him the name of Yankee Jon."

Gordon supposes that the students, upon leaving College, circulated the name through the country, as the phrase "Hobson's choice" was established by the students at Cambridge, in Old England, though the latter derivation is disputed by Mr. Ker, who calls it "a Cambridge hoax."

The second Jonathan Hastings, long the College Steward, was born in 1708, graduated at Harvard in 1730, and died in 1783, aged seventy-five. It was during his occupancy that the house acquired its paramount importance. He was appointed postmaster of Cambridge in July, 1775, as the successor of James Winthrop; and his son Jonathan, who graduated at Harvard in 1768, was afterwards postmaster of Boston. Walter Hastings, also of this family, was a surgeon of the 27th regiment of foot (American), from Chelmsford, at the battle of

Bunker Hill, and rendered efficient service there. Walter Hastings, of Boston, had a pair of gold sleeve-buttons worn by his grandsire on that day. His father, Walter Hastings, commanded Fort Warren, now Fort Winthrop, in 1812.

As early as April 24, 1775, and perhaps immediately after the battle of Lexington, the Committee of Safety established themselves in this house, and here were concerted all those measures for the organization of the army created by the Provincial Congress. It was here Captain Benedict Arnold reported on the 29th of April with a company from Connecticut, and made the proposal for the attempt on Ticonderoga, prompted by his daring disposition. It was, without doubt, in the right-hand room, on the lower floor, that Arnold received his first commission as colonel from the Committee, May 3, 1775, and his orders to raise a force and seize the strong places on the lakes. Thus Massachusetts has the dubious honor of having first commissioned this eminent traitor, whose authority was signed by another traitor, Benjamin Church, but whose treason was not then developed.

> " 'T is here but yet confused :
> Knavery's plain face is never seen till used."

Arnold was the first to give information in relation to the number and calibre of the armament at Ticonderoga.

As all that relates to this somewhat too celebrated personage has a certain interest, we give the substance of a private letter from a gentleman who was in Europe when General Arnold arrived there, and whose acquaintance in diplomatic circles placed him in a position to be well informed.

The revolution in England respecting the change of ministry was very sudden, and supposed to have been influenced by the honest representations of Lord Cornwallis relative to the impracticability of reducing America, which rendered that gentleman not so welcome in England to the late Ministry as his brother-passenger, General Arnold, who, from encouraging information in favor of the conquest of America, was received with open arms by the king, caressed by the ministers, and all imaginable attention showed him by all people on that side of the question. He was introduced to the king in town, with whom he had the honor of many private conferences; and was seen walking with the Prince of Wales and the king's brother in the public gardens. The queen was so interested in favor of Mrs. Arnold as to desire the ladies of the court to pay much attention to her. On the other hand, the papers daily contained such severe strokes at Arnold as would have made any other man despise himself; and the then opposition, afterwards in power, had so little regard for him, that one day, he being in the lobby of the House of Commons, a motion was about to be made to have it cleared in order to get him out of it, but upon the member (the Earl of Surrey) being assured that he would not appear there again, the motion was not made.

The name of the corporal who with eight privates constituted the crew of the barge in which Arnold made his escape from West Point to the Vulture, was James Lurvey, of Colonel Rufus Putnam's regiment. He is believed to have come from Worcester County. Arnold meanly endeavored to seduce the corporal from his flag by the offer of a commission in the British service, but the honest fellow replied, "No, sir; one coat is enough for me to wear at a time."

This mansion was probably occupied by General Ward at a time not far from coincident with its possession by the Committee of Safety, but of this there is no other evidence than that his frequent consultations with that body would seem to render it necessary. He received his commission as commander-in-chief of the Massachusetts forces on the 20th of May, 1775, at which time headquarters were unquestionably established here. It must be borne in mind, however, that the committee exercised the supreme authority of directing all military movements, and that General Ward was a subordinate.

The fact that this was the Provincial headquarters has been doubtfully stated from time to time, but is settled by the following extract from the Provincial records, dated June 21, 1775 : —

"Whereas, a great number of horses have been, from time to time, put into the stables and yard of Mr. Hastings, at headquarters, not belonging to the Colony, the Committee of Safety, or the general officers, their aids-de-camp, or post-riders, to the great expense of the public and inconvenience of the committee, generals, &c."

General Ward's principal motive for quitting the army was a painful disease, which prevented his mounting his horse. His personal intrepidity and resolution are well illustrated by the following incident of Shays's Rebellion.

The General was then chief justice of the court to be held in Worcester, September, 1786. On the morning the court was to open, the Regulators, under Adam Wheeler, were in possession of the Court House. The judges had assembled at the house of Hon. Joseph Allen. At the usual hour they, together with the justices of the sessions and members of the bar, moved in procession to the Court House.

A sentinel challenged the advance of the procession, bringing his musket to the charge. General Ward sternly ordered him to recover his piece. The man, an old soldier of Ward's own regiment, awed by his manner, obeyed. Passing through the multitude, which gave way in sullen silence, the cortege reached the Court House steps, where were stationed a file of men with fixed bayonets, Wheeler, with a drawn sword, being in front.

The crier was allowed to open the doors, which, being done, displayed another party of infantry with loaded muskets, as if ready to fire. Judge Ward then advanced alone, and the bayonets were presented at his breast. He demanded, repeatedly, who commanded the people there, and the object of these hostile acts. Wheeler at length replied that they had met to prevent the sitting of the courts until they could obtain redress of grievances. The judge then desired to address the people, but the leaders, who feared the effect upon their followers, refused to permit him to be heard. The drums beat and the guard were ordered to charge. "The soldiers advanced until the points of their bayonets pressed hard upon the breast of the chief justice, who stood immovable as a statue, without stirring a limb or yielding an inch, although the steel, in the hands of

desperate men, penetrated his dress. Struck with admiration
by his intrepidity, the guns were removed, and Judge Ward,
ascending the steps, addressed the assembly."

> " Says sober Will, well *Shays* has fled,
>   And peace returned to bless our days.
>   Indeed, cries Ned, I always said,
>   He 'd prove at last a *fall back Shays.*"

When the army first assembled under Ward, officers were
frequently stopped by sentinels for want of any distinguishing
badge of rank. This led to an order that they should wear
ribbons across the breast, — red for the highest grade, blue for
colonels, and other colors according to rank.

It is well known that Washington spoke of the resignation
of General Ward, after the evacuation of Boston, in a manner
approaching contempt. His observations, then confidentially
made, about some of the other generals, were not calculated to
flatter their *amour propre* or that of their descendants. It is
said that General Ward, learning long afterwards the remark
that had been applied to him, accompanied by a friend, waited
on his old chief at New York, and asked him if it was true that
he had used such language. The President replied that he did
not know, but that he kept copies of all his letters, and would
take an early opportunity of examining them. Accordingly, at
the next session of Congress (of which General Ward was a
member), he again called with his friend, and was informed by
the President that he had really written as alleged. Ward then
said, " *Sir, you are no gentleman,*" and turning on his heel
quitted the room.

It is certain that the seizure of Dorchester Heights was resolved upon early in May, 1775, or nearly a year before it was
finally done by Washington. Information conveyed to the
besiegers from Boston made it evident that the enemy were
meditating a movement, which we now know from General
Burgoyne was to have been first directed upon the heights of
Dorchester, and secondly upon Charlestown.

On the 9th of May, at a council of war at headquarters, the
question proposed whether such part of the militia should be

called in to join the forces at Roxbury as would be sufficient to enable them *to take possession of and defend Dorchester Hill*, as well as to maintain the camp at Roxbury, was passed unanimously in the affirmative. Samuel Osgood, Ward's major of brigade, signed the record of the vote. On the 10th of May an order was sent to all the colonels of the army to repair to the town of Cambridge, — " as we are meditating a blow at our restless enemies," — the general officers were directed to call in all the enlisted men, and none were allowed to depart the camps till the further orders of Congress.

For some reason the enterprise was abandoned, but it shows that both belligerents were fully conscious from the first that the heights of Dorchester and Charlestown were the keys to Boston. Burgoyne says the descent on Dorchester was finally to have been executed on the 18th of June, and gives the particulars of the plan of operations, — a scheme which the intrenchment on the heights of Charlestown rendered abortive.

The next whose personality is involved with the old house is Joseph Warren. The account preserved in the Hastings family is, that the patriot President-general was much pleased with Rebecca Hastings, who was then residing with her father, the College steward. The previous day the General had presided at the deliberations of the Congress at Watertown, where he passed the night, coming down to Cambridge in the morning. His steps tended most naturally to the old house where were his associates of the Committee, and the commanding general. There was perhaps a fair face at the window welcoming him with a smile as he, for the last time, drew up before the gate and alighted from his chaise.

Warren, risen from a sick-bed, to which overwork and mental anxiety had consigned him, dressed himself with more than ordinary care, and, silencing the remonstrances of his more cautious colleague, Elbridge Gerry, proceeded to the scene of action at Bunker Hill on foot.

The old farm-house is not yet to lose its claim as a worthy memorial of the varying destinies through which our country passed. Washington made it his headquarters upon his arrival at camp, remaining in it three days, or until arrangements for his permanent residence could be made. He first dined at Cambridge with General Ward and his officers, — an occasion when all restraint appears to have been cast aside in the spontaneous welcome which was extended him. After dinner Adjutant Gibbs, of Glover's, was hoisted (English fashion), chair and all, upon the table, and gave the company a rollicking bachelor's song, calculated to make the immobile features of the chief relax. It was a generous, hearty greeting of comrades in arms. Glasses clinked, stories were told, and the wine circulated. Washington was a man ; we do not question that he laughed, talked, and toasted with the rest.

The headquarters being here already, it was natural for the General to choose to remain for the present where the archives, staff, and auxiliary machinery enabled him to examine the condition and resources of the army he came to command. Consultations with General Ward were necessarily frequent. It was no doubt in this house Washington penned his first official despatches.

Eliphalet Pearson, Professor of Hebrew and Oriental languages, became the next inhabitant after what may be called the Restoration, when the sway of warlike men gave place on classic ground to the old reign of letters. Professor Pearson was noted for the sternness of his orthodoxy, as exhibited in his resistance to the entrance of Rev. Henry Ware into the Hollis professorship, and for his opposition to Andrew Craigie's efforts to secure a charter for his bridge, — efforts exerted in both instances for the behoof of the College, though in widely different spheres of action.

Following him came Rev. Abiel Holmes, pastor of the First Church, early historian of Cambridge, whose ministry was suspended by a revolution in his parish, which resulted in the overthrow of the old and the elevation of the new. Dr. Holmes's widow, the daughter of Judge Oliver Wendell, continued to live in the house some time after the decease of her husband in 1837. Oliver Wendell Holmes, their son, did not permanently reside in the old house after he left college.

The lines to Old Ironsides, to which allusion has been made, were composed in this old house when the poet was twenty years old. They were written in pencil, and first printed in the " Boston Daily Advertiser." Genuine wrath at the proposed breaking up of the old frigate impelled the young poet's burning lines : —

> " And one who listened to the tale of shame,
> Whose heart still answered to that sacred name,
> Whose eye still followed o'er his country's tides
> Thy glorious flag, our brave Old Ironsides !
> From yon lone attic on a summer's morn,
> Thus mocked the spoilers with his school-boy scorn."

## CHAPTER XII.

### CAMBRIDGE COMMON AND LANDMARKS.

"The country of our fathers! May its spirit keep it safe and its justice keep it free!"

PURSUING our circuit of the Common, "on hospitable thoughts intent," we ought briefly to pause before the whilom abode of Dr. Benjamin Waterhouse. This house may justly claim to be one of the most ancient now remaining in Cambridge, having about it the marks of great age. The strong family resemblance which the dwellings of the period to which this belongs bear to each other renders a minute description of an individual specimen applicable to the greater number.

Here are still some relics of the "American Jenner," and some that belonged to an even older inhabitant than he. In one apartment is a clock surmounted by the symbolic cow. At the head of the staircase, in an upper hall, is another clock, with an inscription which shows it to have been presented, in 1790, to Dr. Waterhouse, by Peter Oliver, former chief justice of the province. The old timekeeper requests its possessor to wind it on Christmas and on the 4th of July. There is also a crayon portrait of the Doctor's mother, done by Allston when an undergraduate at Harvard. The features of Henry Ware, another inhabitant of the house, look benignly down from a canvas on the wall. Some other articles may have belonged to William Vassall, who owned and occupied the house, probably as a summer residence, before the war. Still another occupant was the Rev. Winwood Serjeant, rector of Christ Church.

Dr. Waterhouse is best remembered through his labors to introduce in this country vaccination, the discovery of Jenner, which encountered as large a share of ridicule and opposition as inoculation had formerly experienced. Several persons are remembered who were vaccinated by Dr. Waterhouse.

At one time the old barracks at Sewall's Point (Brookline) were used as a small-pox hospital. This was in the day of inoculation, when it was the fashion to send to a friend such missives as the following : —

"I wish Lucy was here to have the small-pox. I wish you would persuade her to come here and have it. You can't think how light they have it."

The visitor will find some relics formerly kept at the State Arsenal on Garden Street, in several pieces of artillery mounted on sea-coast carriages and arranged within the Common. These guns were left in Boston by Sir William Howe, and, thanks to the care of General Stone, when that gentleman was adjutant-general of the State, were preserved from the sale of a number of similar trophies as *old iron*. As the disappearance of the arsenal left them unprotected it is to be hoped that the State of Massachusetts can afford to keep these old war-dogs which bear the crest and cipher of Queen Anne and the Second George. The largest of the cannon is a 32-pounder. All have the broad arrow, but rust and weather have nearly obliterated the inscriptions impressed at the royal foundry. The oldest legible date is 1687. Besides these, were two diminutive mortars or cohorns. Within one of the houses were two beautiful brass field-pieces, bearing the crown and lilies of France. Each has its name on the muzzle, — one being the Venus and the other Le Faucon, — and on the breech the imprint of the royal arsenal of Strasburg, with the dates respectively of 1760 and 1761. A further search revealed, hidden away in an obscure corner and covered with lumber, a Spanish piece, which, when brought to light by the aid of some workmen, was found literally covered with engraving, beautifully executed, delineating the Spanish Crown and the monogram of Carlos III. It is inscribed, —

> "El Uenado.
> Barcelona J8DE
> Deceimbre De J767."

Inquiry of the proper officials having failed to enlighten us

as to the possession of these cannon by the State, we conclude
them to be a remnant of the field artillery sent us by France
during the Revolution. The Spaniard, when struck with a
piece of metal, gave out a beautifully clear, melodious ring, as
if it contained an alloy of silver, and brought to our mind those
old slumberers on the ramparts of Panama, into whose yet molten
mass the common people flung their silver reals, and the old
dons their pieces of Eight, while the priest blessed the union
with the baser metal and consecrated the whole to victory.

Whitefield's Elm, under which that remarkable man preached
in 1744, formerly stood on a line with its illustrious fellow the
Washington Elm, and not far from the turn as we pass from
the northerly side of the Common into Garden Street. It obstructed the way, and the axe of the spoiler was laid at its root
two years ago.

Dr. Chauncy and Whitefield were not the best friends
imaginable. They had mutually written at and preached
against each other, and reciprocally soured naturally amiable
tempers. The twain accidentally met. "How do you do,
Brother Chauncy," says the itinerant laborer. "I am sorry to
see you," replies Dr. C. "And so is the devil," retorted
Whitefield.

In the early part of his life this gentleman happened to be
preaching in the open fields, when a drummer was present,
who was determined to interrupt the services, and beat his
drum in a violent manner in order to drown the preacher's
voice. Mr. Whitefield spoke very loud, but the din of the
instrument overpowered his voice. He therefore called out to
the drummer in these words : —

"Friend, you and I serve the two greatest masters existing, but
in different callings. You may beat up volunteers for King George,
I for the Lord Jesus Christ. In God's name, then, don't let us interrupt each other ; the world is wide enough for us both, and we
may get recruits in abundance."

This speech had such effect that the drummer went away in
great good-humor, and left the preacher in full possession of
the field.

THE WASHINGTON ELM.

Many a pilgrim daily wends his way to the spot where Washington placed himself at the head of the army. Above him towers

> " A goodly elm, of noble girth,
>     That, thrice the human span —
>   While on their variegated course
>     The constant seasons ran —
>   Through gale, and hail, and fiery bolt,
>     Had stood erect as man."

He surveys its crippled branches, swathed in bandages ; marks the scars, where, after holding aloft for a century their out-stretched arms, limb after limb has fallen nerveless and de-cayed ; he pauses to read the inscription lodged at the base of the august fabric, and departs the place in meditative mood, as he would leave a churchyard or an altar.

Apart from its association with a great event, there is some-thing impressive about this elm. It is a king among trees ; a

monarch, native to the soil, whose subjects, once scattered
abroad upon the plain before us, have all vanished and left it
alone in solitary state.   The masses of foliage which hide in a
measure its mutilated members, droop gracefully athwart the
old highway, and still beckon the traveller, as of old, to halt
and breathe awhile beneath their shade.   It is not pleasant to
view the decay of one of these Titans of primeval growth.   It
is too suggestive of the waning forces of man, and of that

"Last scene of all,
That ends this strange eventful history."

As a shrine of the Revolution, a temple not made with hands,
we trust the old elm will long survive, a sacred memorial to
generations yet to come.   We need such monitors in our public
places to arrest our headlong race, and bid us calmly count the
cost of the empire we possess.   We shall not feel the worse for
such introspection, nor could we have a more impressive coun-
sellor.   The memory of the great is with it and around it ;
it is indeed on consecrated ground.

When the camp was here Washington caused a platform to
be built among the branches of this tree, where he was accustomed to sit and survey with his glass the country round.   On
the granite tablet we read that

UNDER THIS TREE
WASHINGTON
FIRST TOOK COMMAND
OF THE
AMERICAN ARMY,
JULY 3D, 1775.

On the spot where the stone church is erected once stood an
old gambrel-roofed house, long the habitat of the Moore family.
It was a dwelling of two stories, with a single chimney standing in the midst, like a tower, to support the weaker fabric.
In front were three of those shapely Lombard poplars, erect
and prim, like trees on parade.   A flower-garden railed it in
from the road ; a porch in front, and another at the northerly
end, gave ingress according as the condition of the visitor might
warrant.

The Moores occupied the house in the memorable year '75, and saw from the windows the cavalcade conducting Washington to his quarters, — this being, as before stated, the high-road from Watertown to Cambridge Common. On the following day the family might have witnessed the ceremonial of formal assumption of command by the chief, on whom all eyes were fixed and in whom all hopes were centred.

Deacon Moore — does he at length rest in peace ? — was, while in the flesh, much given to patching and repairing his fences, outbuildings, and the wooden belongings of his domain in general. He bore the character of an upright, downright, conscientious deacon, walking in the odor of sanctity, and was regarded with childish awe by the urchins of the grammar-school whenever he chose to appear abroad. The deacon's house had its inevitable best room, into which heaven's sunshine was never allowed to penetrate, and which was rarely opened except to admit a stranger or hold a funeral service. There are yet such rooms in New England, with their stiff, black hair-cloth furniture, their ghostly pictures, and dank, mouldy odors. The carefully varnished mahogany has a smell of the undertaker ; every sense is oppressed, and the soul pleads for release from the funereal chamber. We repeat, there are still such " best rooms " in New England.

Upon the decease of Deacon Moore it was discovered that some peculations had been made from the treasury of Dr. Holmes's church. These were laid at the door of the departed deacon. Now comes the startling revelation. Night after night the ghost of Deacon Moore revisited his earthly abode, and made night hideous with audible pounding, as if in the act of mending the fence, as was the deacon's wont in life. The affrighted neighbors, suddenly roused from slumber, fearfully drew their curtains aside, and peered forth into the night in quest of the spectre ; but still invisible the wraith pursued its midnight labors.

The Jennisons succeeded the Moores, and at length the shade came no more. Not many years ago the old house was demolished. A vault was discovered underneath the kitchen, walled up with rough stone, and in this receptacle were two human skeletons.

What tale of horror was here concealed, what deed of blood had caused the disappearance of two human beings from the face of the earth, was never revealed. For an unknown time they had remained sealed up in the manner related, and the later dwellers in the house were totally unconscious of their horrid tenants. A family servant had long slept immediately above these bones, and we marked, even after years had passed away, a strange glitter in his eye as he recalled his couch upon a tomb.

The remains were of adult persons, one a female. What motive had consigned them to this mysterious hiding-place is left to conjecture. Was it domestic vengeance, too deadly for the public ear? We answer that two individuals could not have been suddenly taken out of the little community without question. Were they some unwary, tired wayfarers who had sought hospitable entertainment, and found graves instead?

> "But Echo never mocked the human tongue ;
> Some weighty crime that Heaven could not pardon,
> A secret curse on that old building hung,
> And its deserted garden."

We have lived to have grave doubts whether, as the old adage says, "Murder will out." Inspect, if you have the stomach for it, our calendar of crime, and mark the array of names which belonged to those whose fate is unknown, and who are there set down like the missing of an army after the battle. The record is startling ; only at the final muster will the victims answer to the fatal list, and speak

> "Of graves, perchance, untimely scooped
> At midnight dark and dank."

In Spain an ancient custom constrains each passer-by to cast a stone upon the heap raised on the scene of wayside murder, until at length a monument arises to warn against assassination. The peasant always pauses to repeat an *ave* to the souls of the slain. On this spot a church has reared its huge bulk, piling stone upon stone until its steeple, overtopping the Old Elm, stands a mightier monument to the manes of the unknown dead.

The events in the life of Washington which have most impressed us are, the day when he unsheathed his sword beneath the Old Elm ; the morn of the battle of Trenton ; the address to his despairing, mutinous officers at Newburg ; and the farewell to his generals at New York.  As he was mounting his horse before Trenton, an officer presented him with a despatch.  His remark, " What a time to bring me a letter ! " is the sequel of his thoughts, — all had been staked on the issue.   When he rose from his bed early in the morning of the meeting at Newburg, he told Colonel Humphreys that anxiety had prevented him from sleeping one moment the preceding night.   Unwilling to trust to his powers of extempore speaking, Washington reduced what he meant to say to writing, and commenced reading it without spectacles, which at that time he used only occasionally.   He found, however, that he could not proceed without them.   He stopped, took them out, and as he prepared to place them, exclaimed, " I have grown blind as well as gray in the service of my country."   In these instances we see the patriot ; in the adieu to his lieutenants, we see the man.

When Washington rode into town after the evacuation of Boston, he was accompanied by Mrs. Washington, who, in accordance with our old-time elegant manners, was styled " Lady " Washington.   Upon reaching the Old South, the General wished to enter the building.   Shubael Hewes, who at this time kept the keys, lived opposite, and the General therefore drew up at his door.

With his usual courtesy the General inquired after the health of the family, and was told that Mrs. H. had, the day before, been delivered of a fine child.   At this Mrs. Washington insisted upon seeing the infant, born on an occasion so auspicious as the repossession of Boston by our troops, and it was accordingly brought out to the carriage and placed in her lap.

The General, alighting, went into the meeting-house, and, ascending to the gallery, where he could fully observe the havoc made by Burgoyne's Light Horse, remarked to the person who accompanied him that he was surprised that the English, who so reverenced their own places of worship, should have shown such a vandal disposition here.

Washington died at sixty-seven; Knox, by an accident, at fifty-six; Sullivan, at fifty-five; Gates, at seventy-eight; Greene, at forty-four; Heath, at seventy-seven; Arnold, at sixty; and Lee, at fifty-one. Putnam lived to be seventy-two, and Stark to be ninety-three, so that it was commonly said of him, that he was first in the field and last out of it.

But other scenes await us, and though we feel that it is good for us to be here, we must reverently bid adieu to the Old Elm. It could perchance tell, were it, like the Dryads of old, loquacious, of the settlers' cabins, when it was a sapling, of the building of the old wooden seminary, and of the multitudes that have passed and repassed under its verdant arch. The smoke from a hundred rebel camp-fires drifted through its branches and wreathed around its royal dome in the day of maturity, while the drum-beat at the waking of the camp frighted the feathered songsters from their leafy retreats and silenced their matin lays. The huzzas that went up when our great leader bared the weapon he at length sheathed with all honor made every leaf tremulous with joy, and every brown and sturdy limb to wave their green banners in triumph on high. We salute thy patriarchal trunk, thy withered branches, and thy scanty tresses, O venerable and yet lordly Elm! *Vale!*

It is much more a matter of regret than surprise that we have not in all New England a specimen of antique church architecture worthy of the name. Rigid economy dictated the barn-like structures which were the first Puritan houses of worship. Quaint they certainly were, and not destitute of a certain sombre picturesqueness, with their queer little towers and wonderful weather-vanes; and even their blackening rafters of prodigious thickness, their long aisles, and carved balustrades, gave modest glimpses of a Rembrandt-like interior. But the beautiful forms of Jones and of Wren were left behind when the Mayflower sailed, and not a single type of Old England's pride of architecture stands on American soil. Simplicity in building, in manners, and in dress, as well as in religion, were the base on which our Puritan fathers builded. Had the means not been wanting, it may be doubted whether they would have been applied to the erection of splendid public edifices. The motives which enforced the adherence of the first settlers to the gaunt and unæsthetic structures of their time ceased, in a great measure, to exist a hundred years later, but no revival of taste appeared, and even the Episcopalians, with the memories of their glorious Old World temples, fell in with the prevailing lethargy which characterized the reign of ugliness.

Christ Church stands confronting the Common much as it looked in colonial times. The subscription was originally formed in Boston, the subscribers being either resident or engaged in business there. The lot included part of the Common and part of the estate of James Reed. The building was at first only sixty-five feet in length by forty-five in width, exclusive of chancel and tower, but has been much enlarged, to accommodate an increasing parish, — a work which its original plan, and the material of which it is constructed, rendered easy. Peter Harrison, the architect of King's Chapel in Boston, was also the designer of this edifice, and seems to have followed the same plan as for that now venerable structure. Service was first held here on October 15, 1761, the Rev. East Apthorp, whom we have already visited, officiating. Of Dr. Apthorp's father it is written that he studied to mind his own business, — a circumstance so rare as to wellnigh deserve canonization.

In the alterations which have been called for the primitive appearance of the building has been, in a great measure, preserved. The exterior is exceedingly simple, but harmonious, the tower, placed in the centre of the front, giving entrances on three of its sides. The old bell-tower appeared rather smaller than its successor, and had a pointed roof, surmounted, as at present, by a gilded ball. The symbolic cross, which the Puritans hated with superstitious antipathy, did not appear on the pinnacle, out of deference perhaps to the feeling which abominated a painted window, a Gothic arch, or chancel rail, as the concomitants of that Episcopacy against which the Cromwellian iconoclasts had waged unrelenting war in every cathedral from Chester to Canterbury.

Upon the Declaration of Independence by the Colonies, all the taverns and shops were despoiled of their kingly emblems. A Boston letter of that date says : —

" In consequence of Independence being declared here, all the signs which had crowns on them even the Mitre and Crown in the organ loft of the chappell were taken down, and Mr. Parker, (who is the Episcopal minister in town) left off praying for the king."

The interior of Christ Church is quiet and tasteful, with

"Storied windows richly dight,
Casting a dim religious light."

The Corinthian pillars of solid wood and the original choir are still remaining. And, very like, the stiff, straight-backed pews are a relic of ancient discomfort. The tablets bearing the Ten Commandments are mementos of Old Trinity in Boston when the wooden edifice was taken down, and have by this means survived their mother church, which the great fire of 1872 left a magnificent ruin. A silver flagon and cup, now in use to celebrate the Holy Communion, were presented by Governor Hutchinson in 1772. These vessels were the property of King's Chapel, Boston, which then received a new service in exchange for the old. They are inscribed as

The Gift of
K. William and Q Mary
To y$^e$ Rev$^d$ Samll. Myles
For y$^e$ use of
Theire Majesties' Chappell in N. England.
MDCXCIV.

Dr. Apthorp was succeeded by Rev. Winwood Serjeant, in whose time, the Revolution having converted his wealthy and influential parishioners into refugees and driven him to seek an asylum elsewhere, the church became a barrack, in which Captain Chester's company, of Wethersfield, Connecticut, was quar-

CHRIST CHURCH.

tered at the time of Bunker Hill, and after them one of the companies of Southern riflemen. It appears also to have been some time occupied as a guard-house by our forces, rivalling in this respect the wanton usage of the Boston churches by the king's troops. But was not Westminster Abbey occupied by soldiery in 1643 ? General Washington, himself a churchman, attended a service here, held at the request of Mrs. Washington, on Sunday, the last day of 1775. The religious rite was performed by Colonel William Palfrey, one of the General's aids. Mrs. Gates and Mrs. Custis were also present. There is a tradition that Washington continued to attend service here, but the General was probably too politic to have adopted a course so little in accord with the views of the army in general. He attended Dr. Appleton's church at times, and always showed himself possessed of true Christian liberality. On at least one occasion he partook of the Sacrament at the Presbyterian table. His generals were, in this respect, mindful of his example. At the baptism of a son of General Knox, in Boston, Lafayette, a Catholic, and Greene, a Quaker, stood godfathers to the child, Knox himself being a Presbyterian.

From 1775 until 1790 Christ Church remained in the condition in which the war had involved it. During that time it had neither parish nor rector, but in the latter year it was reopened, the Rev. Dr. Parker of Trinity, Boston, officiating for the occasion. A chime of thirteen bells was placed in the belfry in 1860. For many interesting particulars of the history of this church the reader is referred to the historical discourse of Rev. Nicholas Hoppin, a former rector.

The remains of the unfortunate Richard Brown, a lieutenant of the Convention troops, were deposited under this church. We have briefly referred to the shooting of this officer on Prospect Hill, as he was riding out with two women. It gave rise to a paper war between General Phillips and General Heath, in which, every advantage being on the side of the latter, he may be said to have come off victorious. An inquest pronounced the shooting justifiable, but the British officers, exasperated to the highest degree by this melancholy affair, affected to believe themselves the objects of indiscriminate slaughter.

It was at the time the church was opened for the interment of Lieutenant Brown, according to the rite of the Church of England, that the damage to the interior took place. Ensign Anbury asserts that the Americans then seized the opportunity "to plunder, ransack, and deface everything they could lay their hands on, destroying the pulpit, reading-desk, and communion table, and, ascending the organ-loft, destroyed the bellows and broke all the pipes of a very handsome instrument." This organ was made by Snetzler.

The burial-place which lies between the churches has received from the earliest times of our history the ashes of freeman and slave, squire and rustic. In its repose mingle the dust of college presidents, soldiers of forgotten wars, and ministers of wellnigh forgotten doctrines. The earliest inscription is in 1653, but the interments antecedent to this date were made, in many cases doubtless, without any graven tablet or other stone than some heavy mass selected at hazard, to protect the remains from beasts of prey. In still other instances the lines traced on the stones have been effaced by natural causes, and even the rude monuments themselves have disappeared beneath the mould.

> "The slumberer's mound grows fresh and green,
>     Then slowly disappears ;
> The mosses creep, the gray stones lean,
>     Earth hides his date and years."

Among the earlier tenants of God's Acre, as Longfellow has reverently distinguished it, are Andrew Belcher, the innkeeper, Stephen Day, the printer, and Samuel Green, his successor, Elijah Corlet, master of the " faire Grammar Schoole," Dunster, first President of the College, and Thomas Shepard, minister of the church in Cambridge, who succeeded Hooker when he departed to plant the Colony of Connecticut. In their various callings, these were the forefathers of the hamlet; Old Cambridge is really concentrated within this narrow space.

The consideration which attached to the position of governor of the College is indicated by the long, pompous Latin inscriptions, to be deciphered only by the scholar. Classic lore, as dead to the world in general as is the subject of its eulogium, followed them to their tombs, —

> "But for mine own part it was all Greek to me," —

and is there stretched out at full length in many a line of sounding import. Dunster, Chauncy, Leverett, Wadsworth, Holyoke, Willard, and Webber lie here awaiting the great Commencement, where Freshman may at once attain the highest degree, and where College parchment availeth nothing.

The disappearance of many of the leaden family-escutcheons has already been accounted for by their conversion into deadly missiles. Necessity, which knows no law, led to these acts of sacrilege, and yet we should as soon think of fashioning the bones of the dead themselves into weapons as rob their tablets of their blazonry. The cavities in which were placed the heraldic emblems are now so many little basins to catch the dews of heaven, — our precious and only Holy Water.

The Vassall tomb, a horizontal sandstone slab resting on five upright columns, is one of the most conspicuous objects in the cemetery. On the face of the slab are sculptured the chalice and sun, which may have been borne upon the banner of some gallant French crusader; for the Vassalls were lords and barons in ancient Guienne. Hospitality and unsullied reputation are in the heraldic conjunction reduced to knightly or kingly subjection in the name. Whether amid the sands of Holy Land, the soil of sunny France, or the clay of Cambridge churchyard, the slumberers calmly await the summons of the great King-of-Arms.

Near Christ Church is a handsome monument of Scotch granite, erected by the city in 1870 to the memory of John Hicks,

William Marcy, and Moses Richardson, buried here, and of Jabez Wyman and Jason Russell, of Menotomy, who fell on the day of Lexington battle.

Here is the form of an invitation to a funeral of the olden time.   Rev. Mr. Nowell died in London in 1688.

" ffor the Reuerend Mr. Mather.   These —

REUEREND S<sup>R</sup>, — You are desired to accompany the Corps of M<sup>r</sup> Samuell Nowell, minister of the Gospell, of Eminent Note in New England, deceased, from M<sup>r</sup> Quicks meating place in Bartholemew Close, on Thursday next at two of the clock in the afternoon p<sup>r</sup>cisely, to the new burying place by the Artillery ground."

An epitaph has been described as giving a good character to persons on their going to a new place, who sometimes enjoyed a very bad character in the place they had just left.   There is something touching about an unknown grave.   Even the ignorant crave some memento when they are gone, and the dread of being wholly forgotten on earth is depicted in Gray's incomparable lines : —

> " Yet even these bones from insult to protect,
>     Some frail memorial still erected nigh,
>   With uncouth rhymes and shapeless sculpture decked,
>     Implores the passing tribute of a sigh."

Occasionally we see a stone splintered or wantonly defaced. Sometimes an old heraldic device is obliterated by a modern chisel, to give place to some new-comer who has thus, through the agency of a soulless grave-digger, possessed himself of the last heritage of the former proprietor.

" I think I see them at their work those sapient trouble tombs."

While we are beautifying our newer cemeteries, and making them to " blossom as the rose," our ancient burial-places remain neglected.   Cambridge churchyard was long a common thoroughfare and playground, from which the stranger augured but ill of our reverence for the ashes of our ancestors.   The place is much better kept than formerly, but we marked the absence of all attempt at beautifying the spot.   There are

neither shady walks nor blooming shrubs in a place so public
as to meet the eye of every wayfarer. The older stones, half
hidden in the tangled grass, threaten total disappearance at no
distant day. Pray Heaven all that is left of ancient Newtown
does not return to a state of nature.

Governor Belcher, one of Harvard's best friends, and the
patron of Princeton College, died at his government in New
Jersey in 1757. He was much attached to Cambridge, his
Alma Mater, and the friends of his youth. In his will he desired to be buried in the midst of those he had loved, and
accordingly his remains were deposited in this burying-ground
in a tomb constructed a short time previous. It appears that
the governor and his bosom friend Judge Remington had expressed the desire to be buried in one grave, so that when Belcher was laid in the tomb the body of his friend, who had
preceded him, was disinterred and laid by his side. The monument which the governor had directed to be raised over his
resting-place was never erected, and in time the memory of the
place of his interment itself passed away with the generation to
which he belonged. The tomb became the family vault of the
Jennisons. On the decease of Dr. Jennison, it was found to
be completely filled with tenants. The old sexton, Brackett,
upon being questioned, recollected to have seen at the bottom
of the vault the fragments of an old-fashioned coffin, covered
with velvet and studded with gilt nails. This was believed to
be that of Governor Belcher, whose granddaughter was the wife
of Dr. Jennison. The tomb of Belcher and that of Judge
Trowbridge (since known as the Dana tomb) are near the gateway. In the latter were placed the remains of Washington
Allston.

There have been funerals in New England with some attempt
at feudal pomp. When Governor Leverett died, in 1679, the
pageant was rendered as imposing as possible. Though the
governor had carefully concealed the fact of his knighthood by
Charles II. during his lifetime, the customs of knightly burial
were brought into requisition at his interment in Boston.
There were bearers, carrying each a banner roll, at the four

corners of the hearse.   After these came the principal gentlemen of the town with the armor of the deceased, the first bearing the helmet, the last the spur.   The procession closed with
the led horse of the governor followed by banners.

The home of Judge Trowbridge was on the ground on which
the First Church now stands.   Trowbridge, who had been
attorney-general, and who was, at the breaking out of the Revolution, judge of the Supreme Court, resigned soon after the
battle of Lexington, and retired to Byfield, where he enjoyed
for a time the companionship of his pupil, Theophilus Parsons,
whose character he no doubt impressed with his own stamp.
Judge Trowbridge presided at the trial of Captain Preston with
a fairness and ability that commanded respect.   He was well in
years when the Revolution burst forth in full vigor, and although offered a safe conduct, declined to leave the country,
saying, "I have nothing to fear from my countrymen."   He
returned to Cambridge, and died here in 1793.

A little time after the battle of Lexington Judge Trowbridge
stated to Rev. John Eliot that, "it was a most unhappy thing
that Hutchinson was ever chief justice of our court.   What
Otis said, 'that he would set the province in flames, if he
perished by the fire,' has come to pass."   At the last court
held under the charter, Peter Oliver was chief justice, and Edmund Trowbridge, Foster Hutchinson, William Cushing, and
William Brown were the judges.   Of these, Cushing was the
only one who afterwards appeared on the bench.

> "The scene is changed !   No green arcade,
>           No trees all ranged arow."

The old Brattle house, on the street of that name, is the first
you meet with after passing the spot where formerly stood a
hotel under the familiar designation of the Brattle House, but
more recently occupied as a printing house.   The buildings,
now entirely demolished, occupied a part of the Brattle estate,
which was once the most noted in Cambridge for the elegance
of its grounds and the walk laid out by the proprieter, known
in its day as Brattle's Mall.   Miss Ruth Stiles, afterwards the

mother of Dr. Gannett of Boston, penned some beautiful lines
to this promenade : —

> " Say, noble artist, by what power inspired
> Thy skilful hands such varied scenes compose ?
> At whose command the sluggish soil retir'd,
> And from the marsh this beauteous mall arose ? "

The walk, which once conducted to the river's side, was the
favorite promenade for the nymphs and swains of Old Cambridge, as on a moonlit eve they wandered forth
to whisper their vows, chant a love-ditty under
the shadows of the listening trees, or idly cast
a pebble into the current of the shimmering
stream.   Besides the mall, was a marble grotto
in which gurgled forth a spring, where love-
draughts of singular potency were quaffed, en-
chaining, so 't was said, the wayward fancies of
the coquette, or giving heart of grace to bashful
wooer.   Reader, the spring has coyly with-
drawn beneath the turf, though its refreshing pool is indicated
by a ruined arch nigh the wall of the enclosure ; the mall, too,
is gone, but still, perchance,

BRATTLE.

> " Light-footed fairies guard the verdant side
> And watch the turf by Cynthia's lucid beam."

The elder Thomas Brattle was an eminent merchant of Boston, and a principal founder of Brattle Street Church.   From
him, also, that street took its name.   He was the brother of
William, the respected minister of Cambridge.   William Brattle,
the tory brigadier, went into exile in the royalist hegira, de-
serting his house and all his worldly possessions.   The soldiery
were not long in scenting out and making spoil of the good
liquors contained in the fugitive's cellars, until this house, with
others, was placed under guard, and the effects of every sort
taken in charge for the use of the Colonial forces.

Thomas Brattle, the son of the brigadier, was the author of
the improvements which made his grounds the most celebrated
in New England.   He left the country in 1775 for England,

but returned before the close of the war, and had the good fortune to obtain the removal of his political disabilities. His character was amiable, and his pursuits prompted by an enlightened benevolence and hospitality. One of the last acts of his life was to erect a bath at what was called Brick Wharf, for the benefit of the students of the University, many of whom had lost their lives while bathing in the river. Brattle was an enthusiastic lover of horticulture, and devoted much of his time to the embellishment of his grounds.

General Mifflin occupied the Brattle mansion while acting as quartermaster-general to our forces. Mifflin and Dr. Jonathan Potts, the distinguished army-surgeon of the Revolution, married sisters. The former was small in stature, very active and alert, — qualities which he displayed in the Lechmere's Point affair, — but withal somewhat bustling, and fond of telling the soldiers he would get them into a scrape. His manners were popular, and he appeared every inch a soldier when on duty. Despite the cloud which gathered about Mifflin's connection with the conspiracy to depose Washington, he nobly exerted himself to reinforce the wreck of the grand army at the close of the campaign of 1776.

Mrs. John Adams paid a visit to Major Mifflin's in December, 1775, to meet Mrs. Morgan, the wife of Dr. Church's successor as director-general of the hospital. In the company were Generals Gates and Lee. Tea was drank without restraint.

"General Lee," says Mrs. Adams, "was very urgent for me to tarry in town and dine with him and the ladies present at Hobgoblin Hall, but I excused myself. The General was determined that I should not only be acquainted with him, but with his companions too, and therefore placed a chair before me, into which he ordered Mr. Spada to mount and present his paw to me for better acquaintance. I could not do otherwise than accept it. 'That, Madam,' says he, 'is the dog which Mr. —— has made famous.'"

Mrs. Adams further says : —

"You hear nothing from the ladies but about Major Mifflin's easy address, politeness, complaisance, etc. 'T is well he has so agreeable a lady at Philadelphia. They know nothing about forts, intrenchments, etc., when they return ; or if they do, they are all forgotten and swallowed up in his accomplishments."

It is evident that the Major was a gallant cavalier, and would have been called in our day a first-rate ladies' man. Margaret Fuller and Motley the historian both lived in this house, now the property of the Cambridge Social Union.

To understand what was this old Colonial highway in which we are now sauntering, contract its breadth, expanded at the cost of the contiguous estates ; rear again the magnificent trees sacrificed to the improvement, save here and there a noble specimen spared at the earnest intercession of the near proprietors, or where protected, like the "spreading chestnut-tree," by the poet's art, — would that he might dedicate his muse to every one of these mighty forest guardians ! — some relics of the dispersed sylvan host yet clings to the soil ; carry the boundaries of Thomas Brattle to those of the Vassalls ; obliterate the modern villas, with their neutral tints and chateau roofs ; restore the orchards, the garden glacis, the fragrant lindens, and cool groves; and you have an inkling of the state of the magnificos of "forty-five" and of the most important artery of old Massachusetts Bay.

Near where stood the horse-chestnut, by whose stem Longfellow has located the village smithy, we ought to pause a moment before the long-time dwelling of Judge Story, — a plain, three-story brick house, with small, square upper windows, and veranda along its eastern front. This house was built about 1800, and in it Story died, and from it he was buried.

The old Judge was wont, they say, when weighty matters occupied him, to take his hat into his study, where he remained secure from intrusion ; while the servant, not seeing his head-covering in its accustomed place in the hall, would say to comers of every degree that he was not at home.

"In the summer afternoons he left his library towards twilight, and might always be seen by the passer-by sitting with his family under the portico, talking, or reading some light pamphlet or news-paper ; oftener surrounded by friends, and making the air ring with his gay laugh. This, with the interval occupied by tea, would last until nine o'clock. Generally, also, the summer afternoon was varied, three or four times a week in fine weather, by a drive with my mother of about an hour through the surrounding country in an open chaise. At about ten or half past ten he retired for the night, never varying a half-hour from this time." *

William W. Story, the son of Judge Story, passed his college life in this house, was married in it, and here also made his first essays in art. The beautiful statue of the jurist in the chapel of Mount Auburn is the work of his son's hands. Judge Story's widow remained but a little time in the house after her husband's decease. Edward Tuckerman, professor of botany at Amherst, lived here some time, a bachelor ; and Judge William Kent, son of the celebrated chancellor, resided here while pro-fessor in the Law School. In his time gayety prevailed in the old halls, often filled with the *élite* of the town, and sometimes distinguished by the presence of the eminent commentator him-self. In this house, could we but make its walls voluble, we might write the annals of bench and bar. It stands amid the frailer structures stanch as the Constitution, while its old-time, learned inhabitant has long since obeyed the summons of the Supreme Court of last resort, where there is no more conflict of laws.

Ash Street is the name now given to the old highway lead-ing to the river's side, where formerly existed an eminence known as Windmill Hill, later the site of Brattle's bathing-house, from which the way was known as Bath Lane. The mill is mentioned as standing in 1719, and, in all probability, occupied the same ground as the earlier mill of the first plant-ers, removed in 1632 to Boston, " because it would not grind but with a westerly wind." The firm ground extends here quite to the river, so that boats freighted with corn could unload at the mill. Down this lane of yore trudged many a weary rustic with his grist for the mill.

* Judge Story's Memoir, by his son.

The house, lately the residence of Samuel Batchelder, Esq., was built about 1700, and may claim the respect due to a hale, hearty old age.   It was originally of rough-cast, filled in with brick.   The east front, unfortunately injured by fire, was restored to its ancient aspect, except that the dormer windows of that part have not been replaced.   The brown old mansion

BELCHER.

incloses three sides of a square, and offers a much more picturesque view from the gardens than from the street.   On the west was the court-yard and carriage entrance, paved with beach pebbles, now a street; the east front opened upon the spacious grounds, now somewhat shrunken on the side of the highway by its enlargement.   During this improvement the low brick wall on Brattle Street, as it now appears on Ash Street, was taken down, and replaced by one more elegant.   The recessed area at the back has a cool, monastic look, with shade and climbing vines, — a place for meditative

GOVERNOR BELCHER.

fancies.   The garden is thickly studded with trees, shrubbery, and flowers, as also was the dreary waste once Thomas Brattle's, during the time of that right worthy horticulturist.   At the extremity of Mr. Batchelder's garden remains of what were believed to have belonged to the early fortifications were discovered.   The situation coincides with the location as fixed by Rev. Dr. Holmes.

The estate came, in 1717, into the possession of Jonathan Belcher while he was yet a merchant and had not donned the cares of office. He was one of the most elegant gentlemen of his time in manners and appearance, — a fact for which his portrait will vouch. While governor he once made a state entry into Hampton Falls, where the Assemblies of Massachusetts Bay and New Hampshire were in session on the vexatious question of the dividing line between the governments. We append a contemporary pasquinade on the event : —

> " Dear Paddy, you ne'er did behold such a sight
> As yesterday morning was seen before night.
> You in all your born days saw, nor I did n't neither,
> So many fine horses and men ride together.
> At the head the lower house trotted two in a row,
> Then all the higher house pranc'd after the low;
> Then the Governor's coach gallop'd on like the wind,
> And the last that came foremost were troopers behind ;
> But I fear it means no good to your neck nor mine,
> For they say 't is to fix a right place for the line."

The mansion afterwards became the property of Colonel John Vassall, the elder, whose sculptured tombstone we have seen in the old churchyard. This gentleman conveys the estate (of seven acres) to his brother, Major Henry, an officer in the militia, who died in this house in 1769. The wife of Major Vassall, *née* Penelope Royall, left her home, at the breaking out of hostilities, in such haste, it is said, that she carried along with her a young companion, whom she had not time to restore to her friends. Such of her property as was serviceable to the Colony forces was given in charge of Colonel Stark, while the rest was allowed to pass into Boston. The barns and outbuildings were used for the storage of the Colony forage, cut with whig scythes in tory pastures.

It is every way likely that the Widow Vassall's house at once became the American hospital, as Thacher tells us it was near headquarters, and no other house was so near as this. There is little doubt that it was the residence, as it certainly was the prison, of that inexplicable character, Dr. Benjamin Church, whose defection was the first that the cause of America had experienced. Suspicion fell upon Church before the middle of September. He was summoned to headquarters on the evening of September 13, before a council of the generals, where he probably learned, for the first time, that he was the object of distrust.    When questioned by Washington he appeared utterly confounded, and made no attempt to vindicate himself.

A treasonable letter, written in cipher, which he was attempting to send to his brother in Boston, by the hands of his mistress, was intercepted, and disclosed Church's perfidy.    The letter itself, when deciphered, did not contain any intelligence of importance, but the discovery that one until then so high in the esteem of his countrymen was engaged in a clandestine correspondence with the enemy was deemed sufficient evidence of guilt.    He was arrested and confined in a chamber looking upon Brattle Street.    The middle window in the second story will indicate the apartment of his detention, in which he employed some of his leisure in cutting on the door of a closet,

" B Church jr "

There the marks now remain, their significance awaiting a right interpretation by Mrs. James, to whom they were long familiar, without suspicion of their origin.    The chamber has two windows in the north front, and two overlooking the area on the south.

The doctor was called before a council of war, consisting of all the major-generals and brigadiers of the army, besides the adjutant-general, General Washington presiding.    This tribunal decided his acts to have been criminal, but remanded him for the decision of the General Court, of which he was a member. He was taken in a chaise, escorted by General Gates and a guard of twenty men, to the music of a fife and drum, to Watertown meeting-house, where the court sat.    It would be difficult to produce a more remarkable instance of special pleading than Church's defence.    The galleries were thronged with people of all ranks.    The bar was placed in the middle of the broad aisle, and the Doctor arraigned.    He was adjudged guilty and expelled.    His subsequent confinement by order of the Continental Congress, his permission to depart the country, and his mysterious fate are matters of history.

A letter from Dr. Church's brother, to which the treasonable document was a reply, contains the following among other re-markable passages, — it refers to Bunker Hill : —

" What says the psalm-singer and Johnny Dupe to fighting British troops now ?   They are at Philadelphia, I suppose plotting more mischief, where I hear your High Mightiness has been Ambas-sador extraordinary : take care of your nob, Mr. Doctor ; remember your old friend, the orator ; * he will preach no more sedition."

What Paul Revere says, together with other corroborative evidence, leaves but little doubt that Dr. Church was in the pay of General Gage.   Revere's account is, in part, as fol-lows : —

" The same day I met Dr. Warren.   He was president of the Committee of Safety.   He engaged me as a messenger to do the out of doors business for that committee ; which gave me an opportunity of being frequently with them.   The Friday evening after, about sunset, I was sitting with some, or near all that committee in their room, which was at Mr. Hastings's house in Cambridge.    Dr. Church all at once started up.   ' Dr. Warren,' said he, ' I am deter-mined to go into Boston to-morrow.'   (It set them all a staring.) Dr. Warren replied, ' Are you serious, Dr. Church ?   They will hang you if they catch you in Boston.'   He replied, ' I am serious, and am determined to go at all adventures.'   After a considerable con-versation Dr. Warren said, ' If you are determined, let us make some business for you.'   They agreed that he should go to get medi-cine for their and our wounded officers."

* Warren.

## CHAPTER XIII.

### HEADQUARTERS OF THE ARMY.

" Somewhat back from the village street
Stands the old-fashioned country-seat."

EXCEPT Mount Vernon, the shrine at which every American means some day to render homage, the house once
the residence of Mr. Longfellow is probably the best known of
any in our country.   It is not to be wondered at that the footsteps of many pilgrims stray within the pleasant enclosure.
The house has often been described, and is an object familiar
to thousands who have visited it, and who would regret its
disappearance as a public misfortune.

A score of years gone by the writer accompanied a gentleman
from a distant State, then accredited to a foreign court, to view
the historic localities of Old Cambridge.   " Ah ! " said the
visitor, as we paused before this mansion, " there is no need to
account for the poet's inspiration."   Be it our task, then, after
repeating something of its history, to stand at the entrance door,
and, like Seneschal of old, announce in succession those who
claim our service in the name of master of the historic edifice.

Standing at some distance back from the street, the mansion
is in the style of an English country house of a hundred and
fifty years ago.   It is built of wood without, walled up with
brick within, giving strength to the building and comfort to its
inhabitants.

The approach is by a walk rising over two slight terraces by
successive flights of sandstone steps.   The first of these terraces
is bordered by a neat wooden balustrade.   Four pilasters with
Corinthian capitals ornament the front of the mansion ; one
standing at each side of the entrance, while others relieve the
corners.   A pediment raised above the line of the cornice rests

upon the central pilasters, and gives character to the design. A dormer window jutting out on either side of the pediment, a pair of substantial chimneys, and a balustrade at the summit of the roof complete the external aspects of the house. The verandas seen on either side are the taste of a modern proprietor. Yellow and white, the poet's colors, are the outward dress which has been applied to this house since a time when the memory of man runneth not to the contrary.

One day we stood on the broad stone slab before this door. We had time to mark the huge brass knocker which seemed to court a giant's grasp, but, O Vulcan ! what a lock was its fellow on the other side. The key might have been forged at the smithy of a Cyclop, and would have done no discredit to the girdle of the keeper of the Bastile or of the White Tower.

It was probably the poet's mental stature that made us expect to see a taller man. His handsome white hair, worn long ; his beard, which threescore and six completed years had blanched, gave him a venerable appearance by no means consistent with his mental and bodily activity. A warm, even ruddy complexion; an eye bright and expressive; a genial smile, which at once allayed any well-founded doubts the intruder might entertain of his reception, made Mr. Longfellow's a countenance to be remembered. Looking into that face, we felt at no loss to account for the beauty, purity, and high moral tone which pervade the poet's productions.

An apparent aroma of fragrant tobacco indicated that, like Tennyson, our host found solace in the weed. The large front room, one of four into which the first floor is divided, and which opens at your right hand as you enter the hall, was reserved by the poet for his study, and here, among his books, antique busts, and other literary paraphernalia, the magician wove his spell.

The windows look upon the lawn and walk by which you approach the house. The grounds are embellished with shrubbery and dominated by some fine old elms ; but the eye is soon engaged with, and lingers on, the broad expanse of meadow through which the river winds unseen, and whose distant margin is fringed with the steeples and house-tops of Brighton. Beyond are the rounded hills and pleasant dales of Brookline, and from the upper windows you may see, on a clear day, the blue masses of Milton Hills. Thus it looked to the early proprietor and to Washington, and thus the present memorial, by the recovery of a large portion of the original acres, perpetuates at once the poet and his landscape.

Lighting a taper, our host first led the way to the cellars, with timely caution to take heed of the solid timbers overhead, as we descended the stairs. He made us remark the thickness of these beams and of the outer walls of the building proper. In extent and loftiness these cellars were not unworthy some old convent in which many a butt of good Rhenish — unless we do them foul wrong — has consoled the jolly friars for days of mortification in downright bacchanalian wassail. We passed beneath arches where light was never meant to enter, for fear of offending the deep, rich glow of the port, or the pale lustre of the Madeira, — recesses out of which we almost expected to see the phantom of the Colonial proprietor appear and challenge our footsteps.

The house is spacious and elegant throughout. From the hall of entrance the staircase winds to the upper floor, giving an idea of loftiness such as you experience in looking up at the vault of a church. The principles of ventilation were respected by the builder in a manner which savors strongly of a West-Indian life. Not a sign of weakness or decay is apparent in the woodwork; wainscots, panels, capitals, and cornices are in excellent taste and skilfully executed.

The old proprietor's farm, for such it was, at first consisted of a hundred and fifty acres or more. The Sewall mansion, since that of John Brewster, Esq., was then the nearest on that side, and at the back the grounds embraced the site of the Observatory, where formerly stood a summer-house. From this hill the waters of a spring were conducted to the house by an aqueduct, still visible where it entered the foundation-wall. The greenhouses were formerly on the spot where the new dormitory has since been erected; the capacious barn is still standing on the west side of the house. Nothing seems to have been wanting to render the estate complete in all its appointments.

The house was probably erected in 1759 by Colonel John Vassall, the same at whose tomb we have paid a passing visit. His family was a distinguished one, both in Old and New England. In King's Chapel, Boston, the visitor may see a beautiful mural monument, commemorative of the virtues, loyalty, and sufferings of Samuel Vassall, a member, and one of the Assistants, of the Massachusetts Company. The escutcheon displays the same emblems as the horizontal slab in Cambridge churchyard. The crest is a ship with the sails furled, adopted, no doubt, to honor the services of that brave John Vassall who fought with Howard, Drake, and Hawkins, against the armada of Philip II. The Vassalls were from Cambridge in Old England.

There could be no fitter name for so stanch a loyalist as Colonel John Vassall. It is said he would not use on his arms the family device, " *Sæpe pro rege, semper pro republica.*" He took an active part against the whigs in the struggles preliminary to active hostilities, and early in 1775 became a fugitive under the protection of the royal standard. In Boston he occupied the time-honored mansion of the Faneuils, where he, no doubt, often saw his fellow-tories assembled around his board. His Cambridge and Boston estates were both confiscated, and not the least curious of the freaks which fortune played in those troublous times was the occupation of the first-named house by Washington, while that of William Vassall, in Boston, afterwards the residence of Gardiner Greene, was for some time the lodgings of Sir William Howe, and also of Earl Percy. Colonel Vassall retired to England, where he died in 1797, after eating a hearty dinner.

Having witnessed the hurried exit of the first proprietor, it becomes our duty to throw wide the portal and admit a battalion of Colonel John Glover's amphibious Marblehead regiment. As the royalist went out the republicans came in, and the halls of the haughty tory resounded with merriment or echoed to the tread of many feet. Colonel John the first gave place to Colonel John the second. Truth compels us to add that the man of Marblehead has left a more enduring record than the marble of the Vassall.

The little colonel, though small in stature, was as brave as Cæsar. His patriotism was full proof. Besides his service at the siege of Boston, his regiment brought off the army in safety after the disastrous affair of Long Island, where they showed that they could handle ashen as well as steel blades. He was a great favorite with Lee, with whom he served two campaigns. It was Glover who, after the ever-memorable passage of the Delaware, made the discovery that the thickly falling sleet had rendered the fire-arms useless. Meaning glances were exchanged among the little group who heard the ill-omened announcement. "What is to be done?" exclaimed Sullivan. "Nothing is left you but to push on and charge," replied St. Clair. Sullivan, still doubtful, sent Colonel William Smith, one of his aids, to inform General Washington of the state of his troops, and that he could depend upon nothing but the bayonet. General Washington replied to Colonel Smith in a voice of thunder, "Go back, sir, immediately, and tell General Sullivan to *go on!*" Colonel Smith said he never saw a face so awfully sublime as Washington's when he spoke these words.

Knox, whose superhuman efforts on that night to get his artillery across the Delaware entitle him to lasting praise, pays this tribute to the brave men of Glover's command : —

"I could wish that they [he was speaking to the Massachusetts Legislature] had stood on the banks of the Delaware River in 1776, on that bitter night when the commander-in-chief had drawn up his little army to cross it, and had seen the powerful current bearing onward the floating masses of ice which threatened destruction to whosoever should venture upon its bosom. I wish that, when this occurrence threatened to defeat the enterprise, they could have heard that distinguished warrior demand, ' *Who will lead us on?* ' and seen the men of Marblehead, and Marblehead alone, stand forward to lead the army along its perilous path to unfading glories and honors in the achievements of Trenton."

Glover was himself a fisherman and wore a short round-jacket like his men. Two of his captains, John Selman and Nicholson Broughton, engaged in the first naval expedition of the Revolution. A third, William Raymond Lee, finally became Glover's successor in the command of the regiment. Glover had been out with the Marblehead militia when Leslie attempted to force his way into Salem. The regiment reported to General Ward on the 22d of June, 1775.

Graydon, whose illiberal and sweeping abuse of the New England troops renders his praise the more remarkable, makes an exception in favor of Glover's regiment, which he saw in New York in 1776. He says : —

"The only exception I recollect to have seen to these miserably constituted bands from New England was the regiment of Glover from Marblehead. There was an appearance of discipline in this corps ; the officers seemed to have mixed with the world, and to understand what belonged to their station. But even in this regiment there were a number of negroes, which, to persons unaccustomed to such associations, had a disagreeable, degrading effect."

Glover served in the Northern army in the campaign against Burgoyne. He commanded the troops drawn up to receive the surrender, and, with Whipple, escorted the forces of the Convention to Cambridge. An excellent disciplinarian, his regiment was one of the best in the army. But the Provincial Congress has ordered the house cleared for a more illustrious tenant, and our sturdy men of Essex must seek another location. On the 7th of July they received orders to encamp. In February, 1776, the regimental headquarters were at Brown's tavern, while the regiment itself lay encamped in an enclosed pasture to the north of the Colleges.

From the records of the Provincial Congress we learn that Joseph Smith was the custodian of the Vassall farm, which furnished considerable supplies of forage for our army. It was at the time when the haymakers were busy in the royalist's meadows that Washington, entering Cambridge with his retinue, first had his attention fixed by the mansion which for more than eight months became his residence.

> "Once, ah ! once, within these walls,
> One whom memory oft recalls,
> The father of his country dwelt ;
> And yonder meadows broad and damp,
> The fires of the besieging camp
> Encircled with a burning belt."

Washington probably took possession of this house before the middle of July, as he himself records, under date of July 15, that he paid for cleansing the premises assigned him, which had been occupied by the Marblehead regiment. The Committee of Safety had ordered it vacated early in May for their own use, but there is no evidence that they ever sat there.

BALL'S WASHINGTON STATUE.

Whatever relates to the personality of Washington will remain a matter of interest to the latest times. The pencils of the Peales, of Trumbull, Stuart, of Wertmüller, and others have depicted him in early manhood, in mature age, and the decline of life; while the chisel of a Canova, a Houdon, and a Chantrey have familiarized Americans with his commanding figure and noble cast of features : —

> " A combination and a form indeed,
> Where every god did seem to set his seal
> To give the world assurance of a man."

One of Rochambeau's generals has left by far the most satisfactory account of Washington's outward man : —

"His stature is noble and lofty, he is well made and exactly proportioned ; his physiognomy mild and agreeable, but such as to render it impossible to speak particularly of any of his features, so that in quitting him you have only the recollection of a fine face. He has neither a grave nor a familiar air, his brow is sometimes marked with thought, but never with inquietude ; in inspiring respect he inspires confidence, and his smile is always the smile of benevolence."

Says another : —

"With a person six feet two inches in stature, expanded, muscular, of elegant proportions and unusually graceful in all its movements, — his head moulded somewhat on the model of the Grecian antique ; features sufficiently prominent for strength or comeliness, — a Roman nose and large blue eyes deeply thoughtful rather than lively, — with these attributes the appearance of Washington was striking and august. Of a fine complexion, he was accounted when young one of the handsomest of men."

That Washington wore his famous blue and buff uniform on his arrival at Cambridge there can be as little doubt as that he appeared in his seat in Congress in this garb ; and, as these became the colors of the famed Continental army, their origin becomes a subject of inquiry.

The portrait of the elder Peale, painted in 1772, represents Washington in the uniform of the provincial troops, which, for good cause, was varied from that of the British line. In the former corps the coat was blue faced with crimson, in the latter scarlet faced with blue, — colors which had been worn since their adoption in the reign of Queen Anne. To continue Peale's delineation of Colonel Washington's uniform, the coat and waistcoat, out of which is seen protruding the "order of march," are both edged with silver lace, with buttons of white metal. An embroidered lilac-colored scarf falls from the left shoulder across the breast and is knotted at the right hip, while suspended by a blue ribbon from his neck is the gorget bearing the arms of Virginia, then and afterwards a distinctive emblem, as the fusee he carries by a sling was the companion of every officer. This was the very dress he wore on the day of Braddock's signal defeat.

Blue — than which no color can be more soldierly — had its precedent, not only in the British Horse Guards, but in the French and other armies of Continental Europe. It is to Sweden, however, that we must look for the origin of the celebrated blue and buff, as we find the Royal Swedes wearing it as early as 1715. In 1789 they were attired in the very costume of the Continentals.

The General wore rich epaulettes and an elegant small sword. He also carried habitually a pair of screw-barrelled, silver-mounted pistols, with a dog's head carved on the handle. It also appears that he sometimes wore the light-blue ribbon across his breast, between coat and waistcoat, which is seen in Peale's portrait painted for Louis XVI. This badge, which gave rise to the mistaken idea that Washington was a Marshal of France, was worn in consequence of an order issued in July, 1775, to make the persons of the generals known to the army. By the same order the major and brigadier generals were to wear pink ribbons, and the aides-de-camp green. An old print of General Putnam exhibits this peculiarity. Cockades of different colors were assigned by orders in 1776 as distinguishing badges for officers.

Peale's portrait of Colonel Washington, together with other valuable paintings at Arlington House, were removed by Mrs. Lee when she left her residence in May, 1861. Although considerably injured by the rough usage of war times, every lover of art will be glad to know that they have been preserved. The gorget which has been mentioned as having been worn by Washington when he sat to the elder Peale is now preserved as a precious relic in the Quincy family, of Boston. A pair of epaulettes worn by the General at Yorktown, together with some other mementos, are in the cabinets of the Massachusetts Historical Society.

The commander-in-chief, upon taking possession of his headquarters, selected the southeast chamber for his sleeping-apart-

ment.  What vigils he kept here in the silent watches of the
night, what invocations were made for Providential aid and
guidance, when, escaping from the sight of men, he unbosomed
himself and bowed down beneath the weight of his responsi-
bilities, the walls alone might tell.

> " Yes, within this very room,
>   Sat he in those hours of gloom,
>   Weary both in heart and head."

Washington was very exact in his habits.  It is said he
always shaved, dressed himself, summer and winter, and answered his letters by candle-light.  Nine o'clock was his hour
for retiring.

The front room underneath the chamber, already mentioned
as the poet's study, was appropriated by the General for a similar purpose.  This opens at the rear into the library, an apartment occupied in the day of the great Virginian by his military
family.  In the study the ample autograph was appended to
letters and orders that have formed the framework for contemporary history ; the march of Arnold to Quebec, the new organization of the Continental army, the occupation of Dorchester Heights, and the simple but graphic expression of the final
triumph of patient endurance in the following order of the
day : —

" HEAD QUARTERS, 17th March 1776.
" Parole *Boston*.  Countersign *St. Patrick.*"
" The regiments under marching orders to march to-morrow
morning.  Brigadier of the Day, General Sullivan.
" By His Excellency's Command."

Here, too, our General rose to his full stature when, in his
famous letter to General Gage, he gave utterance to the feelings
of honest resentment called forth by the supercilious declarations of that officer in language which must have stung the
Briton to the quick : —

"You affect, sir, to despise all rank not derived from the same
source with your own.  I cannot conceive one more honorable than
that which flows from the uncorrupted choice of a brave and free
people, — the purest source and original fountain of all power."

Napoleon, when in exile at St. Helena, remarked to an Englishman while arguing against the foolish attempt to make him relinquish the title of Emperor, " Your nation called Washington a leader of rebels for a long time, and refused to acknowledge either him or the constitution of his country ; but his successes obliged them to change and acknowledge both."

The phrase of " military family," in which was included the entire staff of the General, originated in the British army. The custom of embracing the suite of a general in his household, and of constituting them in effect members of his family, was not practised in the armies of Continental Europe. Washington was fortunately able to support the charge of this practice, as well as to control the incongruous elements sometimes grouped about his person. Of his first staff, Gates, the head, became soured, and, fancying his position far beneath his merits, a restraint soon appeared in his demeanor. Mifflin, the first aid, afterwards governor of Pennsylvania, became involved in the Conway cabal ; and Reed, the General's secretary and most trusted friend, became at one time so doubtful of the success of the American arms, that he is said to have received a British protection. But Reed's patriotism was proof against a most artful attempt to bribe him through the agency of a beautiful woman. When assured of her purpose, he addressed her in these words : " I am not worth purchasing, but such as I am, the king of Great Britain is not rich enough to do it."

Trumbull, the painter, who was made an aid in the early days of the siege, confesses his inability to sustain the exigencies of his position. He relates that the scene at headquarters was altogether new and strange to him.

" I now," he says, " found myself in the family of one of the most distinguished men of the age, surrounded at his table by the principal officers of the army, and in constant intercourse with them ; it was further my duty to receive company and do the honors of the house to many of the first people of the country of both sexes. I soon found myself unequal to the *elegant* duties of my situation, and was gratified when Mr. Edmund Randolph (afterwards Secretary of State) and Mr. Baylor arrived from Virginia, and were named aids-du-camp, to succeed Mr. Mifflin and myself."

George Baylor, who Washington said was no penman, having expressed a desire to go into the artillery with Knox, the General appointed Moylan and Palfrey to fill the places of the former and of Randolph, who was obliged to leave Cambridge suddenly on his own affairs. Baylor is the same officer who, as colonel of dragoons, was surprised and made prisoner by General Grey at Tappan, with the loss of the greater part of his men inhumanly butchered while demanding quarter. Moylan, a gay, rollicking Irishman, was appointed commissary-general, — a place he soon left for the line. Harrison, who succeeded Reed as secretary, lacked grasp for his multifarious duties, though he continued in the staff until 1781. David Humphreys, the soldier-poet, was, for his gallantry at Yorktown, selected to carry the captured standards to Congress, as Baylor had carried the news of victory at Trenton, — Humphreys had first been aid to Putnam. Alexander Hamilton, who served Washington as a member of his military family with singular ability, left the General in anger on account of a scolding he had received from him for some delay in sending off despatches at Yorktown. Tench Tilghman was a dashing cavalier and an excellent scribe. He served Washington nearly five years, during which he was in every action in which the main army was engaged. General Lloyd Tilghman, a descendant, who fought on the Confederate side in the late war, was captured at Fort Henry, and confined for some time at Fort Warren, in Boston harbor. At the festival of the Society of the Cincinnati in 1872, a representative of the Patriot officer was present.

While loitering in the apartments devoted to official business, it may not be uninteresting to refer to the chirography of the leaders of the Continental army, most of whom handled the sword and pen equally well. Washington's characters were large, round, and never appear to have been penned in haste. Knox wrote indifferently when he entered the army, but his hand soon became straggling and difficult to decipher, his mind being so much more active than his pen that his MS. is filled with interlineations. Greene wrote a fair, clear, running-hand ;

CRAIGIE—LONGFELLOW MANSION, CAMBRIDGE.

his language couched in good, terse phrase.  Wayne, far from being the boor that André's epic makes him, not only held a fluent, but a graphic pen, as witness his despatch : —

"STONEY POINT, 16th July, 1779, — 2 o'clock, A. M.

"DEAR GENERAL,— The fort and garrison, with Colonel Johnston, are ours.  Our officers and men behaved like men who are determined to be free.  Yours most sincerely,

"ANT᙮ WAYNE."

Gates wrote a handsome, round hand ; so did Schuyler, St. Clair, Sullivan, and Stirling.  Lee took rather more care of his handwriting than of his dress ; his characters are bold and legible.  Lafayette wrote like a Frenchman.  Steuben's and Chastellux's were rather an improvement on Lafayette's diminutive strokes.

Whatever may be said of Washington's Fabian policy, it is certain the pugnacious element was not wanting in his character.  He wished to carry Boston by assault, but was overruled by his council ; he wished to fight at Germantown, with an army just beaten ; and again at Monmouth against the advice of a council of war, with Lee at its head.  In the latter battle, where he was more than half defeated, disaster became victory under his eye and voice.  Here he is said to have been fearfully aroused, appearing in an unwonted and terrible aspect.  An eyewitness of one of those rare but awful phenomena, a burst of ungovernable wrath from Washington, related that on seeing the misconduct of General Lee, he lost all control of himself, and, casting his hat to the ground, stamped upon it in his rage.

" In every heart
Are sown the sparks that kindle fiery war ;
Occasion needs but fan them and they blaze."

This battle has always reminded us of Marengo, where Desaix, arriving on the field to find the French army beaten and retreating, calmly replied to the question of the First Consul, "The battle is lost ; but it is only two o'clock, we have time to gain another."  But Lee was not Desaix, and the chief, not the lieutenant, saved the day.  Lafayette always said Washington was superb at Monmouth.

Another incident, perfectly authentic, exhibits Washington's personal magnetism and prowess. It is related that one morning Colonel Glover came in haste to headquarters to announce that his men were in a state of mutiny. On the instant the General arose, and, mounting his horse, which was always kept ready saddled, rode at full gallop to the mutineers' camp, accompanied by Glover and Hon. James Sullivan. Washington, arrived on the spot, found himself in presence of a riot of serious proportions between the Marblehead fishermen and Morgan's Riflemen. The Yankees ridiculed the strange attire and bizarre appearance of the Virginians. Words were followed by blows, until an indescribable uproar, produced by a thousand combatants, greeted the appearance of the General. He had ordered his servant, Pompey, to dismount and let down the bars which closed the entrance to the camp ; this the negro was in the act of doing, when the General, spurring his horse, leaped over Pompey's head, cleared the bars, and dashed among the rioters. " The General threw the bridle of his horse into his servant's hands, and, rushing into the thickest of the fight, seized two tall, brawny riflemen by the throat, keeping them at arm's length, talking to and shaking them." His commanding presence and gestures, together with the great physical strength he displayed, — for he held the men he had seized as incapable of resistance as babes, — caused the angry soldiers to fall back to the right and left. Calling the officers around him, with their aid the riot was quickly suppressed. The General, after giving orders appropriate to prevent the recurrence of such an affair, cantered away from the field, leaving officers and men alike astonished and charmed with what they had witnessed. " You have both a Howe and a Clinton in your army," said a British officer to a fair rebel. " Even so ; but you have no Washington in yours," was the reply.

On the occasion when Colonel Patterson, Howe's adjutant-general, brought to Washington at New York the letter addressed to " George Washington, Esq., &c., &c.," an officer who was present at the interview says his Excellency was very handsomely dressed and made a most elegant appearance.

Patterson appeared awe-struck, and every other word with him was "may it please your Excellency," or "if your Excellency please." After considerable talk on the subject of the letter, the Colonel asked, "Has your Excellency no particular commands with which you would please to honor me to Lord and General Howe?" "Nothing but my particular compliments to both," replied the General, and the conference closed.

Of his generals, Washington's relations with Knox were the most intimate and confidential. Lafayette fully shared in the feelings of love and veneration with which Knox regarded his hero. The appointment of Mad Anthony to command the army against the Northwestern Indians showed that the President had great confidence in his courage and ability. Greene was thought to have possessed greater influence in the councils of the general-in-chief than any other of his captains. None other of the superior officers appear to have stood on as familiar a footing as these. St. Clair was a Scotsman, Montgomery an Irishman, as was also General Conway, while Lee and Gates were Englishmen by birth.

It is not a little surprising that in our republican army there should have been an officer born on our soil who not only claimed the title to an earldom, but also to be addressed as "My Lord" by his brother officers. He signed himself simply "Stirling." A *bon vivant*, he was accused of liking the bottle fully as much as became a lord, and more than became a general. On convivial occasions he was fond of fighting his battles over.

One of Stirling's daughters, Lady Kitty, made a private marriage with Colonel William Duer, who acted so noble a part during the memorable cabal in Congress to elevate Gates to the chief command. Lady Kitty kept her secret so well that even her father's most intimate friends were not informed of it, and when Colonel Duer stated that he was married he was supposed to be jesting, until it was announced that the pair had passed the night together at the house of a friend.

Lafayette always kept a huge bowl of grog on his table for all comers. Despite his deep red hair, he was one of the finest-

looking men in the army.    His forehead was good, though re-
ceding ; his eyes hazel ; his mouth and chin delicately formed,
exhibiting beauty rather than strength.    His carriage was
noble, his manner frank and winning.    He never wore powder,
but in later years became quite bald and wore a wig.

The Marchioness was not critically handsome, but had an
agreeable face and figure, and was a most amiable woman.
Mademoiselle and Master George were considered in their youth
fine children, and the friends of the Marquis thought he made
a great sacrifice of domestic happiness in espousing the cause
of our country as warmly as he did.    His son, George Washington Lafayette, who was confided to a Bostonian's care during one of the stormy periods of his father's career after his
return to France, accompanied the Marquis to America in 1824,
and died at La Grange in 1849.

Count Rochambeau could not speak a word of English, nor
could the brothers, Baron and Viscount Viomenil, the Marquis Laval, or Count Saint Maime.    The two Counts Deux
Ponts, on the other hand, spoke pretty well, while General
Chastellux had fully mastered the language.    During the stay
of the French at Newport, an invitation to the *petites soupers*
of the latter officer was eagerly welcomed by intelligent Americans.

It has been said there is not a proclamation of Napoleon to
his soldiers in which glory is not mentioned and duty forgotten ; there is not an order of Wellington to his troops in which
duty is not inculcated, nor one in which glory is even alluded
to.    Washington's orders contain appeals to the patriotism,
love of country, and nobler impulses of his soldiers.    He rebuked profligacy, immorality, and kindred vices in scathing
terms ; he seldom addressed his army that he did not confess
his dependence on that Supreme guidance which the two preceding illustrious examples ignored.

In this study probably assembled the councils of war, at
which we may imagine the General standing with his back to
the cavernous fireplace, his brow thoughtful, his lips compressed
beyond their wont, while the glowing embers paint fantastic

pictures on the wainscot, or cast weird shadows of the tall figure along the floor. Around the board are Ward, Lee, and Putnam in the places of honor, with Thomas, Heath, Greene, Sullivan, Spencer, and Knox in the order of rank. If the subject was momentous, or not finally disposed of to his satisfaction in the council, it was Washington's custom to require a written opinion from each of the generals.

Opposite the study, on your left as you enter, is the reception-room, in which Mrs. Washington, who arrived in Cambridge at about the same time as the news of the capture of Montreal, — twin events which gladdened the General's heart, — received her guests. These, we may assume, included all the families of distinction, either resident or who came to visit their relations in camp. On the day of the battle of Bunker Hill the untoward and afflicting scenes so affected one delicate, sensitive organization that the lady became deranged, and died in a few months. This was the wife of Colonel, afterwards General, Huntington.

But the gloomy aspect was not always uppermost, and gayety perhaps prevailed on one side of the hall, while matters of grave moment were being despatched on the other. It would not be too great a flight of fancy to imagine the lady of the household looking over the list of her dinner invitations while her lord was signing the sentence of a court-martial or the order to open fire on the beleaguered town. Mrs. Washington entered this house on the 11th December, 1775, having for the companions of her journey from Virginia Mrs. Gates, John Custis and lady, and George Lewis. The General's wife had very fine dark hair. A portion of her wedding dress is highly prized by a lady resident in Boston, while a shoe possessed by another gives assurance of a small, delicate foot.

We pass into the dining-room, in which have assembled many of the most distinguished military, civil, and literary characters of our country. Washington's house steward was Ebenezer Austin, who had been recommended to him by the Provincial Committee. Mrs. Goodwin of Charlestown, the mother of Ozias Goodwin, a well-known merchant of Boston, was his housekeeper; she had been rendered homeless by the destruction of Charlestown. The General had a French cook and black servants, — then as common in Massachusetts as in the Old Dominion.

The General breakfasted at seven o'clock in the summer and at eight in the winter. He dined at two, and drank tea early in the evening; supper he eschewed altogether. His breakfast was very frugal, and at this meal he drank tea, of which he was extremely fond. He dined well, but was not difficult to please in the choice of his viands. There were usually eight or ten large dishes of meat and pastry, with vegetables, followed by a second course of pastry. After the removal of the cloth the ladies retired, and the gentlemen, as was then the fashion, partook of wine. Madeira, of which he drank a couple of glasses out of silver camp cups, was the General's favorite wine.

Washington sat long at table. An officer who dined with him says the repast occupied two hours, during which the General was toasting and conversing all the time. One of his aides was seated every day at the bottom of the table, near the General, to serve the company and distribute the bottles. Washington's mess-chest, camp equipage, and horse equipments were complete and elegant; he broke all his own horses.

Apropos of the General's stud, he had two favorite horses, — one a large, elegant chestnut, high-spirited and of gallant carriage, which had belonged to the British army; the other a sorrel, and smaller. This was the horse he always rode in battle, so that whenever the General was seen to mount him the word ran through the ranks, "We have business on hand." Washington came to Cambridge in a light phaeton and pair, but in his frequent excursions and reconnoitring expeditions he preferred the saddle, for he was an admirable horseman. Billy, the General's black groom and favorite body-servant, has become an historical character.

In order that nothing may be wanting to complete the in-door life in this old mansion in 1775 and 1776, we append a dinner invitation, such as was issued daily, merely cautioning the reader that it is not the production of the General, but of one of his family : —

"The General & Mrs Washington present their compliments to Col? Knox & Lady, begs the favor of their company at dinner on Friday half after 2 o'clock

"Thursday Evening Feby 1st."

Among other notables who sat at the General's board in this room was Franklin, when he came to settle with his fellow-commissioners, Hon. Thomas Lynch of Carolina, and Benjamin Harrison of Virginia, the new establishment of the Continental army. General Greene, who was presented to the philosopher on the evening of his arrival, says : —

"I had the honor to be introduced to that very great man, Doctor Franklin, whom I viewed with silent admiration during the whole evening. Attention watched his lips, and conviction closed his periods."

We do not know whether grace was habitually said at the General's table or not, but the great printer would have willingly dispensed with it. It is related, as illustrative of the eminently practical turn of his mind, that he one day astonished that devout old gentleman, his father, by asking, "Father, why don't you say grace at once over the whole barrel of flour or pork, instead of doing so three times a day ?" Neither history nor tradition has preserved the respectable tallow-chandler's reply.

The first steps taken by Washington to form a body-guard were in orders of the 11th of March, 1776, by which the commanding officers of the regiments of the established army were directed to furnish four men each, selected for their honesty, sobriety, and good behavior. The men were to be from five feet eight to five feet ten inches in height, handsomely and well made, and, as the General laid great stress upon cleanliness in the soldier, he requested that particular attention might be paid to the choice of such as were "neat and spruce." The General stipulated that the candidates for his guard should be drilled men, and perfectly willing to enter upon this new duty. They were not required to bring either arms or uniform, which indicates the

General's intention to newly arm and clothe his guard. This was the origin of the celebrated *corps d'élite*.

FLAG OF THE BODY-GUARD.

Caleb Gibbs of Rhode Island was the first commander of the Life Guard. He had been adjutant of Glover's regiment, and must have recommended himself to the commander-in-chief. After the war he resided in Boston, and was made naval store-keeper, with an office in Battery-march Street.

Washington took his departure from the Vassall house between the 4th and 10th of April, 1776, for New York. On the 4th he wrote from Cambridge to the president of Congress, and on the 11th he was at New Haven *en route* to New York. On the occasion of his third visit to Boston, in 1789, he again passed through Cambridge and stopped about an hour at his old headquarters. He then received a military salute from the Middlesex militia, who were drawn up on Cambridge Common with General Brooks at their head.

The next person to claim our attention is Nathaniel Tracy, who became the proprietor after the war. He kept up the traditions of the mansion for hospitality, though we doubt whether his servants ever drank choice wines from pitchers, as has been stated. Tracy was from Newburyport, where, with his brother, he had carried on, under the firm name of Tracy, Jackson, and Tracy, an immense business in privateering. Martin Brimmer was their agent in Boston. He fitted out the first private armed vessel that sailed from an American port, and during the war was the principal owner of more than a score of cruisers, which inflicted great loss upon the enemy's marine. The following extract will enable the reader to form a correct estimate of the hazard with which this business was conducted : —

"At the end of 1777 his brother and he had lost one and forty ships, and with regard to himself he had not a ray of hope but in a single letter of marque of eight guns, of which he had received no news. As he was walking one day with his brother, discussing with him how they should procure the means of subsistence for their families, they perceived a sail making for the harbor, which fortunately proved a prize worth £ 20,000 sterling.

"In 1781 he lent the State of Massachusetts five thousand pounds to clothe their troops, with no other security than the receipt of the State Treasurer."

Mr. Tracy was generous and patriotic. Benedict Arnold was his guest while preparing to embark his troops for the Kennebec in 1775. He had entertained in 1782, at his mansion at Newburyport, M. de Chastellux and his aides, Isidore Lynch, De Montesquieu, and Talleyrand the younger. The Frenchmen could manage his good old Madeira and Xeres, but the home-brewed punch, which was always at hand in a huge punch-bowl, proved too much for De Montesquieu and Talleyrand, who succumbed and were carried drunk to bed.

Tracy went to France in 1784, where he met with due return for his former civilities from Viscount Noailles and some of his old guests. In 1789, when again a resident of Newburyport, he received Washington, then on his triumphal tour ; and in 1824 Lafayette, following in the footsteps of his illustrious commander, slept in the same apartment he had occupied.

Next comes Thomas Russell, a Boston merchant-prince, accredited by the vulgar with having once eaten for his breakfast a sandwich made of a hundred-dollar note and two slices of bread.

Following Thomas Russell came, in March, 1791, Dr. Andrew Craigie, late apothecary-general to the Continental army, in which service it is reported he amassed a very large fortune. For the estate, then estimated to contain one hundred and fifty acres, and including the house of Harry Vassall, — designated as that of Mr. Batchelder, but then occupied by Frederick Geyer,

— Mr. Craigie gave £ 3,750 lawful money, — a sum so small in comparison with its value that our reader will pardon us for mentioning it.

Craigie was at Bunker Hill, and assisted in the care of the wounded there. He was at Cambridge during the siege of Boston, and doubtless dispensed his nostrums liberally, for physic was the only thing of which the army had enough, if we may credit concurrent testimony. He was with the Northern army, under General Gates, in 1777 and 1778, and was the confidant of Wilkinson, Gates's adjutant-general, in his correspondence with Lord Stirling, growing out of the Conway imbroglio. Craigie was a director and large proprietor in the company which built the bridge connecting East Cambridge with Boston, to which his name was given. After his decease his widow continued to reside here.

Craigie entertained two very notable guests in this house. One of them was Talleyrand, the evil genius of Napoleon, who said of him that he always treated his enemies as if they were one day to become his friends, and his friends as if they were one day to become his enemies. "A man of talent, but venal in everything." The world has long expected the private memoirs of this remarkable personage, but the thirty years which the prince stipulated in his will should first elapse proved too short for his executors. Without doubt, the private correspondence of Talleyrand would make a record of the most startling character, and give an insight into the lives of his contemporaries that might reverse the views of the world in general in regard to some of them. Few dared to fence with the caustic minister. "Have you read my book?" said Madame de Staël to the prince, whom she had there made to play a part as well as herself. "No," replied Talleyrand; "but I understand we both figure in it as women."

In December, 1794, the Duke of Kent, or Prince Edward as he was styled, was in Boston, and was received during his sojourn with marked attention. He was then in command of the forces in Canada, but afterwards joined the expedition, under Sir Charles Grey, to the French West Indies, where he so greatly distinguished himself by his reckless bravery at the storming of Martinique and Guadaloupe that the flank division which he commanded became the standing toast at the admiral's and commander-in-chief's table. The Duke was a perfect martinet, and was so unpopular with the regiment he commanded under O'Hara, at Gibraltar, that it repeatedly mutinied. He was the father of Queen Victoria.

The prince was accompanied to Boston by his suite. He was very devoted to the ladies, especially so to Mrs. Thomas Russell, whom he attended to the Assembly at Concert Hall. He danced four country-dances with his fair companion, but she fainted before finishing the last, and he danced with no one else, at which every one of the other eighty ladies present was much enraged. At the British Consul's, where the prince held a levee, he was introduced to the widow of a British officer. Her he saluted, while he only bowed to the other ladies present, which gave rise to feelings of no pleasant nature in gentle breasts. It was well said by one who knew the circumstance, that had his Highness settled a pension on the young widow and her children it would indeed have been a princely salute. The prince visited Andrew Craigie. He drove a handsome pair of bays with clipped ears, then an unusual sight in the vicinity of Old Boston.

In October, 1832, Mr. Sparks married Miss Frances Anne Allen, of New York, and in April, 1833, he began housekeeping in the Craigie house. He was at this time engaged on his " Writings of George Washington," and notes in his journal under the date of April 2 : —

" This day, began to occupy Mrs. Craigie's house in Cambridge. It is a singular circumstance that, while I am engaged in preparing for the press the letters of General Washington which he wrote at Cambridge after taking command of the American army, I should occupy the same rooms that he did at that time." *

Edward Everett, whose efforts in behalf of the Mount Vernon fund associate his name with our memorials of Washington,

* Rev. Dr. Ellis's Memoir.

resided here just after his marriage, and while still a professor in the University of which he became president. Willard, Phillips, and Joseph Emerson Worcester, the lexicographer, also lived in the house we are describing.

We now return to Mr. Longfellow, who became an inmate of the house in 1837, with Mrs. Craigie for his landlady. The Harvard professor, as he then was, took possession of the southeast chamber, which has been mentioned as Washington's. In this room were written "Hyperion" and "Voices of the Night," and to its inspiration perhaps we owe the lines, —

> " Lives of great men all remind us
>     We may make our lives sublime,
> And, departing, leave behind us
>     Footprints on the sands of time."

Nearly all of Longfellow's productions, except "Coplas de Manrique" and "Outre Mer," which were written at Brunswick, have been penned in the old Vassall homestead.

It is related that one day, after patiently exhibiting his grand old mansion to a knot of visitors, to whose many questions he replied with perfect good-humor, the poet was about to close the door on the party, when the leader and spokesman accosted him with the startling question, —

" Can you tell me who lives in this house *now* ? "

" Yes, sir, certainly.   I live here."

" What name ? "

" Longfellow."

" Any relation to the Wiscasset Longfellers ? "

This house will ever be chiefly renowned for its associations with the Father of his Country, and when it is gone the spot will still be cherished in loving remembrance.   Yet some pilgrims there will be who will come to pay tribute to the literary memories that cluster around it ; soldiers who conquer with the pen's point, and on whose banners are inscribed the watchword, " Peace hath her victories no less renowned than war."

## CHAPTER XIV

### OLD TORY ROW AND BEYOND.

"Damned neuters, in their middle way of steering,
Are neither fish nor flesh, nor good red herring."
DRYDEN.

THE house standing at the corner of Brattle and Sparks Streets, almost concealed from view by a group of giant, sweet-scented Lindens, has replaced the one formerly occupying that site, now removed farther up the street. The old, two-storied house, seen in our view, has been bodily raised

from its foundations, on the shoulders of a more youthful progeny, as if it were anxious to keep pace with the growth of the trees in its front, and still overlook its old landscape.

Of about the same length of years as its neighbor which we have but now left, this house was in ante-Revolutionary times first the abode of Richard Lechmere, and later of Jonathan Sewall, — royalists both. To the former, a Boston distiller, we have already alluded; but the latter may well claim a passing notice. He belonged to one of the old distinguished families of Massachusetts, and was himself a man of very

superior abilities.   He was the intimate friend and associate of
John Adams, and endeavored to dissuade him from embarking
in the cause of his country.   To Sewall, Adams addressed the
memorable words, as they walked on the Great Hill at Portland, " The die is now cast ; I have now passed the Rubicon :
swim or sink, live or die, survive or perish, with my country is
my unalterable determination."   " Jonathan and John " again
met in London, — the former a broken-down, disappointed man ;
the latter ambassador of his country at the very court upon
whose niggardly bounty the loyalist had depended.   Sewall
came to Nova Scotia, where he had been appointed Judge of
Admiralty.   He married Esther, the sister of Dorothy Quincy,
wife of Governor Hancock.   Sewall's house was mobbed in
September, 1774, and he was forced to flee into Boston.   Old
MacFingal asks, —

> " Who made that wit of water gruel
>   A judge of Admiralty, Sewall ? "

Sewall's house was at length assigned to General Riedesel as
his quarters.   His accomplished lady has left a souvenir of her
sojourn, in her autograph, cut with a diamond on the pane of
a west window, though we ought, perhaps, to say that the signature is considered as the General's by his biographer.   Unfortunately, in removing the glass from the sash the pane was
broken, an accident much regretted by Mr. Brewster, the
present owner of the premises.

Here the Germans enjoyed a repose after the vicissitudes
they had undergone, and in which we hardly know how sufficiently to admire the fortitude and devotion of the Baroness.
The beautiful lindens were a souvenir of the dear Rhineland,
— not unworthy, indeed, to adorn even the celebrated promenade of Berlin.   The Baroness frankly admits that she never
was in so delightful a place, but the feeling that they were
prisoners made her agreeable surroundings still echo the words
of old Richard Lovelace : —

> " Stone walls do not a prison make,
>   Nor iron bars a cage."

They had balls and parties, and duly celebrated the king's birthday. All the generals and officers, British and German, came here often, except Burgoyne, between whom and Riedesel a coolness existed. When Phillips was put under arrest General Heath recognized Riedesel as chief in command. Madame Riedesel had here an opportunity of returning the civilities of General Schuyler in a measure, by attentions to his daughter, who had married a gentleman named Church, and who, for reasons of his own, lived in Boston under the assumed name of Carter. Church was an Englishman, of good family, who had been unfortunate in business in London. He came to America, became a good whig, and, in connection with Colonel Wadsworth of Connecticut, secured a principal share of the contract for supplying the French troops in our service. After the peace he returned to England.

The uniform of the Germans was blue, faced with yellow, which came near causing some awkward mistakes where they were engaged. The poet describes the enemy's battle-array at Monmouth in this wise : —

> " Britons with Germans formed apart for fight,
> The left wing rob'd in blue, in red the right."

The Baroness relates that she found Boston pretty, but inhabited by violent, wicked people. The women, she says, regarded her with repugnance, and were even so shameless as to spit at her when she passed by them. She also accuses " that miserable Carter" of having proposed to the Americans to chop off the heads of the generals, British and German, salt them down in barrels, and send one over to the Ministry for every hamlet or town burned by the king's forces. Madam the baroness, it appears, was not less credulous than some foreign writers that have appeared since her day.

The way in which the German contingent saved their colors after the surrender of Saratoga is worthy of mention. The flags were not given up on the day when the troops piled their arms, as the treaty required, but were reported to have been burnt. This was considered, and in fact was, a breach of military faith, but, being supposed to have occurred through the pardonable chagrin of veterans who clung to the honor of their corps, was overlooked. Only the staves, however, were burned, the flags being concealed with such care by General Riedesel that even his wife did not know of it until the Convention troops were ordered to Virginia, when the Baroness sewed the flags in a mattress, which was passed into the enemy's lines at New York among the effects of an officer.

The next of the seven families which Madame Riedesel mentions as forming the exclusive royalist coterie of Old Cambridge was that of Judge Joseph Lee, whose house is still standing, not far from that of Mr. Brewster's, in our progress towards the setting sun.

This house has the reputation of being the oldest in Cambridge, although another situated on Linnæan Street may, we think, dispute the palm with it. Evidently the building now appears much changed from its primitive aspect, both in respect to size and distinctive character. Externally there is nothing of the Puritan type of architecture, except the huge central chimney-stack, looking as if the very earth had borne it up with difficulty, for its outline appears curved where its bulk has settled unequally. The west end is of rough-cast, and the whole outward structure as unæsthetic and austere as possible.

Judge Lee was a loyalist of a moderate stamp, who remained in Boston during the siege. He was permitted to return to Cambridge, and ended his days in his antique old mansion in 1802.

The large square house at the corner of Fayerweather Street is comparatively modern, belonging to the period of about 1740–50, when we find a large proportion of the mansions of the Colonial gentry sprang up, under the influence of rich harvests from the French War, which gave our merchant princes an opportunity of thrusting their hands pretty deeply into the exchequer of Old England. Captain George Ruggles owned the estate in Shirley's time, but before the Revolution it became the residence of Thomas Fayerweather, for whom the street is named.

ELMWOOD.

The house passed into the possession of William Wells, in whose family it still remains.

Having brought the reader a considerable distance from our point of departure, we at length come to a halt and consult our guide-book of only fifty odd years ago. It tells us we have arrived at "the cross road south of the late Governor Gerry's, now Rev. Charles Lowell's, seat." This is Elmwood, the residence of James Russell Lowell.

It is a pleasure to happen upon an old Colonial estate retaining so much of its former condition as this. It embodies more of the idea of the country-house of a provincial magnate than is easily supplied to the limited horizons and scanty areas of some of our old acquaintances. The splendid grove of pines is a reminiscence of the primitive forest; the noble elms have given a name to the compact old mansion-house and its remaining acres; and there are still the old barn and outbuildings, with the remnant of the ancient orchard. It is easy to see that the poet's pride was in his trees, and one lordly elm, seen from his library window, is worthy to be remembered with Milton's Mulberry or Luther's Linden. The grounds in front of the house are laid out in accordance with modern taste, but at the back the owner may ramble at will in paths all guiltless of the gardener's art, and imagine himself threading the solitudes of some rural glade remote from the sights and sounds of the town.

Of old the road, like a huge serpent, enveloped the estate in its folds as it passed by the front of the house, and again stretched along the ancient settlement of Watertown where were its first humble cottages, its primitive church, and its burial-place. It is almost in sight of the spot, now the vicinity of the Arsenal, where the English landed by Captain Squeb at Nantasket, in May, 1630, made their way up Charles River, and bivouacked in the midst of savages. Sir Richard Saltonstall's supposed demesne is still pointed out in the neighborhood, and at every step you meet with some memorial of the founders. According to old town boundaries, the estate of which we are writing was wholly in Watertown, and extended its fifteen acres quite to Fresh Pond, on the north ; it is now within the limits of Cambridge.

It has often been stated that this house was built by Colonel Thomas Oliver (of whom anon) about 1760 ; but as the estate was only leased by him until the year 1770, when he acquired the title by purchase of the heirs of John Stratton, of Watertown, we do not give full credence to the assertion. The house is older in appearance, both without and within, than its usually assumed date of construction would warrant. Moreover, in the conveyance to Oliver the messuage itself is named.

The house is of wood, of three stories, and is, in itself, without any distinctive marks except as a type of a now obsolete style of architecture. A suit of yellow and white paint had freshened the exterior, as the powder of the colonial proprietor might have once rejuvenated his wrinkled countenance. The tall trees bend their heads in continual obeisance to the mansion, like so many aged servitors ranged around their master. Inwardly the woodwork is plain, and destitute of the elaborate enrichment seen in Mr. Longfellow's. As you went in, when Mr. Lowell occupied the house, you saw the walls were covered with ancestral portraits and with quaint old engravings, rare enough to have dated from the birthday of copperplate. An antique bust occupied a niche on the staircase ; the old clock was there, and in every apartment were collected objects of art or specimens of ancient furniture, which seemed always to have belonged there, so perfectly did they accord with wainscot, panel, and cornice. The reception-room was on the south side of the house, with the library behind it. The poet's study, in which nearly all his poems have been written, was on the third floor.

Since Mr. Lowell's death an effort has been making, begun by Miss Lucia Ames, to preserve Elmwood for all time, as a memorial of the poet and of his work, after the plan adopted by the Longfellow Memorial Society in securing his favorite outlook. Sufficient funds having been raised to secure the land, the effort is expected to succeed. Taken altogether, Elmwood is an earthly paradise to which few would be unwilling to attain, and were we sure its atmosphere were contagious, we could haunt the spot, inhaling deep draughts in its cool and grassy retreats.

Thomas Oliver, the last of the lieutenant-governors under the crown, dwelt here before the Revolution. He belonged to the Dorchester family, and claimed no relationship with Andrew Oliver, the stamp-master and successor of Hutchinson as lieu-tenant-governor. The Olivers were of Huguenot descent, re-nowned in ancient French chivalry, where the family patro-nymic, now shortened by a letter, was deemed worthy to be coupled with that of a Roland, a Rohan, or a Coligny. Thomas inherited a plentiful estate from his grandfather, James Brown, and his great-uncle, Robert Oliver, so that his father did not deem it necessary to provide further for him in his will than to bequeath some testimonials of affection.

This dapper little man, as the crown-deputy was called, pleasant of speech and of courtly manners, was in no public office previous to his appointment under Hutchinson, — a choice so unexpected that it was currently believed that the name of Thomas had been inserted by accident in the commis-sion instead of that of Peter, the chief justice. But our Machia-velli, who had planned the affair, knew better.

One fine afternoon in September, 1774, the men of Middle-sex appeared in the lieutenant-governor's grounds and wrung from him a resignation, after which he consulted his safety by a flight into Boston. How bitter to him was this enforced surrender of his office, may be gathered from the language in which it is couched : —

"My house at Cambridge being surrounded by four thousand people, in compliance with their commands I sign my name, Thomas Oliver."

The house was utilized as a hospital after Bunker Hill, the opposite field being used as the burying-ground for such as died here. In opening new streets, some of the remains have been exhumed, — as many as eight or ten skeletons coming to light within a limited area.

The royalist's habitation became the seat of his antipodes, —

a democratic governor, later vice-president, who resided here while holding these offices. Elbridge Gerry's signature is affixed to the Declaration of Independence, and he was one of the three commissioners sent by Mr. Adams to France in 1797. He was chosen by the Provincial Congress, of which he was a member, to attend the Gascon Lee, in his proposed interview with Burgoyne, who was to the full as bombastic, and who doubtless thought of his former companion in arms,

> "Nay an' thou 'lt mouth,
> I 'll rant as well as thou."

As one of the delegates to frame the Federal Constitution at Philadelphia, in 1787, Mr. Gerry refused to sign that instrument, and opposed its adoption by the Convention of Massachusetts. The result was for a time doubtful, but when the scale seemed to incline in favor of the federalists, Gerry kept close at Cambridge, and his adherents made no motion for his recall. Hancock, by the offer of a tempting prize, — supposed to be no less than the promise of the support of the Massachusetts leaders for the presidency in case Virginia failed to come in, — was induced to appear and commit himself in favor of ratification. Adams came over, and with the aid of Rufus King, Parsons, Otis, and the rest, the measure was carried. This scrap of secret history came to light long afterward.

But Mr. Gerry will doubtless be recollected as well for the curious political manipulation of the map of Old Massachusetts, which gave a handle to his name by no means flattering to the sensibilities of its owner, and notoriety to one of the most effective party caricatures of his time. Briefly, he was the means of introducing the word " Gerrymander " into our political vocabulary. The origin of the name and of the caricature have been subjects of quite warm discussion.

The democratic or republican party having succeeded in re-electing Mr. Gerry in 1811, with both branches of the Legislature in their hands, proceeded to divide the State into new Senatorial districts, so as to insure a democratic majority in the Senate. Hon. Samuel Dana, then President of the Senate, is

considered the author of the scheme, which has also been attributed to Joseph Story, who was Speaker of the House until
January 12, 1812, when he resigned. The bill passed both
branches early in February, 1812, and received the approval of
the governor. Under this new and then audacious arrangement, the counties of Essex and Worcester were carved up in
such a manner as to disregard even the semblance of fairness.
County lines were disregarded and public convenience set at
naught, in order to overcome the federal majorities in those
counties.

The singular appearance of the new Essex district, where a
single tier of towns was taken from the outside of the county,
and Chelsea, in Suffolk, attached, caused a general outcry from
the federalists. The remainder of the county was completely
enveloped by this political deformity, which, with its extremities in the sea at Salisbury, and Chelsea, walled out the remaining towns from the rest of the State. The map of Essex, which
gave rise to the caricature, was drawn by Nathan Hale, who,
with Henry Sedgwick, edited the "Boston Weekly Messenger,"
in which the geographic-political monstrosity first appeared,
March 6, 1812.

At a dinner-party at Colonel Israel Thorndike's house in
Summer Street, Boston, — the site of which, previous to the
great fire of 1872, was occupied by Gray's Block, — this map
was exhibited and discussed, and its grotesque appearance gave
rise to the suggestion that it only wanted wings to resemble
some fabled monster of antiquity. Upon this Tisdale, the
artist and miniature-painter, who was present, took his pencil
and sketched the wings. The name of Salamander being proposed, Mr. Alsop, it is said, suggested that of Gerrymander,
which at once won the approval of the company ; but it is not
so clear who has the honor of inventing this name, — an honor
claimed also for Ben Russell and Mr. Ogilvie. With this
designation the Gerrymander appeared in the "Boston Gazette"
of March 26, 1812. The artist succeeded in forming a very
tolerable caricature of Governor Gerry out of the towns of
Andover, Middleton, and Lynnfield. Salisbury formed the

head and beak of the griffin, Salem and Marblehead the claws.
The design of this famous political caricature has been errone-
ously attributed both to Stuart and to Edward Horsman.
The word "Gerrymander," though fully incorporated into our
language, has but lately found a place in the dictionaries.

Upon the death of Mr. Gerry the property passed into the
possession of Rev. Charles Lowell, father of the poet, by purchase from Mrs. Gerry.    The new owner greatly improved and
beautified the estate, the splendid elms giving it the name of
Elmwood.    Dr. Lowell is best remembered as the pastor of the

LOWELL.

West Church in Boston, where more
than half a century's service had so
fully incorporated his name with that
historic edifice that it was long better
known as Lowell's than by its ancient
designation.    Dr. Lowell succeeded
Rev. Simeon Howard, in whose time
the dismantled appearance of the West
Church gave occasion to a scene not
usually forming a part of the services.

As a couple of Jack Tars were passing by the meeting-house
on a Sunday, observing the remains of the steeple, which was
cut down by the British troops in the year 1775, "Stop, Jack,"
says one of them, "d—n my eyes, but this ship is in distress ;
she has struck her topmast.    Let's go on board and lend her a
hand."    Upon which they went in, but, finding no assistance
was required of them, they sat down until service was ended.
On their going out they were heard to say, "Faith, the ship
which we thought was in distress has the ablest pilot on board
that we've seen for many a day."

Elmwood comprised about thirteen acres, and is separated
only by the road from Mount Auburn, where the mould en-
closes the remains of two of the poet's children.

> "I thought of a mound in sweet Auburn,
>     Where a little headstone stood,
> How the flakes were folding it gently,
>     As did robins the babes in the wood."

James Russell Lowell, after leaving college, became, in 1840, a member of the Suffolk bar, and opened an office in Boston. In this he was true to the traditions of his family. His grandsire filled the office of United States District Judge by the appointment of Washington; his father studied law first and divinity afterwards; while his uncle, the "Boston Rebel" of 1812, was also bred to the bar. From another uncle, Francis Cabot, the city of Lowell takes its name; and those delightful intellectual feasts, the Lowell lectures, arose from the bounty of another member of this family. Mr. Lowell soon relinquished the law, and his arguments are better known to the world through the medium of his essays and verse than by the law reports. In 1843 Lowell joined with Robert Carter in the publication of the "Pioneer," a magazine of brief existence. The broad humor and keen satire of the "Biglow Papers," which appeared during the Mexican War, are still relished by every class of readers, — the Yankee dialect, now so seldom heard in its native richness, giving a piquancy to the language and force to the poet's ideas. We have the assertion of a popular modern humorist * that his productions made no impression on the public until clothed in the Yankee vernacular, so much is the character associated with the idea of original mother-wit and shrewd common-sense.

> "Agin' the chimbly crooknecks hung,
> An' in amongst 'em rusted
> The old queen's arm thet gran'ther Young
> Fetched back from Concord busted."

The inquiry seems pertinent whether we are not on the eve of passing into a period of mediocrity in literature as well as of statesmanship. Prescott, Cooper, Irving, Everett, and Hawthorne, Longfellow, Bryant, Lowell, Holmes, and Taylor, Emerson, Bancroft, and Motley are no more numbered among the living, and the names of those who are to take their places are not yet written. The coming generation will perhaps look back upon ours as the Golden Age of American Letters, com-

* Henry W. Shaw (Josh Billings).

parable only to the Golden Age of Statesmen in the day of Webster, Clay, Calhoun, and their contemporary intellectual giants.

As respects our catalogue of native authors, few, if any, have ever had their pens sharpened by necessity or dipped in the ink of privation. Most of them have been endowed with sufficient fortunes, gravitating naturally into literature, which they have enriched, to the great fame of American culture at home and abroad. Longfellow, it is said, is more read in England than any native poet, Tennyson not excepted; Lowell is also a favorite there; and the works of Irving, Cooper, and Hawthorne are to be found, in and out of the author's mother tongue, in the stalls of London, on the Paris quays, and in the shops of Leipsic and Berlin. Perhaps in the multitude of young authors now earning their daily bread in intellectual labor, some may yet rise on the crest of the wave worthy to receive the golden stylus from these honored hands, for in no one respect is the growth of our country more remarkable than in the enlarged and still increasing area of the literary field by the multiplication of vehicles of information.

Nearly opposite the Lowell mansion once stood the white cottage of Sweet Auburn, some time the home of Caroline Howard, who became the wife of Rev. Samuel Gilman, of Charleston, in 1819, and is widely known as an authoress of repute. At the age of sixteen she commenced a literary career with her first composition in poetry, "Jepthah's Rash Vow," which was followed by other efforts in prose and verse. Perhaps her best-known work is the "Recollections of a Southern Matron."

Miss Howard was the daughter of Samuel Howard, a shipwright of North Square, Boston. Her father dying in her infancy, Caroline came to live with her mother at Sweet Auburn, whose wild beauty impressed her young mind with whatever of poetic fire she may have possessed. Indeed, it is her own admission that her childhood days, passed in wandering amid the tangled groves, making rustic thrones and couches of moss, stamped her highly imaginative temperament with its subtle influences. In girlhood she was fairy-like; her long oval face, from which the clustering curls were parted, having a deeply peacefully contemplative expression. She was a frequent visitor at Governor Gerry's, where she found books to feed, if not to satisfy, her cravings. Owing to changes of residence, her education was indifferent; but her mind tended most naturally to the beautiful, music and drawing superseding the multiplication-table. When she was about fifteen she walked, every week, four miles to Boston, to take lessons in French.

We close our chapter, a little out of the order of chronology, with a fragment of revolutionary history, which subtracts nothing from the interest of Elmwood. When, on the twenty-first of April, about noon, intelligence reached New Haven of the Battle of Lexington, the local militia company was immediately called out by its captain, Benedict Arnold, and forty of its members assented to his proposal to march at once to join the American army as volunteers. They left New Haven the next day. On the way they passed through Pomfret, and were joined by General Israel Putnam. Arriving at Cambridge, they were quartered in the "splendid mansion of Lieutenant-Governor Oliver." This was the only company on the ground completely uniformed and equipped; and, owing to its soldier-like appearance, it was selected to deliver the body of a British officer who had died of wounds received at Lexington. The company remained three weeks in Cambridge, when, with the exception of twelve of its number, who accompanied Arnold on his adventurous expedition to Canada, it returned to New Haven.

## CHAPTER XV.

### MOUNT AUBURN TO NONANTUM BRIDGE.

"Crown me with flowers, intoxicate me with perfumes, let me die to the sounds of delicious music." — *Dying words of* MIRABEAU.

IT would be curious to analyze the feelings with which a dozen different individuals approach a rural cemetery. Doubtless repulsion is uppermost in the minds of the greater number, for death and the grave are but sombre subjects at the best, and few are willingly brought in contact with the outward symbols of the King of Terrors.

ENTRANCE TO MOUNT AUBURN.

Much of the aversion to graveyards which is felt by our country people may be attributed to the hideous and fantastic emblems which are sculptured on our ancestors' headstones.

The death's-head, cross-bones, and hour-glass are but little employed by modern art. We are making our cemeteries attractive, and — shall we confess it ? — that rivalry displayed along the splendid avenues of the living city finds expression in the habitations of the dead.

The city of the dead has much in common with its bustling neighbor. It has its streets, lanes, and alleys, its aristocratic quarter, and its sequestered nooks where the lowlier sleep as well as they that bear the burden of some splendid mausoleum. It has its ordinances, but they are for the living. Here we may end the comparison. Statesmen who in life were at enmity lie as quietly here as do those giants who are entombed in Westminster Abbey with only a slight wall of earth between. Pitt and Fox are separated by eighteen inches.

> "But where are they — the rivals ! a few feet
> Of sullen earth divide each winding-sheet."

Authors, learned professors, men of science, ministers, soldiers, and magistrates people the silent streets. Every trade is represented. The rich man, whose wealth has been the envy of thousands, takes up his residence here as naked as he came into the world. Sin and suffering are unknown. There is no money. Night and day are alike to the inhabitants. The distant clock strikes the hour, unheeded. Time has ended and Eternity begun.

Perhaps Franklin expressed the idea of death as beautifully as has been done by human lips, to Miss Hubbard on the death of his brother. He says : —

"Our friend and we are invited abroad on a party of pleasure that is to last forever. His chair is first ready, and he is gone before us, — we could not all conveniently start together, and why should you and I be grieved at this, since we are soon to follow, and we know where to find him ?"

Mount Auburn is a miniature Switzerland, though no loftier summits than the Milton Hills are visible from its greatest elevation. It has its ranges of rugged hills, its cool valleys, its lakes, and its natural terraces. The Charles might be the

Rhine, and Fresh Pond — could no fitter name be found for so lovely a sheet of water ? — would serve our purpose for Lake Constance. A thick growth of superb forest-trees of singular variety covered its broken, romantic surface ; deep ravines, shady dells, and bold, rocky eminences were its natural attributes. You advance from surprise to surprise.

Art has softened a little of the savage aspect without impairing its picturesqueness ; has hung a mantle of green tresses around the brow of some gray rock, or draped with willows and climbing vines each sylvan retreat. The green lawns are aglow with rich colors, — purple and crimson and gold set in emerald. Every clime has been challenged for its contribution, and the palm stands beside the pine. " How beautiful ! " is the thought which even the heavy-hearted must experience as they pass underneath the massive granite portal into this paradise. Nature here offers her consolation to the mourner, and man is, after all, only one of the wonderful forms sprung from her bosom.

> " Lay her i' the earth ;
> And from her fair and unpolluted flesh
> May violets spring ! "

As you thread the avenues, the place grows wonderfully upon you. The repugnance you may have felt on entering gives way to admiration, until it seems as if the troubles of this life were like to fall from you, with your grosser nature, leaving in their stead nothing but peace and calm. Turn into this path which sometimes skirts the hillside, and then descends into a secluded glade environed with the houses of the dead. Here the workmen are enlarging the interior of a tomb, and the click of chisel and hammer vibrates with strange dissonance upon the stillness which otherwise enfolds the place. And one fellow, with no feeling of his office, is singing as he plies his task !

Who shall write the annals of this silent city ? A sarcophagus on which is sculptured a plumed hat and sword ; a broken column or inverted torch ; a dove alighting on the apex of yonder tall shaft, or is it not just unfolding its white wings for flight ? the sacred volume, open and speaking ; a face transfigured, with holy angels flitting about in marble vesture. Here in a corner is one little grave, with the myrtle lovingly clustering above ; and here is no more room, for all the members of the family are at home and sleeping. Each little ridge has its story, but let no human ghoul disturb the slumberer's repose.

Pass we on to the tower and up to the battlement. Our simile holds good, for here in gray granite is a counterfeit of some old feudal castle by the Rhine. Here we stand, as it were, in an amphitheatre, hedged in by walls whose green slowly changes into blue ere they lose themselves where the ocean lies glistening in the distance. The river, making its way through the hills, is at our feet. The rural towns which the city, like some huge serpent, ever uncoiling and extending its folds, is gradually enveloping and strangling, nestle among the hillsides. Seaward, the smoke from scores of tall chimneys seams and disfigures the delicate background of the sky, while they tell of life and activity within the vast workshop beneath. Let the great city expand as it will, here in its midst is a city of graves, its circle ever extending. It needs no soothsayer to tell us which will yet enroll the greater number.

A view of Mount Auburn by moonlight and from this tower we should not commend to the timid. The white monuments would seem so many apparitions risen from their sepulchral habitations. The swaying and murmuring branches would send forth strange whisperings above, if they did not give illusive movement to the spectral forms beneath. But none keep vigil on the watch-tower, unless some spirit of the host below stands guard upon the narrow platform waiting the final trumpet sound.

Mount Auburn has always been compared with the great cemetery of Paris, originally called Mont Louis, but now everywhere known by the name of old François Delachaise, the confessor of Louis Quatorze, and of whom Madame de Maintenon said some spiteful things. The celebrated French cemetery was laid out on the grounds of the Jesuit establishment, and first used for sepulture in 1804, nearly thirty years previous to the occupation of Mount Auburn for a similar purpose. The area of the American considerably exceeds that of the Parisian cemetery, while its natural advantages are greatly superior.

The two oldest survivors among the founders of Mount Auburn were Dr. Jacob Bigelow, its earliest friend, and Alexander Wadsworth, who made the first topographical survey. It should afford singular gratification to have lived to witness not only their creation serving as a model for every city and village in the land, but also to see that it has been the actual means of preserving the remains of those gathered within its compass from that miscalled spirit of progress which threatens the existence of the most ancient of our city graveyards. It is as like as not that the remains of Isaac Johnson, the founder of Boston, will be disturbed erelong, as it is true that the old enclosure which contains the ashes of John Hancock and of Samuel Adams has been much encroached upon. Should this continue, we hope the relics of these patriots will be removed to some of the rural cemeteries, where their countrymen may rear that monument to their memory the lack of which savors much too strongly of the ingratitude of republics.

But this experience in regard to cemeteries is not peculiar to American cities. The old burial-ground of Bunhill-Fields in London, called by Southey the "Campo Santo of the Dissenters," and where Bunyan, George Fox, Isaac Watts, and De Foe lie, was only preserved, in 1867, after considerable agitation. The ancient custom of entombment under churches may also be considered nearly obsolete. The old English cathedrals are vast charnel-houses, in which interments are prohibited by act of Parliament, special authority being necessary for interment in Westminster Abbey. The mandates of health alone were long disregarded, but the absolute insecurity of this method of sepulture has been too sharply demonstrated by the great fire in Boston to need other examples.

Neither are the rural cemeteries totally exempt from adverse contingencies. War is their great enemy, and as they are usually located upon ground the best adapted to the operations of a siege, they have often become the theatre of sanguinary conflict. The shattered stones at Gettysburg, where the dead once lay more thickly above ground than beneath, will long bear witness of the destructive power of shot and shell. Cave Hill, the beautiful burial-place of Louisville, Ky., long bore the scars made by General Nelson's trenches.

We do not now need to cite the customs of the ancients who often built their cemeteries without their walls, since the practice of interment within the limits of our larger cities is now generally expressly forbidden. Our own ancestors chose the vicinity of their churches, as was the custom in Old England. Sometimes burials were made along the highways, and not unfrequently in the private grounds of the family of the deceased. This custom, which has prevailed to its greatest extent in the country, has, in many instances, been productive of consequences revolting to the sensibilities. Often the fee of a family graveyard has passed to strangers. We have seen little clusters of gravestones standing uncared for in the midst of an open field ; we have known them to lie prostrate for years, and even to be removed where they obstructed the mowing.

There was a curious resemblance between the manner of sepulture practised by the ancient Celts and Britons with that in vogue among the American aborigines. The former buried their dead in cists, barrows, cavities of the rocks, and beneath mounds. The deceased were often placed in a sitting posture, and their arms and trinkets deposited with them. The latter heaped up mounds, or carefully concealed their dead in caves. The implements of war or the chase, belonging to the warrior, were always laid by his side for his use in the happy hunting-grounds. Some analogy in religious belief would justly be inferred from this similarity of customs. The Indian remains are commonly found in a sitting posture also, except where circumstances do not admit of inhumation, when they are frequently placed on scaffolds, in a reclining posture, in the branches of trees and out of the reach of wild animals. This disposition of the dead appears to be peculiar to the red-men of North America.

Our own sepulchral rites have altered but little in a century. Mankind yet craves " the bringing home of bell and burial."

A hundred years ago, carriages being as yet confined to the few, the greater part of the mourners often walked to the grave. Decorum, indeed, exacted that the immediate relatives of a deceased person should walk in procession, no matter what the weather might be. These were followed by acquaintances, who paid with simulated sorrow the duties required of them by fashion. A train of empty carriages brought up the rear, while the bells were tolled to keep the devil at a respectful distance. The custom of the nearest friends following the body to the grave in their moments of greatest affliction originated, it is said, with us in New England. It is worthy of being classed with that other agonizing horror which compelled the mourner to listen to the fall of the clods upon the coffin.

Hired mourners have not yet made their appearance among us ; but if, while we stand here in Mount Auburn, we scan the faces of the occupants of yonder long train of vehicles, how many shall bear the impress of real grief?

"*Hor.* My lord, I came to see your father's funeral.

"*Ham.* I pray thee, do not mock me, fellow-student; I think it was to see my mother's wedding."

The increasing cost of funerals is becoming a matter of serious solicitude. The equality of the grave is by no means applicable to these displays. The rich, who can afford to be lavish, are copied by the poor, who cannot afford it. The trappings of the hearse, the number and elegance of the carriages, are noted for imitation. "Such a one made a poor funeral," or "There were but half a dozen carriages," followed by an expressive shrug, are not uncommon remarks, serving to fix the worldly condition of the deceased.

Pomp at funerals is an inheritance which lapsed into the observance of a few simple forms under our Puritan ancestors. It grew under the province into such proportions as called for the intervention of positive law to prevent the poorer classes ruining themselves, for it was long the custom to present mourning scarfs, gloves, and gold rings to all the friends and relatives.

In England Lord Chesterfield was among the first to discountenance ostentatious funerals. His will, marked by peculiarities, provides for his own last rites in these words : —

"Satiated with the pompous follies of this life, of which I have had an uncommon share, I would have no posthumous ones displayed at my funeral, and therefore desire to be buried at the next burying-place to the place where I shall die, and limit the whole expense at my funeral to one hundred pounds."

Not unfrequently, however, the will of a deceased person is thwarted, as was the case with Governor Burnet, whose friends were determined that his exit should not be made without noise or ceremony, in accordance with his request.

The Irish may claim pre-eminence for singularity in the funereal rite. With us the house of mourning is sacredly devoted to silence and sorrow. We step as lightly as if we feared the slumberer's awakening. The light burns dimly in the chamber of death, casting pale shadows on the recumbent, rigid figure, robed for eternity. Hushed and awe-stricken watchers flit noiselessly about. It is difficult, therefore, to comprehend the orgies which usually attend on a "wake." All we know is, it is a custom, and as such is respected, though to our mind "more honored in the breach than the observance."

Our veneration for the dead is not of that fine, subtle quality that guards the place of sepulture, even of the great, with jealous care. The mother of Washington long slept in an unknown grave ; the place where the ashes of Monroe were deposited was wellnigh forgotten, while that of President Taylor is neglected. It is but lately that a stone has been placed above the last resting-place of Samuel Adams. Michel Ney has no monument in Père la Chaise. What better illustration of the doom of greatness than the cash entry upon the parish records of the Madeleine ? "Paid seven francs for a coffin for the Widow Capet."

Low as we are inclined to estimate our own reverence for the departed, it is infinitely greater than exists in England or France at the present day. Just now we related that the

graves of the martyrs were only preserved in London by a
narrow chance. In the so-called work of restoration in the grand
old cathedrals like Chester and Bath, it is stated that the
bones of bishops, judges, and the magnates of the time, whose
remains were supposed to have been consigned to everlasting
rest, have been dug up from the cellars and carted away like
so much rubbish !

In Père la Chaise you may see half an acre of gravestones
collected in a certain part of the cemetery. These once belonged
to graves, the leases of which having expired or purchase not
being completed within a specific time, the headstones are removed, the remains disinterred and consigned to a common
trench. In the face of that morbid sentimentality displayed by
the French in the construction of their tombs and their decoration at certain periods with chaplets, wreaths, and *immortelles*, it
is believed that no other civilized nation regards the burial of
the common people with so much indifference. Even the poor
Chinese sells himself to obtain a coffin in which to bury his
father ; and one of the most pleasing features of the American
cemetery is the space set apart for the interment of strangers.

Hamlet inquired of the grave-digger how long a man will lie
in the earth ere he rot. This question has been answered in a
manner from time to time where measures of identification have
become necessary. The body of Henry IV. was recognized in
Canterbury Cathedral after nearly four and a half centuries.
The remains of Charles I. were also fully identified by the
striking resemblance to portraits and the division of the head
from the trunk. The bodies, in these cases, were of course em-
balmed. Henry VIII. had been interred in the same vault in
which Charles I. had been deposited. The leaden coffin of
Henry, which was enclosed in one of wood, had been forced
open, exhibiting the skeleton of the king after the lapse of 266
years. The disinterment of bones in Egypt, Pompeii, and
elsewhere, after they have lain in the earth more than a thousand years, renders it impracticable to fix any limit for their
preservation.

A city like Mount Auburn, which counts its eighteen thou-

sand inhabitants, requires time to observe.    There are the
natural beauties of tree, shrub, and flower; there are the
tombs, the monuments, and the simple stones.    Then there are
the epitaphs, some of which even the casual visitor may not
read without emotion.    He may stand before the tablets of
Kirkland, Buckminster, Everett, Story, Channing, or wander
about until the name of Margaret Fuller or of Mrs. Parton
stays his footsteps.    Not far from the entrance is the tomb of
the gifted Prussian, Spurzheim, a chaste and beautiful design.
Bowditch's statue, in bronze, by Ball Hughes, challenges our
respect for the man who was the equal of Laplace in everything
but vanity.    Longfellow and Sumner, lifelong friends, also lie
here.

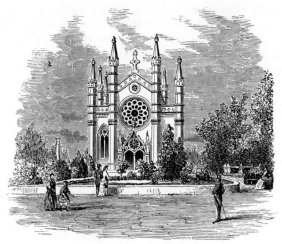

THE FIRST CHAPEL.

Mount Auburn boasts of other architectural features besides
its tombs, of which so many are now being built above ground
that the avenues will, in time, acquire a certain resemblance to
Père la Chaise, where one seems always walking in the streets
of a city.    The Chapel is a gem of its kind, a cathedral in the
diminutive.    It has become a central object of attraction, from
the works of art it contains, — the most remarkable specimens
of statuary in America.    They were designed to represent four

distinct periods of American history, — the Colonial, Revolutionary, Assumption of Sovereignty, and the Supremacy of the Laws.

The first phase is exhibited by John Winthrop, who appears " in his habit as he lived," with ruff, doublet, and hose. The figure is seated, and has a contemplative air. This was the work of Horatio Greenough.

Crawford selected James Otis as a type of the Revolution. His conception is grand and impressive in treatment, noble and striking in form and feature, though to us there appears a superabundance of drapery. Some fault has been found by critics with the pose, as too theatrical, but this objection does not find support in the very general admiration bestowed upon the work, which, to be judged by the groups that assemble before it, is considered the peer among these marbles. Vinnie Ream visited the Chapel when she was engaged in modelling her statue of Abraham Lincoln, and studied the figure of Otis attentively.

The artist, who, we believe, became totally blind before this work was completed, did not succeed in creating the ideal of Otis as a ' flame of fire,' but rather, as it seems to us, of calm and conscious power. But this strength is expressed with great skill. Otis is given to us by Blackburn with a countenance rather cheerful than severe. He was a merry companion, irascible to a degree, but magnanimous, — the life of the clubs and detestation of the crown officers. He might have appeared in the very attitude in which Crawford's chisel has left him when making his celebrated reply to Governor Bernard. Having cited Domat, the famous French jurist, the Governor inquired who Domat was. " He is a very distinguished civilian," answered Otis, " and not the less an authority from being unknown to your Excellency."

Opposite the statue of Otis is that of John Adams, by Randolph Rogers. It possesses much animation and character, being attired in the costume of the time, so that one sees the man as he really appeared, and not a lay figure. The garb of 1776, male and female, civil and military, was worn with as much ease and grace as any more modern costume has been, nor will it in after time appear a whit more awkward than that which happens to be the fashion of the present generation. John Adams in toga and sandals would be no greater anachronism than Julius Cæsar in trousers and French boots.

No doubt the proudest moment Mr. Adams ever knew was the day on which he was presented to George III. as the first American Ambassador. " Sir," said the king, " I was the last man in my kingdom to consent to your independence, and I shall be the last to do anything to infringe it," — a manly as well as kingly speech.

Judge Story's statue has a singular appropriateness in this place. He was the early friend of Mount Auburn, and delivered the beautiful and impressive address of consecration. He often visited its precincts, and lies couched, as he wished to lie, beneath its green turf. His son, William W. Story, wrought on his labor of love many years, and produced a masterpiece.

Besides these more prominent subjects there are in the grounds of Mount Auburn numerous works from the chisels of Dexter, Brackett, Carew, and others. There is also the monumental urn erected in Franklin Street, Boston, in the day of the Old Crescent, in memory of Franklin, since placed above the tomb of Charles Bulfinch, one of the authors of that improvement. The first monument in the cemetery was erected over the remains of Hannah Adams, the historian.

Powers and Crawford and the elder Greenough, after making the name of American art respected at home and abroad, now live only in their works. At the first Great Exhibition at Sydenham our sculptors bore off the palm for beauty, leaving to their European brethren the award for rugged strength. Of either of the triumvirate of deceased sculptors we have named it would be possible to say, —

" He dated from the creation of the beautiful."

The cemetery of Mount Auburn, which is worthy of being compared with no other than itself, owes its origin to the Massachusetts Horticultural Society. Within that body the idea originated with Dr. Jacob Bigelow, whose professional experience condemned the practice of burials beneath the city churches, while the overcrowded state of the graveyards was an evil calling even more loudly for remedy. A meeting was held at Dr. Bigelow's house in Summer Street, Boston, as early as November, 1825, at which were present John Lowell, George Bond, William Sturgis, Thomas W. Ward, Samuel P. Gardiner, John Tappan, Dr. Bigelow, and Nathan Hale. From this time the purpose seems never to have been lost sight of by Dr. Bigelow. The credit of originating the idea of a rural cemetery in the vicinity of Boston belongs to William Tudor, who before 1821 suggested this very remedy for the evils attendant upon burials within the city. His plan did not differ from that eventually carried out in Mount Auburn.

The Horticultural Society having been incorporated in 1829, an informal meeting was held at the Exchange Coffee House in November of the next year, to initiate steps to bring before the public a plan for the purchase of a garden and cemetery. From this meeting others proceeded, until a committee was formed with authority to secure a suitable site. George W. Brimmer, Esq., was then the proprietor of the tract known as Sweet Auburn, but previously as Stone's woods, which he had secured with the view of making himself a residence and park. These woods had, up to this time, been a favorite resort for parties of pleasure, but the axe had already begun its work of ruin when Mr. Brimmer appeared on the scene to arrest it. This gentleman, who had seen Père la Chaise, became an active sympathizer with the object of establishing a cemetery on that plan. He had given $6,000 for Sweet Auburn, which he now tendered to the Horticultural Society for this sum. The offer was accepted. The names of the most prominent and influential members in the community are allied with the foundation. Webster, Story, and Everett took an active part. The one hundred subscribers required, at sixty dollars each, to complete the purchase, were quickly secured. On the 24th of September, 1831, Mount Auburn was formally dedicated. The first interment took place during the following year.

Clashing interests between the society and the lot-holders soon called for new measures. A small beginning had been made with the proposed garden, but the income from the cemetery, greater than had been expected, promised to increase beyond the calculations of the most sanguine. It became evident that the whole tract would be wanted for a cemetery. The idea of separation from the parent society under a government of its own suggested itself, and was at length proposed by Marshall P. Wilder. The discussion on this point was warm and protracted ; so much so that Judge Story, who acted as chairman of the cemetery committee, one day took his hat and left the meeting in anger, but was induced to return. The terms of separation were finally arranged and incorporated into the charter of the Mount Auburn Association. The society relinquished its rights upon payment, annually, of one fourth of the income of the cemetery, after deducting a fixed sum for its expenditures.

This most popular of our societies has already received a very large income from this source, — sufficient to enable it to expand and beautify with its touch the most remote parts of the Union. Taste is developed. A hanging garden is suspended above the door of every cottage, and Hesperides gives up its golden treasures at our command. Not the least of its benefits is the inauguration of Mount Auburn, where the weary

> " Choose their ground
> And take their rest."

In his address on the occasion of laying the corner-stone of Old Horticultural Hall, in 1845, Mr. Wilder well said : —

" And be it ever remembered, that to the Massachusetts Horticultural Society the community are indebted for the foundation and consecration of Mount Auburn Cemetery, — that hallowed resting-place, that garden of graves."

We entered the cemetery with a funeral *cortège*, and we now depart with one. Once past the gate the staid and solemn collection of carriages becomes dismembered, and its sinuous black line parts in fragments. The driver cracks his whip, the horses break into a rattling pace, while the countenances of the so-called mourners are cleared as suddenly as if a cloud had passed from beneath the sun. Here comes the hearse to join the homeward race, and even the still weeping, reluctant friends are whirled away in spite of themselves. Is it a burial with military honors? At entering the band plays a dirge, the comrades following with arms reversed, downcast eyes, and measured tread. The coffin is lowered into the grave and a volley discharged. Once beyond the gate arms are shouldered, the music strikes up a lively air, and the company marches away as gayly as on a field-day. Decorum would seem to challenge such observances. The contrast is somewhat too strongly defined; the revulsion from grief to joyousness something discordant and unworthy.

Emerging from Mount Auburn, we take counsel of the swinging sign pointing to the lane leading to Fresh Pond, which lies but a little distance away, embosomed among the woody hills. In England our ponds would be called lakes, and our lakes might vie with Caspian or Euxine. But our ponds have this advantage, that, while bearing their miniature billows in summer, they become in winter solid acres of ice, to be harvested within the huge storehouses on their banks. Nature has fixed these reservoirs where they may best slake the thirst of the cities, so that whether ten or twenty miles away we may drink of their waters.

Fresh Pond seems to be the natural source of numerous underground streams, which are found whenever the earth is penetrated to any depth between it and Charlestown. Its shores have been looked upon with peculiar favor for country-seats by such as have known its natural advantages; we would not attempt to fix a period when it was not a famed resort for recreation. Big-wigged magistrates and college students came here under the Colony, boating, angling, or haunting the cool groves. It was from the effects of exposure during a fishing excursion here that poor Governor Burnet got his death.

Historically the place has its claims as having served as a

refuge for the panic-stricken women and children of the neighborhood on the 19th of April, 1775. One of these fugitives thus relates her experience : —

"A few hours with the dawning day convinced us the bloody purpose was executing ; the platoon firing assuring us the rising sun must witness the bloody carnage. Not knowing what the event would be at Cambridge at the return of these bloody ruffians, and seeing another brigade despatched to the assistance of the former, looking with the ferocity of barbarians, it seemed necessary to retire to some place of safety till the calamity was passed. My partner had been confined a fortnight by sickness. After dinner we set out, not knowing whither we went. We were directed to a place called Fresh Pond, about a mile from the town ; but what a distressed house did we find it, filled with women whose husbands had gone forth to meet the assailants, seventy or eighty of these (with numberless infant children), weeping and agonizing for the fate of their husbands. In addition to this scene of distress we were for some time in sight of the battle ; the glittering instruments of death proclaiming by an incessant fire that much blood must be shed, that many widowed and orphaned ones must be left as monuments of British barbarity. Another uncomfortable night we passed ; some nodding in their chairs, some resting their weary limbs on the floor."

Time out of mind the shores of the pond belonged to the Wyeths, and one of this family deserves our notice in passing. Nathaniel J. Wyeth was born and bred near at hand. Of an enterprising and courageous disposition, he conceived the idea of organizing a party with which to cross the continent and engage in trade with the Indian tribes of Oregon. He enlisted one-and-twenty adventurous spirits, who made him their leader, and with whom he set out from Boston on the 1st of March, 1832, first encamping his party on one of the harbor islands, in order to inure them to field life. The voyagers provided themselves with a novel means of transportation, — no other than a number of boats built at the village smithy and mounted on wheels. With these boats they expected to pass the rivers they might encounter, while at other times they were to serve as wagons. The idea was not without ingenuity, but was

founded on a false estimate of the character of the streams and
of the mountain roads they were sure to meet with.

Wyeth and his followers pursued their route *via* Baltimore
and the railway, which then left them at the base of the Alle-
ghanies, onward to Pittsburg, at which point they took steam-
boat to St. Louis, arriving there on the 18th of April. Hitherto they had met with only a few disagreeable adventures.
They were now to face the real difficulties of their undertaking.
They soon discovered that their complicated wagons were useless, and they were forced to part with them. The warlike
tribes, whose hunting-grounds they were to traverse, began to
give them uneasiness ; and, to crown their misfortunes, they
now ascertained how ignorantly they had calculated upon the
trade with the savages.

St. Louis was then the great depot of the Indian traders,
who made their annual expeditions across the Plains, prepared
to fight or barter, as the temper of the Indians might dictate.
The old trappers who made their abode in the mountain region
met the traders at a given rendezvous, receiving powder, lead,
tobacco, and a few necessaries in exchange for their furs. To
one of these parties Wyeth attached himself, and it was well
that he did so.

Before reaching the Platte five of Wyeth's men deserted their
companions, either from dissatisfaction with their leader, or
because they had just begun to realize the hazard of the enterprise. Nat Wyeth, however, was of that stuff we so expressively
name clear grit. There was no flinching about him ; the Pacific
was his objective, and he determined to arrive at his destination
even if he marched alone. William Sublette's party, which
Wyeth had joined, encountered the vicissitudes common to a
trip across the plains in that day ; the only difference being that
the New England men now faced these difficulties for the first
time, whereas Sublette's party was largely composed of experienced plainsmen. They followed the course of the Platte, seeing
great herds of buffalo roaming at large, while they experienced
the gnawings of hunger for want of fuel to cook the delicious
humps, sirloins, and joints, constantly paraded like the fruit of

Tantalus before their greedy eyes.  They found the streams turbulent and swift ; the Black Hills, which the iron-horse now so easily ascends, were infested with bears and rattlesnakes. Many of the party fell ill from the effects of drinking the brackish water of the Platte, Dr. Jacob Wyeth, brother of the captain and surgeon of the party, being unluckily of this number.

Sublette, a French creole, and one of those pioneers that have preceded pony-express, telegraph, stage-coach, and locomotive, in their onward march, had no fears of the rivalry of the New England men, and readily took them under his protection.  Besides, they swelled his numbers by the addition of a score of good rifles, no inconsiderable acquisition when his valuable caravan entered the country of the treacherous Blackfeet, the thieving Crows, or warlike Nez-Perces.  The united bands arrived at Pierre's Hole, the trading rendezvous, in July, where they embraced the first opportunity for repose since leaving the white settlements.

At this place there was a further secession from Wyeth's company, by which he was left with only eleven men, the remainder preferring to return homeward with Sublette.  Petty grievances, a somewhat too arrogant demeanor on the part of the leader, and the conviction that the trip would prove a failure, caused these men to desert their companions when only a few hundred miles distant from the mouth of the Columbia. Before a final separation occurred, a severe battle took place between the whites and their Indian allies and the Blackfeet, by which Sublette lost seven of his own men killed and thirteen wounded.  None of Wyeth's men were injured in this fight, but a little later one of those who had separated from him was ambushed and killed by Blackfeet.

Wyeth now joined Milton Sublette, the brother of William, under whose guidance he proceeded towards Salmon River. The Bostons, as the northwest coast Indians formerly styled all white men, arrived at Vancouver on the 29th of October, having occupied seven months in a journey which may now be made in as many days.  The expedition was a failure, indeed, so far as gain was concerned, and Wyeth's men all left him at the Hudson's Bay Company's post. The captain, nothing daunted, and determined to make use of his dearly bought experience, returned to the States the ensuing season. His adventures may be followed by the curious in the pleasant pages of Irving's Captain Bonneville. Arriving at the head-waters of the Missouri, he built what is known as a bull-boat, made of buffalo-skins stitched together and stretched over a slight frame, in which, with two or three half-breeds, he con-signed himself to the treacherous currents and quicksands of the Bighorn. Down this stream he floated to its confluence with the Yellowstone. At Fort Union he exchanged his leather bark for a dug-out, with which he sailed, floated, or paddled down the turbid Missouri to Camp (now Fort) Leavenworth. He returned to Boston, and, having secured the means, again repaired to St. Louis, where he enlisted a second company of sixty men, with which he once more sought the old Oregon trail.

This was sixty years ago. Since then the Great American Desert, as it was called, has undergone a magical transforma-tion. Cities of twenty thousand inhabitants exist to-day where Wyeth found only a dreary wilderness ; from the Big Muddy to the Pacific you are scarcely ever out of sight of the smoke of a settler's cabin. In looking at the dangers and trials to which Wyeth found himself opposed, it must be admitted that he exhibited rare traits of courage and perseverance, allied with the natural capacity of a leader. His misfortunes arose through ignorance, and perhaps, to no small extent also, from that vanity which inclines your full-blooded Yankee to believe him-self capable of everything, because the word " impossible " is expunged from his vocabulary.

Fresh Pond has a present significance due wholly to its limpid waters. In Havana, in San Francisco, and even in Calcutta, you may have read the legend "Fresh Pond Ice. What, ice afloat on the Ganges ! New England winter transported in crystals to the bosom of the sacred stream ! How wondrous the first transparent cubes must have looked to the gaping Hindoo, and how old Gunga would have shivered had one of the solid blocks fallen into his fiery tide !

Little did John Winthrop and his associates dream that the ice and granite which they saw with such foreboding would prove mines of wealth to their descendants. The traffic in ice was originated by Frederick Tudor in 1805, by shipping a single cargo in a brig to Martinique. It was characterized by the sagacious merchants of Boston as a mad project, and the adventurer was laughed at by the whole town. The cargo arrived in perfect condition. The business prospered. Mr. Tudor found other markets open to him, but want of means prevented his extending his trade to the East Indies for nearly thirty years after he had shipped his first cargo. He leased or purchased rights at Fresh Pond, Spot Pond, Walden Pond, and Smith's Pond, — a railway being built to the former, solely for the transportation of ice.

In 1835 Mr. Tudor was unable to meet his indebtedness, but by favor of his creditors was enabled to go on and pursue with energy the business he had inaugurated. He discharged every obligation in full. His house owned property in Nahant, Charlestown, New Orleans, Jamaica, Calcutta, Madras, and Bombay, so that it was almost possible for him who at twenty-two had founded a traffic so extraordinary to repeat the proud boast of England, " that the sun never set on his possessions."

Let us once more take the route of the old Watertown road. And first we greet the ancient hostelry standing in the angle formed by the intersection of Belmont Street. This was known in Revolutionary times as Edward Richardson's tavern, though, as we have seen, it dated much farther back. The house has been removed a short distance from its original location, and has experienced changes in its exterior ; but within are still intact bar-room, kitchen, and dining-room, with the spacious fireplace, beside which hung the loggerhead. This was one of the places where the Colony cannon and intrenching tools were concealed. It was also a famous place of resort for Burgoyne's officers, on account of the cock-pit kept on the other side of the road. Some of these gentlemen, from the West of England, were very partial to this cruel sport. We relate the answer of a poor woman to whom they applied to purchase a pair of fine birds.

" I swear now you shall have neither of them; I swear now I never saw anything so bloodthirsty as you Britonians be; if you can't be fighting and cutting other people's throats, you must be setting two harmless creatures to kill one another. Go along, go. I have heard of your cruel doings at Watertown, cutting off the feathers, and the poor creatures' combs and gills, and putting on iron things upon their legs. Go along, I say."

Suiting the action to the word, the old woman raised her crutch, and threatened to execute summary justice on the officers, who did not consider it indiscreet to beat a hasty retreat. This tavern — subsequently Bird's, and also kept by Bellows — also was the residence of Joseph Bird, known through his efforts to discover a remedy for the prevention of conflagrations.

It is not known where Rev. George Phillips, first pastor of the church of Watertown, lies buried, but tradition having assigned the little knoll a short distance beyond the tavern and near the highway as his resting-place, Mr. Bird caused excavation to be carefully made there, without finding evidence of any remains.

A short walk brings us to the ancient burial-place of Watertown. It is not a garden but a field of graves. Many stones are scarcely visible above the clover-tops and daisies. The red brick and blue slate contrast somewhat sharply with the marble and granite of the neighboring cemetery. If anything, the place wears an even more sombre appearance than its contemporary of Old Cambridge. The very cedars seem dying. The mossy old stone-wall which forms one side of the enclosure is half concealed by climbing vines. Though reputed one of the oldest grounds in New England, no stone is found of an earlier date than that of Sarah Hammond, in 1674. There also is a monument erected to the memory of Joseph Coolidge, who fell at Lexington, April 19, 1775.

This graveyard is thought to have been used as early as 1642, although the situation before mentioned on the Bird estate was conjectured to have preceded it, — a supposition which the examinations of Mr. Bird may be considered to have settled. Opposite, and well withdrawn from the highway, is the house which tradition, that *ignis fatuus* of history, alleges to have been the home of Rev. Mr. Phillips, — perhaps that built for him by Sir Richard Saltonstall. This would place it in the front rank of old houses, where it clearly belongs, though it has for fifty years lost the distinctive English character it once possessed.

The second graveyard in the town, according to its present limits, is at the junction of Mount Auburn and Common Streets. It was established about 1754, the year the meeting-house afterwards used for the sessions of the Provincial Congress was built on the same ground. The neighborhood of the first cemetery is the supposed site of the first or second meeting-house, it being usually placed beside Mr. Phillips's house. The almost invariable custom of that day would seem to indicate its location within the limits of the old burial-place.

The church, to which the sittings of Congress gave political consequence, had a lofty steeple with square tower and open belfry. The entrance was on the east side. It had galleries, and was furnished with the old-fashioned box pews, having those movable seats which every one at the conclusion of the service felt obliged to turn back with a concussion repeated throughout the house like an irregular volley of small-arms. Rev. William Gordon, author of the History of our Revolution, officiated here as the chaplain of Congress. The vane which belonged to this house now adorns the pinnacle of the Methodist church.

Before you came to the bridge in Watertown, first built in 1660, there was still standing, within the foundry-yard of Miles Pratt & Co., an old dwelling-house notable for its dilapidation. It seemed scarcely able to bear its own weight, and, as it encumbered the ground, was pulled down. During the work of demolition the workmen found a number of old copper coins, which had remained concealed in chinks or crevices a century or more. This is said to have been the old printing-office of Benjamin Edes, who removed his type and press from Boston in the spring of 1775. He printed for the Provincial Congress, and many of the old broadsides of the time bear his imprint.

Crossing the bridge, the first old house on the east side of the way — once the residence of Mr. Brigham — is the Coolidge tavern of Revolutionary times, kept by Nathaniel Coolidge from 1764 to 1770, and afterwards by "the Widow Coolidge." Contemporary with this was Learned's tavern, on the site of the Spring Hotel. Nathaniel Coolidge's was known in 1770 as the "Sign of Mr. Wilkes near Nonantum Bridge." The house was appointed as a rendezvous for the Committee of Safety in May, 1775, in case of an alarm. President Washington lodged here in 1789, and styled the Widow Coolidge's house a very indifferent one indeed.

Opposite Mr. Brigham's, and near the river-bank, is another old house, which is situated on ground belonging from the earliest settlement to the Cook family. John Cook lived here during the Revolution, and some of the officers of our army boarded with him at the time of the siege, of whom Colonel Knox and Harry Jackson, bosom friends, enjoyed each other's companionship during brief intervals of rest. It was probably to this place Knox afterwards brought his wife. In a chamber of this house Paul Revere engraved his plates, and, assisted by John Cook, struck off the Colony notes emitted by order of the Provincial Congress. Lying contiguous to this estate along the river were the old fishing-wier lands of the town.

Our rambles extend no farther in the direction we have pursued than the vicinity of the "Great Bridge," so called in the day of small things. Newton, it is true, abounds in pleasant walks, while not a few of its worthies have made a figure in history. Of these Captain Thomas Prentice, the famous Indian fighter in Philip's time, may, in the order of chronology, justly claim precedence. Reputed to have been one of Old Noll's soldiers, he was a sort of second Myles Standish, tough as hickory, seasoned in war, and of approved conduct. He is said to have killed with an axe, on his farm in this town, a bear which attacked one of his servants. This old trooper lived in the saddle all his life, and died at eighty-nine of a fall from his horse. His place was at the corner of the road leading to Brookline, occupied of later years by the Harbacks.

Joseph Ward, who built in 1792 the old mansion opposite the Skinner place, was appointed by General Heath his aide-de-camp the day after the battle of Lexington, and was the first to hold such a position in the American army. He was, in May following, with Samuel Osgood of Andover, appointed to a similar position by General Ward, subsequently holding the office of Commissary of Musters in the Continental Army.

Michael Jackson, colonel of the 8th Massachusetts, has been met with in our pages. Joining his company at the Lexington alarm, in the absence of commissioned officers, he was chosen to command for the day. He immediately stepped from his place in the ranks as a private, and gave the order, *Shoulder arms, platoons right wheel, quick time, forward march !* When he got to Watertown meeting-house the officers of the regiment were holding a consultation. Finding they were likely to consume valuable time in speeches, he led all that would follow him where they could strike the British. He fell in with Percy's column, and that gallant gentleman received him with all the honors of a hot discharge of musketry. Jackson's men were at first demoralized, but rallied and gave shot for shot.

In the old Newton burying-ground the seeker will find the tomb in which were placed the remains of General William Hull and of his wife, Sarah (Fuller) Hull. A plain marble slab is inscribed,

> "GENL. WILLIAM HULL
> An officer of the Revolution
> died Nov. 29th 1825 aged 72 years.
> MRS SARAH HULL
> died August 2d 1826 aged 67 years."

However he may read the history of the campaign which culminated in the surrender of Detroit, the student may not in this place withhold his sympathy for the misfortunes of a brave but ill-fated soldier. That he was not deficient in courage his conduct on some of the hardest-fought fields of the Revolution — Trenton, Monmouth, and Stony Point — sufficiently attest ; that he should suddenly have become a coward is as incredible as the charge of his being a traitor is absurd. Yet a military tribunal pronounced him guilty of cowardice, and but for the interposition of President Madison he would have been shot. Public sentiment was about equally divided in opinion as to whether Hull was the more coward or traitor, and current report had it that wagon-loads of British gold had been seen after the surrender going to his house at Newton.

This case has always presented to our mind a parallel with that of Admiral Byng, an officer of distinguished bravery, who, in obedience to popular clamor, was shot for cowardice on the quarter-deck of his own ship, meeting death like a hero. Fortunately General Hull was not called upon to refute a slander with his life. It is needless to recite instances of the fallibility of courts-martial, or of the power of a ministry or a cabinet to disgrace an officer for what is not unfrequently its own culpability. No one need be reminded that the conqueror of Vicksburg, of Chattanooga, and of Richmond was once on the eve of being permanently as he was temporarily superseded. The victor of Nashville and the present general of the armies of the United States were near meeting this destiny which others of lesser note are even now fulfilling.

After General Hull's return to Newton at the close of the Revolutionary War, he resided first at Angier's Corner in a wooden house formerly standing on the west side of the road from Watertown. Here he lived ten or twelve years, until, after his return from Europe in 1799, he built the large brick house on the opposite side of the street, in which he resided until he went, in 1805, to Detroit, when he sold it to John Richardson. This was the house subsequently enlarged into a hotel, and known as the Nonantum House.

At the peace, in 1783, General Hull had embarked in large land speculations, being one of the owners of the "Connecticut Reserve," on which the city of Cleveland now stands, besides having interests in Georgia and elsewhere of a similar charac-

ter. But his public life had always interfered with these speculations. When he went to Detroit as governor, he invested
most of his funds in real estate in the then frontier village, and
was obliged to build a house for a residence. After he left
Detroit all his property there was sacrificed. He had advanced
large sums for the defence of the Territory, which, together with
his salary as governor, mostly remained unpaid until his death,
and were only obtained by his family after repeated petitions to
Congress for relief.

The farm in Newton of nearly three hundred acres, owned
and occupied by General Hull up to the time of his death, was
first occupied by Joseph Fuller, born in 1652. He was the
son of John Fuller, who came over in 1635 with John Winthrop, Jr., and settled in Cambridge Village (New Town) in
1644. In 1658 he bought a tract of one thousand acres in the
northwest part of the town, long known as the Fuller Farm.
His son Joseph, when he married Lydia, daughter of Edward
Jackson, in 1680, received twenty acres of land from his father-
in-law. This was part of a tract of five hundred acres which
had belonged to Governor Bradstreet in 1646, and which the
governor had bought of Thomas Mayhew of Watertown in
1638 for six cows. Here Joseph Fuller built his house in
1680, and together with about two hundred acres inherited
from his father, it formed the farm which descended to his son
Joseph, his grandson Abraham who added to it, and his granddaughter Sarah Fuller, who married Colonel William Hull in
1781. After the death of Mrs. Hull the place was sold and
divided, a part coming into the possession of William Claflin,
who has improved and embellished it with much taste. It
might be called the "Governors' Farm," having been owned by
Simon Bradstreet, William Hull, and William Claflin.

About 1767 Abraham Fuller removed a part of the old house
built in 1680, and replaced it with one more modern. The
portion of the original structure retained by him remained until
1814, when General Hull removed it, putting in its place the
one he occupied till the time of his decease. The mansion,
composed of the two structures built by Judge Fuller and his

son-in-law, was long to be seen at Newtonville, near the railway station, in turn occupied as a residence and a club-house, until torn down to make room for a brick block.

While this house was building the General resided in Boston, leaving to his son-in-law, Dr. Samuel Clarke, the care of its construction. Dr. Clarke was the father of James Freeman Clarke, who wrote an able vindication of the General, and of Samuel C. Clarke. Upon taking possession of the farm in 1814 the General devoted himself to agriculture, and was one of the first in New England to practice what is known as "high farming." He had little society except the members of his own family circle and a few friends and neighbors. Among these latter were Lucius M. Sargent, William Sullivan, William Little, George A. Otis, David Henshaw, and Nathaniel Greene, of Boston; Madam Swan, of Dorchester; Barney Smith, of Milton; Gorham Parsons and S. W. Pomeroy, of Brighton; Dr. Morse and Marshall Spring, of Watertown. He had numerous correspondents among his old comrades in arms. Governor Eustis and General Dearborn were of the number of his enemies.

General Hull was about five feet eight, of florid complexion, and had blue eyes. He sat to Stuart, in 1821, who obtained an excellent likeness. At this time he was of portly figure, weighing perhaps one hundred and eighty pounds. Of active habits, he might be seen early and late walking or riding about his farm. At seventy he still crossed his saddle with military grace. His manners were courtly and pleasing. At a dinner given him in 1825 by citizens of Boston, those guests belonging to a newer generation were surprised to remark in him the fine old manner now quite gone out of fashion. The General received a visit from Lafayette in 1825.

A pilgrimage to Nonantum Hill might revive shadowy glimpses of a scene worthy the pencil of Angelo, Guido, or Raphael, — the Apostle Eliot preaching to the Indians in 1646. The reverend man of God, offering the Evangel with one hand, friendship and peace with the other, would be the central figure. The grave, attentive savages should be grouped in picturesque attitudes about him. Eliot's was an example we can always contemplate with satisfaction as compensating largely for the malevolent persecution so often meted out to the red-man in the name of the Master.

Having traversed the utmost limits of the Continental lines in Middlesex, from the Mystic to the Charles, and so far as in us lies set the camps in order, rebuilt and garrisoned the works anew, sought out the captains, and fitted together the parts of the rude machinery of government, we now entreat the reader to bear us company in our *résumé* of the first and last attempt of an enemy to penetrate into the interior of Massachusetts.

## CHAPTER XVI.

### LECHMERE'S POINT TO LEXINGTON.

"A single drop of blood may be considered as the signal of civil war."
EDWARD G

IF the British grenadier had not gone into a shop with his accoutrements on, or if the Province House groom had not been indiscreet, perhaps Gage would have succeeded in his plan of surprising the Americans, destroying the stores at Concord, and returning his troops with the prestige of a successful expedition. This would have made a capital despatch for the Ministry, had the event not fallen out otherwise. North would have chuckled and Barré sulked, while Gage would have remained master of the situation.

John Ballard was the hostler at the stables on the corner of Milk and old Marlborough Streets, to whom the groom imparted the intelligence that "there would be hell to pay to-morrow"; but even he little thought how prophetic his language would become. Ballard was a liberty boy, but his informant did not suspect it. His hand trembled so much with excitement that he could hardly hold his curry-comb. Begging his friend to finish the horse he was cleaning, and feigning some forgotten errand, Ballard left the stable in haste. Not daring to go directly to Revere's house, he went to that of a well-known friend of liberty in Ann Street, who carried the news to Revere.

Revere had concerted his signals; Robert Newman hung them in Christ Church steeple. The former crossed the river in his boat, mounted his horse, and the first part of Gage's plan dissolved with the morning mists.

> "And yet, through the gloom and the light,
>     The fate of a nation was riding that night,
>     And the spark struck out by that steed in his flight
> Kindled the land into flame with its heat."

It is time the idea should be buried out of sight that the expedition to Lexington was a mere marauding foray upon a collection of unarmed, inoffensive peasants. It was not the fault of the British general that he was not met and resisted at every step from Lechmere's Point to Lexington Green, if, indeed, his troops had ever succeeded in reaching that place. It was not the fault of the Americans that they did not oppose his march with the greater part of the twelve thousand minutemen they were engaged in equipping for the field. They knew they were levying war, they knew the regulars were preparing to strike ; they were surprised, — that is all.

Before the battle of Lexington, the Americans had twelve light field-pieces, with proper ammunition, for which they were organizing six companies of artillery, and had accumulated as many as eleven hundred tents, fifteen thousand canteens, with other camp equipage in proportion. We say nothing of the magazines of small-arms, brimstone, saltpetre, bullets, provisions, and medicines, which they were collecting in vast quantities. They had resolved five months before that the precise moment to begin hostilities was when the British marched into the country with their baggage, artillery, and ammunition. If General Gage had quietly permitted these preparations to go on, he would have deserved the appointment of generalissimo of the provincial forces.

The provincials had undoubtedly received information that their stores were in danger, for, on the very day the troops left Boston, orders were given for the dispersion of their magazines among several towns. It is evident that a movement on Concord was apprehended. The leaders knew they were not quite ready for battle, and they labored under the disadvantage of expecting the blow without knowing precisely where it was to fall. The secret had been well guarded ; so well that it is said Haldimand, Gage's second in command, did not know the troops had marched until the next morning. But this the reader may or may not believe ; for our own part we do not believe it. Nevertheless, General Gage had always the advantage of a movable force, ready to launch at any moment.

In the latter part of February, 1775, by order of General Gage, Captain Brown of the 52d, and Ensign Berniere of the 10th, went on a reconnoissance through Suffolk and Worcester Counties as far as the town of Worcester. Their mission was purely military, and seems to point to an intention entertained by the General to march into the interior in force. The officers were to observe the country as adapted to military operations, and were to take sketches of the streams, defiles, and any obstacles likely to be encountered by an army in a hostile country. They were disguised, and attempted to pass themselves off as surveyors, but were everywhere recognized, watched, and harassed. In March the same officers were despatched on a similar errand to Concord. The British general was as well informed of the hostile preparations as, on their side, the provincials were that he was meditating a blow. Such was the situation of the parties on the 18th of April, 1775.

Massachusettensis says Gage swore when he came to Boston, " I came to put the acts of the British Parliament in force, and by G—d I will do it." This declaration seems so clearly to ignore the other side of the question that we cannot help repeating the remark of Dr. Franklin to the Britons, who complained to him of the scurvy treatment the king's troops had met with at Lexington, from the Yankees getting behind stonewalls and firing at them. The Doctor replied by asking them *whether there were not two sides to the walls !* This anecdote was repeated with a good deal of unction on the battle-ground by Washington, when on his tour in 1789. The retort would have won for the philosopher in our time the now celebrated sobriquet of " Stonewall."

It must have been after eleven o'clock when Colonel Francis Smith, of the 10th, with his eight hundred, landed at Lechmere's Point from the boats of the men-of-war. It was a fine moonlight night. The men were in light marching order, and took no rations. Smith called his officers around him and told them they were in no event to fire unless fired upon. The roads were all picketed by Gage's order the previous evening, and it is probable that if Revere — who was by this time on his errand — had not fallen in with one of these patrols he would have ridden plump into the main body. The troops moved by old Charlestown Lane, later Milk Street, so that Revere's route intersected their line of march. Samuel Murray, a tory, and the son of a pestilent tory, was their guide.

The morning was chilly, the way unfrequented, and not a sound came out of the gloom in which the cohort was enshrouded, save, perhaps, the rattling of scabbards in unison with the measured tramp, or where some amphibious batrachian sent up a dismal croak from the stagnant pools. The gallant Welsh, the gay marines, and the gracious, well-bred officers of the light companies must have felt their spirits not a little infected by their inglorious undertaking. Smith unconsciously held in his hand the wedge which was to split the British Empire in twain.

The column moves on in silence past the old Davenport tavern, then standing at the corner of North Avenue and Beech Streets. Afar off the note of alarm had begun to sound with the awakening day. Revere had roused the Medford bands. Bells were beginning to ring out, and gunshots to explode on the morning air, as we have heard them many a time since in some country village at the return of this day. Smith halts ; the surprise has ended, and certes, we should say the soldiers' faces might brighten at the prospect. Pitcairn moves off with his six companies. An express goes back to the General for help. Then the word is " Forward ! " and the column presses on. It passes the last rendezvous of the Revolutionary Committee at the Black Horse in Menotomy, now Arlington, and Elbridge Gerry, Orne, and Lee, escaping half dressed into the fields, throw themselves flat on their faces among the stubble. The watch-dogs bark, but the shutters of the houses in the village are kept close drawn, while eager eyes peer forth into the darkness. " Close your ranks ! " " Press on ! " are the oft-repeated commands. Beside the old Tufts' tavern the soldiers halt to slake their thirst at a well now filled up, but which was formerly in the space between the tavern and the store. Men roused from sleep at the tread of the British phalanx warily look out into the morning's obscurity. They see the moonlit points of eight hundred bayonets glittering coldly above a moving mass, which seems like the illusive images of a phantasmagoria. They count the platoons, then, seizing their muskets, take to the fields, where they meet their neighbors, all striving, with a common impulse, to get ahead of the regulars' column.

It is a tradition in Arlington that the first person to give the alarm here was Cuff Cartwright, a negro slave, who lived at his master's on the road, not far from the pond. An officer gave the black a dollar to silence him, but as soon as the detachment had passed Cuffee struck across the fields and roused the neighborhood.

In Smith's ranks were a number of young officers belonging to the fleet, who embraced the opportunity for a run ashore with all the enthusiasm and careless disregard of danger which characterizes the blue jacket the world over. Among them was Philip d'Auvergne, Duke of Bouillon, who was then a lieutenant on board the Asia, under Captain, afterwards Admiral, Vandeput, then lying in Boston harbor. On this day D'Auvergne narrowly escaped being made prisoner. He afterwards attended in the boats at Bunker Hill, and was in the expedition to Falmouth. It is worthy of remark that D'Auvergne and Nelson were the only two officers under age who were permitted to join the expedition to the Arctic in 1773 in the Carcass and Racehorse.

The British officers were fond of riding out into the country, and under the pretext of parties of pleasure had picked up a good deal of knowledge of the roads and of the inhabitants. Pitcairn himself had been out on this business, as had also Samuel Graves, afterwards a British admiral. The Britons were fond of chaffing the countrymen, but were often unhorsed in a tilt of wits. It is related that one day a little knot of these officers were approaching Waltham, when they observed a countryman sowing what appeared to be grain. "Ho, fellow!" says one of the officers, "you may sow, but we shall reap." "Waal," replied the native, "p'r'aps you will; I'm sowing hemp." The Britons pushed on a short distance, laughing at their own discomfiture, but soon returned and insisted that the Yankee should accompany them to the next tavern, where he drank as coolly as he had retorted at their expense, and returned to his labor. This anecdote has done duty in other connections. Owing to the celerity of the march and the success of his precautions, Smith's brigade arrived within a mile and a quarter of the Lexington parade-ground before the militia had any notice of their approach.

It is daybreak. The "Foot of the Rocks," a mile above the centre of the village of Arlington, is reached and passed. Smith and Pitcairn debouch on the fatal plain of Lexington. They hear the rebel drum, and the word is passed to halt, prime, and load. The ground is littered where they stand with the cartridge-ends, while eight hundred nervous arms are forcing the lead down into as many musket-barrels. Forward! The leading companies wheel out of the road and into the Common, where they see Parker's minute-men drawn up at the north end of the Green, near the Bedford road. The armed forces of authority and of rebellion here meet for the first time face to face. A British volley pealed out the knell of British ascendency in the New World.

Poor Pitcairn's memory has suffered all the obloquy of having given the order to fire. A thousand orators and writers have attacked his memory in manner and form from that day to this. It is only just to observe that British authorities are united in saying that the Americans gave the first fire. Lieutenant-Colonel Smith, who was not with the vanguard when the fatal firing took place, asserts it in his official report to General Gage, which was based upon that of Major Pitcairn, and of other officers who were present, to himself. Nothing more conclusively shows the unreliability of some of the depositions taken by direction of the Massachusetts Congress than the statement that Colonel Smith was with the advance.

Mrs. Hannah Winthrop, the wife of Dr. Winthrop of Cambridge, has left her impressions of the scenes of horror and dismay that took place when the news passed from house to house that the regulars were out. She could never forget, nor could time erase from her mind, the terrors created by the midnight alarm, when the peaceful inhabitants were roused from their beds by beat of drum and clang of bells, with all the clamor, confusion, and dread which such an event could inspire, — the men hurriedly arming and hastening to the fray; women lamenting and wringing their hands in despair; children weeping and clinging to their parents; while the very house-dogs howled with fright at the untoward sounds from the steeples.

But all were not bereft of reason by the sudden summons to arms. We have glimpses of the fond wife, pale but resolute, girding up the loins of her warrior ere he sets out for the field of blood; of the mother buckling on the son's sword with a lingering caress and benediction; and of the aged sire taking down from its lodgement over the fireplace the old queen's arm he bore at Louisburg, which he now places in more youthful hands, and commends to eyes yet able to sight along the clouded barrel.

> " Ah! then and there was hurrying to and fro,
>  And gathering tears, and tremblings of distress,
>  And cheeks all pale which but an hour ago
>  Blushed at the praise of their own loveliness."

To comprehend the affair of the 19th of April, 1775, the situation of the buildings about the Common on that day must be understood. Approaching with the troops from the direction of Cambridge, the roads separated as they now do, — that leading to Concord passing to the left, that to Bedford and Billerica diverging to the right. Within the triangular area formed by these roads was the Common, or Green, then unenclosed. Upon a little elevation near the apex or southerly extremity of the Green stood the old church, built in 1714, — a barn-like structure of three stories, with a pitched roof. The building had no proper belfry, but on a little structure placed a short distance north of the meeting-house was a bell-tower, from which pealed forth the alarm on the memorable morning. The church presented its side to the Concord road and its end to the Bedford road. It was taken down in 1794, and a new edifice with a tower erected near the spot. This building was destroyed by fire, and was then rebuilt where it now stands, at

A View of the Green in Lexington where the British Troops
First Fired on the Americans in 1775.

the northwesterly corner of the Common. The flagstaff is now placed not far from the site of the old meeting-house, but since the day when it stood here the southerly point of the Common has been somewhat elongated. An oak-tree or two stood about the meeting-house, and the Common itself was covered here and there with low brush. The little belfry stood on the site of the monument. It was removed to the old Parker farm, on the Waltham road, better known as the birthplace of Theodore Parker, was bought by the local historical society, and placed on Belfry Hill, back of the Hancock School.

On the right of the Bedford road and nearly opposite the old church was John Buckman's tavern, in which many of Parker's men assembled before the arrival of the troops, and which served as a refuge for some of the Americans afterwards. The fugitives fired upon the Britons from this house, and the shot-holes still seen in the clapboards attest that they drew the regulars' fire. Some of the British wounded were left here on the retreat. The old inn, long owned by the Meriam family, remains nearly as it was in 1775, and is the most conspicuous landmark of the battle-ground. The first post-office in the town was here located. Some Lombardy poplars that formerly stood about the building have now disappeared. The tavern, with its barn and outbuildings, and the meeting-house and belfry, are shown in old views of the Common.

On the southwest side of the Concord road, and looking upon the Common, were two houses, at least one of which is still standing. On the north side of the Green were two dwellings, with a blacksmith's shop between. The one nearest the Bedford road was that of Jonathan Harrington, one of the victims of the regulars' fire, whose wife witnessed his fall and the convulsive efforts made by him to reach her side. The other house, then that of Daniel Harrington, was torn down shortly after the Centennial celebration of 1875, and not rebuilt. In front of it are some of the most magnificent specimens of our grand American elm to be seen far or near. Doolittle's picture of the battle-ground was drawn from this house. On the east of it was the well at which the king's men quenched their thirst, and behind the house now occupied by the families of Harrington and Swan was to be seen the quaint little blacksmith's shop with one of those ugly orifices in the door made by a leaden ball. This completes our view of Lexington Green in 1775. Except that the avenue on the north side was a mere lane, and that the space has been enlarged at the southern extremity, the place is topographically the same as on the day of the fight.

The British main body marched up the Concord road and remained there while the attack took place. A body of grenadiers moved into the Common by the Bedford road, deploying in front of the Americans, who were paraded some four or five rods east of the monument and near the Bedford road. At the first alarm the minute-men assembled between the tavern and the meeting-house.

Lexington Common, as we see it to-day, bears little resemblance to the green where the first death-volley rattled in 1775. There is a triangular enclosure, bordered by a double row of elms, some of large growth, others of more recent planting. The fence, composed of stone posts with wooden rails, seen in the accompanying picture has been removed.

LEXINGTON MONUMENT.

The battle-monument stands near the west corner of the enclosure, not far from the ground where the first victims were stretched in their blood, and at a dozen paces from the south side. It is placed on a little knoll, is surrounded by an iron fence, and has the front with the inscription facing south. It is enough to say of this monument, that its insignificant appearance, when compared with the object it is intended to perpetuate, can arouse no other than a feeling of disappointment in the mind of the

BUCKMAN TAVERN, LEXINGTON.

pilgrim.   The shaft is of granite, with a marble tablet bearing the following inscription, written by Rev. Jonas Clark of Lexington.   Lafayette and Kossuth have both read it.

"Sacred to the Liberty and the Rights of Mankind ! ! !   The Freedom and Independence of America — Sealed and defended with the blood of her sons — This Monument is erected by the Inhabitants of Lexington, under the patronage and at the expense of the Commonwealth of Massachusetts, to the memory of their Fellow-citizens, Ensign Robert Monroe, Messrs. Jonas Parker, Samuel Hadley, Jonathan Harrington, Junr., Isaac Muzzy, Caleb Harrington and John Brown, of Lexington, and Asahel Porter, of Woburn, who fell on this Field, the first victims of the Sword of British Tyranny and Oppression, on the morning of the ever-memorable Nineteenth of April, An. Dom. 1775.   The Die was Cast ! ! !   The blood of these Martyrs in the cause of God and their Country was the Cement of the Union of these States, then Colonies, and gave the Spring to the Spirit, Firmness and Resolution of their Fellow-citizens.   They rose as one man to revenge their Brethren's blood, and at the point of the Sword to assert and defend their native Rights. They nobly dared to be Free ! ! !   The contest was long, bloody, and affecting.   Righteous Heaven approved the Solemn Appeal ; Victory crowned their Arms, and the Peace, Liberty, and Independence of the United States of America was their glorious Reward. Built in the year 1799."

The bodies of the seven individuals belonging to Lexington were originally enclosed in long wooden boxes made of rough boards, and buried in one grave in a corner of the town burying-ground, separate and distinct from all other graves.   A few days prior to the celebration in 1835, the remains were disinterred and placed in a wooden coffin enclosed in lead and made air-tight, the whole being then placed in a mahogany sarcophagus.   At the conclusion of the exercises on that occasion the sarcophagus was deposited in the tomb constructed near the base of the monument.   When the bodies were exhumed the coffins were completely decayed.   The bones were also more or less decayed.

The people of Lexington, sensible of the impression which the monument gives the beholder, have some time contemplated the building of a new one on a more enlarged plan. This idea has finally obtained expression in four memorial statues, which are placed in the Town Hall; two of which represent a soldier of 1775 and of 1861; and two others of life size, John Hancock and Samuel Adams. The figure of Hancock, by Gould, is a work of great elaboration. Its left hand holds a scroll, having the words, " We mutually pledge to each other our lives, our fortunes, and our sacred honor." The statue of Adams is by Milmore. We must say that it does not appear from this measure how the defects of the old monument, with its too lengthy inscription, are to be remedied. The memorials placed within four walls fail to inculcate any moral lesson, and are completely shut out from the observation of the passer-by. The old monument, not being of itself a relic of the Revolution, its materials might be included in a new structure more properly commemorative of the event. It stands just where it should, — on the spot where the tocsin first sounded " To arms ! " It should not be inferred that visitors are not admitted with all courtesy to view the statuary, but we should much like to see a shaft national in its character and worthy to illustrate one of History's most eventful pages, standing on the ancient parade.

The troops, having finished their bloody work, and being joined by the rear column, re-form, give three huzzas for victory, and push on for Concord. As, however fast they may march we shall be sure to overtake them, we desire the reader to accompany us to the old Clark house so called.

What is now Hancock Street was the old Bedford road in 1775. The parsonage was situated on the west side, a quarter of a mile distant from the old meeting-house.

The house belongs certainly to two, and perhaps to three, periods. It is composed of a main building in the plain, substantial style of the last century, and of a more antiquated structure standing at right angles with it. The first confronts you if you have come down the road from the Common ; the last faces the street, from which the whole structure stands back a little distance, with a space of green turf between. A large willow is growing in front of the main house, and on the

The Hancock-Clarke Parsonage, Lexington, Mass.

verge of the grass-plot stands an elm, its branches interlacing those of a fellow-tree on the other side the way, so as to form a triumphal arch under which no patriot should fail to pass. We have christened the twain Hancock and Adams. Thus, at least, it looked until its removal to a new site across the street and nearer the Common, where it now stands fronting north, instead of south, reverently cared for by the local historical society.

In this house the afterwards proscribed fellow-patriots, Hancock and Adams, were lodging at the time of the night march, of which one object was supposed to be their arrest. They were advised by Gerry that the British officers were patrolling the road with some sinister design. A guard of the town's alarm-list was placed about the house, and when Revere rode up, "bloody with spurring," to warn the patriot leaders, he was requested not to make a noise for fear of waking them. "Noise!" quoth our bluff mechanic, "you'll have noise enough before long. The regulars are coming out!" After some further parley with the Rev. Mr. Clark, Hancock, who recognized his friend's voice, arose and bade him enter. William Dawes, the other messenger sent by Warren, arrived soon after. This was not long after midnight, and sleep, we may suppose, was banished the house for the remainder of the night.

The room occupied by "king" Hancock and "citizen" Adams is the one on the lower floor on the left of the entrance. Care has been taken to preserve its original appearance. The woodwork, of Southern pine, has remained unpainted, acquiring with age a beautiful color. One side of the room is wainscoted up to the ceiling, the remaining walls bearing the original paper in large figures. The staircase in the front hall has also remained innocent of paint, and is handsome enough for a church. Age has given to the carved balusters and panelled casings a richness and depth of hue that scorns the application of any unnatural pigment. The room we have just left is in the southwest corner of the house. Passing to the opposite side of the hall, we enter the best room, which corresponds in finish with that just described, except that the painter's brush has been applied to the wainscot and newer paper to the walls.

In this apartment there is no manner of doubt Hancock courted "Dorothy Q.," while his graver friend discussed state-craft with their reverend host, or, buried in thought, paced up and down the grass-plot by the roadside.  Dorothy, the daughter of Judge Edmund Quincy of Braintree, was at this time living in the house under the protection of Madam Lydia Hancock, the governor's aunt.  When turned of seventy she had a lithe, handsome figure, a pair of laughing eyes, fine yellow ringlets in which scarcely a gray hair could be seen, and although for the second time a widow, was as sprightly as a girl of sixteen.  What her youth was the reader will be at no loss to infer.  Charming, vivacious, and witty, with a little dash of the coquette withal, one might pardon Colonel Hancock, late of the Boston Cadets, for becoming her devoted admirer.

Hancock had aspired to and obtained a military rank.  He was a trifle of a dandy in his attire, particularly in his military garb, when his points, sword-knot, and lace were always of the newest fashion, and rivalled those of any of his Majesty's officers.  Gage revoked Hancock's commission, and the indignant corps disbanded, flinging — figuratively — the governor's standard in his face, which made him as mad as a March hare.  He is supposed to give his wrath utterance in verse : —

> " Your Colonel H——k by neglect,
>     Has been deficient in respect ;
>     As he my sov'reign toe ne'er kiss'd,
>     'T was proper he should be dismissed ;
>     I never was and never will
>     By mortal man be treated ill ;
>     I never was nor never can,
>     Be treated ill by mortal man.
>     O, had I but have known before
>     The temper of your factious core,
>     It should have been my greatest pleasure,
>     To have prevented this bold measure.
>     To meet with such severe disgrace,
>     My standard flung into my face !
>     Disband yourselves ! — so cursed stout ?
>     O had I, had I, turn'd you out ! "

On the 12th of June, 1775, Governor Gage by proclamation

exempted Hancock and Adams from his offer of a general pardon, and declared all persons who might give them aid or shelter rebels and traitors.  Copies of this document were posted in all the public places, and left with every householder in the town of Boston.  This being as far as the authority of the royal governor extended, the objects of his paper decree were never in any apprehension of their personal safety.  Outlawry by the king's government was to make them the two most conspicuous figures in the Colonies, and the selection of Hancock to preside over the Continental Congress partook largely of an act of bravado.  Trumbull's burlesque of Gage's proclamation, which appeared in June, 1775, evidently formed the germ of his humorous epic of MacFingal.

Hancock's martial pride, coupled, perhaps, with the feeling that he must show himself, in the presence of his lady love, a soldier worthy of her favor, inclined him to show fight when the regulars were expected.  His widow related that it was with great difficulty that herself and the colonel's aunt kept him from facing the British on that day.  While the bell on the Green was sounding the alarm, Hancock was cleaning his sword and fusee, and putting his accoutrements in order ; but at length the importunities of the ladies and the urgency of other friends prevailed, and he retired with Adams to a place of concealment.  The astute Adams, it is recounted, a little annoyed perhaps at his friend's obstinacy, clapped him on the shoulder, and exclaimed, looking significantly at the weapons, " That is not our business ; we belong to the cabinet."  It will now be easily understood by the reader why Hancock, who was also a relative of Rev. Mr. Clark, chose to come so far from Concord, where the Congress was sitting, to lodge.

The patriots first repaired to the hill, then wooded, southeast of Mr. Clark's, where they remained until the troops passed on to Concord.  They were afterwards conducted to the house of Madam Jones, widow of Rev. Thomas Jones, and Rev. Mr. Marrett, in Burlington.  From here, upon a new alarm, they retired to Mr. Amos Wyman's, in Billerica, leaving an elegant repast, to which they had just sat down, untasted.  Revere, after his misadventure on the road to Concord, rejoined the patriots, as did also Madam Hancock and her niece.

It was while walking in the fields after hearing the firing that Adams made the observation, " It is a fine day." " Very pleasant," replied one of his companions, supposing him to mean the glories of the dawning day. " I mean," said the patriot seer, " this day is a glorious day for America." The veil was lifted, and perhaps he alone saw the end of which this was the beginning. During the firing random shots whizzed past the house he had quitted, and some of the wounded Americans were brought into it to have their hurts cared for. The whole affair on the Common was visible from this spot.

The house in which we have been loitering was built by Thomas Hancock, the Boston merchant of whom we have already had occasion to speak. He was not born until 1703, served his time with Henchman, the stationer, and had not acquired wealth until a much later period ; so that we suppose the building to have been erected about 1740, although the tablet reads 1698–1734. Thomas Hancock did not build his own princely mansion in Boston until 1737. He was the son of the old Bishop Hancock, as he was called, who was ordained in 1698 over a society which then inhabited this part of Cambridge, called " the farms." The merchant, as soon as his position enabled him to do it, doubtless looked to the more convenient housing of his honored parent, who received his name of bishop on account of his great influence among the ministers. Lexington was incorporated in 1712.

The best room communicates with the ancient or original house, which is seen fronting the street with its single story and picturesque dormer windows and roof. This part was doubtless built by the bishop's parishioners soon after his settlement. It formerly stood nearer the high-road until the new building was completed, when it was moved back and joined upon it. The house is a veritable curiosity, and would not make a bad depository for the household furniture and utensils of the period to which it belongs, being of itself so unique a specimen of early New England architecture. The floors and

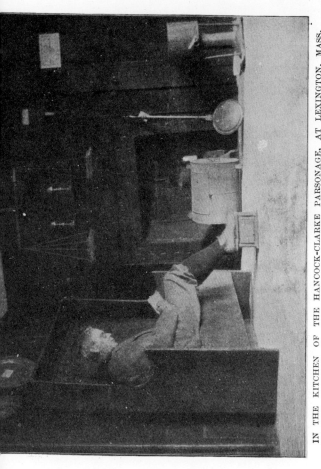

IN THE KITCHEN OF THE HANCOCK-CLARKE PARSONAGE, AT LEXINGTON, MASS. EDWARD DENHAM SITTING IN THE SETTLE. TIN-KITCHEN BEFORE THE FIRE-PLACE, WARMING-PAN TO THE RIGHT OF FIRE-PLACE, WITH OLD STILL AT EXTREME RIGHT. DENHAM'S FEET RESTING ON A FOOT-STOVE. — LEXINGTON, OCT. 15, 1898.

wainscot are of hard wood, upon which time has left not the least evidence of decay. The farmers clearly meant their minister to inhabit a house of a better sort than their own, as is apparent in the curious panelling of the outer door, which still retains its original fastenings, and in the folding shutters of the little study at the back. A cramped and narrow staircase conducts to the chambers above, from the room in which we are standing. The same old dresser is attached to the wall, garnished of yore by the wooden trenchers and scanty blue china of the good bishop's housekeeping. Some old three-legged tables are the only other relics of the former inhabitants. This one room, according to the custom of the times, served as kitchen, dining-room, and for the usual avocations of the family. The little study has the narrow windows which first admitted light upon the ponderous folios of the minister or the half-written sheets of many a weighty sermon. And perhaps he listened here to the tale of domestic wrong wrung in bitterness from some aching heart, or wrestled in prayer with an awakening but still struggling spirit. We see him in the common apartment performing the marriage rite for some rustic swain and his bride, or reading aloud the news from the metropolis, which he alone of all the village receives. Teacher, guide, parent, and friend, the clergyman of the olden time feared not to preach a political sermon or lay bare the abuses of society. In general, if something severe, he kept himself above reproach in his private life. He was steadfast, never confounding his flock with a sudden change of doctrine. These were the men who laid line and plummet to the foundation-stone of New England society, and we yield them the respect their teachings have gained for her sons.

On the day of the battle the clergymen followed their parishioners to the field, with the town stores of ammunition, which they busied themselves in distributing from their chaises. On the Sunday ensuing those who had taken part in the fray stood up in the aisles of the churches, — many with bullet-holes in their garments, — while thanks were publicly offered for their safe return. The country was all on fire. The young men hastened to array themselves for the war that was seen to be inevitable. " Arms ! " was the cry, " give us arms ! " Hearken to one young, ardent spirit : " I would not be without a gun if it costs me five guineas, as I shall be called a tory or something worse if I am without one. Pray don't fail of sending me a gun ! a gun ! a gun and bayonet ; by all means a gun ! a gun ! "

At the celebration in 1783 Hancock, then governor, was present, again sojourning at Mr. Clark's. At the appointed time Captain Munroe appeared with his company, and escorted his Excellency to the meeting-house, where Rev. Mr. Adams of Lunenburgh preached the anniversary sermon. Cannon were fired, and the United States flag hoisted at sunrise over Captain Brown's, and near the spot where the militia were slain. The Rev. Mr. Clark has recounted the events of the day, which he witnessed in part from his own house.

The old burial-ground of Lexington is so secluded that the stranger might pass it without suspecting its vicinity, if some friendly hand did not guide him to the spot. It lies back of the Unitarian Church, and is reached by a little avenue from the street. We looked for the older graves here with the same ill success which has befallen in many similar places. The " forefathers of the hamlet " have scarcely left their traces upon the stones. There is a handsome marble monument over the remains of Governor Eustis, erected by his widow, the daughter of Hon. Woodbury Langdon of Portsmouth. She lived to the great age of eighty-four, and now reposes by the side of her husband. The stone for the governor's monument was quarried in the Berkshire Hills.

The noise which the battle of Lexington made reached England. A subscription was raised in London and forwarded for the relief of the widows and orphans of those who fell here and all along the blood-stained road. Walpole deplored it in a letter to Sir Horace Mann, and Rogers, the poet's father, put on mourning. The fatal news was carried from Salem to England by Richard Derby, reaching there May 29.

PASTURE WHERE PAUL REVERE WAS TAKEN.

## CHAPTER XVII.

### LEXINGTON TO CONCORD.

" Why, our battalia trebles that account ;
  Besides, the king's name is a tower of strength,
  Which they upon the adverse faction want."

SHAKESPEARE.

IT would be difficult to imagine a more beautiful Indian summer's day than that on which we marched from Lexington to Concord with the ghosts of Colonel Smith's command. A heavy frost still incrusted the grasses and shrubbery by the wayside, but the energetic rays of the sun speedily transformed the beautiful crystal masses into commonplace grass and shrub. Some respectable hills, now made more passable by nearly a hundred years' labor of the sturdy tax-payers of old Middlesex, must have tried the sinews of the king's troops, already wearied with their ten miles of hurried tramp from Lechmere's Point. They may have paused, as we did, on the summit of the highest of these, to breathe awhile and glance at the glistening white tower of Bedford Church, before descending into the plain of Concord.

The road over which the troops marched and retreated is in some places disused, except for the accommodation of the neighboring farm-houses. Fiske's Hill, a high eminence a mile and a third from Lexington, is now avoided altogether. Another segment of the old highway, grass-grown and roughened by the washings of many winters, enters the main road at an abandoned lime-kiln, before you reach the Brooks tavern. In this vicinity one of the severest actions of the 19th of April was fought.

It was in the days of the epizoötic, and the highway was as deserted as could have been desired for our purpose. Proceeding onward, a farm-house almost always in view, there seemed a sort of fascination in the old, moss-grown, tumble-down stone-walls. No great stretch of imagination was necessary to convert them into the ramparts of a century ago, behind which the rustic warriors crouched and levelled the deadly tubes.

A grand old elm standing sentinel at the entrance of the town may have murmured a challenge to the advancing war, or waved back the scarlet array with its then youthful arms. But the goal was almost reached. The officers tighten their sword-belts ; the men fasten their gaiters and fix their grenadier caps more firmly. Onward !

The high hill around which the road winds as it enters Concord is the position from which the Americans viewed the approach of the regulars, and which was immediately occupied by a British detachment. By his spies Smith knew the places where the munitions were deposited. The bands disperse to their allotted work.

Concord is one of those places which, not having any scenic features sufficiently marked to arrest the tourist, has yet found — and this apart from its battle reminiscences — a group of writers who have made it one of exceeding and wide-spread attractiveness, so that no town in New England, we will venture to say, is so well known to the world in general. And this, as in the play which but for the excellent acting would be doomed to fatal mediocrity, is what Emerson, Hawthorne, Channing, Thoreau, Alcott, *père* and *fille*, with others unnamed, have done for quiet, inland Concord. Nature knew it in the commonplace pastoral sense. War left the print of her bloody hand there. Man's intellect has breathed upon it, and clothed it with such beauty that we seem to see gems sparkling in the drifts of gravel, nuggets among the river's sands, and feel an uncontrollable desire to view for ourselves all those objects by which our interest has been fixed while regarding the picture from a distance. And a closer acquaintance confirms our pre-possession.

At the very entrance of the town, but at the distance of about a mile from the public square, are several dwellings consecrated by pleasant memories. The hill itself, a brave old headland, throws its protecting arm around the northern and eastern section of the settled portion of Concord. Were a second invasion of the place ever again to occur, a few pieces of cannon posted here would, with the possession of some outlying hills, effectually command the approaches and the town itself. The hill-top forms a generally level plateau, sinking gradually away near the northerly extremity of the public square, where a section of it has been removed to place in orderly array some handsome buildings. Following the base of the hill through the town, with your face to the north, you arrive at the site of the old North Bridge, of which hereafter. Upon the summit and slopes of this eminence is the ancient burial-place, considered by many the oldest in Concord. Here you may command a superb view of the town at your feet; of Concord River, with its fertile meadows; and of the hills which rise and stretch away along the northwest, where the Americans rallied after retreating from the town, and gathered strength for their onset. In this same hillside the first settlers burrowed in caves; and we are left not only to wonder at their endurance, but to marvel at the patience and humility with which they recount their privations. The hill was the key to Concord in 1775, and the British seized and held it until they evacuated the place.

The much renovated house, with its pointed gables and its square tower between, is that in which Hawthorne lived after his return from his English consulate. The house itself is almost hid from view among the masses of evergreen by which it is surrounded. For some distance a cool walk skirts the street, — a row of thickly-set larches next the road, with an inner rank of firs or spruces. These trees were set out by Hawthorne. Back of the house, and dominating above it, the hill ascends in terraces, but so densely is it covered with evergreen-trees, planted by Alcott when he lived here, as to resemble nothing more than a young forest of native growth. The character of the trees which Hawthorne chose to have about him conveys the idea that he loved their constant verdure and balmy breath, if, indeed, he was not susceptible to the subtle and saddening influence of the bared and wintry arms of the statelier woodland varieties.

Partly ancient and in part modern, the novelist's dwelling has little or nothing peculiar to itself except the before-mentioned tower, which he built in defiance of architectural rules on the top of the house. Towards the road, this retreat overlooked a broad reach of sloping meadow in the highest state of tillage. Hill and dale, stream and pool, with all those concomitants of New England landscape which the artist so well knew how to weave into his pen-pictures, are here in the charming prospect. From the back window appeared the dark masses of evergreens with their needles glistening in the sun. As we looked out of the little study, we could not believe pagan ever worshipped fire more than Hawthorne loved nature.

We are told that the astrologers of old always pursued their studies of the heavens from some lofty castle-turret, whither the would-be questioner of Fate was conducted, bewildered by long, winding staircases, to find himself at last in the wizard's cabinet, confronted by all his unearthly and startling paraphernalia. A corner of the arras is lifted, and the man of destiny appears.

Ascending to Hawthorne's watch-tower of genius, the eye was first arrested by two cupboards of stained wood, standing on either side of the single window with which the rear wall is furnished. These closets were each decorated with a motto in white paint, as follows: "All care abandon ye that enter here"; "There is no joy but calm." Above the window was the one word, "Olympus." This, then, thought we, is the abode of the gods, — the summit sung by Homer and the poets. Enclosing the stairs was a pine box with such a movable shelf as is sometimes seen in a country school-house, appropriated to the village pedagogue. This was Hawthorne's desk, at which he is said to have written "Septimius Felton," the last of his works. Perched upon a high stool, with his back to the landscape, and his face resolutely turned towards his blank wall of stained deal, we may picture the sorcerer, with massive, careworn brow and features of the true Puritan stamp, tracing the horoscope of his fleshless creations. The house had since become a boarding-school for young ladies, kept by Miss Pratt, the study appropriated as a sleeping-apartment for school-girls whose dreams were not vexed by its former celestial occupants.

Franklin Pierce, the college chum of Hawthorne at Bowdoin, came here to visit his old friend, whom he had given a highly lucrative appointment abroad. The "Scarlet Letter" was produced while Hawthorne was surveyor of the port of Salem under General Miller, the old hero of Lundy's Lane. With his intimates, in the days of his custom-house experience, — and they were confined to a chosen few, — he was less taciturn than he afterwards became. But even among these he often appeared absent, gloomy, and misanthropical, as if some disappointment weighed upon him and had despoiled him of his young manhood.

Our author is one of those figures best contemplated from a distant stand-point, as some tall peak, lifting itself above its lesser companions from afar, sinks into the general mass at a nearer approach, giving no token of the subterranean fires that glow within its foundations. We know him better by his works than by actual contact with himself, but we have not had in America a mind of so antique a stamp as his, even if his imaginings are something weird, and his characters partake largely of the attributes of spectres who walk the earth because the master wills it.

Some of Hawthorne's productions, when a lad of fourteen, and thought to be authentic, have lately come to light. It appears that his literary tastes were first stimulated by an uncle, the brother of his mother, who resided at Raymond, Maine, whither Mrs. Hawthorne had removed after her husband's death, at Havana, of yellow-fever. These early effusions, which are descriptive of some of the events of his life in Maine, do not exhibit any of those flashes of genius for which the man was famous, although excellent pieces of composition for a youth in his teens. Hawthorne there speaks of the spur which his Uncle Richard's praises gave him.

Hawthorne's intellect was too fine for the multitude. His plane did not conduct to the popular heart. His writings teem with sombre tints, and oftenest lead to a tragic termination ;

but his fancies are always striking and his descriptions often marvellous. He seemed to walk apart, in an atmosphere of his own, seldom, if ever, giving note of what was within. Burns was an exciseman, and Hawthorne a gauger. Both were given to convivial indulgence, but the Scotsman's mood was in general less gloomy than the American's.

Adjoining Hawthorne's is the house which Alcott formerly lived in. Curtis has indulged in some quiet pleasantry at the expense of the practical cast of the philosopher's mind as applied to rural architecture, but for our own part, after having trampled half New England under foot, we can commend the taste which Alcott had applied to the restoration of his dwelling. Not so, however, with the rustic fence which separated his domain from the road. It appeared to have been composed of the relics of sylvan surgery, the pieces being selected with references to knobs, fungi, and excrescences. This is not what we should call putting one's best foot foremost by any means. Who likes to think of a Dryad with a wart on her nose or a woodland nymph with a hump?

Apropos of trees, they bear their ills as well as poor humanity. Go into the forest and see how many are erect and robust and how many bent and sickly. One in a hundred, perhaps, is a perfect specimen, the remaining ninety and nine are subject to some blemish. Nevertheless we do not advocate the collection of the diseased members by the wayside.

Alcott was by all accounts a pattern of industry. He is one of the few men who have kept a daily journal of passing events, in itself a work of no small labor and value. A walking encyclopædia, he is frequently consulted for a date or an incident. "I wish," said Webster, "I had kept a record of my life." And who does not echo the wish?

When Alcott was keeping school at Cheshire, in Connecticut, the fame of his original plan of instruction came to the knowledge of the late Samuel J. May, who invited him to visit him, in order to know more of the man whom he felt assured must be a genius. The result of this visit was an attachment between Mr. Alcott and Mr. May's sister, Abigail, which led to their marriage in 1830. Says Mr. May : —

" I have never, but in one other instance, been so completely taken possession of by any man I have ever met in life. He seemed to me like a born sage and saint. He was radical in all matters of reform ; went to the root of all things, especially the subjects of education, mental and moral culture. If his biography shall ever be written by one who can appreciate him, and especially if his voluminous writings shall be properly published, it will be known how unique he was in wisdom and purity."

It is well known that Alcott was among the little band of antislavery reformers, or agitators, as they were called twenty odd years ago. So deeply was he impressed with the wickedness of supporting a government which recognized slavery, that he refused to pay his poll-tax. As a consequence, one day an officer came with a warrant and arrested the philosopher. His loving wife soon packed a little tin pail of provisions, adapted to the wants of a vegetarian in seclusion, with which Alcott contentedly trudged off to jail. Arrived here, the officer delivered his prisoner up, but the person in charge, astonished to see Alcott there, invited him to sit down in the waiting-room until his cell could be made ready. Word was then sent to one of Alcott's friends, said to be Samuel Hoar, who came forward and paid the tax. Whereat Alcott waxed indignant, for he was as anxious to get into jail as most men would be to get out of it. He stood on high moral, if not financial grounds, and had no idea of rendering unto Cæsar the sinews of evil. So the example was lost, the wheels of government moved on unclogged, and Alcott mournfully returned to his home.

At the time of this episode the idea of communities was a favorite project with the transcendentalists. Brook Farm did not go far enough for philosophers of the ultra school, like Emerson and Alcott. They carried individualism to the point which permits the citizen to choose, absolutely, the form of government under which he shall live. They refused animal food, agreed by tacit league and covenant not to make use of the products of slavery or pay taxes, and believed they could get along without money. The experiment at Harvard resulted, and was in less than a year abandoned by its projectors, who may, nevertheless, claim the merit of having put their design into actual execution while others have only dreamed and talked.

Alcott, with the other reformers, soon realized that society is not to be improved by seceding from it. He then sets himself to work within the hive, talking, writing, printing, and making use of the appliances they were once so ready to surrender. Alcott was above six feet, and but little bent, even when he had exceeded his threescore and ten. His silver hairs and dignified appearance rendered him an object of respectful curiosity, whom few passed without turning for a second glance at his tall figure. He spoke with earnestness and simplicity, conveying the idea of a man thoroughly honest in his convictions, pure in his motives, and faithful in his friendships.

Alcott lived in an old house, which he had made very comfortable without destroying its distinctive antique character. The grounds reach back into the hillside, which here seems indented on purpose for a romantic little dell. The authoress of " Little Women" has, we are told, christened the place " Apple Slump," wherefore, O reader, demand of the sibyl, not of us. Two patriarchal elms, with rustic seats at the foot, are the guardians of Alcott's home, — just such a one in which you would look for an honest, hearty welcome, and find it.

One of Mr. Alcott's daughters, Louisa May, has made a broad and strong mark with her pen. The world knows from her that there are old-fashioned girls with hearts and brains, and little women with great souls. It may interest ambitious young writers to know that when Alcott brought to a certain publisher the MS. of some stories for boys, it was declined with the happy suggestion of " Get your daughter to write a story for girls." " She can do it if she has a mind to ! " exclaimed Alcott, bringing his hand down on the desk, at which he stood, by way of emphasis. " Little Women" was the result.

At the intersection of the Lexington with the old Boston road is Ralph Waldo Emerson's dwelling, built in 1828 by Charles Coolidge, grandson of Joseph Coolidge, one of the magnates of the West End of Old Boston, where he had a fine estate. It is a coincidence which led Samuel Parkman, another old-time resident of Bowdoin Square in that town, to inhabit the ancient rough-cast house which stands somewhat farther on by the burying-ground. The Coolidge house passed into Mr. Emerson's possession in 1835. It is a plain, square building, painted a light color, which you would pass without notice un-unless apprised of its former ownership. By some accident the house was badly injured by fire, during Mr. Emerson's lifetime, but was skilfully restored to its form appearance, to the great delight of his townsmen.

In the grove of pines which stands at the extremity of Mr. Emerson's grounds, Alcott erected with his own hands the summer-house which Curtis says was not technically based and pointed, but which he still speaks of with evident pride. As no vestiges of it now remain, we infer that it fulfilled the adverse destiny predicted for it.

There is amusement and instruction in the story of how, at Emerson's suggestion, Hawthorne, Alcott, Thoreau, and Curtis met at his house for mutual interchange of ideas. The plan was excellent, the failure complete. The elements for spark-ling wit or brilliant thought were there, but the combination would not take place. In vain Emerson, with his keen and polished lance, struck the shield of each with its point. Only a dull thud resulted, instead of the expected coruscation. Haw-thorne was mute, while the rest struggled manfully but in vain to produce the ethereal spark. Three Mondays finished the club.

Some of Mr. Emerson's pupils, when he kept school in the old house at Cambridge, are now white-haired men, who recall with a smile how, for discipline's sake, they were sometimes sent into the Widow Emerson's room to study. As a teacher he was mild and gentle, leaving agreeable impressions on the minds of his scholars. The school was in Brattle Street, oppo-site the Brattle House.

Thoreau, the hermit-naturalist, lived in a house built by him-self in 1845 on the shore of Walden Pond, his literary friends helping him one afternoon to raise it. It is said he never went to church, never voted, and never paid a tax in the State; for which contempt of the tax-gatherer he passed at least one night in jail. It is evident from his writings that Thoreau gloried in Nature, and that his soul expanded while he communed with her. She was his meat and drink. He craved no other society, putting to flight in his own person the crystallized idea that man is a gregarious animal. He calls upon hill and stream as if they would reply, and in truth the Book of Nature was never shut to him. A revival of interest in the character of Thoreau is manifest, an interest which no man is better able to satisfy than his friend Channing.

George William Curtis was for a time a resident of Concord, and Lieutenant Derby, better remembered as "John Phœnix," beyond comparison the keenest of our American humorists, it is said some time tended a shop here. Frederick Hudson, author of "Journalism in America," was also an inhabitant of this town.

Concord, on the day of invasion in 1775, although a place of considerable importance, contained but few houses scattered over a wide area. The old meeting-house, similar in appearance to the one at Lexington, stood in its present position. A square building at the corner of Main Street and the Common, was then known as Wright's Tavern, and was the alarm-post of the provincials. This house alone, of those standing along this side of the Square at that time, is still remaining. On the opposite corner of Main Street, where is now the Middlesex Hotel, was Dr. Minott's residence. Between this and the engine-house, on ground now lying between the latter and the priest's house (formerly known as the county house), was the old court-house, built in 1719, a square building with little old-fashioned belfry, steeple, and weather-vane, bearing the date of 1673. The northerly end of the public square was occupied by the residence of Colonel Shattuck, which, with some alteration, is still on the same spot. This brings us to the point of the hill, previously described, around which the road wound to the river, which it passed by the North Bridge. At this point, where the road diverges from the Square, Mr. Keyes's house formerly stood. Since 1794 the court-house has occupied the side of the Square opposite its old location, while the jail was removed from its situation on Main Street to its late site in the rear of and between the Middlesex Hotel and the priest's. The house described as Minott's became, after the war, a tavern kept by John Richardson of Newton. At no great distance from the soldiers' monument stands a magnificent elm, which once served as the whipping-post to which culprits were tied up.

Main Street, which we now propose to follow a certain distance, conducted towards the South Bridge which crossed the river by Hosmer's. In 1775 it was merely a causeway leading to the grist-mill which then stood on the spot now occupied by stores, next the old Bank and opposite Walden Street. A few steps farther and you reach the second of the burial-places in the town, in which lie the remains of gallant John Hosmer, who, "although in arms at the battle of Concord and a soldier of the Continental Army, was in all his life after a man of peace." Beyond the burying-ground was the second situation of the jail built here in 1770. It was a wooden building with gambrel roof, standing on the estate of the late Reuben Rice. On the same estate was the old tavern formerly known as Hartwell Bigelow's. Prior to the erection of the first jail in 1754, prisoners were confined in Cambridge and Charlestown. Concord, having ceased to be one of the shire towns of Middlesex, now contains neither jail nor malefactors.

In 1775 the tavern mentioned as Bigelow's was kept by Captain Ephraim Jones, who had also charge of the jail. General Gage wrote home to England that the people of Concord were "sulky" while his troops were breaking open their houses, flinging their property into the mill-pond, and killing their friends and neighbors! Of what stuff the inhabitants of Concord were made in the estimation of the king's officer we are unable to conjecture, but we have his word for it that they were "sulky, and one of them even struck Major Pitcairn." Ephraim Jones was the man. He should have a monument for the blow.

Pitcairn went straight to Jones's tavern, where he had often lodged, sometimes in disguise. This time he found the door shut and fastened. As Jones refused to open, Pitcairn ordered his grenadiers to break down the door, and, being the first to enter, rushed against Jones with such violence as to overthrow the unlucky innkeeper, who was put under guard in his own bar, while Pitcairn, with a pistol at his breast, commanded him to divulge the places where the stores were concealed. The crestfallen Boniface led the way to the prison, where the British were surprised to find three 24-pounders in the yard, completely furnished with everything necessary for mounting. The Major destroyed the carriages, knocked off the trunnions of the guns ; and then, feeling his usual good-humor return with certain gnawings of his stomach, retraced his steps to the tavern and demanded breakfast, of which he ate heartily and for which he paid exactly. Jones resumed his *rôle* of innkeeper, and found his revenge in the transfer of many silver shillings bearing King George's effigy from the breeches pockets of the king's men to his own greasy till.

The jail is also connected with another incident of interest. A battalion of the 71st Highlanders, which had sailed from Glasgow in the George and Annabella transports, entered Boston Bay, after a passage of seven weeks, during which they had not spoken a single vessel to apprise them of the evacuation. They were attacked in the bay by privateers, which they beat off after being engaged from morning until evening. The transports then boldly entered Nantasket Road, where one of our batteries gave them the first intimation that the port was in possession of the Americans. After a gallant resistance the vessels were forced to strike their colors. The Highlanders, under the orders of their lieutenant-colonel, Archibald Campbell, fought with intrepidity, losing their major, Menzies, and seven privates killed, besides seventeen wounded. Menzies was buried in Boston with the honors of war, and Campbell sent a prisoner to Reading, while the men were distributed among the interior towns for safety.

This regiment, raised at the commencement of the American war, was one of the most famous levied among the Highland clans. It was composed of two battalions, each twelve hundred strong, and was commanded by Simon Fraser, the son of that

Lord Lovat who had been beheaded in 1747 for supporting the Pretender's cause. Each battalion was completely officered, and commanded by a colonel. Another Simon Fraser was colonel of the second battalion, — the same of which the larger number were captured in Boston Bay.

There was a great desire to enlist in this new regiment, more men offering than could be accepted. One company of one hundred and twenty men had been raised on the forfeited estate of Cameron of Lochiel, which he was to command. Lochiel was ill in London, and unable to join. His men refused to embark without him, but after being addressed with persuasive eloquence, in Gaelic, by General Fraser, they returned to their duty. While their commander was speaking, an old Highlander, who had accompanied his son to Glasgow, was leaning on his staff, gazing at the General with great earnestness. When he had finished the old man walked up to him and said, familiarly, " Simon, you are a good fellow, and speak like a man. As long as you live Simon of Lovat will never die."

When Sir William Howe refused to exchange General Lee, — and it was reported he had been placed in close confinement, — Congress ordered a retaliation in kind. Campbell, one of the victims, was brought to Concord, and lodged in the jail of which we are writing. His treatment was unnecessarily severe, the authorities placing the most literal construction upon the orders they received. He complained in a dignified and manly letter to Sir William, with a description of his loathsome prison. By Washington's order his condition was mitigated, and he was afterwards exchanged for Ethan Allen. In the Southern campaign he fought us with great bravery, and lived to be a British major-general.

But to resume our topography. Main Street was also formerly the old Boston and Harvard road, which left the Common by the cross-way entering Walden Street, opposite the old Heywood tavern, since the property of Cyrus Stow. Within the space between this cross-way and Main Street and Walden Street and the Common was the mill-pond which played so important a part in the transactions of the 19th of April, but the existence of which would not be suspected by the stranger. The mill-pond has, in fact, disappeared along with the dam, — the little brook to which it owed its existence now finding its way underground, and flowing onward unvexed to Concord River. We ask the reader to circumnavigate with us the old mill-pond.

Pursuing our way along the south side of Walden Street, we soon come to what is called the "Hubbard Improvement," a large tract through which a broad avenue has been opened. Upon this land, where the cellar and well were still to be seen, was once a very ancient dwelling, known as the Hubbard House. It had a long pitched roof, which stopped but little short of the ground, and from which projected two chimneys, both stanch and strong. The old well-sweep, now an unaccustomed object in our larger towns, had done unwilling service for the king's men in '75, creaking and groaning as it drew the crystal draughts from the cool depths. The house had been visited by these same redcoats, and its larder laid under severe contribution.

A little farther on was the dwelling and corn-house of Captain Timothy Wheeler, the miller, whose successful *ruse-de-guerre* saved a large portion of the Colony flour, stored along with his own. The story has often been told, but will bear repetition.

When the troops appeared at his door, he received them in a friendly manner, inviting them in, and telling them he was glad to see them. He then asked them to sit down, and eat some bread and cheese, and drink some cider, which they did not hesitate to do. After satisfying themselves, the soldiers went out and were about to break open the corn-house. Wheeler called to them not to trouble themselves to split the door, as, if they would wait a minute, he would fetch the keys, and open himself; which he did. "Gentlemen," said the crafty Yankee, "I am a miller. I improve those mills yonder by which I get my living, and every gill of this flour" — at the same time putting his hand on a bag of flour that was really his own — "I raised and manufactured on my own farm, and it is all my own. This is my store-house. I keep my flour here until such time as I can make a market for it." Upon this the officer in command said, " Well, I believe you are a pretty honest old chap ; you don't look as if you would hurt anybody, and we won't meddle with you." He then ordered his men to march.

Heywood's tavern was vigorously searched by the troops for a fugitive who had brought the alarm from Lexington. He, however, eluded their pursuit by getting up the chimney, where he remained until the search was given over. If the reader is surprised at finding so many houses of entertainment in Old Concord, he must remember it was the ancient seat of justice for Middlesex, and on the high-road from the capital to the New Hampshire Grants.

The hill burying-ground is now thickly covered with a growth of young locust-trees, which somewhat obstruct the view, although they impart fragrance to the air and shade to the close-set graves. The oldest inscription here is dated in 1677. It is credible that the settlers who first made their homes in this hillside should have carried their dead to its summit. We observed here what we considered to be the rude sepulchral stones seen in Dorchester and other ancient graveyards.

One inscription usually attributed to the pen of Daniel Bliss, has been much admired.

> " God wills us free ; — man wills us slaves.
> I will as God wills ; God's will be done.
> Here lies the body of
> JOHN JACK
> A native of Africa who died
> March, 1773, aged about sixty years.
> Though born in a land of slavery,
> He was born free.
> Though he lived in a land of liberty,
> He lived a slave ;
> Till by his honest though stolen labours,
> He acquired the source of slavery,
> Which gave him his freedom ;
> Though not long before
> Death, the grand tyrant,
> Gave him his final emancipation,
> And put him on a footing with kings,
> Though a slave to vice,
> He practised those virtues,
> Without which kings are but slaves."

## CHAPTER XVIII.

### THE RETREAT FROM CONCORD.

"That same man that runneth awaie,
  Maie again fight an other daie."
                                        ERASMUS.

THE area which we have been thus circumstantial in describing was, on the morning of the battle, a scene of mingled activity, disorder, and consternation. The troops were occupied in searching the houses of the suspected, and in destroying or damaging such stores as they could find. Reserve companies stood in the principal avenue ready to move on any point, for Smith was too good a soldier to disperse his whole command. The court-house was set on fire by the soldiers, but they extinguished the flames at the intercession of Mrs. Moulton, an aged woman of over eighty. The garret contained a quantity of powder, which would, in exploding, have destroyed the houses in the vicinity. Colonel Shattuck's was also a hiding-place for public property. The inhabitants, though "sulky," certainly behaved with address and self-possession in the emergency in which they found themselves.

All this time the storm without was gathering head. The troops had entered the town at seven. It was now nearly ten o'clock. So far the British had little reason to complain of their success, but in reality the provincial magazines had met with trifling injury.

A magnetism easily accounted for conducted our footsteps along the half-mile of well-beaten road that leads to the site of the battle-ground, as it is called. A shady avenue, bordered with odoriferous pines and firs, parts from the road at the westward side and leads you in a few rods to the spot. Briefly, this was the old road to Carlisle, which here spanned the river by a simple wooden bridge resting upon piles. The passage of the bridge was secured by Smith's orders, who did not omit to possess himself of all the avenues leading into the town. A detachment under Captain Parsons, of the 10th, crossed the bridge and proceeded to the house of Colonel Barrett, a leader among the patriots, and custodian of the Colony stores. Captain Laurie of the 43d had the honor to command the troops left to protect the bridge.

The monument is built of Carlisle granite, the corner-stone having been laid in 1825 in the presence of sixty survivors of the battle, who listened to an eloquent word-painting of their deeds from the lips of Everett. The Bunker Hill Monument Association aided greatly in advancing its erection. The pilgrim, as in duty bound, reads the inscription on the marble tablet of the eastern face : —

Here
On the 19th of April, 1775,
was made the first forcible resistance to
British Aggression.
On the opposite bank stood the American
militia, and on this spot the first of the enemy fell
in the War of the Revolution,
which gave Independence to these United States.
In gratitude to God, and in the love of Freedom,
This monument was erected,
A. D. 1836.

What need to amplify the history after this simple condensation ! We seated ourselves on a boulder invitingly placed at the root of an elm that droops gracefully over the placid stream, and which stands close to the old roadway. Beyond, where you might easily toss a pebble, were the remains of the farther abutment of the old bridge, for the mastery of which deadly strife took place between the yeomen of Middlesex and the trained soldiers from the isles. For our own part we have never fallen upon so delightful a nook for scholar's revery or lovers' tryst. The beauty, harmony, and peacefulness of the landscape drove the pictures of war, which we came to retouch, clean away from our mental vision. Not a leaf trembled. The

river in its almost imperceptible flow glided on without ripple
or eddy. The trees, which had become embedded in the mould
accumulated above the farther embankment, cast their black
shadows across its quiet surface. A vagrant cow grazed quietly
at the base of the monument, where the tablet tells us the
newly springing sod was fertilized by the life-blood of the first
slain foeman.

> " By the rude bridge that arched the flood,
>     Their flag to April's breeze unfurled,
>   Here once the embattled farmers stood
>     And fired the shot heard round the world."

The ground upon which the monument stands was given to
the town by Dr. Ripley in 1834, for the purpose, and formed
originally a part of the parsonage demesne. We cannot choose
but challenge the anachronism of the inscription as well as the
fitness of the site. The first declares that " here was made the
first forcible resistance to British aggression." By substituting
the word " American " for " British " we should adhere to historic truth; for, to the eternal honor of those Middlesex farmers,
they were the aggressors, while " here " stood the enemy. The
British fired the first volley, but the Americans were moving
upon them with arms in their hands.

When Thomas Hughes, Esq., better known as " Tom
Brown," was here, he is said to have exclaimed, " *British*
aggression ! I thought America was a colony of Great Britain,
and that her soldiers had a right to march where they pleased !"

This ɪonument, therefore, marks the spot where the British
soldiers fought and fell, while the place where the gallant yeomen gave up their lives is commemorated by a statue. A
wealthy citizen of Concord bequeathed by his will a sum to be
applied to the restoration of the old bridge, taken down in
1793, and for the erection of a monument on the farther shore.
A committee of intelligent and patriotic gentlemen have fulfilled the conditions of Mr. Hubbard's legacy, thus permanently
fixing the positions of the combatants when the collision took
place. A spirited figure in bronze, by French, presents to
us the minute-man of 1775 hastening to the conflict. The

artist has succeeded in investing his subject with a good deal of martial fire. Eagerness and determination are well expressed in the attitude of the youthful soldier. The rebuilding of the bridge, too, brings the warlike scene all the more vividly before us.

A few paces from the monument, beside a stone-wall, are the graves of the two British soldiers who were killed here, their place of sepulture marked by two rough stones. One of these has so nearly disappeared by acts of vandalism as to be scarcely visible above the sod. A stone from the North Bridge is placed under the corner of the soldiers' monument in the public square, thus uniting two historic eras in the town's annals.

At this place the river, which before flowed easterly, bends a little to the north. The old road, after passing the stream, ran parallel with it along the wet ground for some distance before ascending the heights beyond. The muster-field of the provincials is now owned by Mr. George Keyes, who has found flints such as were then used where the Americans stood in battle-array. Were they dropped there by some wavering spirit who feared to stain his soul with bloodshed, or were they discarded by some of sterner cast? — a Hayward, perhaps, who drew up his gun at the same moment the Briton levelled his own, and gave and received the death-shot.

Mr. Keyes has also ploughed up a number of arrow-heads, axes, pestles, and other of the rude stone implements of the original owners of the soil, who kept faith with the white man as he had kept faith with them. Hardships fell to the settlers' lot, but peace and concord endured, in token of the name which Peter Bulkley, their first minister, gave the plantation.

The Old Manse has received immortality through the genius of Hawthorne. It was built in 1765, the year of the Stamp Act, for Rev. William Emerson, the fighting parson, the same who vehemently opposed retreating from before the British in the morning at Concord; the same who died a chaplain in the army. The same reverend gentleman likewise officiated as chaplain to the Provincial Congress when it sat in Concord.

Standing back from the road, a walk bordered by black ash-trees, now somewhat in the decline of life, leads to the front door. The house looks as if it had never received the coat of paint, the prospect of which so alarmed Hawthorne's sensibilities. It is of two stories with gambrel roof and a chimney peeping above at either end. The front faces the road, the back is towards the river; one end looks up the street by which you have come from the town, while the other commands a view of the old abandoned road to the bridge, — the boundary of the demesne in that direction. A considerable tract of open land extends upon all sides.

The Manse is among modern structures what a Gray Friar in cowl and cassock might be in an assemblage of fashionably dressed individuals. The single dormer window in the garret looks as if it might have made a quaint setting for the head of the old clergyman, with his silver hairs escaping from beneath his nightcap. If he looked forth of a summer's twilight to scan the heavens, fireflies flitted sparkling across the fields, as if some invisible hand had traced an evanescent flash in the air. Behind the house, among the rushes of the river meadows, the frogs sang jubilee in every key from the deep diapason of the patriarchal croaker to the shrill piping of juvenile amphibian. Discord unspeakable followed the shores of the Concord along its windings even to its confluence with the Assabeth. The din of these night-disturbers seemed to us, as we stood on the river's bank, like the gibings of many demons let loose to murder sleep. And one fellow — doubt it if you will, reader — actually brayed with the lungs of a donkey.

> " As the worn war-horse, at the trumpet's sound,
>   Erects his mane and neighs and paws the ground."

Walking around to the rear of the Manse, we see a section of the roof continued down into a leanto, — a thing so unusual that we make a note thereon, the gambrel being the successor of the leanto in our architecture. The back entrance is completely embowered in syringas, whose beautiful waxen flowers form a striking contrast with the gray walls. Vines climb and cling to the house as if ineffectually seeking an entrance, imparting

CONCORD MANSE.

to it a picturesqueness answerable to and harmonizing with the general effect of the mansion. We give a glance at the garden where Hawthorne grew his summer squashes, of which he talks so poetically. What, Hawthorne delving among potatoes, cabbages, and squashes ! We can scarce bend our imagination to meet such an exigency. It is only a little way down to the river where he moored his boat, in which he floated and dreamed with Ellery Channing.

We enter the house. A hall divides it in the middle, giving comfortable apartments at either hand. Some mementos of the old residents serve to carry us back to their day and generation. A portrait of the Rev. Dr. Ripley, the successor of Mr. Emerson, and inhabitant of the house many years, hangs upon the wall. His descendants long possessed the Manse. On the mantel I noticed an invitation to General Washington's table, addressed, perhaps, to Dr. Emerson. The ink is faded and the grammar might be improved; but the dinner, we doubt not, was none the less unexceptionable.

Hawthorne's study was in an upper room, but let none but himself describe it.

" There was in the rear of the house the most delightful little nook of a study that ever afforded its snug seclusion to the scholar. It was here that Emerson wrote ' Nature ' ; for he was then an inhabitant of the Manse.

" There was the sweet and lovely head of one of Raphael's Madonnas and two pleasant little pictures of the Lake of Como. The only other decorations were a vase of flowers, always fresh, and a bronze one containing ferns. My books (few, and by no means choice ; for they were chiefly such waifs as chance had thrown in my way) stood in order about the room, seldom to be disturbed.

"The study had three windows, set with little old-fashioned panes of glass, each with a crack across it. The two on the western side looked, or rather peeped, between the willow branches down into the orchard, with glimpses of the river through the trees. The third, facing northward, commanded a broader view of the river, at a spot where its hitherto obscure waters gleam forth into the light of history. It was at this window that the clergyman who then dwelt in the Manse stood watching the outbreak of a long and deadly struggle between two nations : he saw the irregular array of his parishioners on the farther side of the river and the glittering line of the British on the hither bank. He awaited in an agony of suspense the rattle of the musketry. It came ; and there needed but a gentle wind to sweep the battle smoke around this quiet house."

In 1843 Hawthorne — whom many here name *Haw*-thorne as they would say " *Haw*-buck " to their oxen — came to dwell at the Manse. The place would not have suited him now. The railway coming from Lexington passes at no great distance, and the scream of the steam-whistle would have rudely interrupted his meditative fancies. He lived here the life of a recluse, receiving the visits of only a few chosen friends, such as Whittier, Lowell, Emerson, Channing, Thoreau, and perhaps a few others. Here he passed the first years of his married life, and here his first child was born. The townspeople knew him only by sight as a reserved, absorbed, and thoughtful man.

The house opposite the Manse, now the residence of Mr. J. S. Keyes, is another witness of the events of that April day. The then resident was named Jones, who, from being a spectator of the scenes at the bridge, maddened at the sight, wished to fire upon the redcoats. It is said that he levelled his gun from the window, but his wife, more prudent, prevented him from pulling the trigger. He at last stationed himself at the open door of the shed as the regulars passed by, when he was fired at, and with evil intent, as you may see by the bullet-hole near the door. Farther our informant did not proceed ; but in the angry swarm that clung to and stung the Britons' column all that day, we doubt not Jones at last emptied the contents of his musket.

In Mr. Keyes's house we saw a marble mantel beautifully sculptured in relief. It is a relic from the old Chamber of Representatives at Washington. On the fender the feet of Adams, Clay, Webster, Calhoun, and the master spirits of that old hall have often rested. Before the emblematic fasces the great Carolinian brooded how to loose the bands. The caucuses, bickerings, and party tactics that fireplace could tell of would make a curious volume. Ascending the hill behind the

MERIAM'S CORNER.

house you have a ravishing landscape, with blue Wachusett looming in the distance.

The Concord deserves to be known in all time as the Rubicon of our history. The affair at Lexington was but a butchery: here the Americans gave shot for shot and life for life. Their blood on fire with the rage of battle and the fall of their friends, it is most unaccountable that the patriots allowed Parsons and his command to repass the bridge unmolested. These last must have stepped over the dead bodies of their comrades stretched in their path, gathering evil augury from the sight.

This ended the advance, and here begins the retreat, which we should say is one of the most extraordinary in the annals of war, for the pertinacity of the pursuit by an armed rabble and for the complete demoralization of eight hundred disciplined soldiers, led by officers of experience. The old song makes the British grenadier recite in drawling recitative : —

> " For fifteen miles they followed and pelted us, we scarce had time to draw a trigger ;
> But did you ever know a retreat conducted with more vigour ?
> For we did it in two hours, which saved us from perdition ;
> 'T was not in *going out* but in *returning*, consisted our *expedition*."

The British detachment from the North Bridge buried one of their slain at the point of the hill as they turned into the square, where the house of Mr. Keyes formerly stood. The wounded were carried into Dr. Minott's. All being at length collected, the troops begin their march, — the main body by the road, a strong flanking column by the burying-ground hill. This hill terminates at the distance of a mile from the centre of the town at Meriam's Corner. The flanking column had to descend the hill at this point, where the road passes the low meadow by a causeway until it reaches the hill beyond. Near the corner was a little bridge thrown over a brook, which the road crossed.

Meriam's house and barn are still seen in the angle where the Bedford road unites with that coming from Lexington. From behind these buildings gallant John Brooks with his

Reading company arrived in time to pour a volley among the enemy as they were passing the bridge. Brooks, a captain in Bridge's regiment, had received his colonel's permission to push on while the regiment halted for refreshment. Loammi Baldwin came up with the Woburn men, who drifted in a cloud along the British flank. The men of Sudbury, of Lincoln, and even Parkers's from Lexington, joined in the race, for race it was beginning to be. The fields grew armed men, and the highway was fringed with fire-arms.

The six miles from Concord back to Lexington were perfectly adapted to the guerilla-fighting of the Americans. They abounded in defiles and places for ambush. On the other hand, the retreating enemy was somewhat covered by the stone-walls as long as the flank guards could keep them clear of foemen; but the column was fired at in front, in rear, and on all sides at once. Ranks, platoons, and the semblance of military order were soon lost. We need no ghost to tell us what such a retreat must have been. The dust trampled into stifling clouds, and enveloping everything; the burning thirst which men brave death to assuage; no time to halt; tongues parched and cleaving to the roof of the mouth; haggard faces, and red, bloodshot eyes; the proud array and martial bearing all gone; burnished arms and uniforms stained with powder and dirt; one by one a comrade dropping with a bullet in his heart, or another falling out, exhausted, to await his fate in dogged despair, — this is what it meant to retreat fighting from Concord to Lexington. The column, like some bleeding reptile, scotched but not killed, dragged its weary length along. Stedman, the British historian, says the regulars were driven like sheep. Harassed, humiliated, and despairing, the men became fiends, divested of every semblance of humanity. Every shot that whistled through the broken battalion proclaimed aloud, "The Province is dead! Long live the Republic!"

That same prowling ensign, Berniere, tells his own tale: —

"At last, after we got through Lexington, the officers got to the front and presented their bayonets and told the men if they advanced they should die. Upon this they began to form under a very heavy fire ; but at this instant the first brigade joined us, consisting of the 4th, 23d, and 47th regiments, and two divisions of marines, under the command of Brigadier-General Lord Percy ; he brought two field-pieces with him, which were immediately brought to bear upon the rebels, and soon silenced their fire. After a little firing the whole halted for about half an hour to rest."

Percy opened his ranks and received the fugitives within his squares. His cannon, a new element for the militia to deal with, were unlimbered and began to play on the hunters. Smith's men threw themselves upon the ground, "with their tongues hanging out of their mouths, like those of dogs after a chase." Certainly, my lord was near being too late.

This was the first appearance of the Royal Artillery in the war. The 4th battalion was in Boston under command of Colonel Cleaveland, who also served on the staff of the army as brigadier, as did most of the colonels of the line regiments. In relation to the report sent to England that the pieces were not well provided with ammunition, Colonel Cleaveland stated that Lord Percy refused to take an ammunition-wagon, which was on the parade, fearing it might retard the march, and did not imagine there could be occasion for more than was in the side boxes. A more serious complaint was preferred against Cleaveland at Bunker Hill, where, according to Stedman, he sent balls too large for the guns, which rendered the artillery useless until the error could be rectified. Allusion is also made to this occurrence in a letter in the British Detail and Conduct of the War, in which it is said, " The wretched blunder of the over-sized balls sprung from the dotage of an officer of rank in that corps, who spends his whole time in dallying with the schoolmaster's daughters." This language is attributed to Sir William Howe, and the Misses Lovell are referred to. Colonel Cleaveland, however, says he sent sixty rounds with each of the twelve guns that accompanied the troops, but that not more than half were fired. The name of a brother of the " schoolmaster's daughters " has been mixed up with this accident, which is also referred to in the song : —

> " Our conductor he got broke
>     For his misconduct, sure, sir ;
>     The shot he sent for twelve-pound guns
>     Were made for twenty-four, sir."

The companies of the Royal Artillery were numbered, and wore in full dress a laced hat with black feather, hair clubbed and powdered, white stock, white breeches and stockings. They were armed with a carbine and bayonet. The Continental artillery were formed upon the same model.

The place where Percy met the fugitives is about half a mile below Lexington Common. One of his cannon was placed upon a little eminence near the present site of the Town Hall. This elevation has since been levelled. The other gun was posted on the hill above the old Munroe Tavern, and back of the residence of the late Deacon Mulliken. These pieces commanded the road for a considerable distance in front, and one of them sent a shot through the old meeting-house.

The old inn of William Munroe, which was used as a hospital for the British wounded during their halt in its vicinity, yet stands, somewhat altered in appearance, but still the same building as in 1775. It presents its end to the high-road, and faces you as you pass up towards Lexington Common. The place is still owned by the Munroe family, the house being at present occupied by William Munroe. A short distance beyond, the road from Woburn unites with that in which we are journeying, which was the old post-road to No. Four, Crown Point, and the New Hampshire Grants.

Gage had received the express, and at nine o'clock despatched the Earl with something less than a thousand men and two field-pieces. The noble Northumbrian marched out over Boston Neck with the Royal Welsh, King's Own, 47th, and his cannon at his heels, to the tune of Yankee Doodle. We feel that allowance must be made for Gordon's statement that a smart boy attracted his Lordship's attention by recalling Chevy Chase to him, — a circumstance at which his Lordship seemed much affected ; but as we now know no other means of ascertaining the truth than by a resort to supernatural agencies, — to which, however, it is possible the noble Earl's ethereal part might fail to respond, — we willingly refer the subject to the reader as a tough historical morsel.

Yankee Doodle, from whatever cause, ceased to be popular with the English after this day. On the return from Lexington one Briton asked a brother officer " how he liked the tune now." " Damn them ! " was the reply, " they made us dance it till we were tired." Yankee Doodle was beat along the American line at the surrender of Burgoyne.

At eight o'clock on the morning of the 19th the people of Boston first knew that a collision between the troops and people had occurred, though an express had arrived at the General's quarters at an earlier hour. The anxiety to know the circumstances was extreme, especially when Percy's brigade was seen under arms. Word was immediately sent to Watertown by a sure hand, and at ten o'clock Trial Bissell mounted his horse, carrying the first intelligence of the events thus far, — namely, the slaughter at Lexington and the momentarily expected arrival of the first brigade. He took the great southern highway. The town committees on the route made copies of his despatch and gave him fresh horses. Worcester, Hartford, New Haven, were in turn reached and electrified. At the time the express rider left Watertown the idea of preventing the junction of Smith with Percy was circulating, but no combination to that end could be effected.

At noon Gage gave out to the inhabitants of Boston, by his aide-de-camp, that no one had been killed. He had not, it is said, been informed of the massacre on Lexington Common until late in the afternoon. Rumors then flew thickly, raising the excitement within the town to the highest pitch. Percy and Haldimand were both reported killed. But the reader knows by what exaggerated accounts the news of battle is usually heralded.

Percy's force was doubtless considered equal to every emergency. His own and Colonel Smith's commands comprised about half Gage's available strength, and included the flower of the army. The relieving troops passed on unassailed through

Roxbury, Brookline, Little Cambridge, now Brighton, to Charles River. At this point they found the "leaves" of the bridge had been removed, but, the rest of the structure being uninjured, they were soon found, replaced, and Percy, after being some time delayed, proceeded. The season was unusually early. The barley was waving in the fields, the pastures were green, and the men plucked branches from the cherry-trees, on which the buds were bursting into bloom. It was a warm and dry day, and the men suffered with the heat. An officer in the detachment observing, as they marched along, that the windows of the houses were all shut, remarked to his commander, that, in his opinion, they would meet but little opposition. "So much the worse," Lord Percy replied, "for we shall be fired on from those very houses."

Percy, having allowed breathing time to the troops, threw out his flankers, faced about, and commenced his retrograde march. Captain Harris, — the same mentioned in a previous chapter as Lord Harris, — senior captain of the 5th, Percy's own regiment, was ordered to cover the retreat. It was now about half past two in the afternoon.

The Americans were joined in the upper part of Arlington by Dr. Warren and General Heath, who were the master-spirits in conducting the attack from this point. The Earl adopted a savage expedient for clearing his way. Parties fell off from the front, entered the houses by the road, first plundered, and then set them on fire. For two miles, after descending into the plain of Arlington, it was a continued scene of arson, pillage, and slaughter. The militia having assembled from the more populous towns near Boston, their numbers were greatly augmented, and the conflict here merged into the proportions of a battle. Led by Warren, and maddened by the sight of the burning dwellings, the fleeing women and children, and the stark bodies of aged men lying dead by their own hearthstones, the patriots fell upon the British rear with fury. Harris was so hard pressed that half his company, with his lieutenant, Baker, were either killed or wounded. When accosted by Percy, the captain, with his grenadier-cap filled with water for the relief of the wounded, offered some of the precious beverage to the Earl, but his Lordship gratefully declined it. Warren had the pin struck from the hair of his earlock by a bullet at this time. A British officer had his bayonet-scabbard shot from his side, and Percy came near realizing his sombre apprehensions, a musket-ball carrying away a button from his waist-coat. The cannon ammunition being expended, the pieces became a useless encumbrance. Smith is wounded, and Bernard of the Welsh has received a hurt. Chevy Chase, indeed!

## ELIPHALET DOWNER'S DUEL.

Dr. Eliphalet Downer left his house in Punch-Bowl Village, in Brookline, early in the morning, first directing his wife and children to a place of safety. He then repaired to the front.

Coming in sight of the main body of the enemy advancing in their retreat, he suddenly encountered one of their flankers, who had stopped to pillage a house. At the same moment the soldier descried Downer, who instantly put himself in the duel-list's posture of defence, presenting his side to his foe. Both levelled their guns, and both missed. The antagonists then closed in deadly struggle. They crossed bayonets, each hoping by superior strength or skill to obtain the advantage. For the little time they looked into each other's eyes, gleaming with fero-city, and read there the bitter resolve to destroy, each knew the supreme moment had come. They lunged, parried, locked bay-onets, and with every muscle strained to its utmost tension strove for each other's life. Downer soon found he was no match for his adversary in dexterous use of the bayonet. He could only protract the contest, while all the time the main body was coming nearer. Gathering himself together for a desperate effort, Downer, with incredible quickness, reversed his firelock and dealt the Briton a terrific stroke with the butt which brought him to the ground. The blow shattered the breech of his gun, that had served him so good a turn. His blood was up, he had fought for life, his enemy was only dis-abled, and he finished him with eight inches of cold steel;

then, possessing himself of the soldier's arms as the spoil of victory, he hastily retreated to a safer position. When the battle was over, he found his forehead had been grazed by a musket-ball. General Heath, in noticing this combat, calls Dr. Downer "an active, enterprising man"!

A little about the bellicose doctor's subsequent career. He immediately joined the army as surgeon. His regiment having disbanded at the conclusion of the siege of Boston, he entered on board the privateer sloop Yankee, Captain Johnson, in a similar capacity. The sloop mounted nine guns, four on a side. In her first cruise in July, 1776, she fell in with two ships, the Creighton and Zachara, heavily laden with rum and sugar. These she took. Our surgeon, compelled to remain below, assisted in working the odd gun in the cabin.

Captain Johnson having sent a number of his men away with the prizes, the prisoners took advantage of the lenity with which they were treated, rose and possessed themselves of the sloop. Their captors, now prisoners, were taken to England, where they were treated with great rigor. Downer found friends, who obtained his removal from prison into a public hospital as an assistant, and in the course of a year made his escape to France. Not finding an immediate opportunity of returning to America, he entered on board the Alliance, then fitting out at a French port for a cruise in the Channel. She had the good fortune to capture eighteen prizes.

The Doctor then took ship for home, but on the passage had the ill-luck to again become a prisoner. The vessel in which he was fought for seven hours and a half, had both her masts shot away, and fired her last round before she surrendered. Downer was severely wounded in the action by a grape-shot. He, with his fellow-prisoners, becames inmates of Portsea Prison, near Portsmouth, where, to use the Doctor's own language, they were worse treated than if they had fallen into the power of savages.

The prisoners contrived to dig a hole under ground for a distance of forty feet, their object being to pass under the prison-wall and into the street. This was effected with no other tool than a jack-knife, and a sack to carry away the earth, which was deposited in an old chimney and beneath the floor. Only one person at a time could work at the excavation, which had to be prosecuted at certain hours of the day, as the noise at night would have discovered them to the sentinel who paced directly above the workman's head. Once they were betrayed, but, the gallery being at length completed, they cast lots for precedence in the order of escape. The Doctor was rather corpulent, and when his turn came he stuck fast in the passage, completely blocking the way until it could be enlarged by the removal of more earth. Owing to the badness of the roads in that chalky country, made worse by rains, many of the fugitives were recaptured and consigned to the black-hole. The Doctor's friends — for Americans had friends even then in the heart of England — concealed him till an opportunity offered for him to cross over to France, from whence he made his way to Boston after an absence of three years. Dr. Downer afterwards served as surgeon-general of the Penobscot expedition, that most melancholy of failures. He was the grandfather of Samuel Downer of Boston.

As you go towards Lexington, at your left hand, nearly opposite the Baptist Church, was an old house rejuvenated with white paint and bright with green blinds. Still, beneath this disguise, and in spite of the modern additions grafted on the parent structure, you would have known it for a veteran by its monstrous chimney and simple outlines. The house stood a little back from the street, with the end towards it, and was the dwelling of Mr. Russell Teel.

We found in this house the mother of Mr. Teel, a sprightly, intelligent lady of eighty-one. She willingly related the tragedy that happened here on the 19th of April, 1775.

After the regulars had passed up to Lexington, a number of minute-men from the eastward, who had collected here, thought a good opportunity would occur to harass them on their return. To this end they made a small breastwork of casks, shingles, and such movables as they could readily obtain near the present gate and next the road. From behind this cover the patriots fired on Percy's van, but they had not taken into account the flank-guards moving across the fields parallel with the main body. Hemmed in between these two columns, the minute-men sought shelter within the dwelling.

"My grandfather, Jason Russell, then lived in this house," continued Mrs. Teel. "He had conducted his wife and children to the high hill back of the house, and was returning, when he was discovered and pursued, with the others, into the house. He was first shot and then bayoneted. The bloody stains remained until quite recently upon the floor, where he with ten others perished while in vain entreating mercy. Several Americans of this ill-fated band, which belonged to Lynn, Danvers, and Beverly, retreated into the cellar, and as they were well armed the British durst not follow them, but discharged several volleys into the entrance." Upon opening the door leading to the cellar, a dozen bullet-holes were plainly visible in the heavy cross-timbers. Jason Russell was an invalid, and it is thought imprudently returned to his dwelling to save some articles of value.

Russell's old store, which is seen with a modern addition not far above the railway-station and on the same side of the main street, was entered by the regulars, who, after helping themselves to the liquors which they found there, left all the spigots turned so as to waste what remained. Right in front of this store a soldier was mortally wounded, and in his agony begged his comrades to finish him.

Opposite the Unitarian Church, the successor of the several houses of the First Parish, is the scene of the following incidents. Two wagons had been despatched from Boston in the route of Percy's brigade, but at some distance in his rear. One contained ammunition, the want of which he had so miscalculated on setting out, the other was loaded with provisions. A guard of seventeen men and an officer accompanied the convoy. Information reached Menotomy that these supplies were coming, and their capture was at once resolved upon. The young men were all in the main action then going on in Lexington, and this affair was managed by some of the elders, led, say the town traditions, by David Lamson, a half-breed, though Gordon claims this honor for Rev. Dr. Payson, of Chelsea.

A low stone-wall then extended in front of the former residence of George Russell. The ground here falls off sharply towards the railway, forming a hollow in which was kept an old cider-mill. Behind this wall the patriots posted themselves, and when the train arrived opposite their ambuscade they rose to their feet, levelled their guns, and called out for the officer to surrender. For answer the drivers lashed their horses, upon which Lamson's party fired a volley, killing and wounding at least four of the escort, besides disabling several of the horses. The officer soon found himself alone and was made prisoner. Several of the guard ran to the pond, into which they threw their guns ; then, continuing their flight for half a mile along its westerly shore, they came to a little valley where they encountered an old woman digging dandelions, to whom they gave themselves up. The wagons became the prize of the Americans.

We frankly admit the doubts which assailed us at first in regard to this old woman digging dandelions. On a day so unfavorable, with Percy's guns rumbling in the distance, the musketry sputtering spitefully at intervals, the spectacle of Mother Batherick calmly digging early greens awoke in our mind a scepticism such as not unfrequently attends the announcement of natural phenomena. The relation being authenticated by persons of high credibility, we are no longer surprised that a squad of his Majesty's grenadiers gave themselves up to such an Amazon. And yet this woman lived and died in poverty. Her figure was tall and commanding, her eye piercing. She led her captives to a neighbor's house, and there delivered them up with the injunction to tell the story of their capture to their king. The home of John T. Trowbridge, the author, is the arena of Mother Batherick's exploit.

The old house which stood opposite the railway-station, on the spot since occupied by the residence of the late Mr. Pierce, was that of Deacon Adams, a leading man in the village. The dwelling was riddled with bullets, and a big elm standing near was spattered with lead, which the youth of West Cambridge were fond of cutting out and displaying as souvenirs. When the old house was pulled down, and the tree, rotten with age, was laid low, many of the leaden mementos were secured.

Another family of this name, so hateful to the British, lived higher up the road. Mrs. Adams was sick in bed, with a new-born infant at her side. The regulars forced open the doors, and, bursting into the room in which she was lying, one of the brutes levelled his bayonet at her breast. The poor woman, in an agony of fear, cried out, "For the Lord's sake do not kill me!" "Damn you!" ejaculated the brute. Another, more humane, interposed, and said, "We will not hurt the woman if she will go out of the house, but we will surely burn it." Strengthened by terror, Mrs. Adams arose, and throwing a blanket about her person crawled to the corn-house with her infant in her arms. Her other little children, concealed by the curtains, remained unsuspected under the bed which she had just left. The soldiers then made a pile of chairs, tables, books, clothing, etc., to which, after helping themselves to as much plunder as they could carry, they set fire. The flames, however, were extinguished at the instant the troops had passed by. A relative of the family, from whom the writer received this narration, has a small Bible which the soldiers had used to kindle the fire at Deacon Adams's. It was much scorched, and although she did not say so much, we could easily see that the owner attributed the preservation of the house to the sacred volume.

At Cooper's whig tavern, now the site of the Arlington House, the king's troops committed similar atrocities. Two unresisting old men, non-combatants, were killed, their skulls crushed and their brains scattered about. More than a hundred shots were fired into the house. Farther on was the tory tavern, to which the British officers were accustomed to resort. At that time four houses stood near together between the Cambridge line and the railway-station in Arlington, all owned by families of the name of Winship. The couplet runs, —

> "Jed' and Jeth', Jason and Jo'
> All lived in Menotomy Row."

Only a single shot was inadvertently fired into the tavern which stood near the position of Mr. Abbott Allen's house. Winship kept here in 1772, and Lem. Blanchard later.

In the same strain the relation might be continued, but enough has been said to show that the severest fighting and most afflicting scenes took place in old Menotomy. Mrs. Winthrop, who passed over the ground shortly after the battle, says : —

"But what added greatly to the horrors of the scene was our passing through the bloody field at Menotomy, which was strewed with the mangled bodies. We met one affectionate father with a cart, looking for his murdered son, and picking up his neighbors who had fallen in battle, in order for their burial."

It is probable that Percy intended to return as he came, but by this time he learned that Brighton Bridge had been effectually disabled. Had this not been done, the villages of Old Cambridge, Brookline, and Roxbury would have each renewed the scenes of Menotomy. To have forced his way for eight miles farther might have been difficult, if not impossible, for Percy. Fortune, therefore, conducted the head of his column back through Charlestown by the way around Prospect Hill. At the old tavern in North Cambridge the officers may have hastily swallowed a mouthful of spirits. At six o'clock the British vanguard began to file across Charlestown Neck, and ranged themselves in battle line on the heights of Bunker Hill, where they remained until the next day. They were then relieved by the marines and the third brigade.

" Says our General we were forced to take to our arms in our own defence ;
    (*For arms read legs,* and it will be both truth and sense.)
    Lord Percy (says he) I must say something of him in civility,
    And that is I never can enough praise him for his great agility."

We annex the whole account of this battle as it appeared in Draper's Boston Gazette of April 20, 1775, which is, we think, worthy of being numbered among the literary curiosities of its day : —

### BATTLE OF LEXINGTON.

"Last Tuesday Night the Grenadier and Light Companies belonging to the several Regiments in this Town were ferried in Long boats from the Bottom of the Common over to Phip's Farm in Cambridge, from whence they proceeded on their way to Concord where they arrived early yesterday. The first Brigade commanded by Lord Piercy with two pieces of Artillery set off from here Yesterday Morning at Ten o'clock as a Re-inforcement, which with the Grenadiers and Light Companies made about Eighteen Hundred men. Upon the people's having notice of this Movement on Tuesday night alarm guns were fired through the country and Expresses sent off to the different Towns so that very early yesterday morning large numbers were assembled from all parts of the Country. A general Battle ensued which from what we can learn, was supported with great Spirit upon both Sides and continued until the King's Troops retreated to Charlestown, which was after sunset. Numbers are killed and wounded on both sides. The reports concerning this unhappy Affair and the Causes that concurred to bring on an Engagement are so various that we are not able to collect anything consistent or regular and cannot therefore with certainty give our readers any further Account of this shocking Introduction to all the Miseries of Civil War."

The American accounts appeared in the form of hand-bills. One, printed in Boston, is embellished with a death's-head, and contains a list of the American killed and wounded. Another has at its head twenty coffins, bearing each the name of one of the slain. It is entitled,

## "BLOODY BUTCHERY

### BY THE

### BRITISH TROOPS

#### OR THE

##### RUNAWAY FIGHT OF THE REGULARS."

"Being the PARTICULARS of the VICTORIOUS BATTLE fought at and near CONCORD, situated Twenty Miles from Boston, in the Province of the Massachusetts Bay, between Two Thousand Regular Troops, belonging to His Britanic Majesty, and a few Hundred Provincial Troops, belonging to the Province of Massachusetts-Bay, which lasted from sunrise until sunset, on the 19th of April, 1775, when it was decided greatly in favor of the latter. These particulars are published in this cheap form at the request of the friends of the deceased WORTHIES who died gloriously fighting in the CAUSE OF LIBERTY and their COUNTRY and it is their sincere desire that every Householder in the Country, who are sincere well-wishers to America may be possessed of the same either to frame and glass, or otherwise to preserve in their houses, not only as a Token of Gratitude to the memory of the Deceased Forty Persons but as a perpetual memorial of that important event on which perhaps, may depend the future Freedom and Greatness of the Commonwealth of America. To which is annexed a Funeral Elegy on those who were slain in the Battle."

In the burying-ground at Arlington we found a plain shaft of granite, nineteen feet high, standing over the remains of the fallen. The monument is protected by a neat iron fence, and has a tablet with this inscription : —

> " Erected by the
> Inhabitants of West Cambridge
> A. D. 1848,
> Over the common grave of
> Jason Russell, Jason Winship,
> Jabez Wyman and nine others
> Who were slain in this Town by the
> British Troops,
> on their retreat from the battles of
> Lexington and Concord,
> April 19th 1775.
> Being among the first to lay down
> their lives in the struggle for
> American Independence."

A plain slate gravestone at the foot of the obelisk has the following : —

> " M<sup>r</sup> Jason Russell was
> barbarously murdered in his own
> House by Gage's bloody Troops
> on y<sup>e</sup> 19th of April 1775 Ætat 59
> His body is quietly resting
> in this grave with Eleven
> of our friends, who in like
> manner, with many others were
> cruelly slain on that fatal day.
> Blessed are y<sup>e</sup> dead who die in y<sup>e</sup>
> Lord."

The memorial was erected by the voluntary contributions of the citizens of West Cambridge ; the remains beneath the old slab being disinterred and placed within the vault under the monument, April 22, 1848. Nine of the twelve victims are unknown.

At Acton, on the 19th of April, 1851, a monument was dedicated to the gallant spirits belonging to that town who fell on the day of Lexington and Concord. The tablet bears the names of Captain Isaac Davis and of privates Abner Hosmer and James Hayward, provincial minute-men.

It was Davis's company which marched in the van to force the passage of the North Bridge. A halt and parley had occurred among the provincial soldiers. None, apparently, were desirous of occupying the post of honor and of facing the British muzzles. Davis, resolute, and ashamed of this ignoble conduct before the enemy, exclaimed, "I have n't a man that is afraid to go"; immediately suiting the action to the word by marshalling his men in the front. He appeared depressed, and had rebuked the gayety of some of his comrades who breakfasted with him on that, to him, fateful morning.

> " 'T is the sunset of life gives us mystical lore,
> And coming events cast their shadows before."

Davis was a tall, athletic man, famed for courage and coolness. He was a gunsmith, and an excellent marksman. At the first volley he was shot through the heart. He leaped convulsively in the air, and fell, still grasping his musket, over the causeway on the low ground. Hosmer was killed by the same fire. Hayward's more tragic death we have briefly alluded to. He was killed, during the pursuit, at the red house on the right as you descend Fiske's Hill, in Lexington, going towards Boston. His adversary's ball perforated his powder-horn, which is still preserved; but before he fired his last shot he had nearly expended the forty bullets with which he had set out.

The remains of these brave men were exhumed from the burial-ground, where they had lain for seventy odd years, and placed in the tomb at the base of the monument. The graves were then filled up, — the gravestones being left standing to tell the future visitor where they had first been interred. The bones were found remarkably well preserved. The orifice in Hosmer's skull through which the ball passed while he was in the act of taking aim was still distinctly visible. These relics were carefully placed in a coffin of three compartments and laid away beneath the monument, while the booming of cannon sounded a soldier's requiem.

Two mementos of the battles of Lexington and Concord may be seen in the Massachusetts Senate Chamber; one is a Tower musket captured from a soldier of the 43d, the other the gun used by Captain John Parker on that day. These weapons were a legacy to the State from Theodore Parker, and were received by both branches of the Legislature assembled in joint convention. Governor Andrew made the address of presentation, during the delivery of which he exhibited much emotion, and as he concluded he pressed the barrel of the Revolutionary firearm to his lips "with effusion." This occurred in 1861, when the opening events of the Rebellion presented a certain analogy in the Governor's mind to the teachings of 1776. Many applauded, while not a few were disposed to ridicule his patriotic fervor.

An internecine war has raged ever since the event of 1775 between Lexington and Concord, as to which town might claim the greater honor of the day. As if there were not enough and to spare for both! To Lexington belongs the glory of having assembled the first force to oppose the march of the king's troops, and of the first bloody sacrifice to liberty. At Concord the Americans first attacked the troops, and with numbers which rendered such a measure justifiable. Concord, too, was the object of the British expedition. The conflict raged during the day within the limits of six towns, each of which might fairly claim a portion of the credit due the whole. The historian will, however, treat the occurrences of the 19th of April as a single event, leaving to local chroniclers the care of separating the golden sands which make their peculiar portion of fame from the fused ingot. All will agree that no similar quantity of powder ever made so great a noise in the world as that burned on the Green at Lexington, and all along the old colonial highway.

## CHAPTER XIX.

### AT THE WAYSIDE INN.

"Ah! who could deem that foot of Indian crew
    Was near? — yet there, with lust of murderous deeds,
Gleamed like a basilisk from woods in view,
    The ambushed foeman's eye."

THE village of South Sudbury lies embosomed in a little valley formed by considerable hills. A few houses mount the slope of the easternmost eminence, which is called Green Hill, while to the southwest of the meadows through which trickles the Mill or Hop Brook, rises what we call a mountain in Massachusetts, — a well-wooded height lying partly in Framingham and still holding to its Indian name of Nobscot. The brook once turned the water-wheel of an ancient saw and grist mill at the foot of Green Hill.

The years 1675–76 were fateful ones for New England. The old chronicler, Hubbard, says, "It was ebbing water with New England at this time, and awhile after; but God shall turn the stream before it be long, and bring down their enemies to lick the dust before them." Philip, the great chieftain of the Wampanoags, had begun hostilities with the whites, and for a time it looked as if he might destroy all their frontier settlements. Had he been able to effect his object of bringing all the savage nations into alliance, the war might have ended with the extermination of the pale-faces.

Indians were everywhere. There had been no formal declaration of war, — nothing of that poetic exchange of rattlesnake-skin filled with arrows for the white man's powder and lead. There was nothing chivalric about it. The war was planned in secret and in treachery; the onset was sudden and wellnigh

WAYSIDE INN, SUDBURY.

irresistible. The first intimation the English had that Philip had dug up the hatchet was in the fatal shot from an ambuscade, or the war-whoop sounded in the midst of the hamlets. At this time the Colony could muster about four thousand foot and four hundred horse, without reckoning the aged or infirm.

On their part, the whites were not more blameless than they now are, more than two hundred years since, when the work of extinguishing the remnant of the red race is approaching the end. Two centuries ago the Indians were powerful enough on the Atlantic shore to render it doubtful for a time whether the English might retain a precarious foothold in the seaports. To-day they are hunted down among the rocky fastnesses of the Pacific.

In 1675 there were, as now, Indian traders without souls, and Englishmen who thought as little of shooting a savage as of outraging a squaw. There was also the fire-water, under the influence of which the savage parted with his birthright, or made his mark at the bottom of a so-called treaty, of which he knew not the meaning. The English fought then for self-preservation, which we know is nature's first law, so that we can well pardon them for dealing blow for blow, — and even their reverend teachers for preaching a crusade against the savages, as Dr. Mather and the clergy generally did. The Indians — did they not suspect it, and did not their wise men foretell it? — were also fighting for self-preservation. The law was as inexorable to them as to the pale-face. Philip was living in a sort of vassalage which his proud spirit rebelled against. Did an Englishman complain of an injury from an Indian, his sachem was instantly cited to appear before the stranger's council. Did an Indian complain of the wrong of a white man, justice was oftentimes both blind and deaf. The Indians warred after a cruel fashion, certainly. They tortured the living and mutilated the dead. But then, after all, they were but savages, and it was the manner in which they had been accustomed to wage war among themselves; until we had civilized them we had little right to murmur if they did not adopt our style of warfare. But what did the English do? With the

Holy Scriptures in one hand, they ordered the beheading and scalping of their red enemies. The Quakers who refused to enlist were compelled to run the gauntlet in Boston streets, and attempts were made to break open the jails and put to death the Indian prisoners. There was a strong dash of heroism in Philip of Pokanoket, and we cannot blame him for making one grand effort for freedom.

When the news came to the Massachusetts capital that the frontier towns were being harried, drums beat to arms, and stout John Leverett summoned his council together. Henchman, Hutchinson, Paige, Willard, and the other captains put on their buff coats and belted their heavy broadswords or rapiers about them. The bands were mustered. In each company was an ensign, who bore aloft a color of red sarsenet, a

KING PHILIP, FROM AN OLD PRINT.

yard square, with the number of the company in white thereon. Another had a white blaze in the centre. Volunteers were demanded, and even the profane seafaring men — "privateers," as they were called — were enrolled. A guard of musketeers was set at the entrance of the town. A busy man was John Fayerweather, the commissary, in providing for the levies. With drums beating, trumpets braying, and standards displayed, the troops defiled through the town-gates. A few encounters, and this bravery of regular war was laid aside. This was above two hundred years ago, and yet we have lately seen our brave men led into an enemy's ambush as unwarily as they were in the year 1675.

Some of the evils which a solemn session of the General Court, convened at Boston at this time, held to lie at the foundation of their misfortunes, were the proud excesses in apparel and hair of which many — " yea, and of the poorer sorte as well as others " — were guilty. The Quakers came in for a liberal share of invective. Excess in drinking, and the toleration of so many taverns, especially in Boston, which the townspeople were too much inclined to frequent, were glaring offences. It was urged that profane swearing had frequently been heard, and steps were taken to suppress and punish it. The fourth and fifth commandments were ordered to be better observed than formerly, and it was decreed that there should be no more such oppression by merchants or laborers as had been. Truly, Philip was working a social revolution among his enemies of Massachusetts Bay !

From these measures we may see that our forefathers were not so well satisfied with themselves as to feel sure of providential aid in their work of killing savages ; but it is set down in the chronicles that on the very day when these new civil regulations were established, the English forces achieved a victory at Hatfield.

During the summer and autumn of 1675 the Indians had almost uninterrupted success. They had ravaged the country from the Connecticut to the shores of Boston Bay, and a stray warrior had appeared within a few miles of Boston Town-House. In November the commissioners of Massachusetts, Plymouth, and Connecticut met at Boston, and agreed to raise an army of a thousand men, of which the Bay Colony furnished more than half. At the head of this force Winslow assaulted the stronghold of the Narragansetts in December, inflicting a terrible defeat upon that nation, and entirely breaking its power.

The Indians resumed hostilities in the early spring of 1676. The English had become more circumspect ; still their losses were heavy, and the path of Philip's warriors could be marked by desolation and ruin. The whites, too, learned at length to make use of the Christian or Praying Indians, to act as runners and scouts, — a measure which we in later times imitated with advantage in the employment of the Warm Springs Indians against the Modocs.

One Sabbath, late in March, the Indians attacked Marlborough, while the inhabitants were at divine worship in their meeting-house. The people sought the shelter of their garrison-houses, which were found in every settlement, leaving the enemy to burn the greater part of the town. Lancaster had previously suffered, and the tale of the captivity and redemption of Mrs. Rowlandson furnishes a graphic chapter of these terrible years.

In April Philip had assembled about four hundred of his followers in the neighborhood of Marlborough, and after burning the few deserted houses they fell with fury upon Sudbury. A small party from Concord, coming to the assistance of their neighbors, were ambushed and slain. The news of the descent on Marlborough having reached Boston, Captain Samuel Wadsworth was despatched with a company of soldiers to its relief. Reaching Marlborough after a weary march of twenty-five miles, Wadsworth learned that his enemy had gone in the direction of Sudbury, and, after giving his men some rest and refreshment, and being joined by Captain Brocklebank, who commanded the garrison at Marlborough, he returned on his own footsteps in pursuit, following, tradition says, the old trail, afterwards the Lancaster road, now closed to travel.

When within what is now South Sudbury, Wadsworth saw about a hundred of the enemy's war-party, with whom, believing them the main body, he endeavored to close. The Indians retired slowly through the woods, until Wadsworth's men were wholly encompassed by enemies lying in concealment, when the terrific war-whoop rang through the forest, and every tree around the devoted band blazed with a death-shot. The English, perceiving theirs to be a desperate case, fought with obstinate bravery, but were at length forced to the top of Green Hill, the circle of enemies all the while drawing closer around them. On this hill they defended themselves valiantly until nightfall, when some of the party, attempting to escape, were followed by others, until a precipitate retreat was the result. The Indians pursued, slaying all but thirteen or fourteen, who sought safety at Noyes's mill, — the same referred to in another place. This mill was fortified after the usual fashion of the garrisons, but had been abandoned by the Sudbury people. Believing it to be still occupied by them, the Indians did not venture to the assault, but withdrew to complete and celebrate their victory. The survivors at the mill were afterwards relieved by Captain Hugh Mason's company from Watertown, who approached the battle-ground by way of Mount Nobscot, where they left the carts containing their baggage and provisions. The Indians were still in the vicinity, but Mason did not feel sufficiently strong to attack them.

The English lost in this battle their captain, Wadsworth; Sharp, their lieutenant; and twenty-six others, besides Captain Brocklebank. Five or six who were captured were put to the torture on the night of the fight. The remains of the fallen Englishmen were gathered and interred near the spot where they fell. Over their common grave a heap of loose stones was piled. This humble monument was in an open field, about thirty rods east of the road, and near a growth of pines and oaks. The soil on the hill-top is light and sandy.

With this victory Philip's onset culminated, and he began to drift down the tide apace. The fierce Maquas and Senecas attacked the undefended villages of his allies, while sickness and disease spread among his people. Disasters overtook him, and he became a hunted fugitive. On the 12th of August, 1676, he fell by the hand of one of his own race, and was beheaded and quartered by the Plymouth authorities, — his head being set on a gibbet, where it was to be seen for twenty years.

A plain slab of blue slate was raised over the remains of Captain Wadsworth and his ill-fated companions by his son, President Wadsworth, of Harvard College. It bears the following inscription : —

Capt. Samuel Wadsworth of Milton, his Lieut. Sharp of Brooklin, Capt. Broclebank of Rowley, with about 26 other souldiers,

fighting for the defence of their country, were slain by y⁰ Indian
enemy, April 18th, 1676, lye buried in this place."

In 1852 the relics were exhumed and removed a little distance to the site of the present monument, — a plain granite
shaft, which was dedicated by an address from Hon. George S.
Boutwell, present Senator for Massachusetts. The old gravestone is placed at the base of the monument, the tablet of
which recites that it was erected by the Commonwealth and the
town of Sudbury, in grateful remembrance of the services and
sufferings of the founders of the State. The same date is exhibited on the monument as is borne on the old slab, namely,
April 18, 1676 ; but as this is a subject of contradiction among
the historians of the time, the committee concluded to adhere
to the date adopted by President Wadsworth.

A fuller research has turned the weight of testimony against
the earlier date, and in favor of April 21 as the time of the
fight. In the midst of discrepancies of this character the narrator has only to accept what is supported by the greatest number of authorities, and these certainly are on the side of April
21, 1676.

In the discussion which has ensued as to the date which
should have been placed on the Wadsworth monument, it was
assumed by the distinguished advocate of the earlier date that
communication with Boston was cut off by Philip between the
17th and 20th of April. Doubts have also been expressed as to
whether intelligence of the fight could have reached the vicinity
of Boston on the same day. The authorities had not neglected
so vital a matter as the arrangement of signals between the garrison attacked and the capital. The firing was, of course, distinctly heard in the neighboring towns, and was communicated
by alarm-guns from garrison to garrison until it reached Boston.
In Hutchinson's History an example is given of the rapidity
with which communication could be transmitted : —

" Sept 23ᵈ (1676) an alarm was made in the town of Boston about
ten in the morning, 1200 men were in arms before 11 and all dismissed before 12. One that was upon guard at Mendon, 30 miles

off, got drunk and fired his gun, the noise of which alarmed the next neighbors and so spread to Boston."

Considering what were then the resources of the Colony, Sudbury fight was as important in its day as a pitched battle with thousands of combatants would be in our own time. It occasioned great depression. The Indians must have lost heavily to have conducted their subsequent operations so feebly.

Though the whites usually ventured to attack them with greatly inferior numbers, they were far from being contemptible foes. The Englishman's buff coat would sometimes turn a bullet, but the Indian's breast was bared to his enemy. His primitive weapons, however, the bow and arrow, had been exchanged for guns and hatchets, which he soon learned to use but too well. The Dutch on one side, or the French on another, kept him supplied with powder and ball. He fought for his hunting-grounds, now parcelled out among strangers. He fell to be received into the elysian fields of the great Manitou.

We cannot forbear our tribute of pity and of admiration for Philip. What though he struck the war-post and chanted the death-song to gather his dusky warriors for one mighty effort to exterminate our ancestors, his cause was the same that has ever received the world's applause. Liberty was as sweet to Philip as to a Tell or a Toussaint, but he failed to achieve it, and the shades of oblivion have gathered around his name. There was a simple yet kingly dignity in Philip's communications to the chief men among the colonists. His neck could not bear the yoke ; he must walk free beneath the sun.

Though the great chief's policy would not have left a single foe alive, it is known that he sent warning to some among the whites who had bound themselves to him by uprightness and honorable dealing. In that part of Taunton now known as Raynham was one of Philip's summer haunts for fishing and hunting. The Leonards had there erected the first forge in New England, if not in North America, and had there lived in amity with the Indian prince. They fashioned him spear and arrowheads with which to strike the red-deer or the leaping salmon, and he repaid them with game, rich skins, and wampum. To them he gave a hint to look to their safety.

It seems passing strange to be standing beside a monument erected to commemorate a victory over our sires by a race wellnigh blotted out of existence.    Every circumstance of our surroundings, every object upon which the eye dwells in the landscape, gives the lie to such an event.    Where the warriors lay in ambush, green and well-tilled fields extend themselves ; where the old mill creaked, steam issues from its successor ; instead of the Indian trail the railway presents its iron pathway ; the rude yet massive garrison-house is replaced by yonder costly villa ; and the simple village meeting, in which the settlers fearfully pursued their devotions with arms in their hands, is renewed where we see the distant and lofty spire.    The virgin forests have disappeared as completely as have the red-men who threaded the greenwood.    All nature is at work for man where once all was repose.    Only the hills and the stream remain as pressed by the moccason or cleft by the canoe.

In Pilgrim Hall, at Plymouth, the stranger is shown some memorials of Philip.    The barrel of the gun through which the bullet passed to his heart, and the curiously woven helmet which he is said to have worn, are there displayed among the bones and implements of his race.    As yet we lack, here in New England, a museum devoted to Indian antiquities, in which we might see the dress, arms, and utensils of the natives of the soil.    It would be a most interesting collection.    They were no effete Asiatics, but a brave, warlike, hardy people.    Their history is filled with poetry and romance.    Even Cooper, while presenting in a Magua the wild, untamable, vindictive savage, depicts on the same scene an Uncas brave, noble, and devoted.

About three miles from Sudbury Mills and four from Marlborough is the old Wayside Inn, which Longfellow has made famous.    It stands in a sequestered nook among the hills which upheave the neighboring region like ocean billows.    For above two hundred years, during the greater part of which it has been occupied as a tavern, this ancient hostelry has stood here with its door hospitably open to wayfarers.

In the olden time the road possessed the importance of a much-travelled highway, but with the building of railways through this region, travel deserted it, and custom the tavern. After being closed for thirty years as a public house, for once, at least, sentiment has prevailed over the logic of events, and once again the old inn, true to its ancient traditions, proffers "entertainment to man and beast" as of yore.

> "As ancient is this hostelry
> As any in the land may be,
> Built in the old Colonial day,
> When men lived in a grander way,
> With ampler hospitality."

The name of the house was the Red Horse, and at the other end of the route, belonging to the same family, in rivalry of good cheer, was the White Horse in Old Boston Town. The horse has always been a favorite symbol with publicans. However tedious the way may have been, however shambling or void of spirit your hackney of the road, the steed on the hostel sign always pranced proudly, was of high mettle, and of as gallant carriage as was ever blazoned on Saxon's shield.

SIGN OF THE WAYSIDE INN.

The Red Horse in Sudbury was built about 1686. From the year 1714 to near, if not quite, the completion of a century and a half, it was kept as an inn by generation after generation of the Howes, the last being Lyman Howe, who served the guests of the house from 1831 until about 1860. The tavern stood about half-way on the great road to Worcester, measuring twenty-three good English miles from Boston Town-House.

Well, those were good old times, after all. A traveller, after a hard day's jaunt, pulls up at the Red Horse. The landlord is at the door, hat in hand, with a cheery welcome, and a shout to the blacks to care for the stranger's beast. Is it winter, a mimic conflagration roars on the hearth. A bowl of punch is brewed, smoking hot. The guest, nothing loath, swallows the mixture, heaves a deep sigh, and declares himself better for a thousand pounds. Soon there comes a summons to table, where good wholesome roast-beef, done to that perfection of which the turnspit only was capable, roasted potatoes with their russet jackets brown and crisp, and a loaf as white as the landlady's Sunday cap send up an appetizing odor. Our guest falls to. Hunger is a good trencherman, and he would have scorned your modern tidbits, — jellies, truffles, and *patés à fois gras*. For drink, the well was deep, the water pure and sparkling, but home-brewed ale or cider was at the guest's elbow, and a cup of chocolate finished his repast. He begins to be drowsy, and is lighted to an upper chamber by some pretty maid-of-all-work, who, finding her pouting lips in danger, is perhaps compelled to stand on the defensive with the warming-pan she has but now so dexterously passed between the frigid sheets. At parting, Boniface holds his guest's stirrup, warns him of the ford or the morass, and bids him good speed.

Our modern landlord is a person whose existence we take upon trust. He is never seen by the casual guest, and if he were, is far too great a man for common mortals to expect speech of him. He sits in a parlor, with messengers, perhaps the telegraph, at his beck and call. His feet rest on velvet, his body reclines on air-cushions. You must at least be an English milord, a Russian prince, or an American Senator, to receive the notice of such a magnate. It is a grave question whether he knows what his guests are eating, or if, in case of fire, their safety is secured. His bank-book occupies his undivided attention. "Like master, like man." Your existence is all but ignored by the lesser gentry. You fee the boot-black, tip the waiter, drop a *douceur* into the chambermaid's palm, and, at your departure, receive a vacant stare from the curled, mustached personage who hands you your bill. At entering one of these huge caravansaries you feel your individuality lost, your identity gone, in the living throng. Neglected, heavy-hearted, but lighter, far lighter in purse than when you came, you pass out under a marble portico and drift away with the stream. Give, O publican, the stranger a welcome, a shake of the hand, a nod at parting, and put it in the bill.

Coming from the direction of Marlborough, at a little distance, the gambrel roof of the Wayside Inn peeps above a dense mass of foliage. A sharp turn of the road, which once passed under a triumphal arch composed of two lordly elms, and you are before the house itself. Formerly the capacious barns and tall sign-posts stood across the old, grass-bordered, country road, which leads straight up to the tavern door. The general appearance of things, however, has been much altered by the building of a new macadam road past the spot, by the State. But let us go in.

The interior of the inn is spacious and cool, as was suited to a haven of rest. A dozen apartments of one of our modern hotels could be set up within the space allotted to his patrons by mine host of the Wayside. Escaping from a cramped stage-coach, or the heat of a July day, our visitor's lungs would here begin to expand "like chanticleer," as, flinging his flaxen wig into a corner, and hanging his broad-flapped coat on a peg, he sits unbraced, with a bowl of the jolly landlord's extra-brewed in one hand, and a long clay pipe in the other, master of the situation.

Everything remains as of old. There is the bar in one corner of the common room, with its wooden portcullis, made to be hoisted or let down at pleasure, but over which never appeared that ominous announcement, "No liquors sold over this bar." The little desk where the tipplers' score was set down, and the old escritoire, looking as if it might have come from some hospital for decayed and battered furniture, are there now. The bare floor, which once received its regular morning sprinkling of clean white sea-sand, the bare beams and timbers overhead, from which the whitewash has fallen in flakes, and the very oak of which is seasoned with the spicy vapors steaming from pewter flagons, all remind us of the good old days before the flood of new ideas. Governors, magistrates, generals, with scores of others whose names are remembered with honor, have been here to quaff a health or indulge in a drinking-bout.

In the guests' room, on the left of the entrance, the window-pane bears the following recommendation, cut with a gem that sparkled on the finger of that young roysterer, William Molineux, Jr., whose father was the man that walked beside the king's troops in Boston, to save them from the insults of the townspeople, — the friend of Otis and of John Adams : —

> " What do you think
> Here is good drink
> Perhaps you may not know it ;
> If not in haste do stop and taste
> You merry folks will shew it.
>
> WM. MOLINEUX Jr. Esq.
> 24th June 1774 Boston."

The writer's hand became unsteady at the last line, and it looks as though his rhyme had halted while he turned to some companion for a hint, or, what is perhaps more likely, here gave manual evidence of the potency of his draughts.

A ramble through the house awakens many memories. You are shown the travellers' room, which they of lesser note occupied in common, and the state chamber where Washington and Lafayette are said to have rested. In the garret the slaves were accommodated, and the crooknecks and red peppers hung from the rafters. This part of the house has been fitted up into bedrooms, by the present proprietor, Mr. Lemon.

Conducted by the presiding genius of the place, Mrs. Dadmun, we passed from room to room and into the dance-hall, annexed to the ancient building. The dais at the end for the fiddlers, the wooden benches fixed to the walls, the floor smoothly polished by many joyous feet, and the modest effort at ornament, displayed the theatre where many a long winter's night had worn away into the morn ere the company dispersed to their beds, or the jangle of bells on the frosty air betokened the departure of the last of the country belles. The German was unknown ; Polka, Redowa, Lancers, were not ; but contra-dances, cotillons, and minuets were measured by dainty feet, and the landlord's wooden lattice remained triced up the livelong night. O the amorous glances, the laughter, the bright eyes, and the bashful whispers that these walls have seen and listened to, — and the actors all dead and buried! The place is silent now, and there is no music, except you hear through the open windows the flute-like notes of the wood-thrush where he sits carolling a love-ditty to his mate.

The road on which stands the old inn first became a regular post-route about 1711, a mail being then carried over it twice a week to New York. But as early as 1704, the year of the publication of the first newspaper in America, there was a western post carried with greater or less regularity, and travellers availed themselves of the post-rider's company over a tedious, dreary, and ofttimes hazardous road.

We have the journal of Madam Knight, of a journey made by her in 1704, to New Haven, with no other escort than the post-rider, — an undertaking of which we can now form little conception. She left Boston on the 2d of October, and reached her destination on the 7th. The details of some of her trials appear sufficiently ludicrous. For example, she reached, after dark, the first night, a tavern where the post usually lodged. On entering the house, she was interrogated by a young woman of the family after this fashion : —

" Law for mee — what in the world brings You here at this time a night. I never see a woman on the Rode so Dreadfull late in all the days of my versall life. Who are You ? Where are You going ? I 'm scar'd out of my wits."

Who that has ever travelled an unknown route, finding the farther he advanced, the farther, to all appearances, he was from his journey's end, or whoever, finding himself baffled, has at last inquired his way of some boor, will deeply sympathize with the tale of the poor lady's woes. At the last stage of her route, the guide being unacquainted with the way, she asked and received direction from some she met.

" They told us we must Ride a mile or two and turne downe a Lane on the Right hand ; and by their Direction wee Rode on, but not Yet coming to y$^e$ turning, we mett a Young fellow and ask't him

how far it was to the Lane which turn'd down towards Guilford.
Hee said wee must Ride a little further and turn down by the
Corner of uncle Sam's Lott.  My Guide vented his spleen at the
Lubber."

No wonder that when safe at home again in Old Boston, she
wrote on a pane of glass in the house that afterwards became
that of Dr. Samuel Mather,—

> " Now I 've returned poor Sarah Knights,
>    Thro' many toils and many frights ;
>    Over great rocks and many stones,
>    God has presarv'd from fracter'd bones."

The use of coaches was introduced into England by Fitz
Alan, Earl of Arundel, A. D. 1580.  At first they were drawn
by two horses only.  It was Buckingham, the favorite, who
(about 1619) began to have them drawn by six horses, which,
as an old historian says, was wondered at as a novelty, and
imputed to him a "mastering pride."  Captain Levi Pease was
the first man to put on a regular stage between Boston and
Hartford, about 1784.

The first post-route to New York, over which Madam
Knight travelled in 1704, went by the way of Providence,
Stonington, New London, and the shore of Long Island
Sound.  The distance was 255 miles.  We subjoin the itin-
erary of the road as far as Providence : —

" From Boston South-end to Roxbury Meeting-house 2 miles,
thence to Mr. Fisher's at Dedham 9, thence to Mr. Whites * 6, to
Mr. Billings 7, to Mr. Shepard's at Wading River 7, thence to Mr.
Woodcock's † 3, from thence to Mr. Turpins at Providence 14, or to
the Sign of the Bear at Seaconck 10, thence to Providence 4, to
Mr. Potters in said town 8."

* Stoughton.                              † Attleborough.

COUNT RUMFORD'S BIRTHPLACE, WOBURN.

## CHAPTER XX.

### THE HOME OF RUMFORD.

*"Fortune does not change men, it only unmasks them."*

THE world knows by heart the career of this extraordinary man. Sated with honors, he died at Auteuil, near Paris, August 21, 1814. Titles, decorations, and the honorary distinctions of learned societies flowed in upon the poor American youth such as have seldom fallen to the lot of one risen from the ranks of the people. The antecedents and character of the man have very naturally given rise to much inquiry and speculation.

Benjamin Thompson was born in the west end of his grandfather's house in North Woburn, March 26, 1753. The room where he first drew breath is on the left of the entrance, and on the first floor. As for the house, it is a plain, old-fashioned, two-story farm-house, with a gambrel roof, out of which is thrust one of those immense chimneys of great breadth and solidity. A large willow which formerly stood between the house and the road has disappeared, and is no longer a guide to the spot. This ancient dwelling has a pleasant situation on a little rising ground back from the road, which here embraces in its sweep the old house and the queer little meeting-house, its neighbor.

A pretty little maiden deftly binding shoes, and an elderly female companion who had passed twenty years of her life under this roof, were the occupants of the apartment in which Count Rumford was born. A Connecticut clock, which ticked noisily above the old fireplace, and a bureau, the heirloom of several generations, were two very dissimilar objects among the furniture of the room. There are no relics of the Thompsons remaining there.

The father of our subject died while Benjamin was yet an infant, and the widowed mother made a second marriage with Josiah Pierce, Jr., of Woburn, when the future Count of the Holy Roman Empire was only three years old. After this event Mrs. Pierce removed from the old house to another which formerly stood opposite the Baldwin Place, half a mile nearer the centre of Woburn.

At the age of thirteen young Thompson was apprenticed to John Appleton, a shopkeeper of Salem, Massachusetts, and in 1769 he entered the employment of Hopestill Capen in Boston. While at Salem, Thompson was engaged during his leisure moments in experiments in chemistry and mechanics, and it is recorded that in one branch of science he one day blew himself up with some explosive materials he was preparing, while on the other hand he walked one night from Salem to Woburn, a distance of twenty odd miles, to exhibit to his friend Loammi Baldwin a machine he had contrived, and with which he expected to illustrate the problem of perpetual motion. His mind appears at this period absorbed in these fascinating studies to an extent which must have impaired his usefulness in his master's shop.

A few doors south of Boston Stone every one may see an antiquated building of red brick, a souvenir of the old town, which was standing here long before the Revolution. Strange freaks have been playing in its vicinity since Benjamin Thompson tended behind the counter there. The canal at the back has been changed into solid earth, and sails are no more seen mysteriously gliding through the streets from the harbor to the Mill-pond. The facsimile of Sir Thomas Gresham's grasshopper, on the pinnacle of Faneuil Hall, is about the only object left in the neighborhood familiar to the eye of the apprentice, who, we may assume, would not have been absent from the memorable convocations which were held within the walls of the old temple in his day. The building with which Rumford's name is thus connected forms the angle where Marshall's Lane enters Union Street, and bears the sign of the descendant of the second oysterman in Boston, himself for fifty years a vender of the delicious bivalve.

Thompson's master, Hopestill Capen, becomes a public character through his apprentice, whom he may still have regarded as of little advantage in the shop by reason of his strongly developed scientific vagaries. Capen had been a carpenter, with whom that good soldier, Lemuel Trescott, served his time. He married an old maid who kept a little dry-goods store in Union Street, and then, uniting matrimony and trade in one harmonious partnership, abandoned tools and joined his wife in the shop. Samuel Parkman, afterwards a well-known Boston merchant, was Thompson's fellow-apprentice. The famous Tommy Capen succeeded to the shop and enjoyed its custom.

Thompson, at nineteen, went to Concord, New Hampshire, then known as Rumford, and from which his titular designation was taken. At this time he was described as of " a fine manly make and figure, nearly six feet in height, of handsome features, bright blue eyes, and dark auburn hair." He soon after married the widow of Colonel Benjamin Rolfe, a lady ten or a dozen years his senior. Rumford himself is reported by his friend Pictet as having said, " I married, or rather I was married, at the age of nineteen." One child, a daughter, was the result of this marriage. She was afterwards known as Sarah, Countess of Rumford.

If Rumford meant to convey to Pictet the idea that his union with Mrs. Rolfe was a merely passive act on his part, or that she was the wooer and he only the consenting party, he put in a plea for his subsequent neglect which draws but little on our sympathy. His wife, according to his biographers, took him to Boston, clothed him in scarlet, and was the means of introducing him to the magnates of the Colony.

The idea forces itself into view that at this time Rumford's ambition was beginning to develop into the moving principle of his life. The society and notice of his superiors in worldly station appears to have impressed him greatly, and it is evident that the agitation which wide differences with the mother country was then causing in the Colonies did not find in him that active sympathy which was the rule with the young and ardent spirits of his own age. He grew up in the midst of troubles which moulded the men of the Revolution, and at a time when not to be with his brethren was to be against them. We seldom look in a great national crisis for hesitation or deliberation at twenty-one.

Certain it is that Rumford fell under the suspicions of his own friends and neighbors as being inclined to the royalist side. He met the accusation boldly, and as no specific charges of importance were made against him, nothing was proven. The feeling against him, however, was so strong that he fled from his home to escape personal violence, taking refuge at first at his mother's home in Woburn, and subsequently at Charlestown.

Thompson was arrested by the Woburn authorities after the battle of Lexington, was examined, and released; but the taint of suspicion still clung to him. He petitioned the Provincial Congress to investigate the charges against him, but they refused to consider the application. He remained in the vicinity of the camps at Cambridge, vainly endeavoring to procure a commission in the service of the Colony, until October, 1775, when he suddenly took his departure, and is next heard of within the enemy's lines at Boston.

In the short time intervening between October and March, — the month in which Howe's forces evacuated Boston, — Thompson had acquired such a confidential relation with that general as to be made the bearer of the official news of the end of the siege to Lord George Germaine. He does not seem to have embraced the opportunity of remaining neutral under British protection, as did hundreds of others, but at once makes himself serviceable, and casts his lot with the British army.

It has been well said that nothing can justify a man in becoming a traitor to his country. Thompson's situation with the army at Cambridge must have been wellnigh intolerable, but he had always the alternative of living down the clamors against him, or of going into voluntary exile. His choice of a course which enabled him to do the most harm to the cause of his countrymen gives good reason to doubt whether the attachment he had once professed for their quarrel was grounded on any fixed principles. Be that as it may, from the time he clandestinely withdrew from the Americans until the end of the war his talents and knowledge were directed to their overthrow with all the zeal of which he was capable.

From this point Rumford's career is a matter of history. At his death he was a count of the Holy Roman Empire, lieutenant-general in the service of Bavaria, F. R. S., Foreign Fellow of the French Institute, besides being a knight of the orders of St. Stanislaus and of the White Eagle.

Rumford had derived some advantage from his attendance at the lectures of Professor Winthrop, of Harvard University, on Natural Philosophy. With his friend, Loammi Baldwin, he had been accustomed to walk from Woburn to Cambridge to be present at these lectures. Being at the camp, he had assisted in packing up the apparatus for removal when the College buildings were occupied by the soldiery. In his will he remembered the University by a legacy of a thousand dollars annually, besides the reversion of other sums, for the purpose of founding a professorship in the physical and mathematical sciences, the improvement of the useful arts, and for the extension of industry, prosperity, and the well-being of society. Jacob Bigelow, M. D., was the first incumbent of the chair of this professorship.

A miniature of Count Rumford, from which the portrait in Sparks's Biography was engraved, is, or was, in the possession of George W. Pierce, Esq. The Count is painted in a blue coat, across which is worn a broad blue ribbon. A decoration appears on the left breast. The miniature, a work of much artistic excellence, bears a certain resemblance to the late President Pierce, a distant relative of the Count. It is a copy from a portrait painted by Kellenhofer of Munich, in 1792, and is inscribed on the back, probably in Rumford's own hand, " Presented by Count Rumford to his much loved and respected mother 1799."

Colonel Loammi Baldwin, the companion of Thompson in early youth, and who manfully stood up for his friend in the midst of persecution, when the name of tory was of itself sufficient to cause the severance of life-long attachments, lived in the large square house on the west side of the road before you come to the birthplace of Thompson. The house has three stories, is ornamented with pillars at each corner, and has a balustrade around the roof. In front is a row of fine elms, with space for a carriage-drive between them and the mansion. The house could not be mistaken for anything else than the country-seat of one of the town notabilities.

Baldwin's sympathies were wholly on the side of the patriots, and he was at once found in the ranks of their army. He was at Lexington, at the siege of Boston, and in the surprise at Trenton, where a battalion of his regiment, the 26th Massachusetts, went into action with sixteen officers and one hundred and ninety men. Wesson, Baldwin's lieutenant-colonel, and Isaac Sherman, his major, were both in this battle, leading Mighell's, Badlam's, and Robinson's companies.

Colonel Baldwin resigned before the close of the war, and was appointed High Sheriff of Middlesex in 1780. He has already been named in connection with his great project, the Middlesex Canal. He discovered and improved the apple known by his name, and if that excellent gift of Pomona is king among fruits, the Baldwin is monarch of the orchard. His son Loammi inherited his father's mechanical genius. While a student at Harvard he made with his pocket-knife a wooden clock, the wonder of his fellow-collegians. The Western Avenue, formerly the Mill Dam, in Boston, and the government docks at Charlestown and Newport, are monuments of his skill as an engineer.

Woburn was originally an appanage of ancient Charlestown, and was settled in 1640 under the name of Charlestown Village. Among its founders the name of Thomas Graves — the same whom Cromwell named a rear-admiral — appears. A confusion, not likely to be solved, exists as to whether he was the same Thomas Graves who laid out Charlestown in 1629, and is known as the engineer. The admiral, however, is entitled to the distinction of having commanded, in 1643, the "Tryal," the first ship built in Boston.

> " Our revels now are ended ; these our actors,
>   As I foretold you, were all spirits, and
>   Are melted into air, into thin air ;
>   And, like the baseless fabric of this vision,
>   The cloud-capped towers, the gorgeous palaces,
>   The solemn temples, the great globe itself,
>   Yea, all which it inherit, shall dissolve,
>   And like this insubstantial pageant faded,
>   Leave not a rack behind."

# INDEX.

## A.

## B.

## W.

Wadsworth, Captain Samuel, killed, 414, 415.

Wapping, 28.

Ward, General Artemas, 61; headquarters, 258; incident of Shays's Rebellion, 259, 260.

Ward, Joseph, 349.

Warren, Joseph, conducts an exchange of prisoners, 8; at Bunker Hill, 60, 61, 261; death, 72; statue of, 77.

Washington Elm, 267.

Washington, General George, collision with Hancock on a point of etiquette, 15, 70, 71; leave-taking of his officers, 174, 208; first headquarters in Cambridge, 262; events in life of, 271, 272; headquarters, 289–308; personal description of, 296; Continental uniform, 297; his staff, 299, 300; at Monmouth, 301; anecdotes of, 301, 302; habits of, 306; his body-guard, 307, 308.

Washington, Lady, 305.

Waterhouse, Benjamin, 264.

Waters, Captain Josiah, 187.

Watertown meeting-houses, 347; Bridge, 347, 348; burial-grounds, 346, 347.

Wayside Inn (Sudbury), 420–425.

Wells, William, 317.

Wesson, Colonel James, 162, 163.

West Church (Boston), anecdote of, 322.

West Boston Bridge, built, 4, 5.

Wheeler, Captain Timothy, ruse of at Concord, 384.

Whitcomb, Colonel Asa, anecdote of, 156.

Whitefield's Elm, 268.

Wilder, Marshall P., 339.

Wilkinson, General James, account of Bunker Hill battle, 70; duel with Gates, 104.

Willard, Joseph, 209.

Willard, Samuel, 211.

Willard, Solomon, architect of Bunker Hill Monument, 75, 79, 80.

Williams, General Otho H., 88.

Windmill Hill (Cambridge), 284.

Winter Hill, fortified and garrisoned, 100–102; German encampment on, 106, 107.

Winthrop, Mrs. Hannah, 359, 360.

Winthrop, Governor John, 95, 96; statue, 336; William, 200.

Woolrich, John, 244.

Worcester, Joseph E., 312.

Wyeth, Nathaniel J., his trip to the Pacific, 341–344.

Wyman, Rufus, M. D., 178.

## Y.

Yankee, origin of the word, 256.

Yankee Doodle, 397.

THE END.

# Other TUT BOOKS available:

**TWO CENTURIES OF COSTUME IN AMERICA**
*by Alice Morse Earle*

**TYPHOON! TYPHOON! An Illustrated Haiku Sequence** *by Lucile M. Bogue*

**ZILCH! The Marine Corps' Most Guarded Secret** *by Roy Delgado*

Please order from your bookstore or write directly to:

**CHARLES E. TUTTLE CO., INC.**
Rutland, Vermont 05701 U.S.A.

or:

**CHARLES E. TUTTLE CO., INC.**
Suido 1-chome, 2–6, Bunkyo-ku, Tokyo 112